The History of British Women's Writing, 1500–1610

The History of British Women's Writing

General Editors: **Jennie Batchelor** and **Cora Kaplan**

Advisory Board: Isobel Armstrong, Rachel Bowlby, Carolyn Dinshaw, Margaret Ezell, Margaret Ferguson, Isobel Grundy, and Felicity Nussbaum

The History of British Women's Writing is an innovative and ambitious monograph series that seeks both to synthesise the work of several generations of feminist scholars, and to advance new directions for the study of women's writing. Volume editors and contributors are leading scholars whose work collectively reflects the global excellence in this expanding field of study. It is envisaged that this series will be a key resource for specialist and non-specialist scholars and students alike.

Titles include:

Caroline Bicks and Jennifer Summit (*editors*)
THE HISTORY OF BRITISH WOMEN'S WRITING, 1500–1610
Volume Two

Ros Ballaster (*editor*)
THE HISTORY OF BRITISH WOMEN'S WRITING, 1690–1750
Volume Four

Jacqueline M. Labbe (*editor*)
THE HISTORY OF BRITISH WOMEN'S WRITING, 1750–1830
Volume Five

Forthcoming titles:

Elizabeth Herbert McAvoy and Diane Watt (*editors*)
THE HISTORY OF BRITISH WOMEN'S WRITING, 700–1500
Volume One

Mihoko Suzuki (*editor*)
THE HISTORY OF BRITISH WOMEN'S WRITING, 1610–1690
Volume Three

History of British Women's Writing
Series Standing Order ISBN 978–0–230–20079–1 hardback
(outside North America only)

You can receive future titles in this series as they are published by placing a standing order. Please contact your bookseller or, in case of difficulty, write to us at the address below with your name and address, the title of the series and the ISBN quoted above.

Customer Services Department, Macmillan Distribution Ltd, Houndmills, Basingstoke, Hampshire RG21 6XS, England

---

The History of British Women's Writing, 1500–1610

Volume Two

Edited by

Caroline Bicks

and

Jennifer Summit

First published 2010 by
PALGRAVE MACMILLAN

Palgrave Macmillan in the UK is an imprint of Macmillan Publishers Limited,
registered in England, company number 785998, of Houndmills, Basingstoke,
Hampshire RG21 6XS.

Palgrave Macmillan in the US is a division of St Martin's Press LLC,
175 Fifth Avenue, New York, NY 10010.

Palgrave Macmillan is the global academic imprint of the above companies
and has companies and representatives throughout the world.

Palgrave® and Macmillan® are registered trademarks in the United States,
the United Kingdom, Europe and other countries.

ISBN 978–0–230–21834–5   hardback

This book is printed on paper suitable for recycling and made from fully
managed and sustained forest sources. Logging, pulping and manufacturing
processes are expected to conform to the environmental regulations of the
country of origin.

A catalogue record for this book is available from the British Library.

Library of Congress Cataloging-in-Publication Data

The history of British women's writing.
     p. cm.
  Vol. 2 edited by Caroline Bicks and Jennifer Summit.
  ISBN 978-0-230-21834-5 (v. 2 : hardback)
  1. English literature—Women authors—History and criticism.
2. Women and literature—Great Britain—History. I. Bicks, Caroline,
1966– II. Summit, Jennifer.
  PR111.H57 2010
  820.9'9287—dc22
                                                            2010026127

10   9   8   7   6   5   4   3   2   1
19 18 17 16 15 14 13 12 11 10

Transferred to Digital Printing in 2011

Contents

Tudor Courts

Part III: Developing Histories

List of Figures

Series Preface

One of the most significant developments in literary studies in the last quarter of a century has been the remarkable growth of scholarship on women's writing. This was inspired by, and in turn provided inspiration for, a postwar women's movement which saw women's cultural expression as key to their emancipation. The retrieval, republication, and reappraisal of women's writing, beginning in the mid-1960s, have radically affected the literary curriculum in schools and universities. A revised canon now includes many more women writers. Literature courses that focus on what women thought and wrote from antiquity onwards have become popular undergraduate and postgraduate options. These new initiatives have meant that gender – in language, authors, texts, audience, and in the history of print culture more generally – is a central question for literary criticism and literary history. A mass of fascinating research and analysis extending over several decades now stands as testimony to a lively and diverse set of debates, in an area of work that is still expanding.

Indeed so rapid has this expansion been, that it has become increasingly difficult for students and academics to have a comprehensive view of the wider field of women's writing outside their own period or specialism. As the research on women has moved from the margins to the confident centre of literary studies it has become rich in essays and monographs dealing with smaller groups of authors, with particular genres and with defined periods of literary production, reflecting the divisions of intellectual labour and development of expertise that are typical of the discipline of literary studies. Collections of essays that provide overviews within particular periods and genres do exist, but no published series has taken on the mapping of the field, even within one language group or national culture.

A History of British Women's Writing is intended as just such a cartographic standard work. Its ambition is to provide, in ten volumes edited by leading experts in the field, and comprised of newly commissioned essays by specialist scholars, a clear and integrated picture of women's contribution to the world of letters within Great Britain from medieval times to the present. In taking on such a wide-ranging project we were inspired by the founding, in 2003, of Chawton House Library, a UK registered charity with a unique collection of books focusing on women's writing in English from 1600 to 1830, set in the home and working estate of Jane Austen's brother.

JENNIE BATCHELOR
UNIVERSITY OF KENT

CORA KAPLAN
QUEEN MARY, UNIVERSITY OF LONDON

Acknowledgments

The editors wish to acknowledge the valuable help of general editors Jennie Batchelor and Cora Kaplan, as well as Paula Kennedy and the anonymous reader for Palgrave Macmillan. We also thank the contributors to this volume, whose work bears witness to the vitality of the field. And finally, we extend personal thanks to our families and our departments, the Department of English, Stanford University, and the Department of English, Boston College.

Notes on Contributors

Caroline Bicks is Associate Professor of English at Boston College. She has published articles on pregnancy, midwifery, and churching in the early modern period and is the author of *Midwiving Subjects in Shakespeare's England* (2003). She is currently writing on girlhood and girl-actors in early modern England.

Heidi Brayman Hackel is Associate Professor of English at the University of California at Riverside. She is the author of *Reading Material in Early Modern England: Print, Gender, and Literacy* (2005) and a co-editor of *Reading Women: Literacy, Authorship, and Culture in the Atlantic World, 1500–1800* (2007).

Pamela Allen Brown is Associate Professor of English at University of Connecticut, Stamford. Her publications include *Better a Shrew than a Sheep: Women, Drama and Jest in Early Modern England* (2003) and a co-edited volume (with Peter Parolin), *Women Players in England, 1500–1660: Beyond the All-Male Stage* (2005).

Christine Coch is Associate Professor of English at The College of the Holy Cross. Her research centers on gender, pleasure, and art in early modern England; she has published essays on Elizabeth I, Spenser, Lanyer, and the image of the woman in the garden in late Elizabethan poetry.

A. E. B. Coldiron, Associate Professor of English, Florida State University, History of Text Technologies program, writes articles and books on late-medieval and Renaissance literature including, *Canon, Period, and the Poetry of Charles of Orleans: Found in Translation* (2000) and *English Printing, Verse Translation, & the Battle of the Sexes, 1476–1557* (2009).

Julie Crawford, Professor of English and Comparative Literature at Columbia University, has written on Shakespeare, Fletcher, Margaret Cavendish, the Sidneys, Anne Clifford, and Mary Wroth, as well as post-Reformation religious and literary culture. She is the author of *Marvelous Protestantism: Monstrous Births in Post-Reformation England* (2005).

Sujata Iyengar teaches Shakespeare, Renaissance Literature, and Medical Humanities in the English Department at the University of Georgia. She is the author of *Shades of Difference: Mythologies of Skin Color in Early*

Modern England (2005) and *A Dictionary of Shakespeare's Medical Language* (forthcoming, 2011). With Christy Desmet, she founded and co-edits the CELJ's 'Best New Journal' of 2007, *Borrowers and Lenders: The Journal of Shakespeare and Appropriation.*

Chris Laoutaris is British Academy Post Doctoral Fellow at University College London and the author of *Shakespearean Maternities: Crises of Conception in Early Modern England* (2008). He is currently writing *The Queen's Soldier: The Life and Wars of Elizabeth Russell.*

Lynne Magnusson is Professor of English at the University of Toronto and writes on Shakespeare's language, the genre of the letter, and early modern women's writing. She is the author of *Shakespeare and Social Dialogue* (1999) and is completing a book on Elizabethan letter-writing.

Catherine Richardson is Director of the Canterbury Centre for Medieval and Early Modern Studies at the University of Kent (UK). She is author of *Domestic Life and Domestic Tragedy in Early Modern England: The Material Life of the Household* (2006) and editor of *Everyday Objects: Medieval and Early Modern Material Culture and its Meanings* (2009).

Carolyn Sale is Assistant Professor in the Department of English at the University of Alberta (Canada). She is currently completing the manuscript for her first book, *Common Properties: The Early Modern Writer and the Law, From Christopher St. German to Elizabeth Cary.*

Edith Snook is Associate Professor in the Department of English at the University of New Brunswick (Canada). She is the author of *Women, Reading, and the Cultural Politics of Early Modern England* (2005) and is now writing a book on beauty in early modern women's writing.

Jennifer Summit is Professor in the Department of English at Stanford University. She is the author of *Lost Property: The Woman Writer and English Literary History, 1380–1589* (2000) and *Memory's Library: Medieval Books in Early Modern England* (2008) and co-editor (with David Wallace) of 'Medieval/Renaissance: After Periodization', a special issue of *Journal of Medieval and Early Modern Studies* (2007).

Ema Vyroubalová is doctoral candidate in English and Comparative Literature at Stanford University, completing a dissertation on the cultural politics of foreign languages in early modern England's linguistic theories, court documents, and theater.

Nancy Bradley Warren is Professor of English and Courtesy Professor of Religion at Florida State University. She is the author of *Spiritual*

Economies: Female Monasticism in Late Medieval England (2001) and *Women of God and Men of Arms: Female Spirituality and Political Conflict, 1380–1600* (2005).

Marion Wynne-Davies holds the Chair of English Literature at the University of Surrey (UK). She has edited *Renaissance Drama by Women: Texts and Documents* and *Women Poets of the Renaissance* (1996) and she has written four monographs: *Women and Arthurian Literature* (Macmillan, 1996), *Sidney to Milton* (Palgrave Macmillan, 2002), *Women Writers of the English Renaissance: Familial Discourse* (Palgrave Macmillan, 2007), and *Margaret Atwood* (2007).

Chronology

Ema Vyroubalová

People are listed under their full names at death; married women's maiden names (where known) are given parenthetically; English monarchs are listed under their regnal names and additional identifying information is included for foreign monarchs.

*c.*1373	Margery (Brunham) Kempe born.
1374	Petrarch (Francesco Petrarca) dies.
1377 (21 June)	Edward III dies; Richard II becomes King of England.
*c.*1394	Eleanor (Malet) Hull born.
1399 (30 September)	Richard II deposed; Henry IV becomes King of England.

1400

1400	Geoffrey Chaucer dies.
1413 (20 March)	Henry IV dies; Henry V becomes King of England.
1415	England defeats France in the Battle of Agincourt.
1420	Treaty of Troyes; Henry V marries Catherine of Valois.
1422 (31 August)	Henry V dies; Henry VI becomes King of England.
1428–1429	English siege of Orléans.
1431 (30 May)	Joan of Arc executed.
*c.*1434	Christine de Pizan dies.
1438 (after)	Margery (Brunham) Kempe dies.
1453	France defeats England in the Battle of Castillon; Hundred Years War ends.
1455	Wars of the Roses begin.
1460	Eleanor (Malet) Hull dies.
1461	Henry VI deposed and flees to Scotland; Edward IV proclaimed King of England.
*c.*1467	Desiderius Erasmus born.
*c.*1468–1470	*Morte Darthur* by Thomas Malory written.
1470 (30 October)	Henry VI reclaims throne.
1471 (April)	Henry VI deposed; Edward IV reclaims throne.

(4 May)	Battle of Tewkesbury; Henry VI defeated and imprisoned.
1473–1474	*Recuyell of the Historyes of Troye*, first book published in English, printed by William Caxton in Bruges.
1478	*The Morale Prouerbes of Cristyne*, Anthony Woodville's translation of Christine de Pizan's verse aphorisms, printed by William Caxton.
1483 (9 April)	Edward IV dies; Edward V becomes King of England with Richard of York as Protector.
(22 June)	Richard III proclaimed King of England.
(6 July)	Richard III crowned.
1485 (22 August)	Richard III defeated and killed in the Battle of Bosworth Field; Wars of the Roses end; Henry VII becomes King of England.
*c.*1489	*Blanchardyn and Eglantine* translated and printed by William Caxton.
1489	*Fayttes of Armes and of Chyualrye* by Christine de Pizan translated and printed by William Caxton.
1491 (28 June)	Henry VIII born.
*c.*1492	William Caxton dies; Wynkyn de Worde takes over Caxton's press.
1492	Christopher Columbus's first voyage to the New World.
1493–1495	Honor (Grenville) Plantagenet (Lady Lisle) born.
*c.*1494	William Tyndale born.

1500

1500–1501	Wynkyn de Worde moves his press from Westminster to London.
*c.*1501	Excerpt from *The Book of Margery Kempe* printed by Wynkyn de Worde.
1501 (14 November)	Prince Arthur marries Katherine of Aragon.
1502 (2 April)	Prince Arthur dies.
*c.*1503	*The Castle of Labour*, anonymous translation (attributed to Alexander Barclay) of Pierre Gringore's *Chasteau de labour*, printed in Paris.
?1505	*The Castle of Labour* printed by Richard Pynson.
1505	Margaret (More) Roper born.

1506	*The Castle of Labour* printed by Wynkyn de Worde.
c.1507	'Tretis of the twa mariit wemen and the wedow' by William Dunbar published.
c.1509	Erasmus writes *The Praise of Folly*.
1509	John Calvin born.
	The Fyftene Joyes of Maryage, anonymous translation (possibly by Robert Copland) of Antoine de la Sale's *Quinze joyes de mariage*, printed by Wynkyn de Worde.
(21 April)	Henry VII dies; Henry VIII becomes King of England.
(11 June)	Henry VIII marries Katherine of Aragon.
(24 June)	Henry and Katherine crowned.
c.1510	*The Gospelles of Dystaues*, Henry Watson's translation of *Les evangiles des quenouilles*, printed by Wynkyn de Worde.
1511	*The Praise of Folly* (*Morias Enkomion* in Greek, *Stultitiae Laus* in Latin) by Erasmus published in Paris.
1512	*The Castle of Labour* reprinted by Wynkyn de Worde.
c.1514	John Knox born.
	Robert Copland sets up his own press after working for Wynkyn de Worde.
1514	Thomas Wolsey becomes Archbishop of York.
	Mary Herrick born.
1515	Thomas Wolsey becomes Cardinal.
1516 (18 February)	Mary I born.
	Utopia by Thomas More published in Leuven.
1517	Martin Luther publishes his Ninety-Five Theses.
1518	*Auctuarium selectarum epistolarum* by Erasmus with dedicatory letter by Thomas More published.
	Colloquies by Erasmus published.
1519	Katherine (Willoughby) Brandon Bertie born.
1520 (June)	Meeting between Henry VIII and Francis I of France at the Field of Cloth of Gold in France.
c.1521	Anne (Askew) Kyme born.
1521	Hernán Cortés conquers the Aztec empire and claims the land for Spain.
	Excerpt from Margery Kempe's *Book* published by Henry Pepwell.

	Booke [of the] Body of Polycye by Christine de Pizan printed by John Skot.
	Cyte of Ladyes, Brian Anslay's translation of Christine de Pizan's *Cité des dames*, published.
c.1524	*Devout Treatise upon the Pater Noster*, Margaret (More) Roper's translation of Erasmus's *Precatio Dominica*, published (edition now lost).
1524	'The Abbot and the Learned Lady' by Erasmus published as part of his *Colloquia*.
?1525	*Interlocucyon, with an argument, betwyxt man and woman* by Alexis Guillaume printed by Wynkyn de Worde.
c.1525	*Seuen Sorowes that Women Haue When Theyr Husbandes Be Deade* compiled and printed by Robert Copland (edition now lost).
	Treatise concerning the fruitful sayings of David by John Fisher published.
c.1526	*Devout Treatise upon the Pater Noster*, Margaret (More) Roper's translation of Erasmus's *Precatio Dominica*, published (first surviving edition).
1526	Mildred (Cooke) Cecil born.
	The New Mother by Erasmus published by the Froben Press.
c.1527	Hans Holbein the Younger paints portrait of the More family.
?1528	Elizabeth (Cooke) Hoby Russell born.
c.1528	Anne (Cooke) Bacon born.
1528 (before)	Richard Hyrde translates Juan Luis Vives's *De Institutione Foeminae Christianae* as *Instruction of a Christian Woman*.
1528	*The Castle of Labour* reprinted by Richard Pynson.
1529	Thomas More appointed Lord Chancellor.
c.1530	*The Payne and Sorowe of Euyll Maryage*, John Lydgate's translation of *De conjuge non ducenda*, printed by Wynkyn de Worde.
1530	Thomas Wolsey accused of treason; dies on his way to trial in London.
	Anne (Vaughan) Lock Dering Prowse born.
1530–1535	Mary (Dudley) Sidney born.
1531	Stephen Gardiner becomes Bishop of Winchester.
	The Book Named the Governor by Thomas Elyot published.

	Le Miroir de l'âme pécheresse by Marguerite de Navarre published in Paris.
1532 (16 May)	Thomas More resigns from Chancellor office.
1533	*A Boke Made by John Frith Prisoner in the Tower of London* by John Frith published.
	Johan Johan and Hys Wyf Tyb by John Heywood published.
(January)	Henry VIII marries Anne Boleyn.
(23 May)	Henry VIII's marriage to Katherine of Aragon declared null by Thomas Cranmer.
(11 July)	Henry VIII excommunicated by the Pope from the Catholic Church.
(7 September)	Elizabeth I born.
1534	*Letter to Alice Alington* written by Margaret (More) Roper.
(March)	First Act of Succession passed (Mary excluded from succession).
(April)	Thomas More imprisoned.
(November)	First Act of Supremacy establishes Church of England with Henry VIII as its head.
1534–1535	Wynkyn de Worde dies.
*c.*1535	*Jyl of Braintford's Testament* by Robert Copland published.
1535	Coverdale Bible published on the Continent (exact place uncertain).
(22 June)	John Fisher executed.
(6 July)	Thomas More executed.
*c.*1536	*The Hye Way to the Spyttell House* by Robert Copland published.
1536	Ten Articles of Religion published by Thomas Cranmer.
	First Act of Dissolution initiates dissolution of monasteries in England and transfer of their property to the Crown.
	Desiderius Erasmus dies.
(19 May)	Anne Boleyn executed.
(30 May)	Henry VIII marries Jane Seymour.
(June)	Second Act of Succession passed (Elizabeth and Mary excluded from succession).
(October)	Pilgrimage of Grace begins in northern England.
(6 October)	William Tyndale executed.

1536–1537	Jane (Grey) Dudley (Lady Jane Grey) born.
1537	Jane (Fitzalan) Lumley born.
(July)	Organizers of the Pilgrimage of Grace executed.
(12 October)	Edward VI born.
(24 October)	Jane Seymour dies.
1538	Religious pilgrimages suppressed in England.
1539	Second Act of Dissolution (Act for the Dissolution of the Greater Monasteries) disbands remaining monasteries.
	Syon Monastery of the Brigittine order in Middlesex seized; order flees to Flanders.
	Coverdale Bible first printed in England.
1540 (6 January)	Henry VIII marries Anne of Cleves; (9 July) marriage annulled.
(28 July)	Thomas Cromwell executed.
(28 July)	Henry VIII marries Katherine Howard.
c.1542	Katherine (Cooke) Killigrew born.
1542 (13 February)	Katherine Howard executed.
(8 December)	Mary Queen of Scots born.
(14 December)	Mary Queen of Scots becomes Queen of Scotland.
1543 (12 May)	Act for the Advancement of True Religion passed.
(July)	Third Act of Succession passed (Mary and Elizabeth restored to succession).
(12 July)	Henry VIII marries Katherine Parr.
1544	Margaret (More) Roper dies.
	Psalms or Prayers taken out of the Holy Scripture, translation of John Fisher's Latin text (possibly by Katherine Parr), published.
1545	Anne (Askew) Kyme first detained and examined.
	Princess Elizabeth (later Elizabeth I) translates Marguerite de Navarre's *Le Miroir de l'âme pécheresse* as 'The Glass of the Sinful Soul' and presents it to Katherine Parr.
	Prayers or Meditations by Katherine Parr published.
(December)	Council of Trent meets for its first session in Italy.
1546	Robert Parsons born.
	Anne (Askew) Kyme examined second time; (16 July) Askew executed.

	The first examinacyon of Anne Askewe, edited by John Bale, published in Germany.
1547	*The lattre examinacyon of Anne Askewe*, edited by John Bale, published in Germany.
	Lamentacion of a Sinner by Katherine Parr published.
(28 January)	Henry VIII dies; Edward VI becomes King of England.
(20 February)	Edward VI crowned.
1548	'The Glass of the Sinful Soul', Princess Elizabeth's (later Elizabeth I) translation of Marguerite de Navarre's *Le Miroir de l'âme péchereuse* edited and published by John Bale.
1549	The Book of Common Prayer introduced.
	Beginning of Katherine (Willoughby) Brandon Bertie's extant correspondence with William Cecil.
	The Praise of Folie: Moriae encomium, Thomas Chaloner's translation of Erasmus's text, published in London.
	C. Hystoryes of Troye, Robert Wyer's translation of Christine de Pizan's *Cent histoires de Troie*, published.
(October)	William Cecil imprisoned.
1550 (January)	William Cecil released from prison.
	John Calvin dedicates his Latin commentary on Isaiah to Edward VI.
	Mildred (Cooke) Cecil presents her *An Homilie or Sermon of Basile the Great* (translation of Basil of Caesarea's homily) to the Duchess of Somerset.
	The Booke of freendship of Marcus Tullie Cicero, John Harington's translation of Cicero's *De amicitia*, published.
1551	Stephen Gardiner stripped of his bishopric.
	Utopia (*A fruteful, and pleasaunt worke of the beste state of a publyque weale*), Ralph Robinson's translation of Thomas More's *Utopia*, published.
*c.*1552	Grace (Sharington) Mildmay born.
?1552	Edmund Spenser born.
1552	Second revised edition of the Book of Common Prayer published.

	End of Katherine (Willoughby) Brandon Bertie's extant correspondence with William Cecil.
1553	Stephen Gardiner restored as Bishop of Winchester and appointed Chancellor.
	Anne (Cooke) Bacon's translation of Bernardino Ochino's Sermons published.
(6 July)	Edward VI dies.
(10 July)	Jane (Grey) Dudley (Lady Jane Grey) proclaimed Queen of England.
(19 July)	Lady Jane Grey and Guildford Dudley imprisoned; Mary I becomes Queen of England.
(1 October)	Mary I crowned.
?1553–1558	Mary (Roper) Clarke Basset translates Eusebius's *Ecclesiastical History*.
1554	Philip Sidney born.
	The Tryumphes of Fraunces Petrarcke, Henry Parker's translation of Petrarch's *I Trionfi*, published.
(Jan.–Feb.)	Wyatt's Rebellion.
(12 February)	Jane (Grey) Dudley (Lady Jane Grey) and Guildford Dudley executed.
(July)	Mary I marries Prince Philip (later Philip II of Spain).
1556 (January)	Prince Philip becomes King of Spain.
(December)	Thomas Cranmer executed.
c.1557	Jane (Fitzalan) Lumley translates Euripides's *Iphigenia at Aulis* as *Iphigeneia*.
1557	Brigittine order returns from exile; Syon monastery reestablished in Middlesex.
	Anne (Vaughan) Dering Prowse Lock flees to Geneva with her children.
	Songs and Sonnets (also known as *Totell's Miscellany*), compiled and published by Edward Totell.
	The Workes of Sir Thomas More published in London by Richard Cawood and Edward Totell.
1558	William Cecil becomes Secretary of State.
	Syon monastery closed; order flees back to the Continent.
(17 November)	Mary I dies; Elizabeth I becomes Queen of England.

1559 (15 January)	Elizabeth I crowned.
	Second Act of Supremacy and Act of Uniformity passed; Church of England reestablished and unified.
	Third revised edition of the Book of Common Prayer published.
	Elizabeth I entertained by the Lumleys and Arundels at Nonsuch Palace; possible performance of Lumley's *Iphigeneia* on this occasion.
1560	Geneva Bible first published in Geneva.
	Anne (Vaughan) Dering Prowse Lock's sonnets and translations of John Calvin's sermons on Isaiah published.
1561	Elizabeth I declines Pope Pius IV's invitation to England's representatives to attend Council of Trent.
	Francis Bacon born.
	Mary (Sidney) Herbert born.
1562–1563	Samuel Daniel born.
1563	Bubonic plague outbreak in London and England.
	Council of Trent meets for its last session.
	Thirty-Nine Articles of Religion published under the direction of Matthew Parker.
	Penelope (Devereux) Rich born.
	Robert Sidney born.
	Acts and Monuments (also known as *Book of Martyrs*) by John Foxe published in London.
	The Treasure of Gladnesse published in London at Elizabeth I's injunction.
1564	William Shakespeare born.
	John Calvin dies.
	Anne (Cooke) Bacon translates John Jewels's *Apologia pro Ecclesia Anglicana* as *Apologie of the Church of England*.
1566	Honor (Grenville) Plantagenet (Lady Lisle) dies.
	Isabella Whitney, first record of literary activity (date of birth unknown).
(19 June)	James Stuart (later James VI of Scotland and James I of England) born.
1567 (8 February)	Mary Queen of Scots executed.
(24 July)	James Stuart becomes James VI of Scotland.

	Parker's Psalter published.
	Xv. bookes of P. Ovidius Naso entytuled Metamorphosis, Arthur Golding's translation of Ovid's *Metamorphoses*, published.
	The Copy of a Letter by Isabella Whitney published.
1568	Bishops' Bible published.
	Christian Prayers and Holy Meditations by Henry Bull published.
1569	Northern Rebellion (Revolt of the Northern Earls).
	Aemilia (Bassano) Lanyer born.
1570	*The Schoolmaster* by Roger Ascham published.
	A Hundred Good Points of Husbandry by Thomas Tusser published.
*c.*1571	'The Doubt of Future Foes' by Elizabeth I written.
1571	Margaret (Dakins) Devereux Sidney Hoby born.
	Anne (Vaughan) Dering Prowse Lock marries Edward Dering.
1572	St Bartholomew Massacre in France.
	Beginning of the Admonition Controversy.
	William Cecil becomes Lord High Treasurer.
	Ben Jonson born.
	Mary (Roper) Clarke Basset dies.
	John Knox dies.
1573	Isabella Whitney's recorded literary activity ends (date of death uncertain).
	Wyll and Testament and *A Sweet Nosegay* by Isabella Whitney published.
1575	Arbella (Stuart) Seymour born.
(July)	Elizabeth I entertained by the Dudleys at Kenilworth Castle.
1576	First purpose-built theater in London.
	Complete edition of Geneva Bible printed in England.
	Anthony Cooke dies.
	Frances (Manners) Neville dies.
1577	Francis Drake starts circumnavigation of the globe.
	William Herbert marries Mary (Sidney) Herbert.
*c.*1578	Philip Sidney starts *Arcadia*.

1578	Jane (Fitzalan) Lumley dies.
	William Roper dies; Margaret (More) Roper reinterred with him at St Dunstan's Church.
	Mirrour of Princely Deedes and Knighthood, Margaret Tyler's translation of the first part of Diego Ortúñez de Calahorra's *Espejo de principes y cavalleros,* published.
1579	Marriage negotiations between Elizabeth I and Duke of Alençon begin.
?1580	*The Life and Good End of Sister Marie* (authors unknown) written.
1580	Francis Drake's expedition returns to England.
	Edmund Spenser goes to Ireland.
	Sister Marie Champney of Syon Monastery dies in London.
	Katherine (Willoughby) Brandon Bertie dies.
1581	Marriage negotiations between Elizabeth I and Duke of Alençon abandoned.
c.1582	'On Monsieur's Departure' by Elizabeth I written.
1582	Joan Newton's will written.
	A Monument of Matrones, compiled by Thomas Bentley, published.
1583	Katherine (Cooke) Killigrew dies.
1584	Walter Raleigh's expedition to North America.
	Discoverie of Witchcraft by Reginald Scot published.
c.1585	*The Birth of Mankind* by Thomas Raynalde reprinted by Joan Jugge.
1585	William Segar paints the 'Ermine Portrait' of Elizabeth I.
	Elizabeth (Tanfield) Cary born.
1586	Mary (Dudley) Sidney dies.
	Philip Sidney dies.
?1587	Mary (Sidney) Wroth born.
1587	*Tamburlaine* by Christopher Marlowe first performed.
1588	The Spanish Armada defeated by the English.
1589	Mildred (Cooke) Cecil dies.
	The Art of English Poesie by George Puttenham published.
	An Abridgment of the Booke of Acts and Monuments [...] *by John Foxe* edited by Timothy Bright published.

French Historie, Anne Dowriche's verse adaptation of Thomas Tymme's prose translation of Jean de Serres's *Commentatorium,* published.

Jane Anger Her Defense for Women published.

(23 November) James VI of Scotland marries Anna of Denmark.

1590 Anne Clifford born.

The Tragedy of Antonie, Mary Sidney Herbert's translation of Robert Garnier's *Marc Antoine,* published.

First installment of *The Faerie Queene* by Edmund Spenser published.

First edition of (the unfinished) *Arcadia* by Philip Sidney published.

Certaine Godly and Verie Comfortable Letters by Edward Dering published.

Of the Markes of the Children of God, Anne (Vaughan) Dering Prowse Lock's translation of Jean Taffin's *Des marqves des enfans de Diev,* published.

1590 (after) Anne (Vaughan) Lock Dering Prowse dies.

1591 *Astrophil and Stella* by Philip Sidney published.

Orlando Furioso in english heroical verse, John Harington's translation of Ludovico Ariosto's *Orlando Furioso,* published.

1592 Bubonic plague outbreak in London.

(May) William Cecil released from prison.

Elizabeth I entertained by the Hobys at Bisham House.

A Discourse of Life and Death, translation of Philippe de Mornay's *Excellent Discours de la vie et de la mort* by Mary (Sidney) Herbert, published.

1593 Christopher Marlowe killed.

Second edition of *Arcadia* with additions and changes by Mary (Sidney) Herbert published as *The Countess of Pembroke's Arcadia.*

1594 (19 February) Prince Henry (son of James VI of Scotland) born.

Nine Years War (Tyrone's Rebellion) begins in Ireland.

Syon Monastery reestablished in Lisbon, Portugal.

Relacion que Embiaron Las Religiosas Del Monasterio de Sion de Inglaterra, Spanish translation of *The Life and Good End of Sister Marie,* published in Madrid.

1595	*An Apology for Poetry* (*The Defense of Poesy*) by Philip Sidney published.
c.1596	*A Midsummer Night's Dream* by William Shakespeare first performed.
1596	Elizabeth Stuart (daughter of James VI of Scotland) born.
	Elizabeth (Brooke) Joscelin born.
	Second installment of *The Faerie Queene* by Edmund Spenser published.
c.1596–1597	*The Merchant of Venice* by William Shakespeare first performed.
?1597	Rachel (Speght) Procter born.
1598	William Cecil dies.
	Palladis Tamia by Francis Meres published.
	Third edition of *Arcadia* together with Philip Sidney's *Lady of May* and *Astrophil and Stella* published by Mary (Sidney) Herbert.
	Earliest dated needlework sampler in England by Jane Bostocke.
	A godlie forme of hovsholde government by Robert Cleaver published.
1599	The Globe Theatre built.
(September)	Essex Rebellion.
	Edmund Spenser dies.
	Margaret (Dakins) Devereux Sidney Hoby starts her diary.
	Mary (Sidney) Herbert presents a copy of her and her brother's Psalm translations to Elizabeth I.
	Basilikon Doron by James VI of Scotland published in Edinburgh.
	Silkewormes and their Flies by Thomas Moffet published.
1600	
c.1600	*Hamlet* by William Shakespeare first performed.
	Mary (Sidney) Herbert translates Petrarch's *Trionfo della Morte* as *The Triumph of Death*.
1600	*Il merito delle donne* by Moderata Fonte published in Italy.
	Quips upon Questions by Robert Armin published.

1601 (25 February)	Robert Devereux (Earl of Essex) executed.
(30 November)	'The Golden Speech' delivered by Elizabeth I.
	The Mothers Blessing by Nicholas Breton published.
c.1602–1604	*Tragedy of Mariam* by Elizabeth (Tanfield) Cary written.
1603	Bubonic plague outbreak in London.
(24 March)	Elizabeth I dies; James VI of Scotland becomes James I of England.
(30 March)	Nine Years War ends in Ireland.
(25 July)	James I crowned.
	Anne Clifford begins writing her first known diary.
	Grace (Sharington) Mildmay starts *Lady Mildmay's Meditations*.
	The Batchelars Banquet (a new edition of *Fyftene Joyes*) published.
	The Essayes, John Florio's translation of Montaigne's *Essais*, published.
1603–1604	*A Treatise of Three Conversions of England from Paganisme to Christian Religion* by Robert Parsons published.
c.1604	Elizabeth (Tanfield) Cary secretly converts to Catholicism.
1604	*Miscelanea, Meditations, Memoratives* by Elizabeth (Bernye) Grymeston published.
1605	Gunpowder Plot foiled.
	Margaret (Dakins) Devereux Sidney Hoby's diary ends.
	A Way of Reconciliation, Elizabeth (Cooke) Hoby Russell's translation of Jean Ponet's *Diallactation viri boni*, published.
1606	*Instructions for My Children*, Elizabeth Richardson's manuscript, dated.
1607	Jamestown Colony founded in Virginia.
	Penelope (Devereux) Rich dies.
	Hole v. *White* trial at Star Chamber.
1609	*Att.-Gen.* v. *Chatterton* trial at Star Chamber.
	Elizabeth (Cooke) Hoby Russell dies.
1610	Robert Parsons dies.
	Anne (Cooke) Bacon dies.
1611	Mary Herrick dies.
	King James Bible published.

	Salve Deux Rex Judaeorum and 'To Cookeham' by Aemilia (Bassano) Lanyer published.
1612 (6 November)	Prince Henry dies.
1613	Frederick V, Count Palatine, marries Elizabeth Stuart.
	The Tragedy of Mariam by Elizabeth (Tanfield) Cary published.
1615	Arbella (Stuart) Seymour dies.
	The English Housewife by Gervase Markham published.
1616	William Shakespeare dies.
	Ben Jonson's First Folio published.
	The Mothers Blessing by Dorothy Leigh published.
	Anne Clifford starts her second diary.
1617	*Ester Hath Hang'd Haman* by Esther Sowernam published.
	A Mouzell for Melastomus by Rachel (Speght) Procter published.
	Katherine Scott of Nettlestead's will written.
1617–1620	Grace Mildmay finishes *Lady Mildmay's Meditations*.
1618	Thirty Years War begins in Europe.
(October)	Walter Raleigh executed.
1619	Frederick V and Elizabeth Stuart become King and Queen of Bohemia.
1620	The *Mayflower* with the Pilgrim Fathers arrives in Plymouth.
	Frederick V defeated by Catholics; flees from Prague with Elizabeth.
	Grace (Sharington) Mildmay dies.
1621	Mary (Sidney) Herbert dies.
1622	Elizabeth (Brooke) Joscelin dies.
	The Countess of Lincoln's Nurserie by Elizabeth (Knevitt) Clinton published.
	Of Domesticall duties by William Gouge published.
?1623	Margaret (Lucas) Cavendish born.
1623	William Shakespeare's First Folio published.
1624	*The Mother's Legacie to her Unborn Child* by Elizabeth (Brooke) Joscelin published.

1625 (27 March)	James I dies; Charles I becomes King of England.
(13 June)	Charles I marries Henrietta Maria of France.
1626	Elizabeth (Tanfield) Cary makes public her conversion to Catholicism; husband abandons her. Robert Sidney dies.
*c.*1627	*History of the Life, Reign, and Death of Edward II* by Elizabeth (Tanfield) Cary written.
1627	Dorothy (Osborne) Temple born.
1630	*A Chaine of Pearl* by Diana Primrose published.
1633	Margaret (Dakins) Devereux Sidney Hoby dies.
1637	Ben Jonson dies.
1639	Elizabeth (Tanfield) Cary dies.
1640	Long Parliament called by Charles I.
1641	English civil wars begin.
*c.*1643–1650	*The Lady Falkland: Her Life* by Elizabeth (Tanfield) Cary's daughters written.
1645	Archbishop Laud executed.
	Aemilia (Bassano) Lanyer dies.
	A Ladies Legacy to her Daughters by Elizabeth Richardson published.
1648	Thirty Years War ends.
1649 (30 January)	Charles I executed.
	Rump Parliament opens; Republican government (the Commonwealth) established in England, Scotland, Wales, and Ireland.
1651	English civil wars end.
1651–1653	Mary (Sidney) Wroth dies.
1653	Parliament dissolved; Protectorate under Oliver Cromwell's rule established.
1658	Oliver Cromwell dies; Cromwell's son becomes Protector.
1660	Monarchy restored, Charles II becomes King of England.
1661	Rachel (Speght) Procter dies.
1662	Elizabeth Stuart dies.
1665	Great Plague of London.
1666 (September)	Great Fire of London; plague epidemic ends.
	The Blazing World by Margaret (Lucas) Cavendish published.

1673   Margaret (Lucas) Cavendish dies.
                             An Essay to Revive the Antient Education of Gentle-
                             women by Bathsua (Reginald) Makin published.
                             The Legacy of a Dying Mother to her Mourning
                             Children by Susanna Bell published.
1680   *History of the Life, Reign, and Death of Edward II*
                             by Elizabeth (Tanfield) Cary published.
1685 (6 February)   Charles II dies; James II becomes King of
                             England.
1688   Glorious Revolution; James II deposed; William of
                             Orange and Mary become monarchs of England.

Introduction

Caroline Bicks and Jennifer Summit

With this volume, we propose a new approach to women's literary history. Rather than inserting women into a pre-existing literary canon or defining an autonomous female tradition, we focus on the diverse practices of women's writing in order to discern a broad but obscure landscape of female literacy and literary practice in the early modern period.[1] The subject of women's writing forces us to rethink at a fundamental level what 'writing' is and has been, and how it interacted with the various histories – religious, social, cultural, and political – that shaped it. The period of our focus, 1500–1610, maintained far less rigid conceptions of authorship, genre, and the literary work than did the modern period. The very term 'literature' in the early modern period meant 'writing' in the broadest sense, rather than the distinctly high-cultural modes of fiction or poetry that the term came to signify for moderns.[2] And just as recent scholarship has established that the idea of the author – as an individual who makes (mostly) his living by his pen – was a relatively recent phenomenon, so too scholarship on the early modern period has uncovered a wide variety of alternative forms – corporate and anonymous, multi-media and socially dispersed – in which writing could and did flourish before the professionalization of the author.[3] Attentive to the multiple textual forms and writing practices that persisted in the shadows of traditional literary authorship, we are better able to understand and appreciate writing by early women.

Our focus on women's participation in writing as a broad cultural field is supported by the very title of this series, *The History of British Women's Writing*. For while the achievements of few women featured in this volume would be recognized under the modern designation 'literature', together they represent the richness and diversity of early modern literacy and textual culture. Women's writing in the period is notable for its hybridity (a term that we borrow from contributor Nancy Bradley Warren) in genre, form, and modes of composition. Many women did write in genres that we now recognize as literary, such as drama, poetry, and imaginative fiction. But our expanded focus on 'writing' allows us to focus too on women's production of a wider range of texts – not only plays, poetry, and narrative, but also letters, compilations, and recipe books. In contrast to the modern expectation of authorship as a singular achievement, these texts are products of a notably social and communal practice that, in turn, demands a new model of literary history to account for it.

This volume moves beyond the traditional concerns of literary history, which have alternately produced 'monumental' accounts of isolated achievements or 'antiquarian' accounts of comprehensive scope.[4] In their place, we seek something approaching a sociology of writing, which attempts to understand individual writing acts within a broad field of literate practice. In this aim we join D. F. McKenzie, for whom 'the sociology of texts' promised a new field (in bibliography) that sought to place books within the 'complex relationships' that established 'the very conditions under which meanings are created'.[5] Likewise, this volume continually returns to questions that plumb the social significance of women's acts of writing and literacy: Who reads? Who writes? And how are these practices fostered or limited by the range of other social activities with which they are entwined?

This volume builds on a generation of scholarship on writing by women in the early modern period. A late but vibrant outgrowth of the second-wave feminist literary scholarship that began in the 1970s and 1980s, the field of early modern women's writing transformed literary study for multiple constituencies: for feminist scholars, it revealed (against the well-known lament of Virginia Woolf for Shakespeare's lost sister) that women writers had been active in the periods before modernity; for Renaissance scholars, it produced a new archive of writings and with it, a profound shift in the understanding of early literary culture; and for students, it opened up genres previously believed to be restricted to men, such as love lyric, historical drama, and even military treatise.[6] The pioneers in the field undertook a massive archaeological task, aiming to uncover, beneath the better-known monuments of the age, forgotten strata of writing by women in all forms. Given the relative scarcity of textual evidence surviving from the period – as compared to the modern fields – scholars of early modern women's writing established a special closeness to the archives. They also found themselves questioning the taxonomies of authorship, genre, and the literary work that had long structured literary study. Instead, scholarship of early modern women's writing was defined in its initial stages by a focus on the material and social conditions of literacy, publication, and access that shaped women's interactions with texts – those that they wrote as well as read. And above all, scholars in early women's writing found themselves confronting the authoritative models of English literary history from which their subjects had long been excluded.

The discovery of early women writers and new attention to their work prompted scholars to redraw the lineages of literary influence and cultural authority that had previously defined the English literary Renaissance. Projects like *The Norton Anthology of Literature by Women* envisioned a 'female tradition' that stretched from the Middle Ages to the present; while *The Norton Anthology of English Literature* and other influential anthologies began to include works by early women writers such as Aemilia Lanyer and Lady Mary Wroth alongside those of their better-known male contemporaries, such as Sidney, Milton, and Shakespeare.[7] But in a simultaneous development, traditional models of literary history – premised on the idea that the history of the literature belonging to an age or nation can be represented through the selection and chronological ordering of its greatest works – began to attract criticism and increasing doubt in the discipline at large. Where poststructuralist criticism encouraged skepticism of the 'grand narratives' that drove traditional literary histories, scholars working on the literatures traditionally excluded from such histories questioned the processes of selection and notions of value and cultural authority that created them. In the wake of these critiques, many began to ask whether literary history itself continued to be a viable enterprise.[8]

More recently, a number of innovative scholarly editorial projects both return to and transform the foundations of literary history. Mario J. Valdés, the editor of a new literary history of Latin America, contrasts what he calls 'effective' or 'open literary history' with the more restrictive models from the past: 'traditional literary history restricts, repeats, and institutionalizes the writing of the past, while effective literary history aims to inform, situate, and contextualize the literature of the past in a literary culture', defined broadly – 'the aim is multiplicity, not totality.'[9] For Franco Moretti, the editor of a five-volume history of the novel, literary history should mobilize 'abstraction, synthesis, and comparative research' to capture the 'flexibility [that] borders on chaos' of its subject, in which 'one encounters the strangest creations, and high and low trade places at every opportunity, as the borders of literature are continuously, unpredictably expanded'.[10] And the editors of The Orlando Project, an online database of women's writing, endorse criticism of traditional literary history 'as monolithic, hegemonic, teleological, dependent upon a single-voiced narrative that obliterates the multiple and ex-centric narratives of writers outside of canonical traditions (including women)' and assert in its place the possibility of a 'rhizomatic' web of 'multiple literary histories' enabled especially by digital forms.[11] These new literary histories stress openness, multiplicity, and flexibility of approach and form, reflecting new perspectives on their subjects: they focus less on the distinctive achievement of isolated individuals than on writing as a social practice, and less on abstract models of tradition or development than on literary culture, defined by changing material and historical contexts.

In keeping with these ideas, we have not organized this volume around individual female authors (with the exception of Elizabeth I), or conventional generic literary categories. Many of the essays here focus not on 'literary' texts or well-known authors, but rather on ordinary women from across the social spectrum and their everyday encounters with the written word. For example, women from 'the technically illiterate to humanist educated', as Lynne Magnusson writes, composed letters to family members and friends (whether or not they penned them themselves) that offered everything from medical to marital to political advice. Such texts indicate the diverse material forms that women's writing assumed across our period, the dynamic networks in which these texts were composed and exchanged, and the far-reaching cultures of literacy in which their readers and writers participated.

As the example of letters shows, modern distinctions between public and private do not hold in the early modern period. The supposedly private household itself, as Julie Crawford establishes, was a center of communal and sometimes political power, 'a headquarters for religious and political activism both at the national and international levels': it was also a center of female writing, as Catherine Richardson shows us, from commonplace books and embroidered family histories, to broadsides pasted on walls. Conversely, the public venue of the street, in Pamela Allen Brown's handling of it, allowed women unexpected avenues for literate expression that are invisible if we believe women to have been restricted to the 'private' home. The multiplicity of women's literate practices challenges us to rethink the boundary between reading and writing in ways that support and expand modern scholars' interests in 'eliminat[ing] the separation between producing and consuming' that has artificially limited our understanding of early literary culture.[12]

The 110 years of English history that define our volume's scope (1500–1610) witnessed a number of seismic shifts in the intersecting landscapes of politics, religion, society, and culture: the Reformation and its multiple effects on theological philosophy and practice, political rule, religious factionalism, and the institution of the Church of England; the centralization of the monarchy; the growth of humanism, with its attendant social and intellectual changes; the rise of print culture; colonial expansion and encounters with foreign cultures. Our aim here is to explore women's writing (from the everyday recording of household expenses and recipes to the penning of widely circulated verse Psalms) as it intersected with and influenced these sixteenth-century movements. In doing so, we hope that this volume can begin to offer alternative models of how texts, their writers and readers (all broadly defined), respond to and participate in their historical moment. Whether sharing a letter, translating a text, or debating a religious motto painted over a mantelpiece during a family dinner, women's experiences of literacy are never socially isolated incidents.

We have organized this volume around three major sections: Part I, Reading and Writing, foregrounds media and literacy (manuscript culture and its relationship to a nascent print culture, literary coteries, and the growth of vernacular literacies). Part II, Writing Places, considers the physical spaces in which women's (and sometimes also men's) literary production occurred, taking into account the various social, political, and cultural ideologies that inflected each of these categories of space. Three subsections consider three different types of space: Domestic Settings; Playing Spaces (which includes traditional theatrical venues as well as alternative performance spaces, such as local festivals and street markets); and Tudor Courts, both royal and legal. Part III, Developing Histories, focuses on the intersection of writing and major historical developments in the period – most notably, the Reformation, the emergence of a national identity through colonial expansion, encounters with racial 'others', and the dissemination and enforcement of monarchical ideologies.

Rather than isolating 'women' as the central focus of our sections and essays, we explore how women and their writings engaged with and shaped literary genres, technologies, and institutions in fundamental ways. Each essay in our volume takes up, from different perspectives, the meanings of gender for the authors and writings under consideration; but, in so doing, our contributors find ways to consider gender difference as a factor within a larger literary or historical problem. The result is a volume that considers women's literary production as fully engaged with the multiple levels of culture, literary and otherwise, in the sixteenth century.

This volume's first section on Reading and Writing offers both an overview of women's writing during the period of our focus and a revisionary perspective on writing and written culture as these entered women's lives. In her chapter 'Reading Women' Heidi Brayman Hackel offers a survey of female literacy that both challenges conventional measurements of literacy rates (which, Hackel contends, historically undercount women) and in their place, examines alternative evidence for women's textual engagements: signatures in books, household accounts, and visual representations of books in female portraiture. Our ability to measure literacy in the period is complicated by the fact that reading and writing were treated (and taught) as distinct skills: while writing leaves material traces, Hackel points out, the traces of reading acts are more difficult to discern. Yet Hackel also mobilizes this insight to call for a new vision of female literacy, one in which writing and reading, production and consumption of texts, are mutually implicated. Attending to women's accounts of their own reading, Hackel contends, reveals that literacy and its practices were culturally dispersed and multi-layered, prompting her to describe a field of diverse 'literacies', with diverse levels of participation, to replace the misleading simplifications contained in the opposition of 'literate' versus 'illiterate', which has for too long consigned women to the latter category.

For Julie Crawford, a similarly multi-layered perspective of female literacy manifests in women's experiences of literary circles and coteries. Joined by familial and regional bonds, these literary circles likewise mingled acts of reading and writing, as the circulation of manuscripts among their members generated textual production as well as consumption. As Crawford establishes, the acts of reading and circulating texts in these milieux become 'primary, rather than secondary, forms of literary production'. Similarly, manuscript becomes a form of 'publication' whose influence and cultural privilege is not compromised by its apparent privacy and restriction. Thus the extended literary circles centered on Anne Vaughan Lock, Mary Sidney Herbert, and the learned Cooke sisters (Mildred, Anne, Elizabeth, and Katherine) represent communities of literacy in which writing forms a distinctly social act whose influence extends far beyond the immediate bonds of readers and writers.

A. E. B. Coldiron likewise focuses on social networks as they comprise early print culture and enable, as she establishes, a surprising degree of female participation and influence. As Coldiron asserts, 'textual authority is up for grabs in the environment of early print.' This new era of textual authority found a defining theme in 'the woman question', in which the comic and didactic exploration of gender roles formed a staple for printers and readers. But the reorganization of textual authority held implications for women as producers and consumers of texts as well as the subject of popular books. While the early printers carried some patronage practices over from late medieval manuscript culture, they also betrayed a keen awareness of the new market dynamics of print's readers and buyers. Both patronage system and marketplace allowed women a range of roles; patrons like Margaret Beaufort and Margaret of Burgundy exerted an influence over the output of early printers, while authors like Christine de Pizan and Margaret More Roper emerged as visible authors in early print. The dispersed social networks comprising early print culture further allowed women's participation as typesetters, compositors, bookbinders, booksellers, and even printers: as Coldiron observes, 'we cannot divide social and commercial authorship along a public–private line, nor along gender lines' in the early print. Rather, like manuscript networks and coteries, print reveals a textual culture in which production and consumption are joined as social acts of collective literacy.

The next part of the volume is organized around Writing Places. The essays that make up the first section, Domestic Settings, collectively challenge traditional studies of the period that have privileged literary forms of writing and conceptions of authorship and audience over the vast field of other writing that took place in domestic spaces. Such studies have occluded the everyday women who wrote letters and diaries, embroidered a memory, or compiled advice to pass on to their children and grandchildren. The early modern women in these essays share an interest in shaping both their households and the world beyond their immediate walls, projecting themselves, through their writing, into family histories, current events, and the behavior of future generations.

Catherine Richardson's chapter 'Household Writing' allows for a much wider view into early modern women's writing than previously has existed, one that includes lower- and middle-status households, and encompasses texts as varied as wills, commonplace books, annotated recipes, and embroidered samplers. At the lower and middle parts of the social spectrum, Richardson considers storytelling, and the production and initializing of textiles, as privileged forms of domestic writing. Upper-status women as well engaged in a 'language of ornament' when they produced samplers and wall hangings. Turning to more elite households, Richardson establishes that letters afforded women a particular kind of political influence as they operated from the base of their households, and 'used letter writing to intervene in the kind of patronage suits and dynastic negotiations which were central to their families' political success'. Diaries, as well, were a form of women's writing that pointed beyond the immediate concerns of the household. Richardson reads Lady Margaret Hoby's diary as elevating 'housework, in terms of the curing of the sick, cooking and needlework' by placing it 'within the spiritual scheme of an individual life'. In this way, Hoby's writing, like the other forms of textual engagement Richardson examines, allows the household 'to rub shoulders with eternity'.

Like Richardson, Edith Snook cautions against privileging particular written forms when approaching domestic writing. Snook's topic is maternal advice, a genre that often is misunderstood as having begun with the printed maternal legacies of the seventeenth century. Snook examines a wide range of sixteenth-century manuscripts that, she argues, all influenced the genre of the printed maternal legacy while engaging in a wide range of social discourses: from Elizabeth Ashburnham's prayers and meditations to her children, to the account book Anne Clifford's mother kept regarding her daughter's clothing. Snook examines letters as well, considering three cases of elite mothers (Elizabeth Russell, Mary Dudley Sidney, and Honor Lisle) attempting to shape, via epistolary advice, their children's upbringings and behavior while away from home. In an extended example of maternal manuscripts' multiple afterlives, Snook traces the familial circulation of Grace Mildmay's autobiography and meditations, which were written for her daughter Mary Fane and eventually passed down to her grandchildren, with Mary's own addenda. 'The advice of women of the Reformation', concludes Snook, 'is a matrilineal inheritance that, more surely than land, can be passed from mother to child.'

Lynne Magnusson calls for a similarly expansive definition of women's writing in her chapter 'Letters'. Mining the rich material offered by the over 3,000 extant manuscript letters written by Englishwomen in the sixteenth century, she focuses on two developed case studies (Mary Herrick and Katherine Bertie) and two briefer samplings (from Mary Sidney Herbert and Juliann Penn). By attending to the 'many diverse elements shaping the contexts of production and reception', Magnusson offers new ways of recognizing women's original contributions to as well as their participation in 'conventional epistolary scripts'. Mary Herrick, the wife of an ironmonger, never penned any of the many letters sent from her home in Leicester to her son in London, yet her involvement in what Magnusson terms the 'collaborative discourse' of letter-writing is evident. The twenty-two letters written by Katherine Bertie, Duchess of Suffolk, to her friend William Cecil offer a very different perspective on women's epistolary involvements: written when they both were involved observers of Edward Seymour's fall from grace as Lord Protector, the letters exhibit a relaxed candor and opinionated stance that Magnusson argues marks Bertie's unconventional treatment of epistolary conventions. Magnusson's final examples illustrate how the genre of the suitor's (or petitioning) letter raised particularly vexed issues of reception for the women who performed them, as it was 'the kind most likely to have consequences beyond the woman herself for her husband, her heirs, her family or a wider network of alliances'.

The two chapters that comprise the next section on Playing Spaces re-define conventional notions of writing and performance spaces, expanding both arenas to include a much wider range of women's voices – on the page and in the air, in the closet and the street. Pamela Allen Brown's chapter 'The Street' considers this crowded, noisy space, 'the prime conduit for news and rumor' in the Elizabethan period, as a 'crucial staging ground for writing and reception', especially for the non-elite. 'Writing occurs in many guises', from doggerel to graffiti to the printed broadside. Brown considers how religious processions, ballads, pilgrim-ages, and 'the bloody street theater of religious reprisal' were all rich sites of female narratives, produced both by anonymous women and well-known figures such as Anne Lock and Anne Askew. Brown also examines how female libelers and gossips 'generated a slew of legal writ-ing' that featured women's testimony; in the same vein, street-mockery informs Isabella Whitney's *Wyll and Testament*, a text that Brown argues should be read for the 'crowded comic situation' it evokes, the 'satiric woman-about-town' who jests and entertains her friends on the street, in the alehouse, and the printseller's shop. Ultimately Brown makes the case that, rather than reading early modern women's writing as a purely private act, separate from the world beyond household walls, we must consider how it engages with the multi-media street culture that per-meated so many early moderns' lives.

In her chapter 'The Theater' Marion Wynne-Davies makes a similarly bold argument for redefining the spaces in which early moderns per-formed. Barred from writing for and acting in conventional theatrical venues like the public stage, sixteenth-century Englishwomen 'had to develop innovative and, often, subversive ways of circumventing the requirements of performance, audience, and stage'. She considers four kinds of alternative playing spaces, all of them sites where wider political and social discourses fomented. Wynne-Davies begins by considering how a martyr's last words could be distributed and textually performed via 'let-ters, accounts, and biographies'. She reads John Foxe's and Margaret More Roper's dramatic recreations of the martyr's last words as wielding the same performative power as the scaffold speech. Tracing the history of the banqueting house as a site of aristocratic self-fashioning, Wynne-Davies next argues that Jane Lumley's translation of Euripides's *Iphigeneia at Aulis* was likely intended to be performed at her father's, the Earl of Arundel's, estate at Nonsuch. The play, which has been recognized for its allegorical references to Arundel's role in Jane Grey's execution, demonstrates Lumley's deft engagement with political affairs as well as her role in valorizing the wealth, power, and virtue of her father. Like Lumley, when Mary Sidney Herbert translated Robert Garnier's *The Tragedie of Antonie*, she intervened in larger ideological debates. Wynne-Davies argues that Sidney Herbert's work 'challenges the supposition that closet dramas – and the women who wrote them – were contained by the patriarchal discourses of the public theater'. Instead, she 'rewrites closet drama as the theater of the bed-chamber or brothel', and turns both into 'playing spaces in which supposed containment and marginality are revealed instead as the loci for a deconstruction of traditional gender roles'. Wynne-Davies concludes with Elizabeth Cary's *Tragedy of Mariam*, the most famous female-authored play from our period, and asks why Cary wrote a play never intended for performance. By analyzing how the female voice is foregrounded just as it is silenced, Wynne-Davies ties the play and its perforce imagined playing space back to her earlier consideration of martyrdom as performance, arguing that it should be understood 'as part of the wider early modern discourses of power, rebellion, and freedom of speech'.

The concluding section of Writing Places focuses on the Tudor Courts. The term 'court', originally designating an enclosed area, came to describe both a manor house or princely residence and a center of administration and law during the late medieval and early modern periods. Courts of both descriptions further belie modern oppositions of public and private and the assumptions of gender difference that undergird them, since courts are both private in their very enclosure and exclusivity but also supremely public in the functions they carry out. And, as Carolyn Sale and Christine Coch establish, the princely and the judicial courts of Tudor England served as privileged spaces for the production of literature and writing as well as the performance of gender.

Though women were marginal to the early modern judicial system, since their gender barred them from serving in official functions, the courts nonetheless offered them resonant sites for inscribing stories, both autobiographical and fictional. As Carolyn Sale establishes, women's very marginality to the courts forced them to produce innovative literary forms in confrontation with the authoritative discourse of the law; thus courts play an unexpectedly generative role in the history of early modern women's writing. The Protestant martyr Anne Askew establishes a model for women's engagement with the court as she produces her own written testimony to challenge the official legal records. If courts produce official writing of legal weight and authority, they also instigate alternative textual forms when women produce counter-narratives in the confessional mode. Thus Isabella Whitney's literary forms playfully appropriate legal distinctions between truth and falsehood and offer themselves as both 'trew' and 'fained'. Whitney's writing emerges from an intimate knowledge of the courts; likewise Elizabeth Cary, whose father, Lawrence Tanfield, was a celebrated lawyer and judge, betrays a familiarity with the court as a place in which women's stories gain heightened social significance. In the work of these women writers, the court emerges as a uniquely productive textual site because of its ability to compel narrative from female agents.

The subject of Christine Coch's chapter, Elizabeth I, occupied a unique position in relation to the princely courts in which she served (or from which she suffered banishment) as a princess and queen. By focusing on the full range of genres in which Elizabeth wrote – translation, prayers, poetry, letters, and speeches – Coch illuminates the multi-faceted nature of literary production in the Elizabethan court. While the female monarch embodied a conflict 'between her feminine private self, naturally inferior to men in mind and body, and her public role', Elizabeth's writing continually negotiates and intermingles the seemingly private genres of poetry, prayer, and letters with the public genres of speeches and official decree. In the process, Elizabeth reveals early modern literature to be a diverse field that, in spanning the political and the personal, the public and the private, allows an ideal medium for the complex self-representation of the female monarch.

The chapters comprising the final section, Developing Histories, examine early modern women's engagement, through their writing, with major historical developments of their time. In the process, they offer powerful counterweight to the assumption that women were marginal to, or absent from, such developments. From the fresh vantage point of women's writing, moreover, these chapters open new perspectives on the historical events and processes at their core, showing that historical agency was not restricted to men in political, religious, and military authority but extended to the unofficial social networks and domestic settings in which women's writing flourished.

Religious and devotional topics formed the bulk of early modern women's writings, both published and unpublished. While piety was a praiseworthy characteristic of early modern femininity, Nancy Bradley Warren shows that women who took up religious topics also engaged directly and boldly with the contentious issue of religious reform. In so doing, she contends, they force us to reconsider the very meanings and manifestations of early modern reform movements. Warren's chapter 'Religious Writing and Reformation' finds through women's writing a more heterogeneous and 'hybrid' religious culture than implied by a more conventional polarity of 'Protestant' versus 'Catholic' during the same period. In light of this heterogeneity, Warren proposes that we view the period as one of dynamic and multi-form 'Reformations', rather than of univocal and unidirectional 'Reformation'. Drawing unexpected parallels between the writings of Protestant wives and cloistered nuns (the Brigittine Nuns of Syon), Warren uncovers common strands of Christocentric devotion that belie the outward division between their confessional orientations. At the same time, she finds 'hybrid, multi-dimensional qualities' in the work of single authors that reveal unexpected diversity. The writings of Henry VIII's last queen, Katherine Parr, show affinity with both Protestant and Catholic faiths, parallel to Parr's devotion to her two princess step-daughters, the Catholic Mary and the Protestant Elizabeth. Similarly, the Protestant gentry woman Grace Mildmay exhibits linguistic and devotional conventions – particularly around her meditations on Christ's passions – that would be more expected from writers identified with Catholic, rather than Protestant, orientations. Rereading the Reformation from the perspective of early modern women's writing, Warren shows, undercuts conventional scholarly expectations of 'a linear, teleological relationship between the medieval and the Catholic and the early modern and the Protestant', thereby forcing us to revise our understanding not only of religious but also historical change.

The two chapters that follow take up different aspects of early modern globalization as it informed early modern English conceptions of national and individual identity. Sujata Iyengar finds in early modern women's writing special insights into nascent theories of race and racial otherness and the 'mythologies of skin color' that upheld them. As Iyengar asserts in her chapter 'Race and Skin Color in Early Modern Women's Writing', women bore a close relation to race because they were believed to be guarantors of bloodlines; thus early modern languages of female beauty and sexual purity are frequently aligned with notions of racial purity, and women are commonly held responsible for the physical distinctions between races. The writings of Mary Sidney Herbert, Elizabeth Cary, and Aemilia Lanyer betray awareness of the cultural conventions linking sexual and racial identity, Iyengar finds, but they also reveal their authors' efforts to manipulate contemporary language of female beauty and sexual purity in order to express and understand complex ideas about the nature of race itself. Skin color – always a charged topic in connection with women, for whom fairness and blushing are common conventions of female beauty – emerges as a privileged marker of rank, class, and inheritance, even as these women's writings reflect considerable diversity around the question of whether race is a fixed or fluid characteristic, an external sign or an indelible mark of identity and character.

Chris Laoutaris's chapter 'Translation/Historical Writing' contends that 'women who translated a work from one particular language or local context into another were manipulating histories: sacred, social, national.' This insight counters a widespread assumption that translation offered women a safe but decidedly marginal form of literary activity, while joining and advancing the work of scholars currently revaluing the work of translation in the early periods. Translation, as Laoutaris finds, is a 'kinetic' act, and the translator herself less a 'dutiful disciple' to her original than an agent of collaboration, transformation, and historical change. Margaret More Roper's translations participated in and facilitated the transformation of international humanism by advancing a prototype of 'learned femininity' consistent with the humanist goal of the cultivation of irenic community and the application of human reason against the prejudices arising from a blind adherence to custom. The famously learned Cooke sisters translated religious works as a means of intervening in the international religious reform, while the historical translations of Mary Sidney Herbert and Anne Dowriche assert English national identity on a global stage. In the work of these and other women, Laoutaris finds, translation attests to the international scope of early modern literary culture, as well as to women's ability to enter and shape it.

Together, these chapters produce literary history in a new key. By rethinking traditional models of the literary work and literary authorship, they allow fresh perspectives not only on women's writing in the period but also on the full range of textual practices and objects that made up early modern literary culture. Our contributors' refusal to privilege the relatively rare act of private literary composition over the more common and diverse acts of writing (whether entirely original, mimetic, or patchwork; performed by a group, an individual, or over time by multiple contributors) informs an important principle of this volume: while we do not seek to diminish the importance of well-known female authors or established literary genres, we do insist that they be considered alongside more socially prevalent (if less conventionally literary) modes of women's writing in our period. Such a perspective ideally enriches our understanding of the multiple kinds of cultural work that different women performed when they engaged with the written word; it also broadens our understanding of the material conditions that shaped literary culture for all its participants, women as well as men.

Notes

1. For a reassessment of the literary history of women's writing, see the essays collected in *Women and Literary History: 'For There She Was'*, ed. Katherine Binhammer and Jeanne Wood (Newark: University of Delaware Press, 2003).
2. As Stephen Greenblatt points out, the early modern term 'literature' was identified with the production of 'literacy', and as such, signaled the high social value of the (then, few) literate individuals, rather than the social value of the special forms of writing that would later be distinguished by the term 'literature' (and thus separated from 'writing'). See Greenblatt, 'What is the History of Literature?', *Critical Inquiry*, 23 (1997), 460–81; see also the editors' introduction and essays included in 'Literacies in Early Modern England', ed. Margaret Ferguson and Eve Sanders. Special issue of *Critical Survey*, 14 (2002), 1–8.
3. Jeffrey Masten, *Textual Intercourse: Collaboration, Authorship, and Sexualities in Renaissance Drama* (Cambridge: Cambridge University Press, 1997) and Marcy L. North, *The Anonymous Renaissance: Cultures of Discretion in Tudor-Stuart England* (Chicago: University of Chicago Press, 2003) reassess the meaning of authorship and literary production in the early modern period.
4. For an analysis of these terms, see David Simpson, 'Is Literary History the History of Everything? The Case for "Antiquarian" History', *SubStance*, special issue: 'Literary History', 28 (1999), 5–16.
5. D. F. McKenzie, *Bibliography and the Sociology of Texts* (Cambridge: Cambridge University Press, 1999), p. 2; see also the special issue, 'The Sociology of Literature', ed. Priscilla Parkhurst Ferguson, Philippe Desan, and Wendy Griswold, *Critical Inquiry*, 14 (1988).
6. Seminal work in the field includes Margaret J. M. Ezell, *Writing Women's Literary History* (Baltimore: Johns Hopkins University Press, 1993) and *Rewriting the Renaissance: The Discourses of Sexual Difference in Early Modern Europe*, ed. Margaret W. Ferguson, Maureen Quilligan, and Nancy J. Vickers (Chicago: University of Chicago Press, 1986).
7. *The Norton Anthology of Literature by Women: The Traditions in English*, ed. Sandra Gilbert and Susan Gubar (New York: W. W. Norton & Company, 1985); *The Norton Anthology of English Literature*, ed. M. H. Abrams, 6th edn, 2 vols (New York: W. W. Norton & Company, 1993), I.
8. David Perkins, *Is Literary History Possible?* (Baltimore: Johns Hopkins University Press, 1992).
9. Mario J. Valdés, 'Rethinking the History of Literary History', in *Rethinking Literary History: A Dialogue on Theory*, ed. Mario J. Valdés and Linda Hutcheon (Oxford: Oxford University Press, 2002), pp. 68, 95.
10. Franco Moretti, 'On *The Novel*', in *The Novel: Volume 1. History, Geography, and Culture*, ed. Franco Moretti (Princeton: Princeton University Press, 2006), pp. ix–x.
11. The Orlando Project, http://orlando.cambridge.org/ [accessed 31 August 2009].
12. Roger Chartier, *Cultural History: Between Practices and Representations* (Ithaca: Cornell University Press, 1988), p. 41.

Part I Reading and Writing

1
Reading Women

Heidi Brayman Hackel

If only a handful of British women writers surface in print during the period covered by this volume, many more women left traces of their writing in manuscript, on flyleaves, in textiles, even on walls.[1] But it is as readers that women arguably made the greatest contribution to literary culture in sixteenth-century England. As daughters listening to their fathers reading, as sisters perusing their brothers' university miscellanies, as mothers instructing their children, as nuns sharing books in convents, sixteenth-century women participated in the development of a culture of engaged reading and book buying. However, it is often with a sideways glance that we spot women readers, for reading on its own is historically invisible, and women's reading in particular was strongly shaped by family roles and practices. Although we may never know with certainty how many early modern women could read, we can recover the details of the circumstances, passions, and consequences of how some women read. Paired with other accounts of literacy and learning, these individual reading women – often so extraordinary in their documentary survival – model early modern experiences of piety, family, recreation, domesticity, and writing alongside and through their practices of reading.

The period from 1500 to 1610 was a transformative century for reading women: these years brought a spread of literacy, a surge in print marketed to women, and the birth of a generation of women who would amass substantial libraries. And yet the period poses significant challenges and cautions for scholars of women's reading. Evidence that has shaped early modern scholarship is scarce for much of this period. We do not have comprehensive quantitative studies of literacy for much of the sixteenth century, especially from 1500 to 1550. David Cressy, in a study that continues to shape the field, offers a 'projection back' to 1500 of 'perhaps 90% of Englishmen illiterate at the turn of the century, with illiteracy claiming as many as 99% of the women'. R. A. Houston's parallel study of Scottish literacy begins with the year 1600, and no similar studies of Irish or Welsh literacy have been published.[2] Literacy studies like Cressy's and Houston's present problems of their own for the study of women's reading, but we don't have them even as base-lines for most of this period. A dramatic increase in print aimed at women also favors the later years in the period. Suzanne Hull counts at least 163 books in 500 editions 'specifically directed to or printed for women readers' before 1640, 85 per cent of which was published after 1570.[3] There are similar gaps in anecdotal evidence. Many of the early modern women who have been recovered as readers and book collectors – Lady Anne Clifford, Frances Bridgewater, Frances Wolfreston, Elizabeth Puckering – were born after or towards the end of the period covered by this volume.

A second critical consideration for the period is the impact of the Reformation on women's reading and learning. On the one hand, the Protestant Reformation emphasized literacy and promoted the vernacu-lar Bible; on the other, the dissolution of convents eliminated impor-tant centers of women's learning and changed the landscape of girls' education. Scholars have identified the years before the Reformation as a time when women traditionally provided basic reading instruction at home and in their communities and when nuns could claim benefit of clergy and secure legal protection with a show of literacy. While con-vents and abbeys provided sanctioned spaces for female literacy and book culture, their walls did not entirely enclose the literate practices within. The nuns' engagement with texts helped shift lay devotion and reading practices, and convent schools served as permanent facilities in significant numbers for educating girls. After the dissolution of these convent schools in the 1530s, little formal schooling was available for girls outside the home, and humanists created a masculine educational sphere with little place in it for mothers and schoolmistresses in the six-teenth century.[4] However, education at home was in some families rig-orous and formalized, resistance to these institutional changes surfaced in sixteenth-century debates about girls' possible entry into grammar schools, and the figure of the religious woman writer helped shape an emergent literary culture.[5] In Ireland, too, the dissolution of monaster-ies affected women even more severely than men. By the seventeenth century, Irish cultural support for female learning of the previous cen-tury had nearly vanished.[6]

In this shifting landscape of women's learning and literacy, the prac-tices of writing and reading are related in complicated ways. Like women's writing, women's reading was 'almost equally a site for conflict and anxiety'.[7] Even so, in their resistance to anxieties about women's writing, in their choice of genres and of rhetoric, women writers often figured themselves as readers. In perhaps the first English defense of women's writing in print, Margaret Tyler presents her translation of a Spanish romance as a means 'to acquaint my selfe with mine olde reading', and she defends women's right to 'pen a story' by establishing authorship as a point on a continuum with the more accepted feminine roles of dedicatee and reader.[8] As translators, compilers, and paraphrasers, Tyler's female contemporaries, if less explicitly positioning themselves as readers, nevertheless figure their writing as gathering. Esther Inglis, who desires that she not 'be estemed impudent in transending the limites of schamefastnes (wherwith our sexe is commonlie adorned)', likens herself to a bee drawing honey from flowers; Anne Wheathill uses a similar metaphor in characterizing her 1584 collection of prayers as the fruits she has 'presumed to gather out of the garden of Gods most holie word'.[9] Mary Sidney too cultivated a 'public persona as a reader [...] even as she broke with convention by acting as a patron, editor, and author'.[10] Identifying themselves first as gatherers and readers, these women writers aligned themselves with the far more common and less controversial of the two skills of reading and writing.

In both formal and informal literacy instruction, students learned to read before they learned to write. Reading, accordingly, was 'a much more socially diffused skill than writing', and literacy generally was economically determined, linked as it was to families' ability to send children to school rather than put them to work. But the attainment of literacy was also highly gendered. Not only did girls typically attend schools for shorter periods of time than their brothers, but writing instruction was regularly excluded from girls' curricula in both England and Scotland well into the eighteenth century.[11] Many early moderns, especially women, could read but not write; most 'reading women', therefore, weren't writing women. The answers to the most basic question about reading women, therefore, are elusive: who could read? Reading is historically invisible unless captured and transformed by another act of production, such as recorded speech, extant writing, or visual representation. As Margaret Spufford has put it, the 'one standard literary skill capable of measurement that can be used as an index of literary skill for the whole population [...] is the ability to sign one's name'.[12] Signature literacy studies count as illiterate anyone who uses a mark rather than a signature to authenticate a loyalty oath, court record, or parish record. Such studies of early modern England and Scotland register women, even by the early seventeenth century, as 'mostly', 'massively', 'almost universally' illiterate.[13]

And yet these calculations distort the reality of sixteenth-century women's literacy for a number of reasons: patterns of instruction yielded far more female readers than writers, legal and state practices led to the severe under-representation of female signers and markers of these documents, and the documents themselves typically did not differentiate women by social class or profession. The flaws are numerous enough that several scholars despair of ever knowing how many early modern women were able to read. Margaret Ferguson dismisses the statistics as 'unreliable' and the method as 'arguably useless'.[14] Arguing that early modern England was 'a much more "literate" environment than has ever been fully appreciated', Adam Fox posits that basic reading literacy is no longer the 'crucial divide' by 1500. He assumes instead among early modern women a 'widespread ability to read print'; Frances Dolan similarly accepts 'that many women could read and/or write'. And indeed, if projections based on later periods hold, as many as 75 per cent of female markers may have been able to read.[15]

The projected figure of 99 per cent illiteracy for women in 1500 fails to capture the range and depth of literate practices that survive in glimpses in the historical and literary record. Unequipped to capture gradations in skill, signature literacy studies presume a binary of literate or illiterate predicated upon the presence of a signature or of a mark. Evidence from the period, however, compels scholars to think of literacy as multiple and varied. Girls' education especially was subject to tremendous variation in this period even among the landed gentry, the extent of training dependent upon social class and parental attitudes. Richard Mulcaster in 1581 allowed for girls 'learning with distinction in degrees, with difference of their calling, with respect to their endes'. The 'endes' of primary education shifted over the course of the century as well. In sixteenth-century Worcester, for instance, instructions in wills for the raising of testators' children center on moral education in the first half of the century and gradually incorporate more practical and vocational skills, particularly reading and writing, over the course of the century.[16] In the sixteenth century, these vagaries of literacy instruction and the proliferation of typefaces and scripts produced a range of literacies. A tentative reader, for example, might be able to handle black letter but not roman type, while a more able reader of print might still find various manuscript hands illegible. Hierarchies in print and manuscript both recognized and reinforced these various literacies: primers and ballads were typically produced in black letter, and secretary hand was considered the preserve of male writers.[17] Paper and parchment, pen and ink were not the only media used by early modern writers and readers: Juliet Fleming has recovered the whitewashed domestic wall as 'the primary scene of writing in early modern England'. In 'paper-short' England, the 'bulk' of writing, she argues, occurred on walls, furniture, and other domestic surfaces.[18] The bulk of reading, it follows, was practiced on these domestic surfaces. In the context of such various media and masteries, Rebecca Krug's distinction between 'literacy' and 'literate practices' is especially useful.[19] Counted as illiterate because of an ink mark on a paper document, a sixteenth-century woman might well have engaged in a range of literate practices, reading cheap print, inscribed rings, and chalked walls. She might have found chancery hand unintelligible but been able to write with charcoal above her own hearth.

Even before 1500, strong evidence survives of women's engagement with manuscripts, printed books, and networks of readers. Much as some London guilds began to require that male apprentices upon entrance 'can write and read' as early as 1469, so the Syon Abbey Additions to the Brigittine Rule stated the expectation that novitiates bring 'bokes' and bedding upon joining the order.[20] Among lay women, 'systematized book exchange was by the mid-fifteenth century a widespread practice, established through mechanisms which were becoming more and more common – or at least more and more visible to us'.[21] Medieval wills 'show us that a much higher proportion of women were book owners and book commissioners than might be supposed on the basis of what is often said about the lack of female literacy in England'. Devotional works – primers, books of hours, psalters, breviaries – constituted by far the largest category of such books, but romances and copies of Boccaccio turn up as well. Female testators frequently describe their books as physical, aesthetic objects, noting their age or binding.[22] This attention to books as material objects shows up in notes in the books themselves as well. Rose Tressham, for instance, owned a French psalter in which she inscribed advice for readers, succinctly conveying the preciousness and usefulness of her book: 'Lerne to kepe your books fayre & ockapy them well & use to clasp them whan you have done.'[23] Tressham's expectations for the care of her psalter and her assumption that others will read her inscription are exemplary of the details to be gleaned from a body of evidence about early modern reading practices that is preserved by chance. If signature literacy studies fail scholars of early modern women, glimpses of the extent and place of women's reading in the period are available in records of book ownership and anecdotes about individual readers. Set alongside contemporary descriptions of literacy and prescriptions for reading instruction, they attest to the range of attitudes, habits, and practices among readers at this historical moment.

In a 1548 preface addressed to Katherine Parr, Nicholas Udall dismisses the learned women celebrated in antiquity as exceptions, as three or four women among thousands of their contemporaries, reserving his praise instead for the ordinariness of female learning in his own 'gracious and blissefull time of knoweleage':

> It is nowe no newes in Englande to see young damysels in nobles houses and in the Courtes of princes, in stede of cardes and other instrumentes of idle trifleing, to have continually in theyr handes eyther Psalmes, [h]Omelies, and other devoute meditacions, or els Paules epistles, or some booke of holy Scripture matters, and as familiarlye both to reade or reason therof in Greke, Latine, Frenche or Italian, as in Englishe. It is nowe a common thing to see young virgins so nouzeled and trained in the studie of letters, that they willingly set all other vayne pastimes at naught for learninges sake. It is now no newes at all to see Quenes and Ladies of most highe estate and progenie, in stede of Courtly daliaunce, to embrace vertuous exercises of readying and wrytyng, and with moste earneste studie both erely and late to applye themselves to the acquiring of knowlage.[24]

Some three decades later, in 1581, Richard Mulcaster also asserts that English female learning is unremarkable, merely an achievement 'we both dayly see in many, and wonder at in some' (p. 168). Rather than the lofty achievements in scriptural exegesis and classical languages that Udall celebrates, however, Mulcaster observes the spread of basic literacy skills among the female population: 'To learne to read is very common, where convenientnes doth serve, & *writing* is not refused, where opportunitie will yeild it' (p. 177). If reading women are unremarkable for Mulcaster, he remains careful to differentiate writing as a discrete skill and one dependent not upon ambition but upon 'opportunitie'.

Educational treatises like Mulcaster's functioned partly as prescriptive literature, and they reveal many of the contemporary attitudes about reading women. Just as we must think of literacies as plural in the period, so it is useful to remember the range of attitudes towards reading women. For nearly every prescriptive account, one can find a competing view or practice. While prescriptive literature alone should not dominate scholarship on reading women, it has a place in the inquiry because of its influence and its articulation of core assumptions about the social hierarchy. The most influential and the first of these treatises was Juan Luis Vives's *A Very Frutefull and Pleasant Boke Called the Instruction of a Christen Woman*, first published in Latin in 1523 and then reissued nine times over the course of the century in English translation. Vives defends women's learning as consonant with virtue, but he is careful to specify its proper form. Sanctioned women's reading, for Vives, was situated squarely within the domestic sphere, grounded in virtue, and contained within the feminine virtues of chastity, silence, and obedience:

> let her lerne for her selfe alone & her yonge children or her sisters in our lorde. For it neither becometh a woman to rule a schole nor to lyve amonge men or speke abrode & shake of her demurenes & honestie [...] it were better to be at home within and unknowen to other folkes. And in company to holde her tonge demurely. And let fewe se her and none at all here her. (sig. E2ᵛ)

While Vives recommends substantial fare – the scriptures and Church Fathers but also Plato, Cicero, and Seneca – for his Christian women readers, he also stresses that a woman should not select her own reading. Further, a woman who persists in reading and handling books of 'war and love' and 'wantonness' should not only be kept from them, but if she brings ill intent to 'good bokes' as well, her father and friends should keep her from all reading until she loses her literacy by lack of use (sigs. E3ʳ–F2ʳ).

Published a half century after Vives's treatise, Mulcaster's *Positions* moves the conversation about girls' education and women's reading forward even as it insists upon its own conformity to current custom. 'Having no president thereof in my countrie', Mulcaster does not promote girls' entry into grammar schools or universities, and even as he embarks upon a chapter on girls' education and asserts the value of writing instruction, he acknowledges the opposing views that girls' education might be 'past over with silence' and should not include writing in its curriculum (pp. 168, 166, 177–78). Like Vives, Mulcaster emphasizes 'good bokes' and insists upon the primacy of piety in women's reading and indeed upon the necessity of '*Reading* [...] for religion, to read that which they must know, and ought to performe'. But he then tacks differently from Vives, broadening the syllabus of acceptable genres and, more crucially, making the case for women's recreational reading:

> Here I may not omit many and great contentmentes, many and sound comfortes, many and manifoulde delites, which those wymen

that have skill and time to reade, without hindering their houswifery, do continually receive by reading of some comfortable and wise discourses, penned either in forme of historie, or for direction to live by. (p. 177)

Certainly, the reading advocated here is constrained by domestic duties, and the books remain 'wise' and didactic. Nevertheless, Mulcaster's attention to women's recreational reading reflects the larger shift in the marketing and consumption of print in the second half of the century.

Between the first and last decades of the period covered by this volume, the output of the London printing presses increased tenfold from roughly 307 items published in the first ten years of the sixteenth century to some 3,221 items in the first ten years of the seventeenth century. Women readers were among those targeted in the print marketplace, even as male printers and authors often communicated their ambivalence about female consumers by circulating stereotypes and sexualizing women's reading. In addition to the 163 books identified by Suzanne Hull as directly addressed to women, another 1,780 printed books were dedicated to individual women before 1640.[25] Hull divides these women's books into four categories: devotional works, practical guides, fiction, and books engaging the controversy about women's roles. Representative of the practical guides, Thomas Raynalde's *The Byrth of Mankind*, a gynecological and obstetrical manual translated from the Latin, was subtitled *The Womans Booke* after its initial publication and explicitly advertised as 'both pleasaunt and fruictfull to all women (for whose sake and only respecte it is set furth) in the readyng thereof' (sig. B7ᵛ). But, as Hull demonstrates, it was not just gynecological and devotional tracts that were marketed to women. In the same year that Mulcaster acknowledged a place for women's leisure reading, the first extant edition appeared of *Riche his farewell to Militarie profession: conteinying verie pleasaunt discourses fit for a peaceable tyme: Gathered together for the onely delight of the courteous Gentlewomen, bothe of Englande and Irelande, for whose oneley pleasure thei were collected together*. The emphatic and repeated 'onely' of the long title, coupled with repeated asides to '(Gentlewomen)' throughout the 1594 edition's dedicatory epistle, explicitly markets this volume to a female readership, whom Riche hopes to please and make 'merie' (sig. C2ʳ).

Like prescriptive literature, these title pages and prefaces conjure female readers. The increase in books addressed to women and the multiple editions of many of these books suggest a degree of accuracy in these representations, but records of women's book ownership bring us closer to actual reading women. Like determining literacy rates, reconstructing book ownership by early modern women is difficult for a number of reasons: the overwhelming majority of printed matter from the period does not survive, the spread of print decreased the economic incentive to inventory books, volumes circulated through many hands in a household, and common law prohibited married women from making wills.[26] In contrast to the reading of nuns and widows, 'what married women or young unmarried women read is altogether more difficult to trace', Mary Erler points out, 'since such reading has no *systematic* conduit to the present, either documentary (these women seldom made wills) or institutional (their books do not survive as part of collective holdings)',[27] and indeed Erler's book contains no accounts of such readers. Further, ownership and reading are not a closed circuit: while a woman's possession of a book does not necessarily mean that she read it, a woman merely needed access to a book, rather than possession of it, in order to peruse it. A girl whose brother brought a verse miscellany home from university might not only read manuscript poems but contribute her own responses.[28] Still, if we accept records of ownership as partial evidence that must be supplemented by other forms, they promise to reveal the kinds of gradations that are invisible in signature literacy studies.

Records of women's book ownership in the sixteenth century appear in wills, book bills, printed book labels, embroidered bindings, manuscript inscriptions, probate inventories, household inventories, and portraits. Scattered and disparate though they are, these records reveal the power of familial relations, the emerging identity of women as book consumers, the continuing primacy of devotional reading, and the integration of reading with other material practices. A few records hint at substantial holdings by aristocratic women in this period: Catherine, Duchess of Suffolk (fl. 1580), for instance, owned a 'chest full' of books.[29] More revealing, however, are the ephemeral book labels printed as a novelty starting around 1590. Elizabeth Stow had one made in 1599; Elizabeth Pindar's more elaborate label displays both her piety and her acquaintance with Latin: 'ELIZABETH PINDAR. / Gods providence is mine / inheritance. / Elizabetha Pindar me jure / possidet. / Anno Dom. / 1608'. These labels suggest a self-consciousness on the part of their commissioners; like the gift-stamp produced around 1591 for the wife of an Oxford printer – 'Ex dono Annae Barnes' – they suggest that these women conceived of a female identity as book consumers.[30]

As both givers and recipients, sixteenth-century women were involved in networks of book exchange. In 1502, the will of John Shukborow, Fellow of King's Hall, Cambridge, was proved; it contains the bequest, 'my premour to my syster Kateryne'. The bequest of Shukborow's primer – in 1502, likely a devotional manual or book of hours rather than an elementary text – suggests that his sister was able to read or would otherwise appreciate the possession of a book.[31] Such gifts reinforced familial relations and confirmed the value of a book as a symbolic object. Devotional titles dominate the lists of individual volumes in wills and inventories; in fact, as Mary Erler has suggested, they may indeed be over-represented in these sources.[32] Two collections of five books each are representative of the titles reported in these documents. Alice Cornelius, a 'respectable' Canterbury widow, left at her death in 1579 a Bible, a New Testament, a *Paraphrase of Erasmus upon the Newe Testamente*, a service book, and Augustine's *Meditations*.[33] A household inventory taken by William More, Esquire on 20 August 1556 includes a long list of the items 'In my wyfes closet'. Alongside a fair desk, three working baskets, a blue pot for flowers, glasses for waters, and three little barrels for pickles are five inexpensive books: 'a boke de parte muliers', 'the pomeander of prayers', and three 'other bokes of prayers'.[34] This list is perhaps most revealing in its catalog of the other objects in this gentlewoman's chamber, for they suggest a constellation of household activities and domestic practices that would have shared space with the reading of devotional books: needlework, planting, distilling, and pickling.

This suggestion of a woman's books and reading in the context of her life shows up most forcefully, if still anecdotally, in diaries, remembrances, memoirs, and elegies from the period. Certainly, these textual glimpses alone cannot produce a comprehensive sense of reading women in the period; however, they provide insight into actual practice, and they alert scholars to habits, circumstances, and networks that may, in fact, be extraordinary only in their survival in the historical record. Evidence about women's reading in this period is scattered and often unfamiliar.[35] From Margaret Hoby, for example, we have a rare surviving diary in which a woman records her reading and from which scholars can tease out her practices as a reader – the titles of the books she read, their integration into her daily life, the company with which she read, the rooms in which she read, the pace at which she read. And yet, the entries themselves are so lean as to be nearly unrecognizable as a diary to a modern reader:

Thursday the :3: [of January 1600]
After I was readie, had praied and broake my fast, I reed of the bible, kept Companie with diuerse ther tell dinner time: after dinner, I walked and Confered of good mattres with Mr Rhodes: after that, I hard him

read tell all most night, then I praied priuatly, and so went to supper: after supper I hard a Lector and, sonne after that, I went to bed.[36]

From this typical individual entry, one gets a sense of the rhythm of Hoby's day. Reading in various forms – whether on her own or as an auditor – punctuates her day, and yet the diary doles out its often near-daily mentions of reading with little remark, interpretation, or reflection. Often the glance that reveals a female reader first brings into view a male relative – a father, husband, brother, or son. John Bois, who later helped translate the King James Bible, wrote on the flyleaf of his mother's Book of Common Prayer:

> This was my mother's book; my good mother's book. Hir name was first Mirable Poolye; and then afterwards Mirable Bois; being so called by the name of her husband, my father, William Bois. ... My mother over-lived my father about ten years. ... She had read the Bible over twelve times, and the Book of Martyrs twice; besides other books, not a few.[37]

John Bois writes this biblio-biography on a flyleaf, adapting the contemporary practice of inscribing Bibles and other devotional volumes with life dates, family histories, and ownership marks. Central to his account of his mother's life is her Protestant reading. Bois memorializes his mother's intensive reading of the Bible and of Foxe's *Book of Martyrs*, but as is so often the case with records of reading women, the hint about the rest of her reading – 'other books, not a few' – is left open. Did Mirable Bois, like Mistress More, read Thomas Becon's *Pomander of Prayers* and other prayer books? Or did she avail herself of the recreational reading allowed by Mulcaster?

One of Elizabeth Cary's daughters also wrote a posthumous biblio-biography of sorts in *The Lady Falkland Her Life*. The preadolescent Cary (née Tanfield) emerges from this manuscript account as a voracious, even compulsive reader. With no companions at hand, she 'spent her whole time in reading; to which she gave herself so much that she frequently read all night; so as her mother was fain to forbid her servants to let her have candles'.[38] Arranging to buy candles on the sly from her servants at extortionate prices, Cary racked up a debt of one hundred pounds – or 800 candles – by age twelve. If her mother seemed to obstruct her reading, 'her father (who loved much to have her read, and she as much to please him) gave her Calvin's *Institutions* and bid her read it' at age twelve (p. 188). Befitting a twelve-year-old ready to take on the *Institutions*, Cary was the subject of a dedicatory epistle to Michael Drayton's *Englands Heroicall Epistles* (1597), in which the poet marveled that her 'tender yeres' made her 'judgement, and reading, the more to be wondred at'.[39] The range of Cary's reading into adulthood might still be 'wondred at'. As her daughter reports it, 'She had read very exceeding much: poetry of all kinds, ancient and modern, in several languages', 'history very universally', all English chroniclers, French histories, ecclesiastical history, 'books treating of moral virtue or wisdom' (Seneca, Plutarch, Pliny, Montaigne, Bacon), the Church Fathers, and religious controversy. 'She had read something of very many other things, but in these she had fixed most' (pp. 268–69).

As Drayton recognized, Cary was an extraordinary reader, a tenth English Muse, but her habit of 'fix[ing] most' on some texts recurs in many other early modern accounts. The impulse to quantify and record devotional reading especially shows up not infrequently in funeral sermons and posthumous recollections. Cary's contemporary Katherine Brettergh (*c*.1579–1601) was memorialized in a 1602 octavo volume containing two funeral sermons and an account of her *Holie life and Christian death*, which was reprinted at least six times over the next four decades.[40] In his funeral sermon, William Harrison establishes her piety and defines it in terms of her reading:

> For matters of religion few went before her. She gave her selfe much to reading: [...] so did she accustome her selfe to reade every day eight chapters in the bible: and would not suffer any occasion to hinder her in that *taske*: yea and moreover at convenient leasure would reade over other godly bookes for her further instruction. (pp. 79–80)

Unlike her female peers who would 'gad abroad [...] to dancing greenes, markets, or publike assemblies', this Lancashire gentlewoman made her daily habit 'to reade, to pray, to sing, to meditate' (p. 3). In addition to her daily practice of Bible reading, Brettergh frequently read other godly books, including Foxe's *Book of Martyrs* 'and was seene to weepe most bitterly, when either shee had read of that which touched her affections neere, or of the cruell matyrdome, which the deere children of God were put unto' (p. 9). Like the pious practices of other women celebrated in funeral sermons, Brettergh's intensely emotional, prayerful reading was not only habitual but also visible to those in her household and at church, and a drama with reading at its center dominated her deathbed crisis of faith. Casting her Bible aside in the throes of illness, Brettergh arrives at her Christian death through reading. Harrison reminds her of her own pious reading and reads aloud to her; she turns again to the Bible, taking it 'in her hand, and joyfully kissing it', quoting Psalm 119, and finally asking her husband to 'reade some part of the scripture' to her, directing him to pause at certain verses, urging him to 'reade on' (pp. 17–19, 24, 26–27). Harrison's description testifies not only to the power of devotional reading but also to the continuing strength of what Jennifer Summit has identified as a pre-Reformation belief that 'the act of reading was an efficacious form of prayer' (p. 114). This deathbed scene exemplifies the range of practices that might constitute reading for an early modern woman: Brettergh listens, she recites, she handles her Bible, she directs another's reading aloud. None of this final prayerful attention to the Bible involves Brettergh's reading in the strictest sense of the word, and yet these surrogate, material practices in every way reveal a 'reading woman'.

As Brettergh's death at twenty-two makes achingly clear, the lives of individual reading women rarely conform to literary and historical periodization. Our final reading woman, however, lived long enough to nearly span the period covered in this volume. In 1610, Rose Throckmorton (1526–1613) set down 'Certaine old stories recorded by an aged gentlewoman a time before her death, to be perused by her children and posterity. Written by her with here hand in the 85th yeere of age, and about the yeer our lord 1610.'[41] Her brief memoir of the first thirty years of her life is emblematic of many aspects of women's reading and their interactions with books and manuscripts, and many of its details are typical of the sixteenth-century women whose reading has survived in the historical record. Though Throckmorton explicitly imagines its endurance and circulation, the memoir survives not in print but in three manuscript copies, one of which was produced in 1667 by a descendant, Elizabeth Locke, as handwriting practice (p. 94).

Throckmorton's memoir and her own literate practices are founded in a family culture of engaged reading and book ownership. 'Certaine old stories' opens with parallel reminiscences about her parents that demonstrate Throckmorton's sense of the central role of books in their lives. As her own habits of reading and piety were shaped by these zealous readers with connections to foreign book markets, so her writing project emerges directly from her reading:

Of my father. In Hollinsheds chronicle I finde this story. [...] Now I his daughter Rose Throckmorton [...] reading this of my father, have thought good to leave to my children this addition to it, [...]

> I remember that I have heard my father say that when he was a yong merchant and used to go beyond sea, Queene Anne Boloin [...] caused him to get her the gospells and epistles written in parchment in French together with the psalms. (p. 97)

Writing as a daughter and as a mother, Throckmorton conveys stories of bookish intrigue across generations, and she hopes to 'move [her children] to continue that thankfullnes to allmight God which I their old mother cannot acknowledge too much nor too often' (p. 98). Piety and filial and maternal love motivate this old woman to transform recollection into writing.

Throckmorton's mother also procured dangerous religious books through her husband's mercantile connections abroad:

> Of my mother. My mother in the dayes of King Henry the 8th came to some light of the gospell by meanes of some English books sent privately to her by my fathers factours from beyond sea: whereupon she used to call me with my 2 sisters into her chamber to read to us out of the same good books very privately for feare of troble bicause those good books were then accompted hereticall, and a merchant named Paginton who used to bring English bybles from beyond sea was slaine with a gun as he went in the streete. Therefore my mother charged us to say nothing of her reading to us for feare of troble. (p. 97)

This scene of furtive family reading corrects any easy equation of women's pious reading with quiet passivity. High anxiety and real danger infused these mother–daughter Bible reading sessions. Reading that was 'very private' and 'close' was, however, also communal, sociable, and aural. Though religious reading dominates the memoir, Throckmorton shows herself conversant as well with books that often go unnamed like Mirable Bois's 'other books, not a few', but even so, these books too have familial connections. Holinshed put her in mind of her father, and she notes that voyages undertaken by her husband and brother 'are spetially recorded by Master Richard Hackluit in his second printed volume of English voyages' (p. 98).

Near the end of her life, this eighty-five-year-old woman, who was born during Henry VIII's reign and who had outlived Queen Elizabeth, was thinking about and wrote down all this drama centered on books – a French psalter placed in the queen's hands, a smuggler of English Bibles gunned down in the street, a mother reading a contraband Bible to her three girls, a husband and a brother voyaging to the other side of the world. It seems a small miracle that these 'Certaine old stories' and the consciousness that animated them have survived. Rose Throckmorton might have complied a lifetime with her mother's charge to 'say nothing of her reading', or she might never have learned to write with pen and ink, or she might not have found it worth the trouble with arthritic hands to record these old stories, or like Katherine Brettergh she might have died at twenty-two. And even once this reading woman did survive and did go to the trouble to write, the manuscript itself might so easily have been discarded by a careless relative, and Elizabeth Locke might well have chosen another copy-text from which to perfect her hand. If it is only in reading many women's lives that we can most nearly recover what it meant to be an early modern reading woman, we are lucky in every survival against such odds.

Notes

I am grateful to Caroline Bicks and Jennifer Summit for the opportunity to return to the subject of 'reading women', and I am indebted to Giulia Hoffmann for research assistance.

1. Bianca F. C. Calabresi, '"you sow, Ile read": Letters and Literacies in Early Modern Samplers', in *Reading Women: Literacy, Authorship, and Culture in the Atlantic World, 1500–1800*, ed. Heidi Brayman Hackel and Catherine E. Kelly (Philadelphia: University of Pennsylvania Press, 2008), pp. 79–104; Juliet Fleming, *Graffiti and the Writing Arts of Early Modern England* (London: Reaktion Books, 2001), pp. 29–72.
2. David Cressy, *Literacy and the Social Order: Reading and Writing in Tudor and Stuart England* (Cambridge: Cambridge University Press, 1980), p. 176; R. A. Houston, *Scottish Literacy and the Scottish Identity: Illiteracy and Society in Scotland and Northern England, 1600–1800* (Cambridge: Cambridge University Press, 1985).
3. Suzanne W. Hull, *Chaste, Silent, and Obedient: English Books for Women, 1475–1640* (San Marino, CA: Huntington Library, 1982), p. 1.
4. Eve Rachele Sanders, *Gender and Literacy on Stage in Early Modern England* (Cambridge: Cambridge University Press, 1998), pp. 13–17.
5. Sanders, *Gender and Literacy*, pp. 13–18, 21–22; Rebecca Krug, *Reading Families: Women's Literate Practice in Late Medieval England* (Ithaca: Cornell University Press, 2002), pp. 188, 191; Rosemary O'Day, *Women's Agency in Early Modern Britain and the American Colonies: Patriarchy, Partnership, and Patronage* (Harlow: Pearson Longman, 2007), pp. 320–37; Jennifer Summit, *Lost Property: The Woman Writer and English Literary History, 1380–1589* (Chicago: University of Chicago Press, 2000), pp. 109–11.
6. Margaret MacCurtain, 'Women, Education and Learning in Early Modern Ireland', in *Women in Early Modern Ireland*, ed. Margaret MacCurtain and Mary O'Dowd (Edinburgh: Edinburgh University Press, 1991), pp. 160–78 (pp. 164–65).
7. Jacqueline Pearson, 'Women Reading, Reading Women', in *Women and Literature in Britain, 1500–1700*, ed. Helen Wilcox (Cambridge: Cambridge University Press, 1996), pp. 80–99 (p. 80).

8. *The Mirrour of Princely deedes and Knighthood*, trans. M[argaret] T[yler] (London, 1578), sigs. A2ʳ, A4ʳ–A4ᵛ. Kathryn Coad calls the epistles the 'earliest English-woman's defence of women's literary work' (*The Early Modern Englishwoman: A Facsimile Library of Essential Works*, Part 1: *Printed Writings, 1500–1640*, vol. 8: *Margaret Tyler* [Aldershot: Scolar Press, 1996], p. x).

9. Esther Inglis, *Argumenta Singulorum Capitum Evangelii Matthae Apostoli*, 1607 manuscript volume dedicated to William Earl of Morton, facsimile available on Perdita (fol. 2ʳ); Anne Wheathill, *A handfull of holesome (though homelie) hearbs* (London, 1584), sig. A2ᵛ.

10. Sanders, *Gender and Literacy*, p. 90.

11. Margaret Spufford, *Small Books and Pleasant Histories: Popular Fiction and Its Readership in Seventeenth-Century England* (Cambridge: Cambridge University Press, 1981), pp. 27, 21; Houston, *Scottish Literacy*, p. 66.

12. Spufford, *Small Books*, p. 21; Cressy, *Literacy*, p. 53. For a fuller discussion of literacy, see my *Reading Material in Early Modern England: Print, Gender, and Literacy* (Cambridge: Cambridge University Press, 2005), pp. 56–68.

13. Cressy, *Literacy*, pp. 119, 106, 145; Houston, *Scottish Literacy*, pp. 57–67.

14. Frances E. Dolan, 'Reading, Writing, and Other Crimes', in *Feminist Readings of Early Modern Culture: Emerging Subjects*, ed. Valerie Traub, M. Lindsay Kaplan, and Dympna Callaghan (Cambridge: Cambridge University Press, 1996), pp. 142–67 (pp. 161–62, n. 6); Cressy, *Literacy*, p. 115; Margaret W. Ferguson, *Dido's Daughters: Literacy, Gender, and Empire in Early Modern England and France* (Chicago: University of Chicago Press, 2003), p. 77.

15. Adam Fox, *Oral and Literate Culture in England, 1500–1700* (Oxford: Oxford University Press, 2000), pp. 409, 19; Dolan, 'Reading, Writing', p. 144; Spufford, *Small Books*, p. 22.

16. Caroline Bowden, 'The Notebooks of Rachael Fane: Education for Author-ship?' in *Early Modern Women's Manuscript Writing: Selected Papers from the Trinity/Trent Colloquium*, ed. Victoria E. Burke and Jonathan Gibson (Aldershot: Ashgate, 2004), pp. 157–80 (p. 159); Richard Mulcaster, *Positions* (London, 1581), p. 168 (subsequent references are cited parenthetically in the text); Alan D. Dyer, *The City of Worcester in the Sixteenth Century* (Leicester: Leicester University Press, 1973), p. 247.

17. Keith Thomas, 'The Meaning of Literacy in Early Modern England', in *The Written Word: Literacy in Transition*, ed. Gerd Baumann (Oxford: Clarendon Press, 1986), pp. 97–131 (pp. 99–101). For rare examples of women writing secretary hand, see Bowden, 'Notebooks', pp. 171–73.

18. Fleming, *Graffiti*, pp. 50, 9, 50.

19. Krug, *Reading Families*, pp. 5–7.

20. Dyer, *City of Worcester*, pp. 298–99; Krug, *Reading Families*, p. 153.

21. Mary C. Erler, *Women, Reading, and Piety in Late Medieval England* (Cambridge: Cambridge University Press, 2002), pp. 2, 28.

22. John B. Friedman, *Northern English Books, Owners, and Makers in the Late Middle Ages* (Syracuse: Syracuse University Press, 1995), pp. 3, 16, 19.

23. Erler, *Women, Reading*, p. 146.

24. Preface to the Gospel of John, in *The First Tome or Volume of the Paraphrase of Erasmus upon the Newe Testamente* (London, 1548), sig. 3A1ᵛ. The typography in this quotation and from all early printed texts throughout has been nor-malized to modern usage.

25. Mary Ellen Lamb, 'Inventing the Early Modern Woman Reader through the World of Goods: Lyly's Gentlewoman Reader and Katherine Stubbes', in *Reading Women*, ed. Brayman Hackel and Kelly, pp. 15–35 (p. 17); Pearson, 'Women Reading', p. 89. The figures come from the *ESTC*.

26. For a fuller discussion, see my *Reading Material*, pp. 214–21.

27. Erler, *Women, Reading*, p. 3.

28. Victoria E. Burke, 'Reading Friends: Women's Participation in "Masculine" Literary Culture', in *Early Modern Women's Manuscript Writing*, ed. Burke and Gibson, pp. 75–90 (p. 77).

29. Lawrence Stone, *The Crisis of the Aristocracy, 1558–1641* (Oxford: Clarendon Press, 1965), p. 794.

30. STC 3368.5; Brian North Lee, *Early Printed Book Labels: A Catalogue of Dated Personal Labels and Gift Labels Printed in Britain to the Year 1760* (Pinner, Middlesex: Private Libraries and Bookplate Society, 1976), no. 39.

31. E. S. Leedham-Green, *Books in Cambridge Inventories: Book-Lists from Vice-Chancellor's Court Probate Inventories in the Tudor and Stuart Periods*, vol. 1: *The Inventories* (Cambridge: Cambridge University Press, 1986), p. 594. See too Calabresi, '"you sow, Ile read"', pp. 89–94, on Elizabeth Tudor's production and offering of a book to Katherine Parr.

32. Erler, *Women, Reading*, p. 3.

33. Peter Clark, 'The Ownership of Books in England, 1560–1640: The Example of Some Kentish Townsfolk', in *Schooling and Society: Studies in the History of Education*, ed. Lawrence Stone (Baltimore: Johns Hopkins University Press, 1976), pp. 95–111 (p. 102).

34. Washington DC, Folger Shakespeare Library, L.b.550, fols. 2–7.

35. The *Reading Experience Database, 1450–1945* is an admirably ambitious, collaborative project to gather in one place these many stray moments: http://www.open.ac.uk/Arts/reading. At present, its records for sixteenth-century reading women are nearly exclusively examples from Margaret Hoby's diary.

36. *The Private Life of an Elizabethan Lady: The Diary of Lady Margaret Hoby, 1599–1605*, ed. Joanna Moody (Phoenix Mill, England: Sutton Publishing, 1998), p. 50.

37. *Translating for King James*, ed. Ward Allen (Nashville: Vanderbilt University Press, 1969), p. 129, cited in O'Day, *Women's Agency*, p. 347.

38. *The Tragedy of Mariam The Fair Queen of Jewry with The Lady Falkland Her Life*, ed. Barry Weller and Margaret W. Ferguson (Berkeley: University of California Press, 1994), p. 187; subsequent references are cited parenthetically in the text.

39. Michael Drayton, *Englands Heroicall Epistles* (London, 1597), sig. G3^v.

40. William Harrison, *Deaths advantage little regarded, and the soules solace against sorrow* (London, 1602); subsequent references are cited parenthetically in the text.

41. Maria Dowling and Joy Shakespeare, 'Religion and Politics in Mid Tudor England through the Eyes of an English Protestant Woman: The Recollections of Rose Hickman', *Bulletin of the Institute of Historical Research*, 55 (1982), 94–102. All references are to this transcription. A facsimile is available through Perdita. See too Ben Lowe, 'Rose Throckmorton', in the *ODNB*.

2
Literary Circles and Communities

Julie Crawford

Many of the best-known literary circles or communities of early modern English letters had women at their centers. Sir Philip Sidney, to take a famous example, claimed he wrote most of his *Arcadia* (c.1580) in his sister Mary Sidney Herbert's presence, 'the rest by sheets sent unto you as fast as they were done'.[1] Indeed Mary Sidney Herbert's country seat, Wilton House, was a center of both literary production and religious and political activism throughout the period. Anne Lock, who has been identified as 'the mother of English religious sonneteering' (1560) was similarly a central figure in an important community of religious, political, and literary activity.[2] Lock's circle also intersected with that of the Cooke sisters, whose family home, Gidea Hall, was known, like Wilton, as a kind of female university. Among other things, the Cooke sisters, Mildred, Anne, Elizabeth, and Katherine, all of whom married into powerful families, translated controversial religious texts, worked collectively on a manuscript presentation volume, and wrote verses in multiple languages. Their work, like Sidney Herbert's and Lock's, was part of a larger religio-political practice as concerned with promoting specific religious and political ends as it was with the production of literature.

In this essay I want to use these three interrelated communities to reconsider both the nature of what scholars have identified as 'literary circles' and women's roles in them. My primary goal is to show how the idea of literary circles or communities, particularly those associated with elite women, expands our sense of how literary production worked in the period. Defined loosely as groups 'whose members are linked by shared social, political, philosophical, or aesthetic interests or values, or who vie for the interest and attention of a particular patron, or who are drawn together by bonds of friendship, family, religion, or location', early modern literary circles have attracted a fair share of critical attention.[3]

Much of this work has focused on well-known or frequently identified groups, such as the Sidney-Herbert Circle, Jonson and the Sons of Ben, the Cavendish or Newcastle network, the group at Little Gidding, and Katherine Phillips's Society of Friendship. Some, however, have questioned the existence of certain literary communities. Margaret Hannay, for example, argued that the so-called 'dramatic circle' around Mary Sidney Herbert was a critical invention, and for others the idea of the literary community itself is suspect altogether.[4] Judith Scherer Herz argues, for example, that the literary circle is most usefully understood as a critical cataloging mechanism and heuristic device rather than as a found object.[5]

Yet the idea has proven widely resilient, particularly as literary scholars examine the relationships between literary activity and minoritarian identities, and between collaborative literary manuscripts and the communities who produced them.[6] Indeed, since Margaret Ezell alerted us to the fact that scholarly focus on print culture and ignorance of women's participation in the circulation of work in manuscript has led to a drastic underestimation of the literary activities of early modern women, scholars have begun to unearth women's activities as authors and co-authors, manuscript compilers, verse collectors, and keepers of commonplace books.[7] Many of these activities were collective in nature, and tell us a great deal about how literature was both produced and circulated in the early modern period.

My secondary goal in this essay is simultaneously to debunk any idealized or restrictive ideas we might have about 'women's' literary circles (that they were, for example, women-only, apolitical, private, domestic, and household-based)[8] and to highlight the roles women played in key moments and movements of textual production and religious and political activism. The literary circles in which women played significant roles were certainly domestic, if we understand such 'domestic' practices as hosting, letter-writing, needlework, and reading to have not only a great deal in common with the production of literary texts, but also significant communicative and political freight. And they can also be productively understood as household-based, if we understand the household not only as a familial and regional power base, but also a headquarters for literary collaboration and religious and political activism at both the national and international levels. The communities discussed in this essay were anything but restrictively belletristic, and their activity and influence extended far beyond their households.

While the idea of a women-specific literary circle certainly had purchase in the period (the Cooke sisters, for example, were seen as Protestant successors to the daughters of Sir Thomas More, and consistently characterized as a group of women), the circles discussed in this essay were in fact both cross-sex and (largely) familial. Yet women's roles in them were not, as has sometimes been argued, fixed or delineated by their relationships to men, whether sororal, affective, or marital.[9] Mary Sidney Herbert's oft-reiterated status as 'Sidney's brother' is as much a critical insistence as it is an accurate description of her role, and it is no clearer that Anne Lock's involvement in the Admonition controversy was solely or even primarily a result of her marriage to the radical minister Edward Dering.[10]

'Family' and 'friends' worked for women in much the same way as they did for men: they were terms both of affection and intimacy and of mutual association and self-interest, and they were mediated, as such relationships are, by common values as well as differences about the best way to pursue those values. While it may be erroneous to claim that the women in these circles were primarily concerned with 'constructing a career path' as authors, it would be equally erroneous to claim that the men they worked with thought that way either.[11] (The debates over whether Sir Philip Sidney should be considered primarily as an author or a Protestant activist, to take a comparable example, indicate that the issue is less about gender than about the inextricable nature of such activities within a given community.) The women discussed in this essay were not versifying, translating, devising entertainments, or epitaphing solely or primarily to establish their reputations as authors. Rather these literary activities, for which their education and privilege prepared them, were equally the products of their skills, interests, literary and reputational ambitions, and the shared beliefs and commitments of the communities in which they were key figures.

The empirical activities of the communities I discuss here are also best understood as textual rather than restrictively literary. The patronage, writing, translation, reading, and circulation of a wide range of books and manuscripts existed alongside of – indeed was inseparable from – other forms of textual transmission and transaction practiced by the circles' members, including the writing of letters and petitions, and from other forms of religious and political activism, such as the promotion of certain persons for office, the protection of dissenters, or the criticism of policy. Indeed the production of texts of all kinds, including literary ones, can productively be understood as a form of these communities' religious and political activism.

The production of such texts, moreover, was collective in ways that contemporary notions of authorship cannot comprehend. For example, in a dedicatory poem to Mary Sidney Herbert the poet Samuel Daniel asks his patron to accept his 'humble Rymes [...] as thine owne | Begotten by thy hand, and my desire'.[12] Daniel certainly flatters Sidney Herbert, but he nonetheless attests to a form of literary production in which patrons, dedicatees, and privileged readers played as important roles as authors: the hands and desires that made literary texts, in other words, were not only the ones that put actual pen to paper. Thus this essay takes women's roles as the patrons, dedicatees, readers, collators/collectors, and circulators of texts, both print and manuscript, as seriously as their roles as authors. Literary circles remind us that collaboration could be a collective as well as a dyadic process, and that supporting, reading, and circulating texts were primary, rather than secondary, forms of literary production. They also remind us that the seemingly meager 'handful' of translations, poems, and epitaphs that can be attributed to sixteenth-century women's pens are only part of the literature they played a part in producing.[13]

This essay thus also reexamines the constituencies of literary communities. Rather than trying to fix or name the players in a given circle, I instead take seriously contemporary assumptions that such a circle did exist, and look at the work of those who wrote from within, or with an eye towards, its investments and interests. Those who participated in literary communities participated in many ways, both in the flesh and virtually, through letters, manuscripts, books, and dedications. They were local, including family members, tutors, and ministers who lived in house, as well as neighbors; national, including privy councilors like Secretary of State William Cecil and major ecclesiastical figures like Bishop John Jewel; and international, including the textual and some-times literal presence of Protestant activists from the Continent like the French Huguenot Philippe de Mornay and the Italian convert Pietro Martire Vermigli. Early modern literary communities were also often celebrated for their inclusion of women. The 'fair ladies' interpellated in the *Arcadia*, to take one example, were based, at least in part, on the actual women who participated in the Sidney circle's activities.[14] The fact that various persons and texts petitioned to be in or imagined them-selves as part of specifically identified literary communities suggests less that such communities were endlessly capacious (authors often sought patronage from individuals and families they had never met and would never meet), than that they were popularly seen or imagined *as* commu-nities. This concept of the collective is as telling for the history of literary criticism as the communities' empirical practices themselves.

In the conclusion of this essay I thus look at these communities' later sixteenth- and early seventeenth-century afterlives in order to see if they were seen as collective entities in subsequent cultural imaginations. Why, for example, does Margaret Hoby spend so much time at the end of the century reading the work of those radical London Puritans the Cooke sisters, particularly her mother-in-law Elizabeth Cooke Hoby Russell, had supported in the 1570s? Why does Lady Anne Clifford read the *Arcadia* in 1616 when she is about to meet with female members of the Sidney family at Penshurst? Do texts carry the traces of the literary circles that created them? Are they, in some ways, both repositories for and reactivating agents of the literary and political – and women-centric – investments of those circles? The concept of the literary community as a heuristic tool may not only be the product of our own critical perception, but may be something that early moderns made use of as well.

The Cookes

Perhaps the most famous women's literary community in post-Reformation England was that of the Cooke sisters, the daughters of the humanist Sir Anthony Cooke of Gidea Hall in Essex. Gidea Hall was, in the words of the Edwardian statesman Walter Haddon, a 'small university', comparable to Cicero's villa where 'the industry of the females was in full vigour'.[15] In his will, while Cooke left his sons his land, and his sons and daughters bequests of plate, each daughter was given her choice of books, two Latin and one Greek, from his library.[16] In the thirty-seventh book of his translation of Ariosto's *Orlando Furioso*, in which 'the praises of women are set downe to the encouragement of all virtuous minded yong Ladies' and 'to the terrifying of all great men that dispose themselves to lawlesse and tyrannous behaviour', the poet Sir John Harrington praises the 'three or four' most learned women of England (after Elizabeth I), namely 'the sisters of that learned Ladie [Elizabeth Cooke Hoby Russell, whose elegies he praises], as witnesse that verse written by the meanest of the foure [Katherine Cooke Killigrew] to the Ladie *Burlie* [Mildred Cooke Burghley], which I doubt if Cambridge or Oxford can mend'.[17]

In these and other encomia, the Cookes' scholarly and literary practices were understood to have political valences: the house they were raised in was like Cicero's villa – a symbol of constitutionally minded intervention in the Roman empire – and they were seen as the enemies of 'lawlesse and tyrannous' men. In the 1550s and 1560s the sisters were part of a circle of national and international Protestants who 'were fighting out just where the consensual center of English institutionalized reform would be'.[18] While their activities played a key role in both the Edwardian and Elizabethan settlements, they also frequently contested the terms of those settlements. In both cases, the sisters were sometimes impeded by men they would have identified as 'lawless and tyrannous'. In 1550 the author and royal tutor Roger Ascham wrote to the German scholar Johannes Sturm to promote the Cookes' accomplishments (and the Protestant cause): 'We now have many honorable women who surpass the daughters of Thomas More in all kinds of learning.'[19] As Jaime Goodrich puts it, the Cooke sisters 'invoked the precedent created by More and Henry VIII by which women's learning could represent the political agendas of their coteries'.[20] Ascham's description suggests that collectives of women were understood as a recognizable and distinct phenomenon, and that their scholarly and religio-political freight could play a determining role in particular battles.

Particularly after their marriages, the Cooke sisters were part of the central nucleus of sixteenth-century English Protestant power. The eldest, Mildred Cooke Cecil, Lady Burghley (1526–89), wife of William Cecil, was a key intermediary between petitioners and her husband in both domestic and international affairs, as well as a book owner, donator, and translator.[21] Her library was one of the most impressive of the period. While she inscribed it as her own, marking her ownership of twenty-six books, the collection also indicates the centrality of family and faction: one book has both her name and her husband's on the binding; one is dedicated to her daughter; and two are explicitly associated with her father – including the work of the Florentine convert Pietro Martire Vermigli, a central figure in the circle's Protestant activism.[22] Her library, begun with her father's three willed books, was both a key arsenal for and a record of her community's activities. It also undoubtedly played a role in the 'private school' she ran in England, in which she fostered more than a dozen aristocratic children, including the Earls of Essex and Oxford.[23]

Mildred was also a renowned translator. Pauline Croft has argued that she was involved with the 1572 revision of the 1568 'Bishops' Bible', and she translated a sermon of Basil the Great from the Greek, which she presented to Anne Seymour, Duchess of Somerset (wife of Edward VI's Protector, and herself a major literary patron) in 1550.[24] While 'going back to the Greeks', was a Protestant strategy for reclaiming the true church from the Catholics, Goodrich argues that the sermon also delivered a coded message warning the Somersets of possible attacks by their political enemies. By framing the translation as a personal gift for Anne Seymour, Mildred simultaneously invoked her political connections and kept the work 'at several removes from William Cecil himself'.[25] She used manuscript circulation as a means of both promoting and protecting her community's interests.

In 1553, another Cooke sister, Anne (c.1528–1610), married the statesman Sir Nicholas Bacon, who celebrated in verse the 'fruits of mind' shared between them, particularly their mutual profit from 'your Tully and my Seneck'.[26] Bacon's phrase suggests that the couple's reading was both a form of what Lisa Jardine and Anthony Grafton call 'studying for action' (the Roman historians and Stoics were key reading for all those who wanted to have political influence), and a collective enterprise. While the Seneca may be Bacon's, the 'Tully', or Marcus Tullius Cicero, was Anne's. The Ciceronian villa-like nature of Gidea Hall, in other words, had spread outwards and continued to inform the sisters' work long after their marriages.

Like her sister, Anne was a powerful intermediary both for her husband, and, eventually, for her sons Anthony and Francis Bacon. In 1553, she published a translation of Sermons by the Sienese Franciscan convert Bernadino Ochino. Along with his compatriot Vermigli – whose work appears in both Mildred's and Anne's libraries – Thomas Cranmer had invited Ochino to England in 1547 to assist with the Reformation of the English church.[27] Anne's Ochino translation was meant to disseminate the views of her reformist community throughout England, and to help make Edwardian England an international center of Protestantism.

In 1564, she translated from the Latin Bishop John Jewel's 1562 *Apologia pro Ecclesia Anglicana*, the official defense of the Elizabethan church. Anne's *Apologie of the Church of England* opens with an epistle 'To the right honorable learned and vertuous Ladie A. B' from Archbishop Mathew Parker himself in which he approves of the translation ('bothe the chiefe author of the Latine worke and I, seuerallye perusinge and conferringe youre whole translation, haue without alteration allowed of it') and authorizes its printing under the aegis of the church. Parker sees her translation as reflecting well on and serving as a model for other women, hoping that 'all noble gentlewomen shall (I trust) hereby be alured from vain delights to doinges of more perfect glory [...] and followe your example'.

It may be a stretch to argue that Parker 'makes explicit the strategic use of a female translator to present the case of a female monarch to other women',[28] but it is clear that the *Apologie* was meant to defend the

Elizabethan church in light of international Catholic attacks, and that Parker understood it as a factional Protestant text. Anne's 'publikely beneficiall' translation has, as he puts it, 'raysed vp great comforte to your friendes'. Indeed the work of serving one's 'friendes', particularly when they are under attack, is one of the hallmarks of women's activities in the period. It is thus likely that Parker understood the translation as a 'model' for women in a religio-political sense as well as a behavioral one.

In her later life and widowhood, Anne reaffirmed her international status as a friend of the Reformation and its activists. In 1581 Théodore de Bèze dedicated his meditations on the psalms to her (and wrote to the minister of the French Huguenot church in London asking him to encourage Anne to write to him); and in 1589 the Puritan leader Thomas Wilcox reminded her of how 'you are made truly famous abroad in forraine Churches and counties, & highly revered of many worthie men there, indued doubtless with singular graces for Gods glory, and the building up of the bodie of the fellowship of Saincts'.[29] She also took a more active role in the Puritan cause in England, pressing Cecil to secure a fairer hearing for the nonconformists deprived under Whitgift's 1583 articles; sheltering preachers at Gorhambury – a place William Urwick called 'the rendezvous of the silenced Puritan ministers of [the] day';[30] and almost certainly supporting the major project to collect and disseminate a register of Puritan documents. (There is strong evidence that *A Parte of a Register* [1593], which is dedicated to Anne, and the larger manuscript collection known as 'The seconde parte of a register', were both financed by Anne and undertaken under her roof at Gorhambury.[31])

Elizabeth (Cooke Hoby) Russell (?1528–1609) was the wife of Sir Thomas Hoby (1530–66) and then, after 1574, of John, Lord Russell (d. 1584), heir to Francis Russell, second earl of Bedford.[32] (Until recently, Elizabeth was most famous for the elegies published on her second husband's tomb.) Like her sisters, Elizabeth was an important intermediary, patron, and Protestant activist. In a 1571 dedication, Geoffrey Fenton highlights the local, Bisham Abbey-based practices of her religious and literary community: her 'boarde (which I did often assist)', he writes, was 'seldome without the fellowship of deepe Devines and Preachers', and he praises her 'gret charge to entertayne men of Artes and learned Faculties, by which [her] house seems an Universitie of learning'.[33] He also, however, draws attention to her wider activities, particularly her 'societie with publike Lectures and Sermons this last winter [1570] in London' (sig. Aii^v), an explicit allusion to an important period of Puritan activism to which we will return below.

In 1592 Queen Elizabeth and her privy council were entertained at the same house with an entertainment 'devised' by Elizabeth Russell and her daughters Elizabeth and Anne, whom Elizabeth hoped the Queen would take on as Maids of Honor.[34] The entertainment features a scene between Pan and two 'Virgins keeping sheepe and sowing their Samples', figures for the Russell girls. While Pan derides them as 'but the Farmers daughters of the Dale', they retort by praising the honor of Virgins, comparing men's tongues to 'double stitch', and highlighting their own work in 'Queenes stitch', a practice evocative of Elizabeth I's own textual practices (she frequently embroidered covers for her own translations).[35] Their words advertise their skills – in both needlework and political perspicacity – as potential Maids of Honor, but they also allude to the female-centric nature of Elizabeth's privy chamber, and, I would argue, to that of the Cooke sisters.

Sybilla, the figure for Elizabeth Russell, praises the Queen to Pan, highlighting – and thereby encouraging – her commitment to the pan-European Protestant cause in which the Cooke sisters were so invested: 'One hand she stretcheth to *Fraunce*, to weaken Rebels', Sybilla says, 'the other to *Flaunders* to strengthen Religion.'[36] Using pastoral to 'glaunce at greater matters [...] under the vailes of homely persons',[37] the entertainment also indicates a sympathy, and mutual dependency, between the Queen and her subjects' 'houses'.[38] By ending with praise of 'the Lady of the farme' (Elizabeth Russell herself), as well as an attestation of her loyalty to Elizabeth I, the entertainment served as a reminder of the importance of aristocratic women to Elizabethan politics, particularly as spokeswomen for international Protestantism. Their 'houses', in this case Bisham Abbey, are identified not only for their loyalty, but also their status as sites of advice and even resistance.

In 1605 Elizabeth published a translation from Latin into English of Bishop John Ponet's treatise on the Eucharist, a text written fifty years earlier in Germany and originally published by her father in 1557, and which she herself probably translated in the 1550s. Elaine Beilin argues that Russell's publication in 1605 suggests her awareness of a growing battle over religious conformity between the new king James I and the Puritans;[39] Goodrich that she was responding to several books published in 1604 by the Catholic controversialist Robert Persons, attacking the Elizabethan settlement of 1559[40] (in which, not coincidentally, the Cooke circle had played a significant role).

The book's opening note to the reader certainly indicates the translator's awareness of the factional nature of her work: 'while I study to make enemies friends', Elizabeth writes, 'perhaps I shall have small thankes of them. Which if it happen, the example of him shal comfort me, which said: *If I should please men, I should not be the servant of Christ.'*[41] Its dedication 'To the Right Honourable my most entirely beloved and onely daughter, the Lady Anne Herbert' (her other Russell daughter, Elizabeth, died in 1600) highlights both the translation's interventionism – the importance of 'yeeld[ing] a reason of [her] opinion' in 'a matter so full of controversie' (sig. A2ᵛ) – and her hopes that her daughter would continue her defense of the true church.

Elizabeth's final work was her own tomb at Bisham, which shows her at a prayer desk, reading, her children both living and dead arranged around her, and her surviving daughter, Anne, given pride of place in front.[42] The monument emblematizes the interconnections between family, texts, and power, but it is also particularly concerned with female genealogy and inheritance. Among other things, Elizabeth's work offers evidence that women who had been active in women-centered communities put particular hope in their female descendants' ongoing commitments to their causes.

The Lock circle

Anne Lock (Dering Prowse) is most famous in literary criticism as the author of the first sonnet cycle written by a woman, 'A Meditation of a Penitent Sinner: Written in Maner of A Paraphrase upon the 51 Psalm of David', appended to the end of her translation of Calvin's sermons on Isaiah (published in 1560). But she was also a key figure in a series of related religious-literary communities, both national and international in scope, that, like the Cookes', illustrate the ways in which women's literary practices were inseparable from religious and political activism. In the winter of 1552–53 Anne Lock was one of a group of city wives who 'shared the company' of Scottish reformer John Knox.[43] Thirteen letters from Knox to Anne Lock survive – he addresses her as 'Deir Sister' – and appear to owe their survival to the Puritan propagandist and organizer John Field,[44] who also figures as a key player in the circle. In 1557 she joined Knox in Geneva – Roland Greene calls her an 'aide-de-camp'[45] – where she spent some time translating Calvin's sermons on the Song of Hezekiah from Isaiah 38, and writing what most scholars believe to be her own sonnets on Psalm 51. The psalms were, as Greene puts it, 'a field for the preoccupations of institutions, sects and coteries', and Lock's were a 'sort of exposition on a scriptural text that was essential to preaching and other forms of religious argumentation'.[46] Her translation and sonnets, in other words, can be understood as a form of Protestant outreach.

While her sonnets served as a model for other polemical translations of the psalms, including, as we will see, Philip and Mary Sidney's, her translation reactivated already extant associations between Calvin's expositions on Isaiah and the English church. As Susan Felch points out, in 1550 Calvin dedicated his Latin commentary on Isaiah to Edward VI, challenging the young king to restore the church to its original condition by following God's instructions as given through his prophet.[47] By publishing her translation of Isaiah 38, which focuses on Hezekiah's afflictions rather than triumphs, when she was back in London and serving as what Patrick Collinson has called 'the main link between Knox (who was *persona non grata* to Queen Elizabeth) and the developing religious revolution in Scotland, and England, and especially with the repatriated remnants of the English congregation in Geneva',[48] Lock's translation served as a model for a regenerating Protestant England and its beleaguered activists.[49] Just as de Bèze sought out Elizabeth Cooke for help with the cause of French Protestantism, so did Knox depend on Anne Lock to intercede with wealthy London Protestants in order to sustain the Scottish congregation – and to send him books. Like the Cookes, Lock was a fulcrum for the interconnected economic, congregational, political, and textual activities of a whole community.

After the death of her first husband in 1571, Anne married Edward Dering (d. 1576), 'the most fiery and popular London preacher of the day'.[50] She married Dering right at the moment when he had become notorious for his role in radical Puritanism, 'unbridling his tongue', as Collinson puts it, to Cecil, Parker, and, 'in the most outspoken Lenten sermon she ever heard', Elizabeth I.[51] This ecclesiastical controversy, precipitated by the 'publike Lectures and Sermons this last winter in London' that Geoffrey Fenton praises Elizabeth Cooke Hoby for attending in 1570, and popularized in the *Admonition to Parliament* published by John Field and Thomas Wilcox in 1572, resulted in a great deal of repression and silencing. Dering, however, enjoyed a huge reputation, both with those whom in a dedicatory epistle he called 'the godly in London', and patrons like Henry Killigrew and Katherine Cooke Killigrew.[52] (Indeed several letters from Dering to Katherine dating from this period were printed in his *Certaine Godly and Verie Comfortable Letters, Full of Christian Consolation* published in Middleburg in 1590,[53] testimony both to the central role women played in the collective labors of 'the godly', and to the increasing imbrication of the Lock and Cooke circles.)

In 1572, the same group of godly women presented a manuscript by Bartholo Sylva, a Protestant convert from Turin seeking favor in England, to the Earl of Leicester which included Greek and Latin epigrams by all four Cooke sisters. Louise Schleiner argues that the manuscript was prepared in the wake of the Dering controversy – he too contributed to the volume – and endeavored to both redeem Dering and to present the reformist circle as simultaneously cosmopolitan and loyal to the Queen.[54] The dedicatory epistle to a James Sanford volume published a few years later praises the same group of women ('noble Gentlewomen famous for their learning, as the right honorable my Lady Burleigh, my Lady Russel, my Lady Bacon, Mistresse Dering, with others'[55]), but, as Felch argues, attempts to align the Queen with women who were outspoken supporters of church reform. In both cases, the Puritan cause is emblematized by a collective of women.

This emblematization was based on substantive activity. John Field relied on Anne Lock Dering (now Prowse) for his 1583 publication of a John Knox sermon on Matthew. The dedication, 'To the Vertuous and my very godly friend, Mrs. Anne Prouze of Exeter', thanks her for providing him with the manuscript and asks her 'if by your selfe or otheres, you can procure any other [Knox's] writinges or letters, here at home or abroad, In Scotland, or in England',[56] identifying her as a central figure in the circulation of Knox's unpublished work. Field both praises her for her work as a long-term 'scholler in [God's] schoole' (sig. A3ʳ), and warns her about the dangers facing the movement. 'Beware of the worlde', he writes, 'and let those be an example to you to stand fast, whome you have sene and see dayly to fall from the love of the truth.' Those who fell were those who conformed with the established church; Whitgift, as we have seen, was busy depriving nonconformists in the very same year.

In 1590, Anne translated Jean Taffin's *Of the Markes of the Children of God, and of their Comfort in Afflictions*, a book 'originally intended for the solace of the oppressed Protestants of the Netherlands' (the Belgian Calvinist Taffin was a minister in Harlem) but refitted by Anne for English ends.[57] In the volume's dedication to the Countess of Warwick, Anne explains her intentions: 'Everie one in his calling is bound to doo somewhat to the furtherance of the holie building, but because great things by reason of my sex I may not doo, and that which I may I ought to doo, I have according to my duetie brought my poore basket of stones to the strengthening of the walles of that Jerusalem whereof (by grace) wee are all both citizens and members.'[58] 'Strengthening the walles of Jerusalem' was a figure that Lock had used in Sonnet 20 of her own verse paraphrase of Psalm 51 (verse 18) when the speaker prays 'That thy Hierusalem with mighty wall | May be enclosed under thy defense, | And bylded so that it may never fall'.[59] But as Margaret Hannay points out, it had also become a code phrase for being active in the Protestant cause.[60] The focus in the dedication on the sufferings of 'the gathering of his Church', both 'of our selves' and 'of our neighbours round about us',[61] indicates, as Micheline White has argued, that Prowse understood the translation as rallying cry for the Puritan cause.[62]

The Countess of Warwick, Anne attests, 'hath been of long time, not onlie a professor, but also a lover of the trueth, whom the Lord (exalting to an higher place of dignitie than may other) hath set up, as it were a light upon a high candlesticke, to give light unto manie' (sig. A3v). Indeed Anne Russell Dudley, Countess of Warwick, sister-in-law of both the Earl of Leicester and Elizabeth Cooke Russell, was a major figure in Puritan-leaning Elizabethan Protestant politics. As was the case with her first publication, Anne's publication of Taffin's collectivizing text appeared at the moment the government was 'delivering a crippling blow to the Puritan movement'.[63] In 1590, as White points out, many of her Puritan associates were literally on trial.[64] Warwick, for example, intervened with her relatives on behalf of the Puritans Thomas Cartwright and John Udall, 'and her assistance would be used as propaganda in the projected *Seconde Parte of a Register*',[65] the manuscript collection likely collated under Anne Cooke Bacon's roof. The women of the Cooke and Lock communities played a substantive role in what Patrick Collinson long ago called the Elizabethan Puritan Movement. If considering only the handful of translations, poems, and epitaphs these women wrote may keep them safely minoritized as women writers, looking at the full range of their related activities shows their profound influence on some of the most important events of the sixteenth century.

Mary Sidney Herbert

Mary Sidney Herbert (1561–1621) was at the center of the most famous literary community of the period. (Her circle, moreover, is the one whose existence is most frequently studied – and called into question – by contemporary scholarship.[66]) Mary was, as Schleiner puts it, 'a second generation Protestant aristocrat',[67] the niece of Henry and Katherine Dudley Hastings, earl and countess of Huntingdon; of Ambrose and Anne Russell Dudley, earl and countess of Warwick; and of the Queen's favorite, Robert Dudley, earl of Leicester, all of whom were Protestant, and often Puritan, activists.[68] The major players in this second-generation circle, Mary, Philip, and Robert Sidney, were patrons (both actual and sought after), authors, and deployers of texts and performances for ends much like those of the Cooke and Lock communities.

Key Sidney-Herbert residences, including Penshurst (Robert and Barbara Sidney's seat in Kent, most famously celebrated in Ben Jonson's country house poem, 'To Penshurst'), Baynard's Castle (the Herbert home in London), and, most centrally, Wilton, Henry and Mary Sidney Herbert's home in Wiltshire, were centers of literary and political activity. Wilton was indisputably the community's main household. Nicholas Breton claimed that Mary had more 'servants' writing poetry to her at Wilton than did Elizabetta Gonzaga, Duchess of Urbino, the patron celebrated in Castiglione's *Courtier*,[69] and Samuel Daniel claimed that he received 'the first notion for the formall ordering of [his poetic] compositions at Wilton, which I must ever acknowledge to have beene my best Schoole'.[70] (As Hannay points out, Mary was a participant in as well as patron of these activities; an early draft of her 'Angell Spirit' was found among Daniel's papers.[71]) Like Gidea Hall, Gorhambury, and Bisham Abbey, Wilton was seen as a kind of 'school' in which women played central roles.

Like those other households, Wilton was also a political center. Many of the circle's participants were local, or had local ambitions, and the literary production associated with Wilton House was intimately related to local and national politics. When he wrote his *Silkewormes and their Flies* (1599), a text that flatters the Countess's literary practices, particularly her community of women readers, at Wilton House,[72] Thomas Moffet lived near Wilton, and had recently, with the help of the Herberts, been elected its MP. Most famously, Philip Sidney wrote *The Countess of Pembroke's Arcadia*, a text widely understood as including shadowed political advice for the Queen, particularly about the cause of international Protestantism, at Wilton House. In his famous epistle dedicatory Sidney tells his sister that he began to write the romance because 'you desired me to doo it', that it was written in her presence, and, most significantly for my purposes, that he wants it to circulate 'bearing the livery of your name'.[73] Sidney's dedication indicates the extent to which Mary was seen as a patron and protector of the genre known as 'political pastoral',[74] but his use of the term 'livery' also indicates the extent to which literary texts were seen as ambassadors or representatives of a given name, household, or community.

In her own life and work, Mary herself often made use of the concept of 'livery', a term which referred both to the 'the characteristic uniform or insignia worn by a household's retainers or servants', and, more generally, to 'a group owing allegiance to a person or organization; a following, faction'.[75] When, after the deaths of her brother Philip and her parents in 1586, she rejoined London political society in November 1588, Mary rode into London with a huge entourage all wearing her blue and gold livery.[76] Her spectacular entrance both signaled the return of her household and faction, and announced her status as its head.

Later, when she finished translating the psalms she had started working on with her brother, she sent them to Elizabeth I with a dedicatory poem that highlighted the Sidney name/nexus in similar terms. Her brother Philip, she suggests, provided the 'warp' (the structural vertical threads) and she 'weav'd [the] webb' of the 'liverie robe', or psalter, she now sends the Queen.[77] The opening stanza of this poem admonishes the Queen to 'dispose | What Europe acts in these most active times' (ll. 7–8), and the closing to 'doo what men may sing' (l. 96). As Hannay et al. point out, 'active times', was code for Protestant activism,[78] and the encouragement to 'doo what men may sing' was direct advice for Elizabeth to listen to the godly psalm translators and activists of whom the Sidneys were the latest instantiation. In metaphorizing the psalms as a livery robe, Mary both advises the Queen about what she should be wearing in international politics ('holy garments') and reminds her that the members of the Sidney circle are responsible for making those garments. In choosing to circulate her psalms in manuscript, Mary consciously made use of the political nature of controlled manuscript circulation.[79] The wide nature of their circulation (there are eighteen extant manuscripts) suggests the extent to which the Sidney psalms both referenced and reactivated the tradition of psalmic interventionism signaled by the de Bèze and Marot psalter and the work of Anne Lock (both of which are cited in the Sidneys' translations).[80]

Like Bisham and Gorhambury, Wilton was also seen as a site of Protestant learning and empowerment. Mary specifically dates her translation of Philippe de Mornay's *Discours de la vie et de la mort* – a continued engagement with the investments and texts of the French Huguenots – 'The 13 of May 1590. At Wilton'. Wilton's chaplain Gervase Babington praises Mary's support of religious education, claims that many of his published works were first rehearsed 'in her hearing',[81] and admonishes her to persevere in 'the studie of God's worde, and all other good learning'.[82] Nicholas Breton, Hannay points out, goes even farther when he asks her to turn from the classics to patronize only religious works: 'thinke not of the ruines of Troie, but helpe to builde up the walles of Jerusalem'.[83] In citing the key phrase of godly Protestant activism used by Anne Lock and others, Breton acknowledges Mary's investment in the same cause.

Like Lock before her, Mary was also a repository for and collator of manuscripts. Robert Sidney addressed his manuscript of poems 'For the Countess of Pembroke', and Philip Sidney seems to have entrusted several of his manuscripts to her, including those of *Certain Sonnets, Astrophil and*

Stella, and the *Lady of May,* which she later had printed in the 1598 edition of the *Arcadia*.[84] The afterlife of the liveried *Arcadia* itself was also intimately associated with Mary, who 'corrected' Fulke Greville's earlier printed edition with her own in 1593. Joel Davis has recently argued that Mary sought to remove Philip Sidney's *Arcadia* from its association with the circle of the earl of Essex that Greville had labored to create, and to associate it instead with the 'long-standing links between the Sidney family and French Neostoic intellectuals', an effort affirmed by her translation and publication of works by de Mornay and Robert Garnier in 1592.[85] Regardless of her specific intentions, Mary's *Arcadia* does make use of her 'livery'; the title page features a bear, part of the Dudley family crest, and a porcupine, part of the Sidney's. As Sidney wished, the *Arcadia,* one of the most famous books of the English Renaissance, did circulate 'bearing [his sister's] livery'. While Mary's edition was reprinted over a dozen times, Greville's was never printed again.[86] If there were disagreements within the community historically recognized as the Sidney circle, it is a notable fact of literary history that a woman was frequently its central determining force.

Afterlives

When Margaret (Dakins) Devereux Sidney married Sir Thomas Posthumous Hoby in 1591 she inherited Elizabeth (Cooke) Hoby Russell as mother-in-law and ally (although it might be more correct to say that Elizabeth inherited Margaret, recognizing as she did that her son would not amount to much).[87] Pauline Croft has noted that Lady Russell's Blackfriars house was the Hobys' main destination when they were in London for Sir Thomas's parliamentary commitments, and that they frequently visited with the other Cooke sisters and the Sidneys while they were in town.[88] What I wish to draw attention to here, however, is how Margaret Hoby's reading practices in Yorkshire – what I identify as a regional literary circle, even if the form of literary production is through reading, rather than writing, texts[89] – were imbricated with and expansive of the Cooke community practices discussed above. Hoby's reading practices also indicate the extent to which the work of literary and religio-political circles was understood and preserved as such even when the original circle was absent or no longer extant.

While much of Hoby's reading was standard Calvinist fare, in the period recorded in her diary (1599–1605), she frequently read the main texts associated with the Puritan activism of the 1570s and early 1590s in which her mother-in-law's circle had been so involved: the key texts of the Admonition controversy, the Presbyterian Directory – either the Directory itself or *The first parte of the register* – and the work of John Field, Thomas Cartwright, George Gifford, Richard Greenham, and John Udall.[90] Her reading of these authors, moreover, was aggressively communal, attempting to keep alive the work of Puritans who had been deprived or gone underground by the period in which Hoby was reading them and keeping her diary.[91]

Like her mother- and aunts-in-law, Margaret also supported unbeneficed and Puritan preachers at her house, Hackness, in Yorkshire, ran intervention for ministers brought up on charges of nonconformity, and read and disputed with a wide range of people, including some of the most controversial ministers in Yorkshire.[92] There is also evidence that Margaret played a role in reactivating the Puritan cause in London during the transition to the Jacobean government. After attending a Stephen Egerton sermon in Blackfriars on 25 November 1604, Hoby records in her diary that 'Mistress Cartwright' – Thomas Cartwright's widow, the equally radical if underappreciated Alice Cartwright – 'came to se my Lady [Elizabeth Cooke Hoby Russell]'. Margaret, in turn, 'delivered Sir Arthure Dakins message' to Cartwright.[93]

Sir Arthur Dakins was Margaret's first cousin and a powerful figure in Northern politics. In the exchange in which Margaret gives Cartwright Dakins's message, we see trafficking between the Puritan gentry of the north and the London underground Presbyterian-Puritan forces that were working, in the first year of James's reign, in the hopes of further Reformation along the models they had unsuccessfully proposed in the 1570s and again in the early 1590s. (It was a few months later in 1605, remember, that Elizabeth Russell published her translation of Ponet in an attempt to rally the old cause.)

One year earlier, in April 1603, Margaret Hoby reports that 'Lady Russill [...] required the names of such as I would trust to passe some Livinge, after hirr death, unto me.'[94] Elizabeth Russell evidently felt that Margaret should carry on her work of protecting and recommending Puritan ministers for benefices. Elizabeth's investment in ensuring a specifically female inheritance of her cause seems to have found better purchase in Margaret Hoby than in her own daughter, Anne. Lady Russell's request indicates two further things: one, that women saw other women as the logical heirs to their work (both textual and activist); and two, that communities and causes were often embodied in and maintained by relatively coherent textual oeuvres and relationships.

Along with her sister, Anne Russell Dudley, Countess of Warwick, and her sister-in-law, Elizabeth Cooke Hoby, Lady Russell, Margaret Russell

Clifford, Countess of Cumberland (1560–1616) was a powerful figure in both Elizabethan politics and the Puritan movement. (In a sermon preached before the young Countess of Cumberland in 1577, Christopher Shute, who became a pre-eminent leader of 'a flourishing and sometimes radical puritan tradition in Craven', the location of many Clifford properties, celebrates Margaret's 'happy and welcome comming into these rude and desert partes', which has 'ministered great solace to the godly'.[95]) Margaret was also the mother of Anne Clifford (eventually Countess of Dorset, Pembroke, and Montgomery) (1590–1676), and hoped, much like Elizabeth Cooke, that her daughter would continue her work as a godly householder and activist. In her will, for example, she writes of her desire that her daughter will 'respecte, favor and countenance Mr. Bradley, parson of Brougham', who 'hath many enimies for my sake, and will find opportunities for speaking the truth'.[96]

Anne Clifford certainly celebrated her family ancestry, both in her own voluminous writings and in the 'Great Picture' that she commissioned – both of which were done chiefly to shore up her rights to inherit the Clifford properties which her father had illegally entailed to male heirs. The 'Great Picture', in fact, specifically celebrates a community of women, and her mother and her aunts receive their own portraits within its frame. In the central portrait of the triptych, a young Margaret Clifford is pictured holding a book of psalms, a detail that seems to reference both Mary Sidney Herbert, who is similarly featured holding a psalter in the famous Simon van de Passe portrait, and the cause for which the psalms had become a rallying cry. As critics have pointed out, Margaret's portrait also features an inscription revealing Anne's presence *in utero*,[97] a detail that emphasizes Anne's role as her mother's heir. In addition to highlighting Anne's female lineage and inheritance, the 'Great Picture' also features a great number of books. Indeed, Anne's self-conscious adoption of both her mother's and the Sidney circle's books, and the causes they represent, suggests the continuing textual life and coherence of that community's work.

Of all the books featured in the 'Great Picture' and in the diary Anne kept between 1616 and 1619, the ones that have attracted the most attention are the literary ones. Susan Wiseman, however, has drawn attention to how Anne's other reading, particularly of architectural and chorographical texts, helped her to articulate her land claim.[98] I am similarly interested in how her use of texts associated with Elizabethan Protestant activism indicates her alignment with a cause, even if the cause itself was interesting to her largely for its collateral concern with political resistance.[99] Anne Clifford, I suggest, saw books as carriers both of the histories of causes, and of the communities who were responsible for producing them.

In August 1617, Anne records being kept from a big gathering at Penshurst, the Sidney seat. (She herself was also living in Kent, at her husband's property, Dorset House, and the couple was fighting bitterly about her pursuit of her Clifford inheritance. Dorset wanted her to take a cash settlement; she wanted the land.) Dorset traveled to Penshurst on 4 August, she recounts, 'but would not suffer me to go with him, although my Lord and my Lady Lisle [Robert and Barbara Gamage Sidney] sent a man on purpose to desire me to come'.[100] The reasons for this visit prevention are obscure, but the diary reports that a few days earlier she had visited with 'Lady Wroth [Robert and Barbara Sidney's daughter; Mary Sidney Herbert's niece], whither my Lady Rich [Sir Philip Sidney's 'Stella'] came from London to see me'.[101] Although it is impossible to determine what the women discussed, their meeting may be the reason her husband wanted to keep her away from the bigger Penshurst gathering.

During the time that her husband is at Penshurst, Anne reports keeping largely to her chamber, and spending 'most of the time in playing glecko and hearing Moll Neville read the Arcadia'.[102] What seem like harmless leisure activities are, however, associated both with the combative backdrop to the forestalled visit, and with the stoic withdrawal of their practitioner. (Anne always 'keeps to her chamber' when making a point to her husband.) Her reading of the *Arcadia* during this period suggests that she sees the book as a kind of compensatory placeholder for not being with the Sidneys themselves. In her marginal comment for the same entry, Anne notes that she was thinking 'much of religion' at the time, and that she persuaded herself 'that this religion in which my mother brought me up in is the true and undoubted religion',[103] comments that indicate her connection between the *Arcadia* and 'her mother's' religion, one associated, like the *Arcadia* itself, with militant Protestantism. Her reading of the *Arcadia* seems to evoke both a family – the Sidneys – and a set of religious and political interests.

A short while after the forestalled visit, Anne records making another visit to Penshurst, visiting with Lady Lisle, Lady Dorothy Sidney, Lady Manners, Lady Norris, her 'cousin Barbara Sidney', and, in particular, Lady Wroth, 'who told me a great deal of news from beyond sea'.[104] Wroth's 'news from beyond sea' was likely concerned with the Thirty Years War and the cause of international Protestantism, and the women – what we might call a group of 'third generation Protestant aristocrats' – are clearly pursuing engagements with one another beyond those of apolitical leisure activities. Evocative, perhaps, of the 'fair ladies' invoked in the *Arcadia*, and certainly of her mother's and Mary Sidney Herbert's past activities, Anne sought out both the romance and the Sidney women for political as well as personal reasons. Indeed two months later, in October 1617, she asks the same women for help with her land claim, and they, she is careful to note, 'commend' her daughter, Margaret.[105] By 'commend[ing]' Margaret, Anne's heir and the embodiment of her future, the Sidney women legitimate both Anne's inheritance rights and her political position. In her engagement with the Sidney women, as well as her reading of the *Arcadia*, Anne relies on and promotes a set of alliances, beliefs, and practices that remained, for all the women involved, a collective, community enterprise.

Notes

1. Philip Sidney, *The Old Arcadia*, ed. Katherine Duncan Jones (Oxford: Oxford University Press, 1999), p. 3.
2. William Stull, 'Why Are Not Sonnets Made of Thee? A New Context for the "Holy Sonnets" of Donne, Herbert, and Milton', *Modern Philology* 80.2 (1982), 129–35 (p. 132).
3. *Literary Circles and Cultural Communities in Renaissance England*, ed. Claude J. Summers and Ted-Larry Pebworth (Columbia: University of Missouri Press, 2000), pp. 1–2.
4. Margaret P. Hannay, 'The Myth of the Countess of Pembroke: The Dramatic Circle', *The Yearbook of English Studies* 11 (1981), 195–202.
5. Herz points out that coteries and communities can be no more than the function of a critic's desire or imagination, 'less found objects than artifacts of the discovery process, constructed to serve varied critical, theoretical and historical ends'. 'Of Circles, Friendship, and the Imperatives of Literary History', in *Literary Circles*, ed. Summers and Pebworth, pp. 10–23 (p. 15).
6. For political and religious minorities, like Catholics, or, during the Interregnum, royalists, literary activity reaffirmed bonds between members of a threatened society. See Earl Miner, *The Cavalier Modes from Jonson to Cotton* (Princeton: Princeton University Press, 1971), and, more recently, Margaret Ezell, '"To Be Your Daughter in Your Pen": The Social Functions of Literature in the Writings of Lady Elizabeth Brackley and Lady Jane Cavendish', *Huntington Library Quarterly* 51.4 (1988), 281–96. On manuscript literary production, see Harold Love, *Scribal Publication in Seventeenth-Century England* (Oxford: Oxford University Press, 1993) and Arthur Marotti, *Manuscript, Print, and the English Renaissance Lyric* (Ithaca: Cornell University Press, 1995).
7. See Ezell, '"To Be Your Daughter in Your Pen"', esp. pp. 294–95. On women and literary manuscripts, see the essays in *Early Modern Women's Manuscript Writing: Selected Papers from the Trinity/Trent Colloquium*, ed. Victoria E. Burke and Jonathan Gibson (Aldershot: Ashgate, 2004), pp. 205–36, 211–12, and *Women's Writing and the Circulation of Ideas: Manuscript Publication in England, 1550–1800*, ed. George L. Justice and Nathan Tinker (Cambridge: Cambridge University Press, 2002). Studies of individual manuscripts kept by women abound. Deborah Aldrich-Watson's *The Verse Miscellany of Constance Aston Fowler: A Diplomatic Edition* (Tempe: Arizona Center for Medieval and Renaissance Studies in conjunction with the Renaissance English Text Society, 2000) focuses on the

collective book of poems kept by the youngest daughter in the Aston family; Betty S. Travitsky's *Subordination and Authorship in Early Modern England: The Case of Elizabeth Cavendish Egerton and Her 'Loose Papers'* (Tempe: Arizona Center for Medieval and Renaissance Studies, 1999) addresses the family papers kept by Egerton; and *The Southwell–Sibthorpe Commonplace Book: Folger MS V.b.198*, ed. Jean Klene (Tempe: Medieval and Renaissance Texts and Studies, 1997), shows how poems by Lady Anne Southwell circulated with those of other members of her family and social circle.

8. Marion Wynne-Davies argues that the households in which women produced literature were 'safe houses', and sequestered from wordly concerns in two related essays on Mary Wroth: 'Penshurst, like all familial houses, functioned as a place where noble women could find pleasure in one another's company without the darker and more dangerous intrigues of the early seventeenth-century court.' '"For Worth, Not Weakness, Makes in Use but One": Literary Dialogues in an English Renaissance Family', in *'This Double Voice': Gendered Writing in Early Modern England*, ed. Danielle Clarke and Elizabeth Clarke (Basingstoke: Macmillan, 2000), pp. 164–84 (p. 170 n. 11). She makes a similar argument in '"So much Worth as lives in you": Veiled Portraits of the Sidney Women', in which she identifies Penshurst as a 'safe house'; *Sidney Journal* 14.1 (1996), 45–56 (p. 49). For similar arguments, see Alison Findlay, *Playing Spaces in Early Women's Drama* (Cambridge: Cambridge University Press, 2006), especially chapter 1, 'Homes'.

9. Collinson comments on the 'spiritually intimate dealings – one is tempted to call them affairs – between women of the leisured classes and certain popular and pastorally gifted divines'. See P. Collinson '"Not Sexual in the Ordinary Sense": Women, Men and Religious Transactions', in *Elizabethan Essays* (London: Hambledon Press, 1994), pp. 119–50. Micheline White focuses on what she calls 'Power Couples', crediting their supportive and connected husbands with a great deal of the women's agency. See 'Power Couples and Women Writers in Elizabethan England: The Public Voices of Dorcas and Richard Martin and Anne and Hugh Dowriche', in *Framing the Family: Representation and Narrative in the Medieval and Early Modern Periods*, ed. Diane Wolfthal and Rosalyn Voaden (Tempe: Medieval and Renaissance Texts and Studies, 2005), pp. 119–38. Alan Stewart suggests that women's literary output should be considered in relation to their (changing) status as maids, wives, and widows. See 'The Voices of Anne Cooke, Lady Anne and Lady Bacon', in *'This Double Voice'*, ed. Clarke and Clarke, pp. 88–102.

10. Mary Sidney Herbert's most famous epitaph is William Browne's description of her as 'Sidneys sister, Pembroke's mother' but Thomas Archer reverses that identification in 1760, calling Sidney 'Brother to the Countesse of Pembroke' (Hannay, *ODNB*).

11. Susanne Woods and Margaret P. Hannay, with Elaine Beilin and Anne Shaver, 'Renaissance Englishwomen and the Literary Career', in *European Literary Careers: The Author from Antiquity to the Renaissance*, ed. Patrick Cheney and Frederick A. de Armas (Toronto: University of Toronto Press, 2000), pp. 302–23 (p. 303).

12. Samuel Daniel, *The Complete Works in Verse and Prose of Samuel Daniel*, ed. Alexander B. Grosart, 5 vols (London: Hazell, Watson, and Viney, 1885), I, p. 35.

13. Mary Ellen Lamb, 'The Cooke Sisters: Attitudes toward Learned Women in the Renaissance', in *Silent But for the Word: Tudor Women as Patrons, Translators, and Writers of Religious Works*, ed. Margaret P. Hannay (Kent, OH: Kent State University Press, 1985), pp. 107–25 (p. 108).
14. See Mary Ellen Lamb, *Gender and Authorship in the Sidney Circle* (Madison: University of Wisconsin Press, 1991) and Julie Crawford, 'Sidney's Sapphics and the Role of Interpretive Communities', *English Literary History* 69.4 (2002), 979–1007.
15. Cited in Lisa Jardine and Alan Stewart, *Hostage to Fortune: The Troubled Life of Francis Bacon, 1561–1626* (London: Victor Gollancz, 1998), p. 25.
16. See Donn L. Calkins's *ODNB* entry on Anthony Cooke.
17. Lodovico Ariosto, *Orlando furioso in English heroical verse, by Sr Iohn Haringto[n] of Bathe Knight* (Imprinted at London: By Richard Field, for Iohn Norton and Simon VVaterson, 1607), p. 315.
18. Louise Schleiner, *Tudor and Stuart Women Writers* (Bloomington: Indiana University Press, 1994), pp. 35 and 32. See also Jaime Goodrich, 'Early Modern Englishwomen as Translators of Religious and Political Literature, 1500–1641' (unpublished doctoral dissertation, Boston College, 2008), p. 142.
19. Cited in Goodrich, 'Early Modern Englishwomen', p. 143.
20. Ibid., p. 172.
21. See Caroline Bowden's *ODNB* entry on Mildred Cooke Cecil. See also Jane Stevenson, 'Mildred Cecil, Lady Burleigh: Poetry, Politics and Protestantism', in *Early Modern Women's Manuscript Writing*, ed. Burke and Gibson, pp. 51–73.
22. Pietro Martire Vermigli's *Loci communes* came into the collection as a presentation copy, inscribed to Mildred Burghley by the editor Robert Massonius. Sir Anthony Cooke knew Vermigli when he lived in Strasbourg. Mildred's sister, Anne, Lady Bacon also owned a copy of the book. See Caroline Bowden, 'The Library of Mildred Cooke Cecil, Lady Burghley', *Library* 6.1 (2005), 3–29 (p. 19). For more on Vermigli, see Mark Taplin's *ODNB* entry.
23. Stevenson, 'Mildred Cecil', p. 61.
24. Pauline Croft, 'Mildred, Lady Burghley: The Matriarch', in *Patronage, Culture and Power: The Early Cecils 1558–1612*, ed. Pauline Croft (New Haven: Yale University Press), pp. 283–300 (pp. 290–91). See also Bowden's *ODNB* entry on Mildred and Retha Warnicke's on Anne Seymour.
25. Goodrich, 'Early Modern Englishwomen', p. 172.
26. Cited in Jardine and Stewart, *Hostage to Fortune*, p. 27.
27. See Mark Taplin's *ODNB* entry on Ochino.
28. Stewart, 'The Voices', p. 94.
29. Cited in ibid., p. 95.
30. Cited in ibid., p. 99. For more on Whitgift's 1583 articles, see Lynne Magnusson's *ODNB* entry on Anne.
31. See Collinson, *ODNB* and Stewart, 'The Voices', p. 98.
32. For details about the uncertainty of Elizabeth Russell's birth date, see Chris Laoutaris's essay in this volume.
33. Geoffrey Fenton, *Actes of conference in religion, holden at Paris, betweene two papist doctours of Sorbone, and two godlie ministers of the Church. Dravven out of French into English, by Geffraie Fenton* (London: H. Bynneman, for VVilliam Norton and Humfrie Toye, 1571), sigs. Aii^v, Aiii.

34. On women as 'devisers' of cultural entertainments, see Peter Davidson and Jane Stevenson, 'Elizabeth I's Reception at Bisham (1592): Elite Women as Writers and Devisers', in *The Progresses, Pageants and Entertainments of Queen Elizabeth*, ed. Jayne Elizabeth Archer, Elizabeth Goldring, and Sarah Knight (Oxford: Oxford University Press, 2007), pp. 207–26 (p. 216 and *passim*).
35. Alexandra Johnston, 'The "Lady of the farme": The Context of Lady Russell's Entertainment of Elizabeth at Bisham, 1592', *Early Theatre* 5.2 (2002), 71–85 (pp. 76–77).
36. Cited in ibid., p. 77.
37. George Puttenham, *The Arte of English Poesie* (1589), in *Elizabethan Critical Essays*, ed. G. Gregory Smith, 2 vols (London: University Press, 1904), II, p. 40.
38. Johnston, '"The Lady of the farme"', p. 78.
39. See Elaine V. Beilin, *Protestant Translators: Anne Lock Prowse and Elizabeth Russell*, selected and introduced by Elaine V. Beilin (Aldershot: Ashgate, 2001), pp. 142 and 141.
40. Goodrich, 'Early Modern Englishwomen', p. 368.
41. John Ponet, *A way of reconciliation of a good and learned man touching the trueth, nature, and substance of the body and blood of Christ in the sacrament. Translated out of Latin by the right honorable Lady Elizabeth Russell, dowager to the right honourable the Lord Iohn Russell, Baron, and sonne and heire to Francis Earle of Bedford* (At London: R. B[arker], 1605), sig. A^v.
42. Jessica L. Malay, 'Elizabeth Russell's Textual Performances of Self', *Comitatus: A Journal of Medieval and Renaissance Studies* 37 (2006), 146–68 (p. 165).
43. See Collinson, *ODNB*.
44. Ibid.
45. Roland Greene, 'Anne Lock's Meditation: Invention Versus Dilation and the Founding of Puritan Poetics', in *Form and Reform in Renaissance England: Essays in Honor of Barbara Kiefer Lewalski*, ed. Amy Boesky and Mary Thomas Crane (Newark: University of Delaware Press, 2000), pp. 153–70 (p. 153).
46. Ibid., p. 157.
47. Susan M. Felch, 'Introduction', in *The Collected Works of Anne Vaughan Lock*, ed. Susan M. Felch (Tempe: Arizona Center for Medieval and Renaissance Studies, 1999), p. li.
48. *ODNB*.
49. See Felch, 'Introduction', p. li. See also Micheline White, 'Renaissance Englishwomen and Religious Translations: The Case of Anne Lock's *Of the Markes of the Children of God* (1590)', *English Literary Renaissance* 29 (1999), 375–400.
50. See Collinson's *ODNB* entry on Dering.
51. Ibid.
52. Ibid.
53. Ibid.
54. Schleiner, *Tudor and Stuart Women Writers*, pp. 40–41; see also White, 'Renaissance Englishwomen', p. 388.
55. Lodovico Guicciardini, *Houres of recreation, or afterdinners which may aptly be called The garden of pleasure: containing most pleasant tales, worthy deedes, and wittie sayings of noble princes [et] learned philosophers, with their morals. No lesse delectable, than profitable. Done firste out of Italian into Englishe by Iames Sandford, Gent. and now by him newly perused, corrected, and enlarged* (London: By Henry Binneman, 1576), sig. A4^r.

56. *A notable and comfortable exposition of M. Iohn Knoxes, vpon the fourth of Mathew, concerning the tentations of Christ* (London: Printed by Robert VValde-graue for Thomas Man, 1583), p. 4. See also White, 'Power Couples'.
57. Collinson, *ODNB* entry on Anne Lock.
58. Jean Taffin, *Of the markes of the children of God and of their comforts in afflictions* (London: Printed by Thomas Orwin, 1590), sigs. A2–A2ᵛ.
59. Felch, *Anne Vaughan Lock*, pp. 1 and 5–7.
60. Margaret Hannay, 'Strengthening the walles of [...] Ierusalem': Anne Vaughan Lock's Dedication to the Countess of Warwick', *ANQ* 5.2/3 (1992), 71–75 (p. 72).
61. Taffin, *Of the markes of the children of God*, sig. A2, sig. A2ᵛ.
62. White, 'Renaissance Englishwomen'.
63. Collinson, *ODNB* entry on Lock.
64. White, 'Renaissance Englishwomen', p. 389.
65. Ibid., p. 391.
66. See Michael G. Brennan, *Literary Patronage in the English Renaissance: The Pembroke Family* (London and New York: Routledge, 1988); Margaret P. Hannay, *Philip's Phoenix: Mary Sidney, Countess of Pembroke* (Oxford: Oxford University Press, 1990); Gary Waller, *The Sidney Family Romance: Mary Wroth, William Herbert, and the Early Modern Construction of Gender* (Detroit: Wayne State University Press, 1993); and Lamb, *Gender and Authorship*.
67. Schleiner, *Tudor and Stuart Women Writers*, p. 52.
68. Hannay, *ODNB* entry on Mary Sidney Herbert.
69. Nicholas Breton, *The pilgrimage to paradise, ioyned with the Countesse of Penbrookes loue, compiled in verse by Nicholas Breton Gentleman* (Oxford: Printed, by Ioseph Barnes, and are to be solde in Paules Church-yeard [London, by Toby Cooke], at the signe of the Tygres head, 1592), sig. A2.
70. Samuel Daniel, *A panegyrike congratulatorie deliuered to the Kings most excellent Maiestie at Burleigh Harrington in Rutlandshire* (London: Imprinted [by R. Read] for Edward Blount, 1603), sig. G3.
71. *ODNB*. Mary's works also circulated outside the immediate household. She asks Edward Wotton to return a poem that she had sent him about 1594, and in 'The Ruines of Time', Spenser claims to have read an unpublished elegy that she had written (Hannay, *ODNB*).
72. Lamb, *Gender and Authorship*, p. 53.
73. Sidney, *The Old Arcadia*, p. 3.
74. David Norbrook, *Poetry and Politics in the English Renaissance*, rev. edn (Oxford: Oxford University Press, 2002), chapter 4.
75. *OED*.
76. Michael G. Brennan, *The Sidneys of Penshurst and the Monarchy, 1500–1700* (Aldershot: Ashgate, 2006), p. 100.
77. Mary Sidney Herbert, 'Even Now That Care', in *The Collected Works of Mary Sidney Herbert, Countess of Pembroke, Volume 1. Poems, Translation and Correspondence*, ed. Margaret P. Hannay, Noel J. Kinnamon, and Michael G. Brennan (Oxford: Clarendon Press, 1998), p. 27.
78. Hannay et al. (eds), *Collected Works of Mary Sidney Herbert*, p. 100.
79. See Love, *Scribal Publication*, passim.
80. See Margaret P. Hannay, 'The Countess of Pembroke's Agency in Print and Scribal Culture', in *Women's Writing and the Circulation of Ideas*, ed. Justice

and Tinker, pp. 17–49. Individual psalms also circulated in private correspondence, including three (51, 104, and 137) that John Harington of Kelston sent to Lucy, Countess of Bedford with *The Triumph of Death* (Hannay, *ODNB*).

81. Cited in Hannay, *Philip's Phoenix*, p. 134.
82. Gervase Babington, *A very fruitfull exposition of the Commaundements by way of questions and answeres for greater plainnesse together with an application of euery one to the soule and conscience of man* (London: Printed by Henry Midleton for Thomas Charde, 1583), sig. A5.
83. Breton, *Pilgrimage to paradise*, sig. A2; see also Hannay, *ODNB*.
84. Hannay, *ODNB*.
85. Joel Davis, 'Multiple Arcadias and the Literary Quarrel between Fulke Greville and the Countess of Pembroke', *Studies in Philology* 101.4 (2004), 401–30 (p. 421).
86. Ibid., p. 430.
87. On Elizabeth's pursuit of Margaret and disappointment in her son, see Elizabeth Farber, 'The Letters of Lady Elizabeth Russell (1540–1609)' (unpublished doctoral dissertation, Columbia University, 1977), pp. 111–14.
88. Pauline Croft, 'Capital Life: Members of Parliament Outside the House', in *Politics, Religion and Popularity in Early Stuart Britain: Essays in Honour of Conrad Russell*, ed. Thomas Cogswell, Richard Cust, and Peter Lake (Cambridge: Cambridge University Press, 2002), pp. 65–83 (pp. 69–72).
89. Julie Crawford, 'Reconsidering Early Modern Women's Reading, or How Margaret Hoby Read Her De Mornay', *Huntington Library Quarterly* 73.2 (June 2010).
90. On 30 July 1601, she 'hard Mr Rhodes read of the true diCeplen of christes church' (Anne Clifford, *The Memoir of 1603 and The Diary of 1616–1619*, ed. Katherine Acheson [Peterborough, ON: Broadview editions, 2007], p. 181), a book that could be either *The Book of Discipline*, or the printed collection of Presbyterian writings known as *A Parte of a register* (the title page of which reads 'Demonstration of the trueth of that discipline which Christe hath prescribed in his worde for the government of his Church').
91. Crawford, 'Reconsidering Early Modern Women's Reading', *passim*.
92. See Margaret Hoby, *Diary of Lady Margaret Hoby, 1599–1605*, ed. Dorothy M. Meads (Boston and New York: Houghton Mifflin, 1930), pp. 174, 219, 290.
93. Ibid., p. 214.
94. Ibid., p. 203.
95. Vivienne Larminie's *ODNB* entry on Shute.
96. George C. Williamson, *Lady Anne Clifford, Countess of Dorset, Pembroke and Montgomery, 1590–1676. Her Life, Letters, and Work* (Kendal: Titus Wilson and Son, 1923), p. 41.
97. Heidi Brayman Hackel, *Reading Material in Early Modern England: Print, Gender, and Literacy* (Cambridge: Cambridge University Press, 2005), p. 225.
98. Susan Wiseman, 'Knowing Her Place: Anne Clifford and the Politics of Retreat', in *Textures of Renaissance Knowledge*, ed. Phillipa Berry and Margaret Tudeau-Clayton (Manchester: Manchester University Press, 2003), pp. 199–221 (p. 215).
99. Julie Crawford, 'Anne Clifford and the Uses of Christian Warfare', in *English Women, Religion, and Textual Production, 1500–1625*, ed. Micheline White (Aldershot: Ashgate Press, forthcoming).

100. Clifford, *Memoir and Diary*, p. 143.
101. Ibid.
102. Ibid., p. 145.
103. Ibid., p. 144.
104. Ibid., p. 145.
105. Ibid., p. 147.

3
Women in Early English Print Culture

A. E. B. Coldiron

Within a year of bringing the printing press to Westminster, William Caxton shows an understanding that 'woman questions' will be important and controversial in the new medium. Evidence of this appears in his revision and printing of the *Dictes or sayengis of the philosophres*, which was long thought to be the first book in English printed in England and is now called the second or third.[1] Caxton restores some misogynist passages that his translator-patron, Anthony Woodville, had suppressed. In doing so, Caxton explains his actions at length in a fascinating epilogue, stressing the suppression and restoration of the missing misogyny. His foregrounded topic – 'certayn and dyuerce conclusions towchyng wymen' attributed to Socrates – generates a discussion of textual authority that is by turns obsequious, sly, serious, and playful. In it he grants readers, specifically including women, their own radical agency with the text, offering readers the option of marking or tearing out the very controversial, misogynist passages he has restored.

In some respects, textual authority is up for grabs in the environment of early print, and this has consequences for women's participation in literary production. The old hierarchies and roles of textual production – *auctor*, *compilator*, translator, *scriptor*, patron, bookseller, and so on, as detailed by A. J. Minnis – did not by any means vanish with the arrival of Caxton in England, nor did the important social and commercial relations that grounded manuscript literature.[2] But new economies were forming, entailing new roles and recalibrated hierarchies of textual production. That is, a newly weighted importance came to be placed on purchasers and readers, with new powers of speed, distribution, iterability, and alterability in the printers' hands.[3] For our purposes, these changing economies and hierarchies of textual production created if not a true public sphere[4] or *Öffentlichtkeit*, as philosopher Jürgen Habermas terms the discursive 'opening' spaces of eighteenth-century salons and newspapers, then at least a new matrix of opportunity in which gender issues might be profitably handled in new ways. Caxton, for instance, in the *Dictes* and elsewhere, acted on his prior texts in ways so assertive that we would now call them authorial: overruling his translator and patron; creating lengthy paratexts that anticipate and direct readers' interpretations; adding, removing, reordering, and restoring whole chunks of text; comparing varying copies and making meaningful choices among them. Caxton's strong textual interventions sometimes touch on questions of gender, though not usually with as much blatant manhandling, if you will, as in the *Dictes*. For Caxton and the early printers following him, women's issues seem to have been unevenly problematic but always marketable. The handling of the problematic missing misogyny in the *Dictes* is a telling early signal of the rapidly broadening, sometimes paradoxical, and usually controversial presences of women in early English print culture.

This essay surveys several aspects of women's presences in early print. I begin with a new reading of Caxton's *Dictes* epilogue and revision as the earliest instance of an English printer's explicit self-consciousness about gender issues and textual agency, a case in some ways paradigmatic for early print culture. I then contextualize the case, first with Caxton's other publications related to women, and next with publications related to women made by the second generation of printers in England. The essay closes with a section surveying early modern women's direct participation in printing. Their complicated engagements with the new means of production were more extensive than scholars have usually assumed.

Missing misogyny, or, manhandling *The Dictes or Sayengis of the Philosophres*

The Dictes is a translation of a French version of the *Mukhtar Al-hikam* ('Beautiful Sayings') by the eleventh-century philosopher-poet Al Mubashshir ibn Al Fâtik. This compilation offers quotations from, anecdotes about, miniature biographies of, and interpretations of a set of twenty-two ancient authorities, including Galen, Pythagoras, Hippocrates, and Socrates.[5] We should not underestimate the power of such a list of *auctores* to call forth the use of scribal conventions of fidelity, even in print. That is, scribal treatment of such authorities had commonly involved claims for the truthfulness and accuracy of the text, and claims of faithfulness to the *auctores*. At a moment when textual authority was a provocative matter – when the new medium was calling all in doubt – Caxton's strong revisions to the *Dictes* exemplify the sometimes surprising agencies the earliest printers felt comfortable seizing, despite the tenacity of such old conventions. Furthermore, immediate social considerations would have encouraged a more cautious, traditional, textual fidelity; Caxton's revisions to his powerful patron's manuscript copies thus also revise the relation between patron and textual producer (here, the printer). It is not that Caxton restores the misogynistic passages quietly. He draws attention to them, creating a whole section in which he speculates about why Woodville might have suppressed the passages, about how to interpret the restored section, and what some possible readers' responses might be. In short, Caxton's additions reveal a special, very early attention to textual agency that is played out on some misogynist 'wisdom'.

Where the missing misogyny of the *Dictes* is concerned, Caxton is caught between the Scylla of *auctoritas* and the Charybdis of patronage. (At least, he presents himself that way in his talky epilogue; he may also have been trying to fill blank pages at the end of a quire with lively, controversial material.) William Kuskin rightly reads Caxton's revisions in terms of a genealogy of literary authority;[6] my interest here is to explore further how these revisions also answer what Kuskin calls the 'demand for gender' and for discussions of women's position in the culture.[7] In addition to the interest that scholars like Kuskin and Curt Bühler have found in the *Dictes*, and in addition to my own interest in the text's multi-culturalism and its unappreciated, playful tone, at stake here is the earliest quasi-debate on women printed in England: in the new medium, when it was entirely unnecessary and socially risky to do so, Caxton started a miniature, paratextual *querelle*.

Caxton's restored version of the missing misogyny attributed to Socrates is only seventeen 'sayings' long, each item separated by paraphs, and the whole occupying only about two pages. There is little unusual here: the passage opens with 'Socrates sayde That women ben thapparaylles to cacche men [...] ther is none so grete empeshement vnto a man as ignoraunce. and women'. Sets of comparisons ensue: 'And he sawe a woman that bare fyre, of whom he saide that the hotter bare the colder¶ And he sawe a woman seke. of whom he saide that the euyll restyth and dwellyth with the euill'. One item in an 'evils of women' series deals with writing: 'And he sawe a long mayde that lerned to write', which 'multiplied euyll vpon euyll'. Traditional advice to men not to listen to women, not to educate them, and not to obey them is followed by a traditional *refutatio* or objection and reply: 'And what sayist thou by our good moders and of our susters. He saide to hem. Suffise you. with that I haue sayde to you, For alle ben semblable in malyce'. A striking pair of similes about women as trees allows the Socrates-speaker to deflect each unnamed questioner's pro-woman points with a misogyny. In one sentence, women are like the fair but poisonous Edelfla tree; in the next, after questioners 'demanded wherfore he blamed so wymen. and that he him self had not comen into this worlde ne none other men also with oute hem, He ansuerd' that women are also like the harmfully prickly yet sweet-fruited 'Chassoygnet' (chestnut).[8]

The restored misogyny is fairly short, which makes Caxton's explanatory epilogue seem the more performative. Deanne Williams, for one, persuasively reads Caxton as antifeminist chiefly by way of his mercantilism;[9] creating a gender controversy would certainly help sell books. Caxton explains the matter of the missing misogyny at such length that it seems staged, not only a marketing tactic but also an excuse to discuss textual authority and agency in the new medium.[10] Woodville, Caxton tells us in the epilogue, gave his translation to Caxton, and asked him to 'ouersee' and then print it. Caxton repeats the word 'ouersee' four times in the space of one page, and it comes to sound overly deferential, almost defensive. Caxton praises his patron Woodville's translation ('a meritory dede [...] wherin [Woodville] had deseruid a singuler lawde & thank' [fol. 73ʳ]) but also explains, again with that coy defensiveness, that Woodville authorized and initiated the textual tampering. The epilogue is too long for full discussion here; to summarize, Caxton consistently flatters Woodville's translation and disingenuously claims a reluctance to change it. In his own close comparative reading of varying texts, he says, he found 'nothyng discordaunt' – well, nothing except 'in the dyctes and sayengys of Socrates, Wherin I fynde that *my saide lord hath left out certayn and dyuerce conclusions towchyng wymen*' (fol. 73ᵛ, emphasis mine). Caxton then speculates cheekily about why Woodville might have removed those misogynist passages from his text, first attributing it to personal motives; perhaps 'som fayre lady hath desired him to leue it out of his booke Or ellyes he was amerous on somme noble lady' (fol. 73ᵛ). This speculation could be topical, as truthful as it is playful, since Woodville's first wife died in 1473; he did not remarry until 1480, and in 1477 he was one of England's most eligible bachelors.[11] Or perhaps Woodville was just generally friendly to women ('for the very affeccion loue and good wylle that he hath vnto alle ladyes and Gentylwomen'). Later in the epilogue, Caxton proposes that some textual gap, or maybe the wind, was responsible for the omission of misogyny: 'for as moche as I am not in certayn wheder it was in my lordis copye or not. or ellis perauenture that the wynde had blowe ouer the leef, at the tyme of translacion of his booke' (fol. 74ʳ). In short, Caxton takes considerable space pointing out this omission to readers, speculating about its causes – *amor*? error?

fortuna? – excusing Woodville but making the authority of Socrates hinge on the value of the passage about women:

> I can not thinke that so trewe a man & so noble a Phylosophre as Socrates was sholde write other wyse than trouth For If he had made fawte in wryting of wymen. He ought not ne sholde not be beleuyd in his other dictes and sayinges. (fol. 73^v)

If the misogynist passages are mistaken, suggests Caxton, then Socrates's overall credibility is in doubt.

Finally Caxton extricates himself from the conflicting obligations to old-textual versus current-social authority with the help of cross-cultural analysis, claiming that Socrates was Greek, 'And men and wymen of other nature than they ben heere in thys contre' (fol. 73^v). In England, women are 'right good, wyse, playsant, humble, discrete, sobre, chast, obedyent to their husbondis, trewe, secrete, stedfast, euer besy, & neuer ydle, Attemperat in speking, and vertuous in alle their werkis *or atte leste sholde be so*' (fol. 74^r, emphasis mine), his hyperbolic praise undercut with a sarcastic wink in that last phrase. His winking admission that these patriarchal ideals are just that nevertheless leaves in doubt the character of real English women – some of whom, he soon says, are his readers.

The flattery of women, undercut in this way, seems an obvious attempt to play both sides of a hot question, as Caxton indeed allows when explaining why he moved the Socratic misogynies to the very end of his long book: it is 'in satisfieng of all parties & also for excuse of the saide socrates I haue sette these sayde dyctes & sayengis a parte in thende of this book' (fol. 75^r). Although he anticipates readers' mixed reactions, he does not assume women readers alone will be offended. On the contrary, he specifies readers or listeners of either gender. And for either gender, the Socratic misogyny is apparently so inflammatory that he fancifully allows for a violent, physical response. Caxton moved the restored misogyny to the very end of the *Dictes*,

> to thentent that yf my sayd lord or ony other persone *what someuer he or she be* that shal rede or here it, that If they be not well plesyd with alle that they wyth a penne race it out *or ellys rente the leef oute of the booke*. (fol. 75^v, emphasis mine)

One thinks here of the doubly ventriloquized account of the Wife of Bath's destruction of her husband's misogynistic book; Caxton might also have been thinking of it, since he printed the *Dictes* and *The Canterbury*

Tales at around the same time. If we read this epilogue 'straight', as if Caxton really expected these passages to incite readers to destroy the book, we miss the payoff of its playful performativity. After all, these same tired misogynies had served as perennial debate topoi in Latinate clerical culture[12] and in Christine de Pizan's *querelle*; no one would have been surprised, but much discussion would have ensued. One imagines readers turning immediately to see just what is in that restored section. In so flamboyantly restaging the debate here in paratext with Woodville, Caxton asserts what Williams calls his shift from 'clerkly servility' to 'professional empowerment'. If the epilogue, then, is a clever marketing tactic complete with Chaucerian allusion, we can infer its success by its presence in editions through 1528. Caxton seizes this chance to highlight both the suppression and the restoration of misogyny; the perennial gender controversy will generate buzz for the brand-new object called the printed book, and will also be the perfect topic with which to discuss older hierarchies of textual authority.

The dialectic on women's value and virtue will flare out in early print soon after this, in varying degrees of fury, beginning openly with Wynkyn de Worde's *Interlocucyon, with an argument, betwyxt man and woman to see which will proue the moste excellent* (?1525), an ancestor of later pamphlet debates.[13] There is also a fair amount of covert gender debating built into other popular verse genres in print before 1557, such as complaints, estates satires, marital narratives, and dream-vision allegories. But in 1477, an implicit *querelle* has already been staged between translator/ patron and printer, wrangling over the printing of such authoritative misogynies and finally asking readers to judge. Caxton's paratext, for all its gossipy playfulness and winking appearance of placating all sides, derives its central energy from this ever-controversial topic.

Representing women in earliest print

Caxton's printing of works related to gender issues and his involvements with female authority were complex but certainly generative and profitable for him. He enjoyed the support of important female patrons (whom he represents in paratexts) at a time when patronage and commercial sales of books created mixed, overlapping systems of revenue.[14] Margaret of Burgundy, he tells us, was patron of his translation and production of the first book printed in English, the *Recuyell of the Historyes of Troye* (published in Bruges in 1473–74) and for subsequent translation and printing projects. His other chief female patron, Margaret Beaufort, mother of Henry VII, was also one of the earliest female writers in

English print; her translations of two French devotional treatises were printed in 1503 and 1506. (Caxton's worth may have been one of the few points of agreement between these two powerful Margarets.) Beaufort was patron and dedicatee of Caxton's translation and printing of the romance *Blanchardyn and Eglantine* (*c*.1489), one of the books Caxton tells us he intended for women's instruction. Jennifer Summit explores thoroughly the implications of Caxton's preface to, and Beaufort's patronage of, this book. Summit finds that, taken in the full context of early print commerce, 'the figure of the patron may be used to serve strategic purposes' such that we should not see the patron 'as an unproblematic symbol of female power'.[15] Caxton may say in 1489 that romance is useful for women's instruction, but during the sixteenth and seventeenth centuries attitudes towards women's reading of romance grow more complex and condemnatory.[16]

Before this, in translating and printing the *Boke of the Knyght of the Towre* (1484), Caxton had made the first printed English conduct book for women, 'in especial for ladyes and gentilwymmen doughters to lords and gentilmen'. The stated aim is for these young women to 'lerne to bihaue them self vertuously/ as wel in their vyrgynyte as in their wedlok and wedowhede' (fol. 1[ʳ]), following the traditional medieval categories of the three estates of women. Although intended for daughters, the work is to serve lifelong, 'in what estat she be'. Mark Addison Amos persuasively reads the work 'as engaged in a sexual allegory of class, inscribing within its figuration of noblewomen the social situation and sins of the threatening merchant class'. Disobedient wives are beaten, and 'the noblewomen who are the book's inscribed audience also function subtextually as body doubles for the powerful commoners against whom the text is rhetorically aimed' – many more such commoners, I would add, would have had access to a printed than to a manuscript version. Amos's point applies beyond the *Towre* that 'women are always the subordinate group [...] [but the text functions] by enforcing class distinctions and by drawing parallels between the situations of the upper (potentially falling) gentry and the lower (potentially rising) merchant class'.[17] In other words, books for, about, and by women are necessarily also situated in other kinds of representational struggles. With the rapidly expanding readerships of early print, such struggles multiply and intensify. Caxton's *Knyght of the Towre* is the first in an important early modern line of printing for women's instruction, a line studied thoroughly in its post-1550 phases by Suzanne Hull, Ruth Kelso, and the many scholars following them.

Beyond staging a paratextual *querelle*, receiving commissions from women, and printing books for women, Caxton prints books by an important woman author, Christine de Pizan. In 1478 he printed Wood-ville's translation of Christine de Pizan's verse aphorisms, *The Morale Prouerbes of Cristyne.* His title and colophon fully acknowledge and honor Christine's authorship and authority; in the colophon, a rhyme-royal poem celebrates her as author and as 'mireur and maistresse' of 'Intelligence', so great is her wisdom. In the re-edition of this work in 1526 by Richard Pynson, Henry VIII's King's Printer, the title and run-ning heads continue to proclaim her authority.[18] Caxton also translated and printed her *Fayttes of Armes and of Chyualrye* (1489), naming her in the paratexts. In publishing these works, Caxton set a trend in Tudor printed literature of honoring and validating Christine's authority. John Skot printed her *Booke [of the] Body of Polycye* in 1521, the same year Henry Pepwell published Henrician courtier Bryan Ansley's trans-lation of her *Cyte of Ladyes.* Robert Wyer printed her *C. Hystoryes of Troye* in 1549.[19] Although Christine's work is, as some critics have said, de-authorized and ventriloquized badly in manuscript translations like that of Stephen Scrope or Thomas Hoccleve,[20] nevertheless, Caxton and other early printers and translators consciously promulgated Christine's authority. Readers of Tudor print knew her in part as we know her now – that is, as a writer of feminist utopian allegory – but overall as an author of political theory, of revisionist mythography, of military history, of wisdom literature.

Printers after Caxton actively produced texts for and about women, if not often *by* women. His successor Wynkyn de Worde printed a number of works about women, including *The Gospelles of Dystaues* (c.1510) a translation of Antoine Fouquart's popular French lore-book about women, household management, morality, and social relations. De Worde's list includes many works we would now call misogynist and/or misogamist. Julia Boffey studies De Worde's apparent misogyny, or most charitably, his enterprising use of misogynist materials.[21] De Worde's prolific work includes such titles as *The Payne and Sorowe of Euyll Maryage* (c.1530) and the satiric *Fyftene Joyes of Maryage* (1509). After *The Fyftene Joyes* was banned and burned in front of Stationer's Hall in 1599, it was resur-rected in a new form as *The Batchelars Banquet* in two editions in 1603, three more by 1631, and several thereafter. While many early printed works about women lost popularity over time, some, like *The Fyftene Joyes*, persisted long into later periods. Like De Worde, Robert Copland devotes considerable publication energy to women's issues, and in his smaller corpus, women's issues seem the more prominent. Copland often uses satiric and sometimes transgressive, racy treatments. His *Seuen Sorowes that Women Haue When Theyr Husbandes Be Deade* (c.1525)[22] is part of a minor early subgenre we might call 'widow literature', in this case including a parodic Eucharist. Copland's is not the earliest widow literature in print; William Dunbar's 'Tretis of the twa mariit wemen and the wedow' (c.1507) reminds us of the fascinating though less well-known terrain of early printing and woman-related texts in Scotland.[23] Although such material may appear recondite now, it was known in later Tudor England. For instance, Copland's *Jyl of Braintford's Testament* (c.1535), with its extended fart joke, is later alluded to in Nashe, Harington, and Shakespeare.[24] Copland also translates and revises a pair of marriage complaints. Although satiric, these do feature more varied tones, including a serious voicing not only of a wife's woes in marriage but also a favorable treatment of a wife's sexual desire (c.1505, c.1518, 1535).[25] In the vein of post-medieval estates satire and fool-literature, Copland's darkly satiric translation, *The Hye Way to the Spyttell Hous* (c.1536), adds a whole misogynist subsection on women, associating them, as is frequent in early print, with poverty and the threat of poverty. In sum, for De Worde, Copland, Pynson, Wyer, and other early printers, the topics of sex, marriage, and women in general proved steadily saleable staples.

One popular early printed work I have not seen discussed in terms of gender is a translation from Pierre Gringore, *The Castle of Labour* (Vérard, c.1503; De Worde, 1506, 1512; Pynson, ?1505 & ?1528). In this working-class dream-vision story, a married couple goes to sleep, and the husband undergoes instructive adventures related to work and poverty, complete with personified vices and virtues jousting in reverse-inked or 'negative' woodcuts in a dreamscape sequence. The book is technologically fascinating, but more immediately relevant is the way this hundred-page poem represents men and women in public and domestic settings. In a striking final woodcut titled 'The House of Rest' (Pynson, 1505, [sig. Iii v], see Figure 1), a man sits at a table by the fire with plate and cup, and a woman bends over the fire apparently preparing the meal. 'Rest' means here a man's rest; the woman is working. The assumptions about gender roles and the elision of women's labor implicit in this image may reproduce misogyny in ways more visible to modern than to early modern readers, and more visible to early modern women than to early modern men. As Molly Hand remarks, this image 'has the subversive potential of revealing gender inequality. Something like an inside joke, it will signify differently for men and women readers' (private correspondence). Even in works not ostensibly making arguments about gender, such representations invite reflection on gender issues; the medium of print issues the invitation to an ever larger, ever broader English readership.

Co reereſſe nature wlthout exceſſe
And ſo dꝛewe me to the hous of reſt

J ſawe teſt whiche dyd me abyde
wlthin his hous wlthouten blame
And my wyfe on the other ſyde
Dꝛeſſed my ſouper wlthout dyſfame
There reſted J in goddys name
ffamplierly nat as a ſtranger
Thankynge god oflmmoꝛtall fame
That J eſcaped was that daunger

❧ The hous of reſt.

Ato the table J went that tyde
Entendyng to ſoupe wlthout outrage
My wyfe ſat on the other ſyde
After my cuſtome and olde vſage
There had we bꝛede wyne and potage
And of fleſſhe a ſmale pytaunce
wlthout to any hutte oꝛ damage
we ſouped togeder at our pleaſaunce

My wyfe voyded the table clene
And vnto me apꝛoched nere
Than on my ſholder dyd ſhe lene
After hyr coſtome and manere
There tolde J hyr of the dauugere
whlcqe J was in the nyght befoꝛe
Howe that ſhe ſlept with mery chere
The whyle that J was troubled ſoꝛe

J tolde hyr that in all my lyfe
J had nat ſo great peruerſyte
Nowe in pleaſour and nowe in ſtryfe
Tourmented fyerſly felt J me
foꝛ fals ſlede/and ſeceſſyte
wyth pouertye/& hyr ſelawe diſtreſſe
Thought & heuyneſſe wyth crueltye
Lay on my bed me to oppꝛeſſe

Dyſconfoꝛt and Dlſeſperaunce
Lay vpon me wlth theyr treaſon
Redy to bꝛynge me to myſchaunce
J.llj.

Figure 3.1 'The House of Rest' (Pynson, 1505, [sig. Iii v]). Published with permission of ProQuest. ©The British Library Board. Shelfmark Huth.29. Further reproduction is prohibited without permission.

Overall in early print, we find several main kinds of works about women. The well-studied romances and courtly poems, and the numerous, largely conventional devotional works; conduct books, household books, medical and gynecological treatises; marriage literature: these and more thrived in earliest print. An important, less well-studied strand of early printed secular literature focuses on representing daily lives, usually non-elite lives. Themes here include the uncomfortable intersections of sex and economics and the unpleasant realities of marriage (i.e. marriage is often depicted as a trap for both men and women, or as the Church's containment system for sexual desire). Bodily discomforts receive colloquial treatment, and women's own voices complain about faithless, stingy men or noisy, expensive children, extending the medieval *mal mariée* tradition considerably, in a newly public voice. Here we find an anti-idealizing strain and an appropriation of decidedly un-Petrarchan Continental discourses. In these earliest printed books we find foundations for the later works for and about women – the initial suggestions to which later writers and printers responded variously. Many early works are simply reprinted, or their themes are reworked, as in the Tudor and Stuart pamphlet debates mentioned above which treat the same issues as the *Interlocucyon* of 1525. Important sources of English discourses about women – the early, powerful appropriations of French material in early print – persist even after the Restoration. In sum, in early print we find distinctive, alternative lines of writing about women. However, they have been much better studied for the later Tudor and Stuart periods,[26] a fact that promises good research opportunities for future scholars of the earlier phases of printing.

While many, varied early printed works represent women and aim at women, the few works by women represent a narrow social and thematic range. The early female authors most often cited are Margaret Beaufort, Margaret More Roper, and Juliana Berners. De Worde may have taken up the St Albans printer's work of 1486, the *Bokys of hawking, hunting and blasing of arms* attributed to Juliana Barnes or Berners (the first book in England to use color printing); STC 3309 shows De Worde still at Westminster printing a version in 1496, adding a fishing treatise to it. However, Berners's authorship and existence are now doubted, so the real interest here would be the story of the use of evidence in constructing, canonizing, and dismantling an early case of female authorship.[27]

Margaret More Roper's existence and the appearance of her work in early print, however, are not doubted. In both editions of her translation, *A deuoute treatise vpon the Pater noster* (Berthelet *c.*1526 and *c.*1531), the subtitle begins with the authority of Erasmus and then specifies her gender, virtue, learning, and youth: '*made fyrst in latyn by the moost famous doctour mayster Erasmus Roterodamus, and tourned in to englisshe by a yong vertuous and well lerned gentylwoman of. xix. yere of age*'. In the edition of 1526, the title woodcut representing her as a decorous, studious figure recalls the famous prosopopoeia woodcut depicting Christine de Pizan in the *Cyte of Ladyes* (see Figure 2).

So by 1526, a style or convention of representing the scholarly or devout woman writer is already available in England, adding to other styles of visually representing women, as we learn from Driver's fascinating discussion of early 'everywoman' woodcuts and images of devout women.[28] And yet, Roper's *Deuoute treatise* points to a mixed story where writing women are concerned: the Henrician humanists who favored Roper's learned book ran in the same circles with the likes of John Rastell, who printed John Heywood's misogynist farce translation, *Johan Johan and Hys Wyf Tyb* in 1533. As raucously misogynist as much Henrician literature is, still, some small space was available for a

Figure 3.2 'A Deuoute treatise vpon the Pater noster' (Berthelet *c*.1525, [title page]). Published with permission of ProQuest. ©The British Library Board. Shelfmark C.37.e.6.(1). Further reproduction is prohibited without permission.

certain kind of acceptable woman writer, the kind who will still be most acceptable in later Tudor and Stuart England: learned, 'vertuous', elite.

In this vein, Margaret Beaufort's early translations can be read as precursors to other royal women's translations, for instance, works associated with Marguerite de Navarre, Katherine Parr, and Elizabeth Tudor, as Anne Lake Prescott, Margaret Hannay, and Tina Krontiris explain.[29] Extending older French habits of female authorship to England, the pattern of royal female authorship also permits noble women to write and even to appear in print (but see cautionary discussion below of women authors' access to script and print systems of production and distribution). Only later, with the devotional poems of Anne Lock (*c*.1560) and the secular poems of Isabella Whitney (1566–67 and 1573), do we see much 'trickle-down' effect where non-elite female authorship is concerned. Yet here again, looking outside elite circles yields new material: Steven May's recent *Elizabethan Poetry* index notes some ninety-four women poets before 1603. Many, like Frances Abergavenny, have received scholarly attention and/or do fit the familiar type of elite authors/religious topics, but many are as yet unknown. May's work will permit future scholars to expand our knowledge of earlier women writers beyond the usual suspects.

After 1560 or so, more and more women authors come into print, as Elaine Beilin's foundational bibliography and later additions to it have shown; recent books by Patricia Demers and Anita Pacheco contain fine examples.[30] Although elite women and translators and writers of religious material continue to dominate, ever-expanding lists of later women writers signal the vitality of the field. Maureen Bell authoritatively surveys the later period, and essay collections by Carol Meale and by Helen Wilcox, respectively, reveal important continuities between late medieval and early modern women's texts, as well as further differences to be explored.[31]

Women using the means of literary production

What of women's direct engagements with the means of textual production? There is good reason to see the world of early print as a site of new opportunities for women's work, if not to view the new technology as a liberating force for women. Although the dominant view of expanding opportunities has not gone unchallenged, Natalie Zemon Davis, Martha Driver, Frances Hammill, and others have shown that women were much more active participants in all phases of the early printing industry than has been generally understood. Deborah Parker, writing of Italian women printers, explains the importance of physical space in making printing a more woman-friendly industry: where wives of masons or builders, for instance, did not share the working space of their husbands, printers' wives worked alongside their husbands and could more easily learn and become involved.[32] This point would apply as well to English women printers like those detailed in Hammill or Driver, or listed by Axel Erdmann.[33]

In one way, this activity is evolution, not revolution: women simply continued their manuscript-culture involvements as patrons, readers, owners, authors, translators, and marginalia-writers, and expanded their roles along with the new technology. Mary Erler offers a well contextualized case from the 1530s;[34] Margaret Ezell, writing about a much later period, notes the 'intertwined nature of the private/public/social spheres' throughout the period and the complex relations between the private and public within manuscript culture.[35] Harold Love and others treating scribal publication have convincingly debunked the idea of a strict, private-script/public-print divide. And Steven May, followed by others, has successfully challenged the 'Mythical Stigma of Print' (previously, scholars had held that for early modern writers, especially women, putting their manuscripts into print was stigmatized as vulgar or unseemly).[36] Yet Margaret Ezell disagrees with Love that any such stigma would have been harder on women: 'unlike Love, I believe that we have little or no sense of the actual scale of women's participation in manuscript culture apart from a few celebrated examples'.[37] Recent scholarship has not made it easier to generalize about women and the two media, since in such a complex circulation and production milieu as the late fifteenth and early sixteenth centuries, we cannot divide social and commercial authorship along a public/private line, nor along gender lines. Binaries will not hold: the two media systems shared readers and producers, and competed for both, although different textual practices developed around each medium.[38] Ezell further warns against any sanguine 'print-lib' narratives for women:

> Print cannot be viewed as a more 'democratic' opportunity for those living [far from London] or in Scotland or Ireland before 1695, where only a single press could be legally in operation. There is also a real question whether the shift from social authorship to commercial was more democratic or easier for women living virtually anywhere, with little financial or social independence to deal with a bookseller directly.[39]

Ezell further remarks that the majority of the literate population may not have been primarily engaged with print culture (something that must have been the more true in the earliest days of print), and that print actually created obstacles for some authors working in manuscript.[40] In short, too restrictive a focus on print culture can obscure important facts about women and early texts.

With these caveats and complexities in mind, we can note additional continuities between periods and media where women's textual work is concerned: The British Book Trade Index lists some thirty-four women working as, for instance, stationers, bookbinders, booksellers, and related trades before 1500, mostly in London and mostly as wives or daughters of tradesmen; in the overlapping period between 1476 and 1640, around 190 women are listed as typesetters, compositors, bookbinders, booksellers, or printers, with a slightly increasing geographic spread. These women often work in familial contexts like those that Parker describes, under the local rules of various guilds or trade associations, and after 1557, in accordance with the Charter of the Company of Stationers.

The harsh rules of economics and marriage-property law always circum-scribed women's work, but in some cases the latter furthered women's printing interests. Sometimes apparent marriage pawns in the passing of a printing business between men, sometimes key players in tak-ing over operations when widowed, women in the printing business negotiated the laws and social customs of the London printing trades variously, as Hammill and Barbara Kreps show.[41] Susan Broomhall's conclusions about French widow printers would seem to apply as well to English printers like Joan Jugge, Alice Charlewood, Joan Butter/Allde, and Joan Robinson/Orwin, among many others. Broomhall's evidence suggests that there is a pattern of women's using whichever name, married or maiden – that is, whichever man's name, the husband's or the father's name – that carried the most clout in the world of publish-ing at the time.[42]

Axel Erdmann's list of sixteenth-century women printers and their output, although incomplete, nevertheless reveals that women print-ers worked across the complete range of kinds of printed books, secu-lar, sacred, practical, literary, and so on. Kreps studies in detail how Elizabeth Redman/Pickering's marital and familial situation inflected her thriving specialty in law publishing. Driver further explains that as a widow she came to use her own name and printer's mark and reworded her colophons such that 'we begin to see [...] an emerging sense of self, a self separate from that of her dead husband, [...] the beginnings of a sep-arate female identity, marking the book, the product, as her own'.[43] The new medium may have loosened one implicit thematic constraint on women to restrict themselves to religious material. Elizabeth Pickering/ Redman's and Joan Jugge's printing lists, among others, suggest that unlike in translations (Hannay), and perhaps more so than in authored books, women printers could readily create secular texts and did not feel restricted to producing religious works. Here again is a pattern of constraint of women interrupted by women's work becoming sporadic-ally but increasingly visible in the more public, secular sphere of the new medium.

Furthermore, women were also engaged in some technically challen-ging book productions; Luborsky and Ingram include at least ten women printers involved with printing illustrated books. Margaret Allde, Alice Charlewood, and Redman are fairly well known, but it is less well known that Joan Orwin produced an illustrated fencing manual in 1595, as well as a book on usury, and in the next year was involved in printing an illustration of the Copernican universe and an image of the familiar 'zodiac man'. Joan Broome produces medical and surgical images in 1591, and Joan Jugge's reprint of the *Birth of Mankind* (c.1585) features very elaborate images of female reproductive organs. Jugge is also responsible for the amazing illustrated volume containing a translation of Cortez's *Art of Navigation* that features not only maps but ten volvelles. Clearly this was a printing house with advanced technical capacity, especially for England where the technology tended to lag considerably. Several foreign women were involved with illustrated books as well: the widow Catherine van Ruremund (active 1536–37) and Françoise de Keyser (active 1532–39) were connected to the sophisticated world of Antwerp printing; French widow printer Jacqueline Vautrollier, who also worked with illustrated books, later married Richard Field, whose business, for an English house, maintained an unusually international emphasis, with all the technological and linguistic skills that emphasis entails.

It is important to recall, however, that despite such women printers who were 'cultural amphibians' in something like the way Caxton had been, working with the latest technology both on the Continent and in England, and despite similarities noted here in the way women's social situations inflected their participation in printing, the world of English printing and the worlds of Continental printing provided very different contexts.[44] Indeed, printers like Caxton, Regnault, Jacqueline Vautrollier, or Françoise de Keyser were the more remarkable in being able to negotiate polyglot worlds that were anything but smoothly seamless. Parker reminds us of the 'comparatively high literacy rate of printing families' on the Continent. Christopher Plantin, for instance, taught all five daughters to read; some Italian women printers were clearly also literate.[45] François Rigolot examines the thriving world of mid-sixteenth-century Lyon printing as an energizing climate for Louise Labé's writing; Roméo Arbour studies the vibrant activity of French literary women in the first half of the seventeenth century.[46] Such patterns are much slower to develop in England. Susan Broomhall, however, claims a surprisingly limited literacy in sixteenth-century France, and, making a point that would also apply in England, traces restrictions on women's literary involvements to medieval manuscript culture:

> In the medieval past, most manuscripts had been transcribed for the Church and universities from which women were largely excluded. Both of these institutions separated 'women from knowledge used by men to produce and reproduce power and privilege'.[47]

Another sobering argument applicable to the English situation comes from Parker. As optimistic as she is about the opportunities women workers enjoyed in Italy, nevertheless, she finds an intractable

> contradiction in the careers of women printers whose status, even as they acted as heads of the firm, was provisional. Women could not aspire to be printers; their participation in this craft was borne [sic] of necessity. It is for the sake of family concerns – maintaining the business for a male heir too young to take over, making dowry payments, supporting one's family – that women could print books. Their careers are supplemental: they transpire, for the most part, between the death of a husband or father and the coming of age of a son or a remarriage. Women gain entry into the industry by affirming values which ultimately prevent further progress. They are allowed to work under certain conditions, but these circumstances are generally seen as exceptional. Society did not easily envision female entrepreneurs entrusted with the control of large amounts of capital.[48]

In another vein, Broomhall cautions future scholars against a potential historiographic fallacy:

> We need to be careful how we read the abundant evidence that the print trades provide. Workers of either sex in the book trades were better able than other occupational groups to record their presence through their access to the written medium. More references to women upon the page should not be correlated to a position better perceived by contemporaries or improved conditions within the trades. [...] [The textual arts] may even have been less encouraging of female participants than other work environments.[49]

Broomhall reminds us not to see print technology as an antidote to patriarchy, since the non-elite women working in the printing trades had an ambiguous status at best.[50]

Keeping in mind such cautions, a longer, broader perspective might remind us of a woman's initiative in a spectacular, very early printing project. From about 764 CE until about 770, one million Buddhist *dharani* (sutras) were printed and distributed throughout Japan. This was done at the command and with the oversight of that tempestuous-lived, sometimes-maligned, early patroness of printing, the Empress Shotoku. Accounts of this astonishing work too often elide or downplay Shotoku's involvement, which is difficult to pin down even for open-minded scholars like Mimi Hall Yiengpruksawan or Peter Kornicki.[51] Similar elisions have plagued the history of early modern women. For instance, nuns worked as compositors and type designers at San Jacobus Ripoli, where 113 editions were printed between 1476 and 1484, including a *Decameron* (1483). Martha Driver explains a double suppression of their work. Driver's example strikes me as unusual only because it is so clearly identifiable *as an elision of women's work*; more often, I suspect, such erasures pass into the record unnoticed:

> Reading the incunable catalogue of The Pierpont Morgan Library, one would never guess that nuns were involved at all [...] [were it not for] a note in pencil on the flyleaf of [...] the *Works of Sallust*, stating that this volume was 'Printed by the monks of the Monastery of St James of Ripoli, Florence, 1478'.[52]

Like the final image of woman's work in *The Castle of Labour*, like the suppressed and restored misogyny of the *Dictes*, Driver's example shows that women's essential yet often elusive presence connects in various ways to other representational struggles (in this case, to the struggle for representation in scholarly canons). To seek women in early print is to revise what we thought we knew: in the *Dictes*, the 'woman question' foregrounds the issue of textual authority for a broadening public; in books about and for women, we find whole segments of non-elite literary culture that were previously invisible; to examine women's authorship in early media is to complicate accepted lines between classes of readers and kinds of books; to read the actual record of women's work in printing is to find whole realms of previously unacknowledged agency.

Shotoku's million *dharani* are the earliest reminder that women's engagements with printing at many times, in many places, in ways the record might not immediately reveal, invite and reward a wholesale re-examination of current knowledge about literary culture. With the recently intensified scholarly interest in book history and textual studies, we are poised for further exciting discoveries.

Notes

1. *Dictes or sayengis of the philosophres*, trans. Anthony Woodville (Westminster: 1477, *c.*1480, 1489; London: De Worde, 1528). This is a translation of the French version by Guillaume de Tignonville of a compilation ultimately based on Mubashshir ibn Al Fâtik's *Mukhtar Al-hikam wa-mahâsin al-kalim*. Paul Needham, 'The Paper of English Incunabula', in *Catalogue of Books Printed in the XVth Century Now in the British Library, BMC Part XI England*, ed. Lotte Hellinga (London: British Library, 2007), pp. 311–34. Lotte Hellinga, *Caxton*

in Focus: The Beginning of Printing in England (London: British Library, 1982), pp. 77–83, first challenged the dating. Thanks to R. Carter Hailey for pointing out Needham's essay and for expert explanation of the issues involving early paper stocks and papermaking on which Needham bases his redating. Thanks to research assistants Meaghan Brown and Albert Peacock (for the *Dictes*) and Molly Hand (for women printers), to the FSU Council on Research for funding them, to Katharine Coldiron for reading an early draft, and to Sylvie Merian at the Pierpont Morgan Library.

2. A. J. Minnis, *Medieval Theory of Authorship: Scholastic Literary Attitudes in the Later Middle Ages* (London: Scholar Press, 1984). Harold Love's *Scribal Publication in Seventeenth-Century England* (Oxford: Oxford University Press, 1993) and Margaret Ezell's *Social Authorship and the Advent of Print* (Baltimore: Johns Hopkins University Press, 1990) are foundational studies of manuscript publication.

3. Such changing economies and hierarchies of textual production have been studied in depth by Elizabeth Eisenstein, *Printing Revolution in Early Modern Europe* (Cambridge: Cambridge University Press, 2005); D. F. McKenzie, *Bibliography and the Sociology of Texts* (Cambridge: Cambridge University Press, 1999); Adrian Johns, *The Nature of the Book: Print and Knowledge in the Making* (Chicago: University of Chicago Press, 1998); Martha Driver, 'Christine de Pisan and Robert Wyer: The *.C. Hystoryes of Troye*, or *L'Epistre d'Othea Englished*', *Gutenberg-Jahrbuch* 72 (1997), 125–39; Martha Driver, *The Image in Print: Book Illustration in Late Medieval England and Its Sources* (London: British Library, 2004); Martha Driver, 'Women Printers and the Page, 1477–1541', *Gutenberg-Jahrbuch* 73 (1998), 139–53; Martha Driver and Cynthia Brown (eds), 'Women and Book Culture in Late Medieval and Early Modern France', *Journal of the Early Book Society for the Study of Manuscripts and Printing History* 4 (2001), 1–258; Marjorie Plant, *The English Book Trade: An Economic History of the Making and Sale of Books* (London: Allen & Unwin, 1965); James Raven, *The Business of Books: Booksellers and the English Book Trade, 1450–1850* (New Haven, CT: Yale University Press, 2007); William Kuskin (ed.), *Caxton's Trace: Studies in the History of English Printing* (Notre Dame, IN: University of Notre Dame Press, 2006); William Kuskin, *Symbolic Caxton: Literary Culture and Print Capitalism* (Notre Dame, IN: University of Notre Dame Press, 2008).

4. Joseph Loewenstein maps this in 'Introduction: Charting Habermas's "Literary" or "Precursor" Public Sphere', *Criticism* 46 (2004), 201–05.

5. They are, as Caxton spelled them, Sedechias, Hermes (i.e. Hermes Trismegistus), Tac, Zalquinus, Omer, Salon (Solon), Sabyon, Ypocras (Hippocrates), Pytagoras, Dyogenes, Socrates, Platon, Aristotle, Alexander the grete, Tholome (Ptolemy), Assaron (Avicenna), Legmon, Anese, Sacdarge, Thesille, Saint Gregorie, and Galyen (Galen). This fascinating, xenophiliac catalogue is outside this essay's scope.

6. Kuskin, *Symbolic Caxton*, pp. 162–65.

7. Ibid., pp. 173, 188.

8. The section ends with a woman's indirect, ambiguous question about the man's desire, 'wylt thou haue ony other woman than me' and the Socrates-speaker's scornful question-reply, 'Arte not thou ashamed toffre thy self to him. that demandeth nor desireth the not.' Although outside our scope here, this richly interesting final question-pair deserves discussion in terms of the *quaestio* and other gender-debate traditions.

9. Deanne Williams, *The French Fetish from Chaucer to Shakespeare* (Cambridge: Cambridge University Press, 2007), pp. 97–104.

10. This work's vernacular transmission and complex stemma also challenge traditional lines of authority, as I discuss in work-in-progress.

11. Michael Hicks's *ODNB* entry explains that 'in 1477 Edward IV promoted him as candidate for Mary of Burgundy [...] Late in 1478 a marriage was actually agreed with James III's sister Margaret of Scotland, to be celebrated at Nottingham in October 1479, but differences with Scotland meant that it did not materialize.' See also Deanne Williams on Caxton as a Pandarus to the '*arriviste* earl-on-the-make' (*French Fetish*, p. 104).

12. Examples are in Francis Lee Utley, *The Crooked Rib: An Analytical Index to the Argument About Women in English and Scots Literature to the End of the Year 1568* (Columbus: Ohio State University Press, 1944), and Alcuin Blamires (ed.), *Woman Defamed and Woman Defended: An Anthology of Medieval Texts* (Oxford: Oxford University Press, 1992).

13. See Diane Bornstein's edition of this first formal gender debate in English print, in *The Feminist Controversy of the Renaissance: Facsimile Reproductions* (Delmar: Scholars' Facsimiles & Reprints, 1980); see also A. E. B. Coldiron, *English Printing, Verse Translation, and the Battle of the Sexes, 1476–1557* (Burlington, VT: Ashgate, 2009), pp. 69–85. For later debates, see the bibliography for works by Katherine Usher Henderson and Barbara McManus; Ann Rosalind Jones and Peter Stallybrass; and Joad Raymond, *Pamphlets and Pamphleteering in Early Modern Britain* (Cambridge: Cambridge University Press, 2003).

14. As explored in Jennifer Summit, 'William Caxton, Margaret of Beaufort, and the Romance of Patronage', in *Women, the Book, and the Worldly*, ed. Lesley Smith and Jane H. M. Taylor (Rochester, NY: D. S. Brewer, 1995), pp. 151–65; Raven, *The Business of Books*; and Kuskin, *Symbolic Caxton*.

15. Summit, 'William Caxton', p. 163; Summit's analysis applies also to Margaret of Burgundy and to other, later female patrons.

16. Ibid., p. 158. See also Steve Mentz, *Romance for Sale in Early Modern England: The Rise of Prose Fiction* (Burlington, VT: Ashgate, 2006); Helen Cooper, *The English Romance in Time: Transforming Motifs from Geoffrey of Monmouth to the Death of Shakespeare* (Oxford: Oxford University Press, 2004); Helen Hackett, *Women and Romance Fiction in the English Renaissance* (Cambridge: Cambridge University Press, 2000); Constance Relihan and Goran V. Stanivukovic, *Prose Fiction and Early Modern Sexuality in England, 1580–1640* (New York: Palgrave Macmillan, 2004).

17. Mark Addison Amos, 'Violent Hierarchies: Disciplining Women and Merchant Capitalists in *The Book of the Knyght of the Towre*', in *Caxton's Trace*, ed. Kuskin, pp. 69–100 (pp. 74, 72, 79).

18. Three scholars have confirmed this against previous opinion: Julia Boffey, 'Richard Pynson's *Book of Fame* and *The Letter of Dido*', *Viator* 19 (1988), 339–54; A. E. B. Coldiron, 'Taking Advice from a Frenchwoman', in *Caxton's Trace*, ed. Kuskin, pp. 127–66; and Kathleen Forni, 'Richard Pynson and the Stigma of the Chaucerian Apocrypha', *The Chaucer Review* 34 (2000), 428–36.

19. See Driver, 'Christine de Pizan and Robert Wyer'.

20. Dhira Mahoney, 'Middle English Regenderings of Christine de Pizan', in *The Medieval Opus*, ed. Douglas A. Kelly (Amsterdam: Rodopi, 1996), pp. 405–27; Jennifer Summit, *Lost Property: The Woman Writer and English Literary History,*

1380–1589 (Chicago: University of Chicago Press, 2000); *Poems of Cupid, God of Love: Christine De Pizan's 'Epistre au Dieu D'Amours' and 'Dit De La Rose'; Thomas Hoccleve's 'The Letter of Cupid', with George Sewell's 'The Proclamation of Cupid'*, ed. Thelma Fenster and Mary Erler (New York: Brill Academic Publishers, 1990).

21. Julia Boffey, 'Wynkyn de Worde and Misogyny in Print', in *Chaucer in Perspective: Middle English Essays in Honour of Norman Blake*, ed. Geoffrey Lester (Sheffield: Sheffield Academic Press, 1999), pp. 236–51.

22. The first extant printing is by William Copland *c.*1565, but editor Mary Erler's strong evidence suggests the date 1525. Robert Copland, *Poems*, ed. Mary C. Erler (Toronto: University of Toronto Press, 1993), p. 110.

23. On women and texts in this period in Scotland, see several works by Priscilla Bawcutt, including: 'Crossing the Border: Scottish Poetry and English Readers in the Sixteenth Century', in *The Rose and the Thistle: Essays on the Culture of Late Medieval and Renaissance Scotland*, ed. Sally Mapstone and Juliette Wood (East Lothian, Scotland: Tuckwell, 1998), pp. 59–76; '"My Bright Buke": Women and Their Bodies in Medieval Renaissance Scotland', in *Medieval Women: Text and Contexts in Late Medieval Britain: Essays for Felicity Riddy*, ed. Jocelyn Wogan-Browne et al. (Turnhout, Belgium: Brepols, 2000), pp. 17–34; 'Women Talking about Marriage in William Dunbar and Hans Sachs', in *The Medieval Marriage Scene: Prudence, Passion, Policy*, ed. Sherry Roush and Cristelle L. Baskins (Tempe, AZ: Arizona Center for Medieval and Renaissance Studies, 2005), pp. 101–14. For examples see Utley, *The Crooked Rib*. On printing in Scotland, see e.g. H. G. Aldis, *A List of Books Printed in Scotland Before 1700, Including Those Printed Furth of the Realm for Scottish Booksellers, with Brief Notes on the Printers and Stationers* (New York: B. Franklin, 1904); Robert Dickson and John Philip Edmond (eds), *Annals of Scottish Printing from the Introduction of the Art in 1507 to the Beginning of the Seventeenth-Century* (Cambridge: Macmillan & Bowes, 1890); John Hinks and Catherine Armstrong (eds), *Printing Places: Locations of Book Production & Distribution Since 1500* (New Castle, DE: Oak Knoll Press, 2005); Paul Watry, 'Sixteenth Century Printing Types and Ornaments of Scotland: With an Introductory Survey of the Scottish Book Trade' (unpublished doctoral thesis, Merton College, Oxford, 1992); and the Scottish Printing Archival Trust's histories of printing in various places.

24. This work, too, was reprinted by William Copland *c.*1563 and *c.*1567, indicating continuing interest in such treatments of women's issues; see Copland, *Poems*, p. 176; on the later allusions, p. 178.

25. Coldiron, *English Printing*, pp. 141–71.

26. The recent scholarship about women and literature in later Tudor and Stuart England is dauntingly, hearteningly vast: not only thriving, regular conferences like the University of Maryland's Attending to Women, the associated Society for the Study of Early Modern Women, or the recently established *Early Modern Women: An Interdisciplinary Journal*, but also web projects like Georgianna Ziegler's mega-site, *Early Modern Women Online*, and projects indexed therein such as *The Perdita Project*, book series like Ashgate's 'Women and Gender in the Early Modern World', and new histories like the present volume. Studies and companions to the field abound – Anna Pacheco's *A Companion to Early Modern Women's Writing* (Malden, MA: Blackwell Publishing, 2002)

is a useful volume; also Caroline Bicks, *Midwiving Subjects in Shakespeare's England* (Burlington, VT: Ashgate, 2003); Jean Brink (ed.), *Privileging Gender in Early Modern England* (Kirksville, MO: Sixteenth Century Journal Publishers, 1993); Douglas A. Brooks (ed.), *Printing and Parenting in Early Modern England* (Burlington, VT: Ashgate, 2005); Patricia Demers, *Women's Writing in English: Early Modern England* (Toronto: University of Toronto Press 2005); Frances E. Dolan, *Whores of Babylon: Catholicism, Gender, and 17th-Century Print Culture* (Notre Dame, IN: Notre Dame University Press, 1999); Heidi Brayman Hackel, *Reading Material in Early Modern England: Poetry, Gender, Literacy* (Cambridge: Cambridge University Press, 2005); Anne Haselkorn and Betty S. Travitsky, *The Renaissance Englishwoman in Print: Counterbalancing the Canon* (Amherst, MA: University of Massachusetts Press, 1999); Constance Jordan, *Renaissance Feminism: Literary Texts and Political Models* (Ithaca, NY: Cornell University Press); Sidney L. Sondergrad, *Sharpening Her Pen: Strategies of Rhetorical Violence by Early English Women Writers* (Selinsgrove, PA: Susquehanna University Press, 2002); Jennifer Summit, *Lost Property* and *Memory's Library: Medieval Books in Early Modern England* (Chicago: University of Chicago Press, 2008); Wendy Wall, *The Imprint of Gender: Authorship and Publication in the English Renaissance* (Ithaca, NY: Cornell University Press, 1993); and many others. There are also major projects recovering women's texts (e.g. Prescott and Travitsky's book series, 'Renaissance Englishwomen in Print', Ashgate), anthologies (e.g. Stevenson and Davidson or Ostovich and Sauer), Brenda Hosington's new study of women translators, and, for Continental women's texts, the University of Chicago Press series of primary works made highly accessible in paperback with translations. All promise continued growth and refinement of the field.

27. Compare, for instance, Rachel Hands, 'Juliana Berners and *The Boke of St Albans'*, *Review of English Studies*, n.s., 18 (1967), 373–86; and Karen Gross, 'Hunting, Heraldry, and the Fall in the *Boke of St. Albans* (1486)', *Viator* 38 (2007), 191–215.

28. Driver, *Image in Print*, pp. 62–68 and 115–50.

29. Anne Lake Prescott, 'Making the *Heptaméron* English', in *Renaissance Historicisms*, ed. James M. Dutcher and Anne Lake Prescott (Newark: University of Delaware Press, 2008), pp. 69–84. Margaret Hannay, *Silent But for the Word: Tudor Women as Patrons, Translators, and Writers of Religious Works* (Kent, OH: Kent State University Press, 1985). Tina Krontiris, *Oppositional Voices: Women as Writers and Translators of Literature in the English Renaissance* (New York: Routledge, 1992).

30. Elaine Beilin, 'Bibliography of English Women Writers, 1500–1640', in *The Renaissance Englishwoman in Print: Counterbalancing the Canon*, ed. Anne Haselkorn and Betty Travitsky (Amherst: University of Massachusetts Press, 1999), pp. 347–60. Demers, *Women's Writing in English*; Pacheco (ed.), *A Companion to Early Modern Women's Writing*.

31. Maureen Bell, 'Women Writing and Women Written', in *The Cambridge History of the Book in Britain, vol. IV: 1557–1695*, ed. John Barnard and D. F. McKenzie (Cambridge: Cambridge University Press, 2002), pp. 431–54. Carol Meale (ed.), *Women and Literature in Britain, 1150–1500* (Cambridge: Cambridge University Press, 1993). Helen Wilcox (ed.), *Women and Literature in Britain, 1500–1700* (Cambridge: Cambridge University Press, 1996).

32. Deborah Parker, 'Women in the Book Trade in Italy, 1475–1620', *Renaissance Quarterly* 49 (Autumn, 1996), 509–41; see pp. 517–18.
33. Frances Hammill, 'Some Unconventional Women Before 1800: Printers, Booksellers, and Collectors', *Papers of the Bibliographical Society of America* 49 (1955), 300–14. Driver, 'Women Printers and the Page. Axel Erdmann, *My Gracious Silence: Women in the Mirror of 16th Century Printing in Western Europe* (Lucerne, Switzerland: Gilhofer and Ranschburg, 1999).
34. Mary Erler, 'The Books and Lives of Three Tudor Women', in *Privileging Gender in Early Modern England*, ed. Brink, pp. 5–21.
35. Ezell, *Social Authorship*, p. 39.
36. Steven May, 'Tudor Aristocrats and the Mythical "Stigma of Print"', *Renaissance Papers* (1980), 11–18.
37. Ezell, *Social Authorship*, pp. 22–23.
38. Ibid., pp. 38–39, 101, & *passim*. Cynthia Brown's exciting new research on the tangible results of the intertwined media, 'hybrid books' that contain elements of both script and print production, is unpublished at this writing.
39. Ibid., pp. 101–02.
40. Ibid., p. 102.
41. Barbara Kreps, 'Elizabeth Pickering: The First Woman to Print Law Books in England and Relations Within the Community of Tudor London's Printers and Lawyers', *Renaissance Quarterly* 56 (2003), 1053–88. For explorations of women in Continental contexts, see e.g. Antonino and Campiono (eds), *'Donne tipografe' tra XV e XIX secolo* (Bologna: Università di Bologna, Biblioteca, 2003); Roméo Arbour, *Les Femmes et les métiers du livre en France, de 1600–1650* (Chicago: Garamond Press, 1997); Susan Broomhall, *Women and the Book Trade in Sixteenth-Century France* (Burlington, VT: Ashgate, 2002); Cynthia Brown, *Poets, Patrons, and Printers: Crisis of Authority in Late Medieval France* (Ithaca, NY: Cornell University Press, 1995); Driver and Brown (eds), 'Women and Book Culture in Late Medieval and Early Modern France'; Erdmann, *My Gracious Silence*; Parker, 'Women in the Book Trade'; Diana Robin, *Publishing Women: Salons, the Presses, and the Counter Reformation in Sixteenth Century Italy* (Chicago: University of Chicago Press, 2007); and François Rigolot, 'Louise Labé and the "Climat Lyonnois"', *The French Review* 71 (1998), 405–41.
42. Broomhall, *Women and the Book Trade*, pp. 68–70.
43. Driver, 'Women Printers', p. 152.
44. On the relatively more active participation of women in Italy, see Antonino and Campiono's *'Donne tipografe'*; Robin, *Publishing Women*, on the implications of women's salons and printing for religious ferment (her introduction is especially provocative by comparison with England); and Parker's authoritative essay 'Women in the Book Trade'.
45. Parker, 'Women in the Book Trade', pp. 519, 522.
46. Rigolot, 'Louise Labé and the "Climat Lyonnois"'. Arbour, *Les Femmes et les métiers du livre*.
47. Broomhall, *Women and the Book Trade*, p. 65, quoting D. Spain, *Gendered Spaces* (Chapel Hill: University of North Carolina Press, 1992), p. 3.
48. Parker, 'Women in the Book Trade', pp. 533–34.
49. Broomhall, *Women and the Book Trade*, p. 70.
50. Ibid., pp. 65–70.

51. Mimi Hall Yiengpruksawan, 'One Millionth of a Buddha: The *Hyakumanto Dharani* in the Scheide Library', *Princeton University Library Chronicle* 48 (1987), 224–38, studies some extant copies. Peter Kornicki, *The Book in Japan: A Cultural History from the Beginnings to the Nineteenth Century* (Leiden: Brill, 1998), pp. 115–18, discusses (e.g.) whether the million *dharani* were printed on metallic plates or woodblocks. Kornicki, rare among male scholars of the topic, neither elides nor maligns: Shotoku's *dharani* 'not only utilized a novel technology but did so on a grand scale that must have consumed considerable human and material resources' (p. 117).

52. Driver, 'Women Printers and the Page', pp. 142–43. This essay uncovers further previously occluded involvements by women, *passim*.

Part II Writing Places

Domestic Settings

4
Household Writing

Catherine Richardson

'Pray to god continually: And learne to knowe him rightfullie.' This text is painted on the wall above the mantelpiece at Pirton Grange in Hertfordshire. The same text is printed in Thomas Tusser's 1570 *A Hundred Good Pointes of Husbandry* as one of several 'Husbandly Poesies' suitable to be written up in the hall, the parlor, the guests' chamber, or 'thine own bed Chamber'. The previous section of the poesie, 'what better fare than well content, agreeing with thy welthe | what better ghest, than trustie friend, in sickness and in health', suggests that it was intended to be read while the family and their guests were eating dinner. So how might women have 'used' such a text? When it was newly painted, it must have formed a talking point within the home and the housewife and her daughters with their male family members must have had cause to think about it self-consciously as they passed it. It may have been read out to them as part of the Christian duties of the householder, providing a moral exemplar for their behavior, and when meals were taken below it they and their guests may well have meditated upon its import, perhaps as a part of the grace before a meal. But in the years to come this kind of text, in this type of prominent everyday location, would promote a particular kind of engagement which in many ways sidesteps literacy – known over many years as a part of the household, its physical presence causes mental or verbal repetition whether or not its letters can be translated into words. Its significance is indicated by its grand scope: the passage continues, 'what worse despayre, than loth to dye for feare to go to hel | what greater faith than trust in god, through christ in heaven to dwell', bringing the widest possible cosmology of heaven and hell into a domestic room.

I wanted to start with this quotation because it opens a window onto the way households might actually have used writing – onto the material connections between the rooms of the house and the texts which those who lived there consumed – but also because it problematizes what we mean by writing and reading. The text was written on the wall either by a member of the household or by a painter, but writing here means physically inscribing, not composing or creating. It was 'written' in that latter sense by Thomas Tusser, and the connection between his published work and this overmantle suggests a trajectory of purchasing and consuming texts which stretches from London where the book was sold to this house in rural Hertfordshire. This textual example draws our attention to the connections between script and print within the early modern household.[1]

I begin with a text interpreted by women but not written by a woman in order to outline one of the key issues in the analysis of women's household writing. Most histories of female writing focus on genres such as poetry or closet drama, and the narrowness of their definition of writing means that they are forced to deal only with women of high social status, obscuring the reading and writing practices of the vast majority of early modern women. If we are fully to understand the relationships amongst household, writing, and women, however, we must address the widest possible range of texts and be prepared to consider women's interest and investment in and use of household writings which they did not either author or inscribe. For that reason, this essay focuses upon the more mundane, pragmatic writings which might truly be said to be household texts.[2]

We do not know how many women could read and write in early modern England. In any case, reading and writing did not necessarily go together as they do now as they were taught separately, about two years apart, and people were therefore much more likely to be able to read than to write as their labor was needed to boost the family economy before they had been taught the latter skill. Education and schooling were two separate things, and it was with respect to the former that women and the household came together – an informal and pragmatic approach to learning by example and instruction within the home in which women were involved as children and as mothers. Here, interaction with the written word was combined, in a period in which households were centers of both production and consumption, with practical training in a variety of domestic skills.

Early modern education was never an end in itself. All learning was undertaken for the practical purpose of fitting the individual for their role in life, and that role was strictly circumscribed by gender and by social status. Between 1580 and 1700, 15 per cent of laborers and 21 per cent of husbandmen, but 56 per cent of tradesmen and craftsmen, and 65 per cent of yeomen in East Anglia could sign their names, the easiest way to quantify literacy. In other words, the higher the individual's status the more access they had to literacy because their possession of property and the business in which they were involved necessitated a facility with the written word. As women's activities did not necessitate literacy, over the same period only 11 per cent could sign their names.[3] And yet we know that women inhabited a world increasingly shaped by the printed word, so knowing whether women could sign their names does not tell us the whole story. We need a much wider definition of literacy if we are to understand the nature of female practice.[4]

The connection between women and the household was a matter of considerable interest in this period, and the majority of women in early modern England were probably aware of the ideologies which surrounded domestic space. As one household manual put it: 'A household is as it were a little common wealth, by the good government whereof, God's glory may be advanced, the common wealth [...] benefited, and all that live in that family may receive much comfort and commodity.'[5] In other words, the commonwealth was only as well ordered as each individual household of which it was comprised. The wife's duties were '1. to order the decking and trimming of the house; 2. to dispose the ordinary provision for the family; 3. to rule and govern maidservants; 4. to bring up children while they are young', and she and her husband were to acquaint children and servants 'with the Scriptures, by reading them dayly in thy house, in their hearing'.[6] These roles were, William Gouge reasoned, the origin of her title: 'it is a charge laid upon wives: *guide the house*; whereby it appeareth that the business of the house appertain and are most proper to the wife: in which respect she is called the *housewife*' (p. 469).

This close association of women and household, the very intertwining of their names, led many of these manuals to include some kind of division of labor along physical lines which defines the wife's place as fittingly within the home and the husband's outside it in the wider community. As Cleaver put it,

The dutie of the husband is, to get goods: and that of the wife to gather them together, and saue them. The dutie of the husband is, to trauell abroad to seeke liuing: and the wiues dutie is to keep the house. [...] The dutie of the husband is, to dispatch all things without doore: and of the wife, to oversee and giue order for all things within the house. (p. 170)

This kind of writing elides concepts of private action and household space, connecting a woman's lack of a public role with spatial confinement. In practice, of course, running a household and organizing its productive capacities for profit involved women in numerous public interactions in the markets of the town at the very least, but the ideal remained that their actions were private in the sense that they were primarily concerned with, centered around, and focused upon, the house.

The marketplace of print, as it has been called, was a public arena very firmly outside this purview, one in which texts made political interventions on a national level. Women should not participate: 'The dutie of the man is, to bee skilfull in talke: and of the wife, to boast of silence' (p. 170). If a woman wished to find a public voice she should 'publish' her ideas through her husband; 'she should not speake but to her husband, or by her husband. And as the voice of him that soundeth a trumpet, is not so lowd, as the sound that it yeeldeth: so is the wisedome and word of a woman, of greater vertue and efficacie, when all that she knoweth, and can doe, is as if it were said and done by her husband' (p. 226). In theory then, only in this way could a woman's mind take shape outside her door, could she achieve a legitimate public voice. Women's reading and writing were closely tied up with these dynamics of household boundaries.

The question of literacy with its central issue of education for a specific kind of lifestyle means that it is crucial to discuss women's engagement with writing in relation to their social status, and this essay goes on to examine the relationship between different genres of household writing and women of high, middling, and low social groups. The highest social groups are most likely to have achieved the top of a scale which reached from the making of a mark on paper to a level of proficiency with language which allows the written word to reflect the opinions, feelings, and identities of an inner self to an outer world. The forms which household writing most frequently took for these women were personal letters and diaries.[7]

Letters fulfill a particular set of functions in relation to any concept of household writing. They presuppose a reader or set of readers who are distant. Such writing mediates between people in different locations and, in so far as it often forms a type of conversation between people who are known to one another, it might be seen as bringing the location of the writer to the reader. For the elite, who lived in different houses at different times of the year or moved between London and the country, letters brought one home into another through their iteration of the concerns and practicalities of household management. 'I need not send to know how my buildings go forwards,' Robert Sidney writes to his wife at Penshurst Place. 'For I am sure you are so good a house-wife as you may be put in trust with them', and then later, 'I hope by this time the plumbers be with you and your lead-works in hand.'[8] The domestic concerns of the contents of personal correspondence bring the context in which it was written palpably to the reader's mind.

There are two distinct but related epistolary concerns which might be described as 'household writing'. Robert Sidney and his wife frequently discussed the pragmatics of domestic life, but they also commented on intimate family relationships, and indeed strengthened their own union through the writings which they sent: 'I pray you send me word [...] how my garden goes forwards,' Robert writes on 26 October 1594, and continues, 'I am exceeding glad that my little ones do so well: I thank God for them, and send me word, I pray you, if you be towards another. Sweetheart, farewell, and I would I were with you. I am Your most lov-ing husband, R. Sidney.'[9] The intersection of notions of the household as a physical space and a set of interpersonal relationships are well represented in this and other letter collections, which indicates how mutually enforcing such concerns must have been, and how much these women's male relatives thought about the place where their families were whilst they were away from it. Women, who moved less often than their husbands, mused on these connections in a writing of emotions sharpened by absence: Joan Thynne, for instance, writes to her husband John, 'I have received your kind letter [...] for which I think myself much beholden unto you for it and the knives and for my petticoat, hose, and pomegranates, and the farthingale, all which I received last week. [...] My love to yourself is such not to be broken by knives or anything else whiles I live.'[10]

Like any genre of writing, letters changed in quality and mode of address to their recipients across the period as the way in which emo-tion could fittingly be expressed in written form altered. At the start of the period, the kind of intimacy between writer and reader which we might expect from a letter was not necessarily present. What Daybell calls 'epistolary privacy' was often compromised by collaborative com-position processes such as the use of secretaries for the physical act of writing, and by the fact that 'Letter-writers regularly entrusted further details to bearers, who also conveyed replies by word of mouth.' Such practices stress the partial nature of even elite women's engagement with the written word. The period on which this volume focuses, however, saw the development of informal modes of address and 'the increasing personalisation of women's letter-writing'. Household concerns in the different forms suggested above became more valid subjects and modes of written expression for women. And as they did so, letters became 'In one sense [...] a "technology of the self", a vehicle through which female letter-writers composed a self or selves through writing' which they viewed in relation to their recipients.[11]

If letters could mediate between households, then their written form and the concerns which it reflects should help to define the nature of the boundary between public and private news and the contexts in which it was exchanged. Penelope Rich, writing to Mr Bacon at Essex House, begged 'while I am in this solitary place, wher no sound of any news can come, I must intreat you to let me here something of the worlde from you'.[12] Here, her written word reaches out to the wider world beyond the household and paints a picture of her location as an enclosed one cut off from the news generated by public events. But scholars have paid increasing attention to the 'often overtly political intent of female letter writers which counters traditional understanding of women's letters as domestic, parochial and non-political'. Daybell claims that 'The early modern letter represents the dominant written form by which women exerted power and influence.'[13] From their base within the household, elite women used letter-writing to intervene in the kind of patronage suits and dynastic negotiations which were central to their families' political success.[14]

They often did so by employing an explicitly domestic form of political engagement. Gary Schneider has argued that 'the manoeuvring of the language of the familiar was a frequently employed rhetorical strategy used in a variety of social situations.'[15] Affection and the construction of a kind of intimacy learned in correspondence with close relatives could be used to sustain less personal relationships too. And, employing 'an indistinguishable mixture of affection and ambition', the political impact of the letters of Anne Newdigate utilized 'the convention of female weakness'.[16] Women employed those ideals of behavior whose principles were so familiar from household manuals, but they did so to unconventional ends – they used domestic ideals for political gain.

A complex interaction between household ideals and female identity was also a key element of female diary keeping. By the end of the period covered by this volume, diaries as we might recognize them today were just beginning to emerge as a form of writing, a fact which suggests that the connections between household writing and the making of identity were strengthening. On 26 March, 'The Lordes day', 1601, in one of the earliest women's diaries, Lady Margaret Hoby wrote 'After I was readie I went to the church and after praers and sermon I Came home and dressed Blackbourns foote after I dined and after I talked and reed to some good wiffes after I praied and reed and wrett notes in my bible of the morninge exercise after I went to the church and after sarmon I dressed a poore mans hand and after that I walked a broad and so Came to privat examenation and praier.'[17] This one extract includes several different textual encounters – reading in public and in private and writing notes in her Bible. Her text makes frequent reference, in other words, to other texts which she both produces and consumes, and these are situated within a daily routine of spiritual activity.

Outside the confines of the church the household itself, as a series of physical spaces, provides a context for these observations. There were significant differences between elite and non-elite houses, not only in terms of size but also in the type of rooms which they contained. Within the elite house the daily tasks of food production, for instance, could be kept much more firmly apart from the rooms in which leisure time was spent. And small, intimate rooms for the use of only one member of the household offered elite spaces where the quality of thought gener-ated by and expressed in the written word might be distinctly different. Lady Margaret's private examinations take place in her closet, and when she goes to join the rest of her household she descends the stairs: 'After privatt praier I went downe and wrought with my maides.'[18] In other words, her most intense spiritual exercises are set apart from the produc-tive areas of the house where at other times she works with her servants and engages in household acts of devotion, and her ability to withdraw herself materially alters the quality of her devotions.

It has been argued that it is Lady Margaret's sense of her developing spir-itual identity that accounts for 'the relationship between the temporal – the ongoing progression from event to event – and the timeless. Her days are spent in those activities [...] that mark an onward temporal progression whose resolution lies within the "real" truth of heavenly transcendence.'[19] This spiritual motivation for committing daily life to written form, one which is shared with other early female diarists such as Lady Grace Mildmay, leads to a writing which connects mundane household actions to a much larger redemptive canvas. The minor and repetitive domestic events which form the fabric of the diary are recorded not as an end in themselves, but as a proof of spiritual commit-ment. And writing then becomes a form of self-examination through an analysis of the performance of tasks appropriate for an 'honest' woman. Housework, in terms of the curing of the sick, cooking, and needlework, with which religious observances are interspersed, is elevated by its place within the spiritual scheme of an individual life; like the mantelpiece phrases with which this chapter began, it allows the household to rub shoulders with eternity.

And as the household is a fundamentally material space which encompasses female lives, we might consider other types of creative work that elite women perform within it as expressive practices akin to writing. Women of all social groups were involved with textile production for the home – Margaret Hoby, as quoted above, 'wrought' with her maids. Lower-status women spun yarn and produced basic undergarments for the family which they sometimes marked with initials, for instance when children went into service. But elite women's activities went much further. They embroidered bedhangings and cushions, they 'monogrammed shirts and bedclothes; they stitched designs onto smocks, caps and gloves; and they composed samplers, book covers, casket covers, mirror frames, and pictures to decorate tables or be hung on walls'.[20] The most creative of these activities clearly approached a kind of language of ornament. The earliest dated sampler combines its maker's name, Jane Bostocke, the date, 1598, and the birth of a child called Alice Lee which had occasioned its production, with a heraldic dog related to the family crest and examples of interlocking fruit and knot patterns in basic stitches and more sophisticated ones such as satin, chain, ladder and coral, French knots, and beadwork.[21] From such 'dictionaries' of ornament, women compiled needlework patterns appropriate to the decoration of household objects, patterns which spoke to their family's social status and identity through the skill and aesthetic judgment which they displayed. Extant examples of designs worked on pieces of clothing, for instance, show the selection and arrangement of a variety of different kinds of pictorial representation and pattern in a way that demonstrates a sophisticated understanding of the relationship between individual elements and the overall impact of the piece.[22] As Giovanni Doglioni says of Moderata Fonte, 'without any kind of pattern or sketch to guide her, she could embroider any subject or design that was suggested to her.'[23] Creativity was valued in elite female needlework, and the prioritizing of aesthetic considerations over practical ones suggests a parity with the use of complex language skills as a mode of expression.

The material work that women undertook was directly linked to various kinds of text, not only because it often included words which developed the significance of the imagery they produced, such as Jane Bostocke's identification of the birth of Alice Lee, but also because the imagery itself sometimes told stories in pictorial narrative form. Hangings in particular depicted both classical and biblical stories, and elite women's production of complex figurative and narrative textiles enabled them to engage with the professionally manufactured objects which comprised the decorative arts of the noble household. Sasha Roberts has identified the ways in which elite beds and their hangings, for instance, were animated with written texts materialized and brought to life in ritual performance. She argues that we should see the relationships between texts recited around the bridal bed, women's work in its decoration, and men's labor in its carving. She points out that 'motifs bearing associations of sexuality, fertility, and virility' were carved on these beds, sharing their themes with the Epithalamion or wedding poem. And familiarity with such classical iconography was fostered through literature such as Spenser's *Faerie Queene*, as 'not only visual but also an extensive verbal register of classical iconography brought by elite patrons'. Appreciating the continuities between the literary and visual aesthetics of elite households helps us to understand how women's contributions to domestic furnishings might have related to a wider set of textual and material narratives which were circulating within its rooms, and hence how they engaged with a largely male textual culture.[24]

Textile work was also important for women of middling status. Federigo Luigini made a distinction between the activities of women of different status groups in which the practical gives way to the aesthetic: 'whereas the poor find only utility in these arts, the rich, the noble, and the beautiful lady wins honour also'.[25] Such a division is crucial to our understanding of the relationship between female creativity and women's domestic labor. Women in between the highest and lowest social groups used their skills to assert their family's status through domestic display, but they did so in a more limited way than their social superiors, creating goods both useful and pleasing to the eye whose aesthetic scope was dictated by other constraints on their makers' time. For them, textile skills were one aspect of an emerging domestic identity centered around the ordering of an increasing range of domestic goods.

These women of middling status inhabited a household in which many more goods were being purchased from markets outside rather than manufactured within, and in which greater numbers of domestic items such as table cloths, chairs, and chests were kept.[26] They had, therefore, to have an intimate knowledge of every inch of their domain: the housewife 'must lay a diligent eye to her household stuffe in euery Roome, that nothing be embezeled away, nothing spoyled or lost for want of looking to, nothing mard by ill vsage, nor nothing worne out by more vsing then is needefull, nothing out of place, for things cast aside, are deemed to be stolen'.[27] Gervase Markham's *The English Housewife* lists some of the processes which she must master in its longer title: *Contayning the inward and outward vertues which ought to be in a compleat woman. As, her skill in Physicke, Cookery, Banqueting-stuffe, Distillation, Perfumes, Wooll, Hemp, Flax, Dayries, Brewing, Baking* [...].[28] The middling-status woman's domestic power as cast in these texts was that of order – a physical and spatial issue of controlling the domestic environment. To put things in good order was, through the connections between objects, their associated routines, and prescriptive behavior, to be an 'honest' woman.[29]

Because middling-status women's lives were so closely tied up with the performance of domestic work, scholars have suggested that writing about household issues might constitute a form of life-writing, even outside genres such as the diary. The 'ways in which women circulated information and preserved knowledge', Margaret Ezell suggests, led them to reflect interior thoughts and feelings, attitudes and outlooks in a range of written forms.[30] We can understand commonplace books and receipt books as forms of the selves who created them by examining the material which their authors selected for inclusion. For instance, Ann Bowyer, daughter of a Coventry draper, compiled a commonplace book in the first decade of the seventeenth century which includes 'rhyming couplets and love poetry [...] handwriting exercises, instructions for limning, and the preservation of a local corpse for 77 years'. The poetry of Spenser, Chaucer, and Drayton sits alongside 'proverbs, moral exempla, and historical information'. The book appears to be part of Ann's education in writing as it includes handwriting exercises and a series of proverbial phrases concerning, for instance, advice against quarreling with influential men and overindulging in wine, which appear to be linked to a printed copy-book used for the purpose.[31] In this case, Ann's choice of extracts to record in her book is very clearly shaped by the texts which she is reading. Her morally inspired selections from Chaucer's 'Man of Law's Tale' are regularly extracted in such commonplace books, but it is the physical act of bringing these extracts together from so many written sources and writing them onto the same manuscript page which goes beyond slavish copying. The choices that lay behind their selection and the circumstances under which those choices were made (for instance the context of the writing lesson) define Ann's outlook and predilections.

Such manuscripts share characteristics with receipt books: often compiled over many years, both included information from different places which might be recorded by different individuals. Middling-status women collected medicinal, culinary, and household material from printed sources, and their written texts were contributed both by the owner of the manuscript and the circle of other readers with whom she shared her book. Women's authority, constructed in relation to their role in new domestic processes, was reflected in an increasing desire to textualize knowledge. In these books, experience met with the written word as women annotated received wisdom by writing comments such as 'proved', suggesting that they had tried and tested the recipe; giving their practice a parity with previously printed male example.[32] The process of producing a woman's own manuscript, of making a text out of her household experience, provides a form of autobiography even if that form is practical, knowledge-based, and quotidian. Because of their new associations with domestic objects and processes, writing the household is always, it is possible to argue, a form of writing the self for middling-status early modern women.

The way these texts mix culinary with medical recipes links them to the conception of household activity which came across so strongly from women's diaries: a conglomeration of routines connected by the day-to-day demands of domestic life and given their form by the need to practice many kinds of skill simultaneously and flexibly depending on the times of the year and the ailments of the household. Dorothy Lewkenore, for instance, put a recipe for curative broth 'to boyle a cocke for restorative' next to one 'to seethe a legg of mutton'.[33] By the mid-seventeenth century these aspects of the texts had been separated out, suggesting a new kind of writing which saw categories much more obviously in terms of print culture – of a more masculine form of organization akin to that found in dictionaries and encyclopedias – generated by male forms of knowledge rather than female forms of domestic experience.[34] Again, this period is a key one for the role of the household in constructing the form of the texts women wrote about it.

These manuscript texts offered a different kind of reflection of the life of early modern women to a printed biography partly because they were open-ended. Things were added throughout a woman's life, and indeed long after it by the children and grandchildren to whom her text was passed.[35] Such sources lack the sense of summation which makes a life-writing self-consciously retrospective, which gives it an element of shaping, which anticipates how it might be read by outsiders. Women of the middling sort, as well as their social superiors and to a much lesser extent their inferiors, did produce such summative texts, however, when they died as spinsters or widows and authored their last wills and testaments.[36]

In these texts, women from all but the lowest social levels divided the possessions which they had amongst individuals who were significant to them in terms of family, friendship, or charity at the point of their death. Wills may well, therefore, be the most copious kind of women's writing from this period, one whose basic form alters little across the social scale. Within the text of their wills, women used the objects they owned to create a narrative of their priorities. In the verbal descriptions which they gave of their goods they distinguished between things with which they were familiar, often imbuing their bequests with the sentiment of direct connection with the spaces of their households. The giving of material goods in the form of the will was, therefore, perhaps the ultimate early modern connection between women and household writing.

Through the differences between these individual wills we can trace the distinct forms of identity which could be recorded with different levels of proficiency in writing. Katherine Scott of Nettlestead in Kent, widow of Sir John Scott, knight, wrote her will 'Considering (out of my late deare husbandes death) the infinite Certaine suddennesse of mans decay, and knowinge by good experituce no earthly greatenesse can from this mortallitie pleade priveledge for more peaceable passage into heaven whensoever the Lord shall call'.[37] In common with her less wealthy sisters, her first bequest, 'as most of all concerninge mee' is that of her soul which she gives 'into the handes of God the father, my maker, hopinge only to bee saved by the merrittes and mercies of Jesus my blessed Redeemer, Confirmed in that expectation by the testimony of the holy Ghost the electes Comforter, renouncinge all vaine confidence in earth and earthly thinges, and placeing my affiance in God alone, with perswasion that itt may prevayle in mee unto the end and in the end, the God of all grace grant thorough Jesus Christ our Lord.' This is worth quoting in full to demonstrate Katherine's self-conscious, eloquent, and celebratory profession of a Protestant faith. The phrases appear to take their confidence from her proficiency with language – a heaven which can be imagined textually can be realized in a material way; writing a faith in salvation whilst facing death must provide a considerable degree of comfort. Katherine's conception of salvation is a product of her elite status, of a level of education which enabled and encouraged a more than pragmatic approach to the choice of words.

We do not know whether Katherine actually put these words onto paper herself. Many wills were actually written down by priests or scribes, and the moving eloquence of her faith may well have been clarified in consultation with a spiritual advisor; it was almost certainly worked out in relation to the kinds of self-conscious meditation on scripture, sermon, and printed interpretive texts in which Margaret Hoby was so frequently engaged. Whatever the balance of female inspiration and male advice, by containing those ideas of salvation on pages which were made her own by her powerful conventional opening 'I Katherine Scott', she bent such ideas to a description which defined her own identity through a distinctive piety. And she goes on to choose objects and people in a similarly selectively personal way, dividing, for instance, her most impressive domestic textiles between the women of the next generation: 'Item I beqeath, of my six turkey carpettes, 4 to be given to each daughter one, and fower cover panes of damaske with pearle buttons, to my fower daughters one.'

Although the element of this text which reads most clearly as 'life-writing' to us is the statement of religious faith, thinking about wills as a kind of household writing makes it possible for us to see the choices of bequest as expressions of identity too. And if we can make such an argument, then the wills of Katherine's lower-status peers also offer us access to those women's sense of themselves through their household writing. For instance, Joan Newton, a widow of St George's parish in Canterbury, divided her household objects carefully amongst her relatives. She gave her married daughter clothing, her wedding ring, a christening sheet and other linen, kitchen equipment, and pewter. To her son Thomas, her executor, she gave a settle, a portal, the glass in her windows, a form, a flockbed with bedding, a great chest, a cupboard, a brass pot, some fire equipment, and the painted cloths. Her granddaughters Margery and Alice received kitchen stuff and Margaret and Alice, Joan's unmarried daughters, the best flockbed in the hall with bedding between them with kitchen stuff, pewter, and linen. Finally, 'my greate sheete and a table cloth I gyve to my three dawghters, for everye one of them to occupie as occupacion shall serve.'[38] We can read Joan's strategy of bequests as indicative of her attitudes towards her family and to questions of gender and household identity. Only female recipients are given kitchen equipment, with the exception of the prestigious brass pot which, with the majority of the furniture and furnishings, is given to her son. Joan's daughters are to share the best bed and the best linen – the former they might sell and divide the proceeds, the latter they would use for important occasions. The focus upon ritual moments which Joan passes to her daughters – wedding ring, christening sheet, and great sheet for marriage bed or childbed – is suggestive of her sense of the role of her own household possessions in her daughters' futures. This straightforward text without expressive language nevertheless gives access to its writer's identity.

From the intimate space of the deathbed chamber in which most wills were written, they moved as texts into a much more public sphere. They were proved in an ecclesiastical court, at which point they were read out and rewritten into the official record by a scribe. The bequests which they contained became public knowledge, often broadcast in the church or other public place. Women's wills were very rarely printed, but they were nevertheless very public documents within the communities to which their authors had belonged. Paying attention to the ways in which women's household writings were publicized on this local level gives us a sense of the impact of their words which captures much more sensitively their contributions to the life of the street, hamlet, village, or town than any broader division between private manuscript and public printed document.

The will of a woman of lower status was usually the only textual evidence which she left behind her. At this social level, women's contribution to a culture of writing was mainly through the connection between the spoken and the printed word. All early modern women were popularly associated by their male peers with uncontrolled speech, and lower-status women in particular with old wives' tales which represented fanciful, wild, and fallacious speech. They were popularly represented as gossips and scolds: 'For words they are women, and deeds they are men', the proverb ran. Lower-status women were associated with an oral culture which drew upon and fed into the written word. They told stories within the home, as entertainment or as instruction for children. They told tales which preserved as entertainment family history and local tradition, but also stories which aimed to instruct, not in the pious forms of Protestant educational practice, but in imaginative terms which instilled discipline through fear. Reginald Scot, writer on witchcraft and distant relative of Katherine, had been frightened by his mother's maids' stories of 'bull beggers, spirits [...] kit with the cansticke [...] the mare, the man in the oke, the hell waine, the firedrake, the puckle' and many other creatures as a child.[39]

These tales represent the furthest reaches of women's association with the written word because they circulated in forms which ran alongside but rarely overlapped with any recoverable type of inscription. Adam Fox says, 'They were told one to another down the generations' but that they ran 'as a stream beneath the surface of literary discourse, scarcely recorded at the time, scarcely recoverable by posterity'.[40] A lost, obscure world with a shadowy presence at the borderlines of print culture, the nursery rhymes which women sang to children in many cases only made it into print many decades or even centuries later. Around the firesides and in the nurseries of early modern England, women of lower and middling status told stories; sometimes the children of much higher-status parents in their care listened to their tales. The range of written words with which even lower-status women were connected was considerable then, and the literary forms traditionally privileged in accounts of women and writing are only the uttermost tip of a considerable iceberg of manuscript and material interventions.

I want to end this essay by extending the example of the mantelpiece with its moral message with which I began, to consider the house itself as a repository for these various forms of writing. Its walls might be decorated with printed matter, pasted there to display 'pictures, poems, prayers, catechisms, mementoes of death, devotional guides'. And a range of texts were inscribed there: 'Political commentary, erotic fixation, personal slander [...] signature [...] games, recipes, school lessons, memorials, house rules, prayers, extracts from the Bible, memoranda to the self and advice to others'. Words were even inscribed on windows, for which purpose special 'writing rings' with 'diamonds set in high bevels with one point outwards' to mark glass were designed, and key phrases intended for a form of domestic meditation on moral issues were marked on household objects such as 'fruit trenchers of wood'.[41]

Householders favored a particular kind of aesthetic, one which envisaged the household as a unified space for the display of narrative and textual sources: 'The Elizabethans regarded every part of the interior of a room, including timber beams and supports, as an appropriate surface for painting.'[42] The physical and material constancy of household spaces – the fact that they were seen night and day and that they were the most frequent resort of women and children who were in particular need of instruction – made clear connections between Elizabethan houses and biblical injunctions to draw the hearts of all Christians to their moral duties on a regular basis. The text of Deuteronomy was frequently depicted: 'And these words, which I command thee this day, shall be in thine heart: and thou shalt teach them diligently unto thy children, and shalt talk of them when thou sittest in thine house, and when thou walkest by the way, and when thou liest down, and when thou risest up. [...] And thou shalt write them upon the posts of thy house, and on thy gates.'[43] Protestants and humanists alike saw the educative potential of such spaces. Thomas Elyot suggests that the householder inscribe 'some monument of virtue' on his walls 'that they which do eate or drinke havyng those wisedoms ever in sighte, shall happen with meate to receive some of them'. Writing on the household should generate discussion and conversation – it is writing meant to be read aloud, shared, and debated amongst friends and family.[44]

The same narratives, with their narrow range of moral themes relating to appropriate family and household behavior, were told on painted cloths, painted on the walls themselves, or pasted upon them as individual printed paper sheets called broadsides.[45] The most common biblical subjects were the stories of Susanna and Tobias and the parables of Dives and Lazarus and the prodigal son, but in general stories with a domestic theme were popular. Thomas Pullen, a Canterbury surgeon, had hanging on the wall in his hall a 'table of Christ's calling of St Peter being a fishing' and a 'little table of Abraham sacrificing of Isaac'.[46] Such images implicitly communicate complex ideas and ideals about family life and Christian responsibility. Broadsides such as Gyles Godet's 'The good hows-holder' were more explicit. Beneath a picture of a sage-looking man dressed in a fur hat a poem extols domestic thrift: 'Not daintie Fare and Furniture of Gold, | But handsome-holsom (as with Health dooth stand)'.[47]

The relationship between domestic imagery and the practices of the women who lived within the house is suggested by Watt's assertion that 'The meaning of the printed object on the wall lay in taking the activities of the household (such as prayer, song, instruction and discipline of children) and freezing them into permanent visual form.' And the applicability of these tales to the nature of household life meant that they were common across a wide section of the social scale: 'The same stories recurred on the walls of the manor houses owned by the gentry and yeomanry, in the town houses of substantial tradesmen, and in the lowly broadside ballad.' Their familiarity meant that even textual decoration was available to be read by women with few or no skills in literacy because these were such ubiquitous narratives. So women of comparatively low social status who would be considered illiterate by the standards of modern measurement still had access to these texts and could 'read' them to the children in their care.[48]

Within this admonitory context which was present in different kinds of media across the social scale – pasted broadsides at the bottom, tapestries at the top – women produced their household writings.[49] Some, like the last will and testament, would have been familiar to all – the opening phrases of such documents were known to literate and illiterate alike. Others, like the personal letter, the receipt book, or the tale of the puckle, were largely the preserve of a particular social group of women. Forms of household work shape all these types of writing, and for this reason other, material, forms of creativity have also been considered here as a kind of domestic authorship appropriate for understanding the contributions that women made to the narratives circulating within the home.

This essay has argued for a conception of women's household writing which makes it possible to explore individuality across the social scale, and it has suggested that household writing might be the only kind of writing which can give us this breadth of access to women's identity. The selection and assembly of ideas, words, and images on a household theme, it has been argued, generate a kind of life-writing because they speak to the processes by which women's identity was molded by the ideals of behavior, the daily tasks, and the material culture of the household. As the lives of women in early modern England were intricately tied up with domestic matters, so their written responses to household life, however mundane, take us closer than any other kind of writing to their experiences of existence. The choices they made of what to record and how to record it place them tangibly within the setting which most clearly shaped their lives.

Notes

1. Juliet Fleming, who quotes this example, says it begs the question '"What is a text?" but, before and besides that, "What is writing?" What kinds of reading and writing skills [...] may have constituted literacy at such a moment?' *Graffiti and the Writing Arts of Early Modern England* (London: Reaktion Books, 2001), p. 10.
2. For analysis of literary writings about the household in this period see Barbara K. Lewalski, 'Literature and the Household', in *The Cambridge History of Early Modern English Literature*, ed. David Loewenstein and Janel Mueller (Cambridge: Cambridge University Press, 2002), pp. 603–32. The approach I take here is much closer to Helen Wilcox's essay in the same volume (on a later period) in its interest in texts associated with or generated by the home, although again her focus is on more traditionally 'literary' works.
3. See David Cressy's articles collected in *Society and Culture in Early Modern England* (Aldershot: Ashgate, 2003) or, for a summary of recent writing, Kenneth Charlton and Margaret Spufford, 'Literacy, Society and Education', in *Cambridge History*, ed. Loewenstein and Mueller, pp. 15–54.
4. For more on this see Frances Dolan, 'Reading, Writing, and Other Crimes', in *Feminist Readings of Early Modern Culture: Emerging Subjects*, ed. Valerie Traub, M. Lindsey Kaplan, and Dympna Callaghan (Cambridge: Cambridge University Press, 1996), pp. 142–67.
5. Robert Cleaver, *A godlie forme of hovseholde government* (London: Thomas Creede, for Thomas Man, 1598), p. 13.
6. William Gouge, *Of domesticall duties* (London: Iohn Haviland for William Bladen, 1622), p. 469; Cleaver, *A godlie forme*, p. 47. Subsequent references to Gouge and Cleaver are cited parenthetically in the text.
7. Both were sometimes produced by women lower down the social scale, as Lynne Magnusson's chapter in this volume demonstrates.
8. Margaret P. Hannay, Noel J. Kinnamon, and Michael G. Brennan (eds), *Domestic Politics and Family Absence: The Correspondence (1588–1621) of Robert Sidney, First Earl of Leicester, and Barbara Gamage Sidney, Countess of Leicester* (Aldershot: Ashgate, 2005), p. 49.
9. Ibid., pp. 57, 61.

10. Alison Wall (ed.), *Two Elizabethan Women: Correspondence of Joan and Maria Thynne 1575–1611* (Devizes: Wiltshire Record Society, 1983), p. 11.

11. James Daybell (ed.), *Early Modern Women's Letter Writing, 1450–1700* (Basingstoke: Palgrave Macmillan, 2001), pp. 5, 13; James Daybell, *Women Letter Writers in Tudor England* (Oxford: Oxford University Press, 2006), p. 7.

12. Grace Ioppolo, '"I desire to be helde in your memory": Reading Penelope Rich through Her Letters', in *The Impact of Feminism in English Renaissance Studies*, ed. Dympna Callaghan (Basingstoke: Palgrave Macmillan, 2007), p. 319.

13. Daybell, *Women Letter Writers*, pp. 3, 26.

14. Vivienne Larminie argues that Anne Newdigate 'could sustain effectively a geographically far-flung circle of correspondents, which included courtiers, office-holders, kin and servants'; 'Fighting for Family in a Patronage Society', in *Early Modern Women's Letter Writing*, ed. Daybell, p. 94.

15. Quoted in Daybell, *Women Letter Writers*, p. 10.

16. Larminie, 'Fighting for Family', pp. 99, 106.

17. *Lay By Your Needles Ladies, Take the Pen: Writing Women in England, 1500–1700*, ed. Suzanne Trill, Kate Chedgzoy, and Melanie Osborne (London and New York: Arnold, 1997), p. 74.

18. Ibid., p. 71.

19. Ronald Bedford, Lloyd Davis, and Philippa Kelly, *Early Modern English Lives: Autobiography and Self-representation 1500–1660* (Aldershot: Ashgate, 2007), p. 182.

20. Ann Rosalind Jones and Peter Stallybrass, *Renaissance Clothing and the Materials of Memory* (Cambridge: Cambridge University Press, 2000), p. 135.

21. Sampler (T.190–1960), Victoria and Albert Museum, London, http://collections.vam.ac.uk/objectid/O46183 (accessed 27 July 2009).

22. See, for instance, the mid-sixteenth-century shirt, Victoria and Albert Museum, London (T.112–1972), http://collections.vam.ac.uk/objectid/O115767 or the jacket (1359–1900), http://collections.vam.ac.uk/objectid/O15345.

23. Jones and Stallybrass, *Renaissance Clothing*, p. 148. In a rather different take on the relationship between needlework and writing they argue that 'The needle could *be* a pen' (p. 144).

24. Sasha Roberts, 'Lying among the Classics: Ritual and Motif in Elite Elizabethan and Jacobean Beds', in *Albion's Classicism: The Visual Arts in Britain 1550–1660*, ed. Lucy Gent (New Haven: Yale University Press, 1996), pp. 336, 338.

25. Jones and Stallybrass, *Renaissance Clothing*, p. 140.

26. See Keith Wrightson, *Earthly Necessities: Economic Lives in Early Modern Britain, 1470–1750* (London: Penguin, 2002); Catherine Richardson, *Domestic Life and Domestic Tragedy* (Manchester: Manchester University Press, 2006), chapter 2.

27. Cleaver, *A godlie forme*, pp. 92, 93.

28. Gervase Markham, *The English Housewife*, ed. Michael R. Best (Kingston: McGill-Queen's University Press, 1986).

29. See also Natasha Korda, *Shakespeare's Domestic Economies* (Philadelphia: University of Pennsylvania Press, 2002). Women's account books should be seen as a product of this process of supervision.

30. Margaret J. M. Ezell, 'Domestic Papers: Manuscript Culture and Early Modern Women's Life Writing', in *Genre and Women's Life Writing in Early Modern*

England, ed. Michelle Dowd and Julie Eckerle (Aldershot: Ashgate, 2007), pp. 33–48 (p. 44).

31. Victoria E. Burke, 'Ann Bowyer's Commonplace Book (Bodleian Library Ashmole MS 51): Reading and Writing Among the "Middling Sort"', *Early Modern Literary Studies* 6.3 (2001), 1–28 (pp. 1, 7, 12).

32. Catherine Field, '"Many hands hands": Writing the Self in Early Modern Women's Recipe Books', in *Genre and Women's Life Writing*, ed. Dowd and Eckerle, pp. 49–64 (pp. 54, 50, 56–57).

33. Quoted in ibid., p. 52.

34. See also Ann Moss, *Printed Commonplace Books and the Structuring of Renaissance Thought* (Oxford: Clarendon Press, 1996).

35. Ezell, 'Domestic Papers', p. 46.

36. On historical interpretations of these documents see *When Death Do Us Part: Understanding and Interpreting the Probate Records of Early Modern England*, ed. Tom Arkell, Nesta Evans, and Nigel Goose (Oxford: Leopard's Head Press, 2007).

37. PCC Prob 11/129, 1617.

38. CCAL PROB 17.45.57, 1582.

39. Adam Fox, *Oral and Literate Culture in England, 1500–1700* (Oxford: Oxford University Press, 2000), pp. 177, 189, 190, 194.

40. Ibid., pp. 202, 192.

41. Tessa Watt, *Cheap Print and Popular Piety, 1560–1640* (Cambridge: Cambridge University Press, 1994), p. 224; Fleming, *Graffiti*, pp. 58, 55, 43.

42. Watt, *Cheap Print*, p. 199.

43. King James Bible, Deuteronomy 6:4–9 and 11:18–21.

44. Fleming, *Graffiti*, p. 139.

45. Watt, *Cheap Print*, pp. 201–02.

46. CCAL PRC 10.11.221, 1580.

47. Illustrated in Watt, *Cheap Print*, p. 226.

48. Ibid., pp. 227, 216.

49. For middling-status aspects of domestic decoration see Tara Hamling, 'Reconciling Image and Object: Religious Imagery in Protestant Interior Decoration', in *Everyday Objects: Medieval and Early Modern Material Culture and its Meanings*, ed. Tara Hamling and Catherine Richardson (Aldershot: Ashgate, 2010).

5
Maternal Advice

Edith Snook

Most of the interest in maternal advice in the early modern period focuses on printed maternal advice books, which appeared in the seventeenth century. Elizabeth Grymeston's *Miscelanea, Meditations, Memoratives* was printed first in 1604, Dorothy Leigh's popular *The Mother's Blessing* in 1616, Elizabeth Clinton's *The Countess of Lincoln's Nurserie* in 1622, Elizabeth Joscelin's *The Mother's Legacie to her Unborn Child* in 1624, Elizabeth Richardson's *A Ladies Legacie to her Daughters* in 1645, and Susanna Bell's *The Legacy of a Dying Mother to her Mourning Children* in 1673. Critics have identified these publications as a genre and argued that their style was influenced by religious or devotional literature, courtesy books, advice by fathers (King James, William Cecil, Lord Burghley, and Sir Walter Raleigh), and by a son (Robert Southwell), as well as by Nicholas Breton's *The Mothers Blessing* (1601), a verse epistle ventriloquizing a maternal voice.[1] Other scholars have highlighted the social practices that enabled the publication of maternal advice books. A resurgence of interest in maternal breastfeeding, the continued authority of the Virgin Mary in seventeenth-century England, the valorization of Elizabeth, Queen of Bohemia as a Protestant mother, and the practice of creating wills and deathbed legacies all afforded mothers access to a social authority that facilitated the printing of maternal advice.[2]

But what of sixteenth-century mothers? By beginning the discussion of maternal advice with printed texts, we have obscured the extent to which women were already offering advice to their children in manuscript form. The printed seventeenth-century maternal advice books reflect the textual practices of manuscript culture. While all of the printed volumes but *The Countess of Lincoln's Nurserie* are legacies, *Miscelanea, Meditations, Memoratives* is, as the title suggests, also a miscellany consisting of an epistle to Grymeston's son, meditations, prayers, a madrigal by her son

Bernye, and proverbs. Elizabeth Richardson composed prayers for her daughters, while Susanna Bell's *Legacy of a Dying Mother* is a spiritual autobiography recounting her emigration to New England. The prose essay style employed by Leigh and Joscelin shares much with King James's *Basilicon Doron* and other paternal advice books, but Joscelin's work also includes a letter to her husband, while Leigh draws specifically on the language of prayer.[3] These are the textual forms that sixteenth-century mothers employed. To advise their children in writing, they not only inscribed set pieces of advice, but they also collected common-places and proverbs, directed their prayers, composed autobiographies and family histories, dispatched instructive letters, and supervised their expenditures, particularly on clothes. If their efforts were only rarely printed, they were no less significant to creating an authoritative dis-course of maternal advice.

In the sixteenth century, however, we do not always see motherhood construed in the individualistic, affective terms often imagined in printed books. Elizabeth Grymeston, for instance, constructs the nuclear family as the primary unit in which motherhood takes shape: 'there is nothing so strong as the force of love; there is no love so forcible as the love of an affectionate mother to hir naturall childe'.[4] Grymeston disparages foster parents and other caregivers, and some sixteenth-century mothers share her concern. Yet other sixteenth-century mothers engaged kin and friends in the labor of child-rearing, not because parent–child relations were remote and oppressive, as Lawrence Stone has argued, but as another form of expression of concern for a child's upbringing.[5] David Cressy stresses the flexibility of ideas of family in the early modern period:

> Kinship involved a range of possibilities, rather than a set of concrete obligations. These possibilities began with acknowledgement, advice and support, stretched to financial help and career encouragement, and also included emotional comfort and political solidarity. At issue is not propinquity, network density or frequency of involvement, but rather the potency and instrumentality of extended family ties.[6]

Elite Tudor mothers and fathers regularly attempted to place their children in the households of people, including relatives, who were wealthier or had a better social position than the parents did themselves. The purpose was to educate children, to help them find marriage partners, and to enhance the social networks of both offspring and parents.[7] Pierre Bourdieu provides a useful way of thinking about the function of maternal advice within such an instrumental family model. He argues that families are actively constituted, on the one hand as 'the sum total of genealogical relationships kept in working order (here called practical kinship)', and on the other, as 'the sum total of the non-genealogical relationships which can be mobilized for the ordinary needs of existence (practical relationships)'.[8] Maternal advice, as a textual form, actively constitutes the family in the sixteenth century, making both types of relationships function. Some mothers write to energize the practical kinship of mother and child, while others use texts to institute practical relationships among children, family, and friends, placing the mother at the center of a network of social connections made to matter in a child's upbringing.

Prayers and meditations

Mothers wrote prayers and meditations to guide their children's devotions, in line with the conduct book dictum that mothers ought to inculcate virtue in their children. Yet prayer was not a simple act. Early modern prayers organized and transformed, if one prayed sincerely. The *Book of Common Prayer, for instance, 'encompassed the whole of a person's life', structuring the spiritual and social occasions that were baptism, catechism, Sundays, holy days, weddings, sickness, childbirth, and funerals.[9] Prayers had the power to effect personal reform, but the ends of prayer were often sociable, for prayers established relationships among members of a household, a church, and a nation. The composers of prayers neatly registered their beliefs about the gender, social, and political order, as well as their theology in their approach to language (Latin or English), addressee (God alone or saints), and extemporaneity (the legitimacy of set prayers). As Timothy Rosendale argues, the Book of Common Prayer 'enacted rather than depicted': 'the Prayerbook was (and is) a *performative* or illocutionary text; it not only emblematized a certain sociopolitical order, but helped to bring that order into being through the authoritative, iterative, and formalized nature of its claims'.[10] Private prayer books were not altogether different. Not only were Protestant primers (prayer books for private devotion) accorded royal authority from the reign of Henry VIII, but the prayers themselves aimed to educate and shape English citizens.[11] Even the books for private prayer that were the successors to the primers, Helen White contends, had to work towards 'the establishment of their position politically and socially as well as religiously, and to the working out of the forms of public worship and church government and discipline that would make the theoretical position a living reality'.[12]

Maternal prayers had similar aims. Designed to encourage both the reform of English women and the favor of Queen Elizabeth, Thomas Bentley's *The Monument of Matrones* (1582) includes a section entitled 'sundrie vertuous Queenes, and other devout and godlie women in our time'. Alongside reprints of Queen Elizabeth's translation of Marguerite de Navarre's *The Mirror of a Sinful Soul* (1548), Katherine Parr's *Lamentacion of a Sinner* (1547), and her *Prayers or Meditations* (1545) is one collection of maternal prayers: 'Prayers Made by the Right Honourable Ladie Frances Aburgavennie, and committed at the hour of her death, to the right Worshipfull Ladie Marie Fane (hir onelie daughter) as a Jewell of health for the soule, and a perfect path to paradise, very profitable to be used of everie faithfull Christian woman and man'.[13] The author of these prayers is Frances (Manners) Neville, Lady Bergavenny (d.1576), the wife of Sir Henry Neville, fourth Lord Bergavenny and the mother of Lady Mary (Neville) Fane (1554–1626). The prayers left to profit Lady Mary Fane take a variety of forms: ecclesiastical prayers for use in church to supplement those in the Book of Common Prayer; quotidian prayers for rising in the morning and going to bed; confessional prayers on the recognition and forgiveness of sin; behavioral prayers for protection against the company of the ungodly, living uprightly and well, avoiding the fear of loss, good judgment in controversies, the inculcation of virtue and the avoidance of vice; and occasional prayers for protection, funerals, prosperity, war, plague, private affliction, or death. The prayers are not for Mary Fane alone, but every faithful Christian, man and woman, and do not address themselves particularly to uniquely female subjects, such as childbirth. They do, however, function as maternal advice, for they provide the daughter who prays with a structure for a day, comfort in hardship, and instruction in how to respond morally to various situations, within a community of other Christians who pray as she does. Prayers oblige rehearsal. As Judith Maltby argues, prayers are '"work", intended not so much to be read in a passive sense, but to be used, performed, experienced'; just as the Book of Common Prayer 'provided a framework of words and actions to address a wide range of human needs', the mother's prayers guide a daughter's life within a community of like-minded believers.[14] Lady Bergavenny's prayers also represent the mother as a writer. In teaching the daughter, the mother becomes a poet, with one other prayer in verse, 'A necessarie praier in Meter against vices', and a concluding acrostic poem on the mother's name. Poetry, too, instructs, for as Ramie Targoff argues, '[t]he choice of verse over prose for vernacular devotion reflects a fundamental didactic impulse'.[15] With the acrostic poem on her own name and the acrostic collection of prose prayers on her daughter's, Lady Bergavenny adopts her most personal tone, addressing her daughter's prayers in particular and highlighting her own penitent example.[16] Yet it is with both these individualized prayers and the prayers addressing a range of topics that the mother instructs her daughter. Together with other readers, prayers guide her in knowing herself and her place in the family, the reformed English church, and the social order as a literate, ever-mindful, Protestant Christian. As the writer of prayers, the mother assumes the moral authority to write and to advise not just her own daughter but 'everie faithfull Christian woman and man'.

Miscellanies

In addition to providing moral and theological instruction through prayer, some literate mothers were specifically concerned with their children's reading.[17] Just as early modern schools used the common-place book as a pedagogical tool, so too did mothers who compiled commonplaces for their offspring. Commonplacing was a practice of remembering – 'a record of what the memory might look like' – a mode of textual production – as the reader became a writer copying texts often treated as malleable – and a structure of authority; 'poetic author-ity', according to Max W. Thomas, 'is based on a reading practice in which authority is derived from other writers'.[18] Elizabeth (Beaumont) Richardson (1576/7–1651) created a manuscript that envisioned mater-nal authority through the work of collecting, as well as through the writing of prayers. We know Elizabeth Richardson best for her printed volume, *A Ladies Legacie to her Daughters*, prayers for her four daugh-ters and two daughters-in-law written after her second marriage to Sir Thomas Richardson. But during her first marriage to John Ashburnam (m.1594), she created a manuscript, dated 1606, entitled *Instructions for My Children*.[19] As her preface explains, with this book of 'Precepts, Instructions, and Prayers', she discharges her care for her children. Although the manuscript remains incomplete, she projects four sec-tions: 'Precepts for a civill and christian life'; 'the vertues & vices w[i]th ye rewardes & punishments'; 'an instruction for prayer'; and 'A Treatise, concerning Life, and Death'.[20] This final section is, accord-ing to Margaret Hannay, a 'précis of and meditation on the Countess of Pembroke's *A Discourse of Life and Death* (1592), her translation of the *Excellent discours de la vie et de la mort* (1576) by Philippe de Mornay'.[21] Hannay notes that this discourse is evidence of 'reading [that] became rewriting, as she entered into the text to mould it to her own needs'.[22]

Ashburnam paraphrases other texts in 'Certaine Sentences worthie often to be remembred' – perhaps part of the projected 'precepts' section, which like the discussion of the Ten Commandments, was unfinished. Such collections of 'sentences' or sayings were common in early modern pedagogy; according to Mary Thomas Crane, 'sententious readings (like the Proverbs of Solomon) could frame a child and serve as an antidote to harmful ideas'.[23] Christine de Pizan used this didactic form in her advice to her son, *Les Enseignements Moraux*, published in England in translation in 1478, as did Elizabeth Grymeston in her memoratives. Ashburnam's sentences are collected from the Bible and include advice on remembering death, repentance, and living well. She concludes the section with the instruction, a paraphrase of Proverbs 27:15 and Ecclesiasticus 11:10, to 'be dilligent in thine owne affaires, but be not hastie to meddle in other folks matters, for a busy bodie is hated'. Another small collection of biblical sentences begins with a hand pointing (a drawing often used in manuscripts for emphasis) at 'Use time well, for it tarieth none'.

Ashburnam places her sentences beside prayers and meditations which reflect on reading. Following a meditation on the profit of wisdom, she places 'A praier for knowledge and understandinge before readinge or studie' (fol. 4). In this way, she considers not just the content of moral precepts, but the learning process itself. Prayer is fundamental to knowledge, for one cannot understand what one reads if one does not have a pure heart: 'ye carnall man per ceaveth not ye thinges of ye spiritt, except yu give him wisdome' (fol. 5). Ashburnam's 'instructions' do not value originality, but teach through quotation of the Bible and the Countess of Pembroke's translated meditation. They emphasize a spiritual reading practice begun in prayer, instructions on which constitute a third, completed section of the manuscript. Prayers and commonplaces together educate, grounding a mother's authority and providing evidence of her knowledge and her intelligent care for her children's moral, intellectual, and spiritual development.

Autobiography and history

Grace (Sharington) Mildmay, Lady Mildmay (c.1552–1620) devised her autobiography and meditations as maternal advice. Lady Mildmay prepared the lengthy manuscript, *Lady Mildmay's Meditations* between 1603 and 1617–20 for her only child Lady Mary (Mildmay) Fane (1581/2–1640), to whom Mildmay had given birth some fifteen years after her marriage to Anthony Mildmay, son and heir of Sir Walter Mildmay,

Queen Elizabeth's Chancellor of the Exchequer. Like Susanna Bell, Lady Mildmay wrote a spiritual autobiography, compiled to commend her daughter and her grandchildren from her experience. The first course of life to which she recommends them is to read Scripture, *Acts and Monuments*, history, law, philosophy, and her own meditations, 'a testimony of the love and presence of God'.[24] In history, she tells her children, 'we may be instructed to imitate and to follow the good examples of true and faithfull subjects and to have their worthy acts and exploits in memory'; by failing to follow the virtuous exemplars of history 'many honourable houses of antiguities and renown and ancient names have been utterly subverted' (p. 23). Her life-writing approaches her own history in similarly exemplary terms, with her autobiography and meditations affording a glimpse of her own mother who offered maternal advice by which both she and her household might be preserved.

Lady Mildmay's mother was Anne (Paget) Sharington, the daughter of a London alderman and the wife of Sir Henry Sharington, who was knighted by Queen Elizabeth in 1574. Lady Mildmay records her mother's influence first as enacted through a practical relationship, for she records at length how her governess proved worthy of the 'trust which my mother reposed in her'; the governess guided her behavior and taught her physic and ciphering (p. 26). Lady Sharington's more immediate instruction is in matters of faith. She taught her daughter her own prayers and meditations, which Grace learned 'by heart', and Lady Sharington guided her children's prayers: '[T]he first prayer that ever she taught me was, that I should beg God a blessed end and departure out of this life' (p. 29). When Lady Sharington instructed her daughter about reading, she limited her to books that were wholly good (the Bible, Musculus's *Common Places*, *The Imitation of Christ*, the *Book of Martyrs*), which, Grace adds, 'gave me the first taste of Christ Jesus and his truth whereby I have found myself the better established in the whole course of my life' (p. 28). Lady Mildmay also records how her mother put her spiritual commitments into practice, directing her daughter's conduct: in dress, she should receive 'jewels and pearl and costly apparel' only when she had been 'furnished with virtue in my mind and decked inwardly'; in conversation, she should not mock others but instead be humble, 'esteeming others better than myself'; and in speech, she should 'consider so long as the word remaineth with me it is mine own, but when I have spoken the same word is no more mine own but every man's that heard it and all others to whom the same shall afterward be uttered' (p. 29). Finally, Lady Mildmay records her mother's good death as another scene of maternal instruction.

She called her children to her privately to tell them to read the Bible every day, final words that are, her daughter recalls, but the verbal expression of her daily example. Lady Mildmay's personal history includes the history of maternal advice, configured as both word and deed. Forging a family genealogy of virtue, Mildmay reaches even further back into the sixteenth century, to her maternal grandmother, 'a godly and religious woman' who likewise 'delighted in the word of God' and was chaste in her conversation (p. 29). This history is recorded so that it can continue to provide a guide to conduct: 'I have here set down for mine own example and to keep the same in memory, that whosoever shall read the same may see and consider what a blessed thing it is to proceed of virtuous parents' (p. 30). The advice of women of the Reformation is a matrilineal inheritance that, more surely than land, can be passed from mother to child. It affords an example that children ignore to the peril of their family name, for Lady Mildmay warns, 'an infamous memory remaineth of them and their generation after them' (p. 30).

Grace, Lady Mildmay's descendants honored her precedent. Two manuscripts that supplement her history of maternal advice were prepared for her grandsons, the sons of her daughter Lady Mary Fane, the Countess of Westmorland, and Francis Fane, the first Earl of Westmorland (1583/4–1629). Mildmay Fane (1602–66), the writer and politician, was the first recipient of *Book of Advice to the Children*, while Francis (d. *c.*1681), a younger son, has a partial copy, into which further instructions from the Countess of Westmorland to him were copied.[25] *Book of Advice to the Children* begins with advice by various family members to Mildmay Fane: by his grandmothers, Mary (Neville) Fane, *suo jure* Baroness le Despencer (the first earl's mother) and Grace Mildmay, Lady Mildmay, and by his mother and father. The manuscript also includes a copy of Sir Walter Mildmay's advice to his son Anthony Mildmay, Mildmay Fane's maternal grandfather. Like Sir Walter Mildmay in his advice to Anthony, the Baroness le Despencer takes a topical approach in her advice to Mildmay Fane, urging her grandson to service to God through reading, loyalty to the king, obedience to parents, humility in society, health and sociability in recreations, moderation in diet and expenses, and consideration of religion and birth in choice of a wife and respect for her in marriage. Baroness le Despencer is the Mary (Neville) Fane who received from her mother, Frances Neville, Lady Bergavenny, the prayers printed in Bentley's *Monument of Matrones*. Thus, both Mary Fanes – the Baroness and the Countess of Westmorland – are continuing a tradition of advice established by their mothers and grandmothers.[26] Lady Mildmay's counsel for her grandson is a letter recommending Bible reading, while the Countess of Westmorland's first takes the form of proverbs. The proverbs, she says, Mildmay should make his own, 'by discoursing in yourself' (fols. 4–14ᵛ). Frances Fane's commonplace book also contains copies of several letters from the Countess of Westmorland to him. In one, written in 1631 when he was 'Ambassador Extraordinary to the Emperour the King of Denmark', she compiles, like her mother and grandmother, a reading list. It begins with the Bible, and includes histories, the counsel of parents, the Psalms, St Augustine, St Bernard, Tully's Offices, and Seneca.[27]

Grace, Lady Mildmay's meditations and autobiography, the later collections of advice for the Countess of Westmorland's sons, and the subsequent redirections of these manuscripts create a long history of exemplary maternal advice. The Countess of Westmorland actually configures the reception history of her own advice to this end, in a letter copied in both manuscripts. She begins by remembering the praise that St Paul had for Timothy's mother and grandmother and ends by contemplating her text's recirculation, how as virtuous ancestors 'have begun this booke, y[ou] and yours may fill it, [and] so make it and evidence of a blessed generation', a directive which Mildmay Fane's first wife, Grace Thornhurst, takes up, adding to the manuscript by recording the births of her five daughters between 1627 and 1633;[28] Mildmay Fane, as the second Earl of Westmorland, also adds, with notes on the births of several sons, his own advice: to Charles (b. 1634), Vere (b. 1644), and Henry, born 'after his Brother Vere'.[29] Addressing the whole of the work to her children in 1695, Rachel Fane, the fourth Countess of Westmorland and wife of Vere Fane, was the last mother to write in the book. Similarly, Francis Fane presented his collection of advice to his son Henry. Echoing her mother's sense of history's moral import in a letter copied in both manuscripts, the first Countess explains why the volume deserves good esteem:

> it shewing unto you not only ther owne inwarde vertues but alsoe their affectionate desires to trans-ferre vertue w[i]th ther blude, [and] fortunes to ther posteritie. To whom, those that make not this use of ther lessons, to become fellow servants w[i]th them to vertue, are noe legitimate heyres, but as bastarde plants shall take noe deep roote, for that house w[hi]ch hath had her foundations layde in vertue, will not be repaired [and] upheld with the untempered morter of vice, but will demolish [and] come to nothing.[30]

Maternal advice is both evidence of virtue and a method for its transmission. Its acceptance confers legitimacy, the right to possess the house, and secures the household's foundations in time to come. For these mothers, and significantly, for their sons, maternal advice is at the very core of the family's history and is fit to stand alongside the advice of a prestigious male ancestor in the maternal line, as Sir Walter Mildmay was. Mildmay Fane redirects the advice of his mother and grandmothers to his children, and it becomes the ground on which he adds his own paternal counsel. Issued in meditations, letters, autobiography, and proverbs, Grace, Lady Mildmay and her daughter configure matrilineal histories of advice in which women possess knowledge, virtue, and blood within families that are spiritual, affective, and political entities. Advice is a serious legacy which, like the Earl of Westmorland's title as Baron le Despencer, is the issue of women as much as men.

Letters

If the letters of all literate mothers were not copied to be preserved for posterity in manuscript advice books, they did nevertheless write letters of advice.[31] Like the other forms which advice took, the advice letter highlights mothers' affective, intellectual, spiritual, and behavioral concerns and the genealogical and practical relationships through which sixteenth-century motherhood took shape. Elizabeth (Cooke) Russell, Lady Russell (?1528–1609) – known as Elizabeth Hoby, Lady Hoby during her first marriage to Sir Thomas Hoby – wrote at least one letter of advice to her adult son, Thomas Posthumous Hoby, a second son born just after her first husband's death in 1566.[32] She informs him of the disposition of the widow Margaret (Dakin) Devereaux, suggests how Hoby might arrange to meet her, confirms that she 'hath her father's consent to match where she list', and accounts for the financing he might have for the marriage. Although in 1591 her instructions failed to have any effect, for Devereaux married Thomas Sidney shortly after the letter was written, after Sidney's death in 1595 Devereaux would become Lady Margaret Hoby, the diarist wife of Thomas Posthumous Hoby.[33] Over ninety letters survive by Lady Russell's sister, Anne (Cooke) Bacon (c.1528–1610) to her sons, Anthony (1558–1601) and Francis (1561–1626), the philosopher.[34] She is a widow, and they are adults, but she writes to warn them against papists and incredulity, especially against too much trust in servants, and to offer medical advice on diet, drink, and rest, for, she says, 'Get health to serve God and your country as he shall enable and call you'.[35] Lady Mary (Dudley) Sidney (1530x35–1586) added a postscript to a 1566 letter of advice from her husband Sir Henry Sidney (1529–86) to their son Philip (1554–86), the poet, then at school at

Shrewsbury.[36] Sir Henry wrote a formal letter of advice with instructions to pray with meditation, to study earnestly, to read with an eye to enriching the wit, and to be courteous to all men, moderate in diet, clean in dress, and mirthful in conversation. Lady Sidney's postscript merely reinforces her husband's 'wise, so learned and most requisite precepts', as she eloquently refuses to say more 'as I will not withdraw your eyes from beholding and reverent honouring the same – no, not so long as to read any letter from me'. If Lady Sidney adds only that Philip should read his father's words every four or five days, Sir Henry calls upon him to remember his maternal ancestors, bringing his son's attention to his mother's legacy. He reminds Philip of the 'noble blood you are descended of by your mother's side; and think that only by virtuous life and good action you may be an ornament to that illustrious family'.[37] If Lady Sidney is not voluble, her ancestry is made to matter in her husband's words and to call her son to virtue.

Epistolary maternal advice could also be directed to recipients other than one's offspring. Few letters survive from Elizabeth Russell, Lady Russell to her children, but there are extant letters about the upbringing of Thomas and Edward to William Cecil, Lord Burghley, her brother-in-law and a powerful royal councilor. Lady Russell, for instance, had attempted to place Thomas at the Inns of Court, but had been told that she should wait until he was bigger. Her son, too, resists the plan, but suspicious of European travel, another option which 'nowadays' brings 'nothing but pride, charge, and vanity', she turns to Lord Burghley in hopes he will take Thomas into his household. This is a question of guidance, for he has, she says, an 'unnatural bad nature and insolency in suspecting me, with disdain to serve me'.[38] While averring she is not a bird to defile her own nest, she nevertheless declaims upon Thomas's 'unnatural hard nature and insolency'. Feeling herself to be rendered ineffectual by her son's resistance, she asks Burghley to mediate the instruction she would have offered. Because the son does not appear to recognize the value of his mother's advice, Lady Russell, rather than remaining silent, writes to a powerful kinsman, a male authority who might put into effect the reformation she desires.

The letters of Honor (Grenville) Plantagenet, Lady Lisle (1493/5–1566) likewise highlight a sociable and communal model for mothering, where surrogates can put a mother's advice into effect. Lady Lisle's surrogates, however, treat the care of her children as a form of service to the parents and profess the desire to follow absolutely her instructions for her offspring. They are not to enhance her authority as Lord Burghley is, but merely to relay it reliably. Honor Plantagenet was the daughter of Sir Thomas Grenville, the widow of Sir John Basset, and the wife of Arthur Plantagenet, Viscount Lisle (before 1472–1542), the illegitimate son of King Edward IV. With Basset, she had seven children: Philippa, Katherine, John, Anne, Mary, George, and James; she was also stepmother to Lisle's children from his first marriage, Elizabeth, Frances (who would become the wife of John Basset), and Bridget, and to John Basset's children from his first marriage, Jane and Thomasine.

When the children were not present to receive their mother's instruction orally, they might still be advised by letter and by surrogates who embodied their mother's views on parenting, their mother's authority, and their mother's nurturing care. The letters documenting the education of two daughters with prominent families in France are perhaps the most telling. Anne Basset, in 1533 then twelve or thirteen, was sent to live with Thybault Rouaud, Sieur de Riou, and Jeanne de Saveuzes and Mary Basset, in 1534, then eleven or twelve, with Thybault de Riou's sister, Anne Rouaud and her husband Nicholas de Montmorency, Seigneur de Bours.[39] Neither Anne nor Mary expressed unhappiness about their circumstances. Anne writes to her mother that 'Had I been their natural daughter they could not better nor more gently have entreated me'.[40] Mary writes similarly of Madame de Bours as a surrogate parent to whom she owes allegiance: 'I shall take pain to follow your commandment, by the grace of our Lord, to serve Him well, and to do good service to Madame de Bours, to whom I am much bound for her good entreatment, and for the pains she taketh for me'.[41] Madame de Bours, for her part, figures herself as Mary Basset's mother; writing to her in 1540 to tell her of the birth of a child to her own daughter d'Agincourt, she addresses Mary as 'My well-beloved daughter and good friend' and signs herself 'Your mother and good friend'.[42] This affection emerges because it is Lady Lisle's due, both from her daughters and from her daughters' caregivers. Lady Lisle responds to Mary's concern about the expense of her education by advising her of her duty: 'serve God and please my lord and lady; and so doing I think the cost of you well employed'.[43] Mary obeys Madame de Bours because it is her mother's desire, while Madame de Bours's direction, for its part, enacts Lady Lisle's own wishes. Reporting how Mary received some velvet her mother sent her, Madame de Bours praises the girl's beauty, virtue, and humility, but adds that when Mary rejoiced in the luxurious fabric, Madame de Bours herself 'admonished her according to your commandment, and this you can be sure of in me, that I shall entreat her as if she were my daughter'.[44] Mother and foster mother together offer both love and discipline to Mary as they guide her in the ethics of aristocratic fashion. In the Lisle family, maternal guidance does not end when children live in other houses but is effected through other practical relationships.

This social form of maternal authority is socially recognizable. In July 1537, at a time when Queen Jane Seymour was considering taking on either Katherine or Anne Basset as a lady in waiting, John Husee wrote to Lady Lisle about the importance of her daughters' behavior. He insists she should

> exhort them to be sober, sad, wise and discreet and lowly above all things, and to be obedient, and governed and ruled by my Lady Rutland and my Lady Sussex, and Mrs. Margery and such others as be your ladyship's friends here; and to serve God and to be virtuous, for that is much regarded, to serve God well and to be sober of tongue. I trust your ladyship will not take this my meaning that I should presume to learn your ladyship what is to be done, neither that I do see any likelihood of ill appearance in them; but I do it only of pure and sincere zeal that I bear to them for your ladyship's sake, to the end I would they should so use themselves that it sound to your ladyship's honour and their worship, time coming. [...] But undoubtedly a good lesson at their departing, and good exhortations of your ladyship's mouth while they shall remain there, will profit them more than all others here, although they be their nigh kin. For your ladyship's words will stick nigh in their stomachs.[45]

For Husee, a family servant, maternal advice is authoritative and effective – more profitable than the advice of all the girls' other kin. Yet that advice can be issued through the governance of Lady Rutland, Lady Sussex, and Mrs Margery who as Lady Lisle's friends embody her parental care and authority. Anne Basset eventually becomes a Lady of the Queen's Privy Chamber, serving Jane Seymour, Anne of Cleves, Katherine Howard, and Katherine Parr, a position in which she is obliged to attempt to use her position to benefit the family.[46]

Lady Lisle seems to have a more tenuous hold on her right to advise her son, however. James Basset had been placed at the household of Monsieur le Gras, a wealthy Parisian merchant. Making himself available to the service of the Lisles, he tells Lady Lisle: 'I shall do all in my power for his welfare and the profit of your said son, sparing neither money nor my own pains therein for the honour of my lord the Deputy and yourself'.[47] Yet when in 1538 James Basset complained to his mother about his circumstances at the home of Pierre du Val, his schoolmaster, Lady Lisle's maternal authority and its limits become visible. Monsieur le Gras had arranged, at the desire of James Basset and with the permission of Lord and Lady Lisle, for James to enter the College of Navarre, a prestigious college of the University of Paris. Unhappy, the eleven- or twelve-year-old James wrote to his mother with grievances, and Lady Lisle asked John Bekinsau, an English scholar then studying in Paris, to investigate them.[48] Despite his position of service to the Lisles – he is also called upon to procure for Lady Lisle things such as bibles, canvas, 'crepyns' (nets for the hair), pearls, and fur – and despite his promise that 'Whatsoever your mind be, we will see him ordered accordingly',[49] he adopts the stance that a boy's studies should remove him from his mother's influence. He recommends that she leave her son to men's watchful, but more disciplined, eyes; she should 'not be moved with every word your son shall send you. [...] I pray you quiet your mind, and let Guyllyam le Gras and me alone for the time your son shall be here'.[50] Guillaume le Gras's response is more deferential, as he reports to Lady Lisle his conclusion that James merely wants a bed to himself.[51] Although Gras, too, is dismissive of the boy's concerns, he reassures Lady Lisle that his desire 'is to do you such pleasure and service as is possible, and to treat your said son as tenderly as I may'.[52] When mothers are apart from their children, the obligations of class underpin and enhance the ability of upper-class mothers to issue and implement their advice through others. In this instance, however, the pressure to create in James the self-governing masculinity admired in the scholar and courtier puts pressure on the authority conferred by Lady Lisle's class, even undermining her maternal authority. Yet for both sons and daughters, letters are one of the literary forms of early modern maternity, the means by which a mother is able to energize practical relations to care for children as she would.

Account books

Finally, clothes were a significant concern of sixteenth-century mothers, and a subject on which mothers issued advice. In the sixteenth century, children wore clothes much like their elders, girls from swaddling and boys from breeching. As Anne Buck contends, '[t]he dress of children shares the complex and changing pattern of adult dress but, provided by parents, it is edited by them for each stage of childhood', giving the clothes of children 'a pattern based on the process of growing up and parental ideas on upbringing'.[53] Some mothers explicitly explain their ideas. Elizabeth Joscelin considers attire in warning against pride, and Lady Lisle's letters testify to her constant supervision of her children's clothes, efforts according to Melanie Schuessler, that show distinctions based on age, sex, and the career and social position for which the child was being trained.[54] Lady Sidney signed the accounts kept by Thomas Marshall, a servant, of Philip's school expenses between 1565 and 1566, when Sir Henry Sidney was in Ireland.[55] Under his mother's supervision, young Philip Sidney acquired boot hose, black silk buttons and lace, a silk girdle, various coats, gloves, a crimson satin doublet, 'a shorte damaske gowne garded withe velvette and laid on withe lace', and a double taffeta coat, amongst other things – some of which relate to a journey to Oxford University during a visit by the Queen. Children needed to know how to dress, for as Sue Vincent contends, in early modern England, 'the way a person dressed had the potential power to determine placement in social ranking. It could also affect the expression of personality, and even produce forms of differently gendered behaviour. Clothing could define and delimit the body, and order its relationship with the body politic'.[56] Clothing also constructed subjectivity. As Ann Jones and Peter Stallybrass argue: '"[f]ashion" can be "*deeply* put on" or, in other words, that clothes permeate the wearer, fashioning him or her within'.[57] What a child wore was significant, inculcating both outward behavior and inwardness.

Account books do not discursively outline ideas of dress, but a youthful account book belonging to Anne Clifford, Countess of Dorset, Pembroke, and Montgomery (1590–1676), created between 1600 and 1602, when Clifford was a girl between the ages of ten and twelve, documents her mother's instruction in fashion. Inscribed by a servant, this account book is not a form of women's writing. Yet it is one of the textual practices of parenting. Valentin Groebner argues that early modern 'bookkeeping is identified with constant vigilance and mistrustful scrutiny, with the observation of one's own body and the bodies of others'.[58] The servant's book-keeping afforded parental oversight of the daughter's purchase of goods and taught Anne the necessity of accounting, a practice she would take seriously as a property owner. Even more, the itemized purchases are records of her mother's advice in the use of goods, particularly in the acquisition of clothes. As a record of consumption practices concerned with obligation, obedience, and social relations, as well as what the child specifically wears, this account book shares the interests of prose maternal advice. Throughout her life, Anne Clifford strongly credits the advice of her mother, Margaret (Russell) Clifford, Countess of Cumberland (1560–1616). Anne Clifford would commemorate her mother by constructing 'The Countess's Pillar' at the spot they took their last leave of each other near Brougham Castle,[59] and with a biography in *The Great Books of Record*, a three-volume family history which notes on each of its title pages that it was by her 'care and painfull industry' that the records were assembled. The family history particularly remembers Margaret Clifford's advice: 'She did with singular care and tendernese of affection educate and bring up her said most deare and only daughter, the Lady Anne Clifford, Seazening her youth with the gryndes of true religion and morall vertue, and all other qualities befitting her Birth'. Like Lady Lisle and others, she engages the help of a surrogate: her 'cheife agent' is the tutor she appoints, Samuel Daniel.[60] But in addition to this mediated instruction, the Countess of Cumberland offered instruction in what befits a lady's birth. This can be traced through the account book's record of the purchase of clothes.

Clifford's account book is in several different hands, although Clifford's signature appears, as do her initials, repeatedly approving entries. The book is addressed to the Earl of Cumberland, who is referred to throughout as 'your Lordship', as in 'at yor Lo[rdship's] appointment', 'paied to yor lo[rdship]', or 'geven by my La[dy] Anne as she went abrod wth yor lo[rdship] to my La[dy] of Warwicke'. Both the Countess and Lady Anne, in contrast, are almost always referred to as 'my Lady her mother', 'my La[dy] of Comberland', and, most often, 'my La[dy] Anne'. The earl surveys the activities of his wife and daughter, but the countess is more intimately involved with arranging Anne's expenditures. Indeed, the earl and countess spent most of their time apart after Lady Anne's birth, formally separating after 1601, with the result that Lady Anne probably saw little of her father in the period covered by the account book.[61] An inscription at the beginning explains that its purpose is to track the disbursement of the 'allowance w[hi]ch my La[dy] her mother alloweth her', and the countess further appears to reimburse her daughter for some of her expenses and to direct others, such as payments of alms and perquisites; Anne likewise must reimburse her mother. She is a child, for whom shuttlecocks, battledors, archery, dancing, and an education must be acquired, but she is also a lady, responsible for the accuracy of the accounts and the care of others, such as little Ned, who needs a new suit, and Dick the footboy, who needs shoes and stockings.[62] Much later, Clifford recalls that in 1603, the year after the account's end, she was much used to go to Court, for there was 'as much hope and expectation of me both for my person and my fortunes as of any other lady whatsoever'.[63] This hope is materialized in the clothes that she buys or is given.

The account book, like Lady Lisle's letters, suggests that maternal instruction can function within a network of a mother's social relationships. Clifford records in the 'Memoir of 1603' that she was 'much bound' then to her mother's sister, the Countess of Warwick, 'for her continual care and love of me',[64] and indeed, Anne (Russell) Dudley, the Countess of Warwick gave Anne Clifford several gifts – gold buttons, two tables (that is, table books), a diet drink, two rabbits, and money.[65] Mr and Mrs Elmes, her mother's aunt and uncle with whom the Countess of Cumberland lived until the age of seven because of the death of her own mother, also gave her money totaling more than five pounds, in addition to tokens.[66] She receives black silk from 'Elizabeth barrett my La Frances woman'; Lady Frances is possibly young Lady Frances Bourchier, Anne Clifford's cousin, friend and the daughter of Elizabeth (Russell) Bourchier, the Countess of Bath and another of Margaret Clifford's sisters.[67] Clifford remembers Lady Frances in her memoir, saying that it was during a visit after the death of Queen Elizabeth that began 'the greatness between us'.[68] A courier, 'my la[dy] of Essex man', brings a 'sleve of silke' on 9 June 1602, likely a gift of Frances (Walsingham) Devereaux, the Countess of Essex, and the wife of Robert Devereaux, the second Earl of Essex, who had been executed in February of 1601. The only reference to a Clifford kinswoman bringing clothes is an entry indicating that fifteen pence was paid to Lady Clifford's man 'for bringing of a scarf of pincke culler and white to my La[dy] Anne'; Lady Clifford might be Grissell (Hughes) Clifford, the wife of Frances Clifford, the Earl of Cumberland's brother and soon to be heir.[69] As gifts, Clifford's clothing is, in part, acquired within a milieu engendered by maternal status and relationships, such that her clothes are not just fashionable but objects of obligation and connection to a wider female culture of kinship and aristocratic relations.

Through gifts as well as purchases, supervised by her mother, Lady Anne Clifford acquires the fashions that can place her at Court: articles of clothing, such as farthingales, waists, girdles, bodices, coifs, whalebone corsets, and linens, such as ruffs, smocks, and cuffs; textiles to make into clothes, such as silk, taffeta, cobweb lawn, shag, and tiffany; the transportation and tailoring of items, such as a 'whyte ryban Sypres gowne' and 'Indean clothes'; many yards of ribbon and lace, some of which trimmed 'my Lady Anns vellet gown'; shoes, including 'shoes of silver and spangles'; and accessories, including masks, a fan, a rabato wire, and gold and pearl pendants.[70] Like Lady Lisle and Lady Sidney, the Countess of Cumberland oversees her daughter's clothing purchases. In this way, Lady Anne learns the codes of hygiene, femininity, and class – for she most often does not go shopping herself – that will allow her to fit in with the acquaintances of her mother and aunt – including the Queen – and eventually to marry an earl herself.

Conclusion

Although women in the sixteenth century did not typically see their advice printed, they did articulate in textual form their wishes for their children's education, spiritual development, moral conduct, and social status. Writing might be produced when the mother–child relationship was disrupted, when a child was sent to school or to another house, but mothers might also write texts that could be read within the household, like prayers and meditations, autobiographies, and family histories. Some of these forms were occasional, such as letters, and practical, such as account books, but others were written for posterity, to be remembered by children and grandchildren and used by Christians. Even in the sixteenth century, even before mother's advice began to be printed, it had an authoritative cultural register attentive to virtue, status, blood, and education. If maternal authority did not go unquestioned, even the most famous powerful, childless woman of the period used it. Elizabeth I identified herself as 'good mother of my Contreye', a metaphor Christine Coch argues allows the queen to 'arrogate [...] the mother's cultural authority to the throne'.[71] James VI of Scotland addressed her in 1585 as 'Madame and Mother' and signed himself as 'Your most loving and devoted brother and son', although his own mother was still alive.[72] And when Grace, Lady Mildmay recalled her father-in-law Sir Walter Mildmay in her autobiography, she praised his sage advice to the Queen: 'he found it the best means to persuade her subjects with arguments of reason and love and tender affection towards them as a nurse and mother of her commonwealth, rather than by harsh and distasteful speeches'.[73] For Lady Mildmay, as for Sir Walter, maternity can figure public policy. Sixteenth-century maternal advice existed and it compelled. If it was not printed and did not always follow established literary models for advice, it nevertheless survives in manuscript in prayer books, commonplace books, autobiographies, histories, letters, and account books.

Notes

1. B. Y. Fletcher and C. W. Sizemore, 'Elizabeth Grymeston's *Miscelanea, Meditations, Memoratives*: Introduction and Selected Text', *Library Chronicle* 1–2 (1981), 53–83 (p. 54); Catherine Gray, 'Feeding on the Seed of the Woman: Dorothy Leigh and the Figure of Maternal Dissent', *ELH* 68 (2001), 563–92 (pp. 567–68); Kristen Poole, '"The Fittest Closet for All Goodness": Authorial Strategies of Jacobean Mothers' Manuals', *SEL* 35 (1995), 69–88 (p. 69); Martha J. Craig, '"Write it upon the walles of your houses": Dorothy Leigh's *The Mothers Blessing*', in *Women's Life Writing*, ed. Linda S. Coleman (Bowling Green: Bowling Green State University Popular Press, 1997), pp. 191–208.

2. Valerie Wayne, 'Advice for Women from Mothers and Patriarchs', in *Women and Literature in Britain, 1500–1700*, ed. Helen Wilcox (Cambridge: Cambridge University Press, 1996), pp. 56–79; Wendy Wall, *The Imprint of Gender: Authorship and Publication in the English Renaissance* (Ithaca: Cornell University Press, 1993); Betty Travitsky, 'The New Mother of the English Renaissance', in *The Lost Tradition: Mothers and Daughters in Literature*, ed. Cathy N. Davidson and E. M. Broner (New York: Ungar, 1980), pp. 33–43; Theresa Feroli, '"Infelix Simulacrum": The Rewriting of Loss in Elizabeth Joscelin's *The Mother's Legacie*', *ELH* 61.1 (1994), 89–102.

3. Edith Snook, 'Dorothy Leigh's *The Mother's Blessing* and the Political Maternal Voice in Seventeenth-Century England', in *The Literary Mother: Essays on Representations of Maternity and Child Care*, ed. Susan Staub (Jefferson, NC: McFarland, 2007), pp. 161–84.

4. Elizabeth Grymeston, *Miscelanea, Meditations, Memoratives* (London: Felix Norton, 1604), sig. A3.

5. Lawrence Stone, *Family, Sex and Marriage in England, 1500–1800* (London: Weidenfeld & Nicolson, 1977), pp. 105–14. See also Keith Wrightson, *English Society, 1580–1680* (New Brunswick, NJ: Rutgers University Press, 1982), pp. 104–18 and Linda Pollock, *Forgotten Children: Parent–Child Relations from 1500–1900* (Cambridge: Cambridge University Press, 1983).

6. David Cressy, 'Kinship and Kin Interaction in Early Modern England', *Past and Present* 113 (1996), 38–69 (p. 49).

7. Barbara Hanawalt, 'Female Networks for Fostering Lady Lisle's Daughters', in *Medieval Mothering*, ed. John Carmi Parsons and Bonnie Wheeler (New York: Garland, 1999), pp. 239–58; Barbara J. Harris, 'Women and Politics in Tudor England', *The Historical Journal* 33.2 (1990), 259–81.

8. Pierre Bourdieu, *Outline of a Theory of Practice*, trans. Richard Nice (Cambridge: Cambridge University Press, 1977), p. 39.

9. John E. Booty, 'Communion and Commonweal: The Book of Common Prayer', in *The Godly Kingdom of Tudor England: Great Books of the English Reformation*, ed. John E. Booty (Wilton, CT: Morehouse-Barlow, 1981), pp. 139–216.

10. Timothy Rosendale, *Liturgy and Literature in the Making of Protestant England* (Cambridge: Cambridge University Press, 2007), pp. 39–40. See also Faye L. Kelly, *Prayer in Sixteenth-Century England* (Gainesville: University of Florida, 1966) and Ramie Targoff, *Common Prayer: The Language of Public Devotion in Early Modern England* (Chicago: University of Chicago Press, 2001).

11. David Siegenthaler, 'Religious Education for Citizenship: Primer and Catechism', in *The Godly Kingdom*, ed. Booty, pp. 219–49.

12. Helen C. White, *The Tudor Books of Private Devotion* (Madison: University of Wisconsin Press, 1951), p. 196.

13. Frances Neville, 'The Praiers Made by the Right Honourable Ladie Frances Aburgavennie', in *Monument of Matrones*, ed. Thomas Bentley, 7 books (London: Henry Denham, 1582), II, pp. 139–213 (p. 139); John N. King, 'Thomas Bentley's *Monument of Matrons*: The Earliest Anthology of English Women's Texts', in *Strong Voices, Weak History: Early Women Writers and Canons in England, France and Italy*, ed. Pamela Joseph Benson and Victoria Kirkham (Ann Arbor: University of Michigan Press, 2005), pp. 216–38.

14. Judith Maltby, *Prayer Book and People in Elizabethan and Early Stuart England* (Cambridge: Cambridge University Press, 1998), p. 3.

15. Targoff, *Common Prayer*, p. 60.
16. Neville, 'Praiers Made', pp. 174–75, 207–13.
17. Kenneth A. Charlton, 'Mothers as Educative Agents in Pre-Industrial England', *History of Education* 23 (1994), 129–56.
18. Max W. Thomas, 'Reading and Writing the Renaissance Commonplace Book: A Question of Authorship?' in *The Construction of Authorship: Textual Appropriation in Law and Literature*, ed. Martha Woodmansee and Peter Jaszi (Durham: Duke University Press, 1994), pp. 401–15.
19. Victoria E. Burke, 'Elizabeth Ashburnham Richardson's "Motherlie Endeauors" in Manuscript', *English Manuscript Studies, 1100–1700* 9 (2000), 98–113.
20. Washington DC, Folger Shakespeare Library, MS V.a.511 [Elizabeth (Beaumont) Ashburnam Richardson, *Instructions for my Children*], fol. 1ᵛ.
21. Margaret Hannay, 'Ashburnam Richardson's Meditation on the Countess of Pembroke's Discourse', *English Manuscript Studies, 1100–1700* 9 (2000), 114–28 (p. 114).
22. Ibid., p. 121.
23. Mary Thomas Crane, *Framing Authority: Sayings, Self, and Society in Sixteenth-Century England* (Princeton: Princeton University Press, 1993), p. 73.
24. Linda Pollock, *With Faith and Physic: The Life of a Tudor Gentlewoman Lady Grace Mildmay, 1552–1620* (London: Collins and Brown, 1993), p. 24. Subsequent references are cited parenthetically in the text. This edition alters the order of Mildmay's autobiographical recollections, changes the syntax and grammar, uses modern spelling, and does not reproduce marginal notations. While less complete and lacking most of the passages cited, Randall Martin's edition better conveys the manuscript's details. See 'The Autobiography of Grace, Lady Mildmay', *Renaissance and Reformation/Renaissance et Réforme* 18.1 (1994), 33–81.
25. Washington DC, Folger Shakespeare Library, MS V.a.180 [*Commonplace Book*].
26. Northamptonshire Record Office, MS M380 W(A) Misc. Vol. 35 [*Book of Advice to the Children*], fols. 2–3ᵛ.
27. Folger MS V.a.180, fols. 15ᵛ–18.
28. Folger MS V.a.180, fols. 20ᵛ–21; NRO MS M380 W(A) Misc. Vol. 35, fols. 13ᵛ, 1.
29. NRO MS M380 W(A) Misc. Vol. 35, fols. 22–34ᵛ; Gerald Morton, *A Biography of Mildmay Fane, Second Earl of Westmorland 1601–1666: The Unknown Cavalier*, Studies in British History, XXII (Lewiston: Edwin Mellen Press, 1990), pp. 19–20.
30. NRO MS M380 W(A) Misc. Vol. 35, fols. 20ᵛ–21; Folger MS V.a.180, fol. 13.
31. James Daybell, *Women Letter-Writers in Tudor England* (Oxford: Oxford University Press, 2006), pp. 179–82, 188–95; Raymond A. Anselment, 'Katherine Paston and Brilliana Harley: Maternal Letters and the Genre of Mother's Advice', *Studies in Philology* 101.4 (2004), 431–53.
32. For details about the uncertainty of Elizabeth Russell's birth date, see Chris Laoutaris's essay in this volume.
33. Lady Elizabeth Russell to Thomas Posthumous Hoby (c.1591), in 'The Letters of Lady Elizabeth Russell', ed. Elizabeth Farber (unpublished dissertation, Columbia University, 1977), pp. 113–14.
34. Lynne Magnusson, 'Bacon [Cooke], Anne, Lady Bacon (c.1528–1610)', *ODNB*.

35. Lady Anne Bacon to Nicholas Bacon (?1591), in *The Letters and the Life of Francis Bacon*, ed. James Spedding, 7 vols. (London: Longmans, 1890), I, pp. 112–15.
36. Lady Sidney's birth date is uncertain. She could have been born in 1530 or after the birth in 1532/3 of her brother Robert Dudley. See Simon Adams, 'Sidney, Mary, Lady Sidney (1530x35–1586)', in the *ODNB*.
37. Lady Mary Sidney and Sir Henry Sidney quoted in Malcolm William Wallace, *The Life of Sir Philip Sidney* (Cambridge: Cambridge University Press, 1915), pp. 68–70.
38. Lady Elizabeth Russell to William Cecil, 25 August 1584, in 'The Letters of Lady Elizabeth Russell', ed. Farber, pp. 100–09.
39. Muriel St Clare Byrne (ed.), *The Lisle Letters*, 6 vols. (Chicago: University of Chicago Press, 1981), III, pp. 134–35.
40. Anne Basset to Lady Lisle, 11 May 1534, in ibid., III, p. 143.
41. Mary Basset to Lady Lisle, 24 March 1536, in ibid., III, pp. 166–67.
42. Madame de Bours to Mary Basset, 5 January 1540, in ibid., VI, p. 11.
43. Lady Lisle to Mary Basset, after 16 April 1536, in ibid., III, p. 167.
44. Madame de Bours to Lady Lisle, 17 November 1536, in ibid., III, p. 173.
45. John Husee to Lady Lisle, 17 July 1537, in ibid., IV, pp. 151–52.
46. Byrne, in ibid., IV, pp. 191–92.
47. Guillaume le Gras to Lady Lisle, 15 March 1537, in ibid., IV, p. 471.
48. Ibid., III, pp. 112–13; Andrew A. Chibi, 'Bekinsau, John (1499/1500–1559)', in the *ODNB*.
49. John Bekynsaw to Lady Lisle, 8 April 1535, in Byrne, *The Lisle Letters*, III, p. 112.
50. John Bekynsaw to Lady Lisle, 4 March 1538, in ibid., IV, p. 498.
51. Guillaume le Gras to Lady Lisle, 17 March 1538, in ibid., IV, p. 501.
52. Guillaume le Gras to Lady Lisle, 17 March 1538, in ibid., IV, pp. 507–08.
53. Anne Buck, *Clothes and the Child: A Handbook of Children's Dress in England, 1500–1900* (New York: Holmes & Meier, 1996), pp. 150, 13.
54. Melanie Schuessler, '"She Hath Over Grown All that Ever She Hath": Children's Clothes in the Lisle Letters, 1533–1540', *Medieval Clothing and Textiles* 3 (2007), 181–200.
55. Wallace, *Life of Sir Philip Sidney*, p. 67 and Appendix 1.
56. Sue Vincent, 'To Fashion a Self: Dressing in Seventeenth-Century England', *Fashion Theory* 3.2 (1999), 197–218 (p. 205).
57. Ann Rosalind Jones and Peter Stallybrass, *Renaissance Clothing and the Materials of Memory* (Cambridge: Cambridge University Press, 2000), p. 2.
58. Valentin Groebner, 'Inside Out: Clothes, Dissimulation, and the Arts of Accounting in the Autobiography of Matthaus Schwartz', *Representations* 66 (1999), 100–21 (p. 114).
59. George C. Williamson, *Lady Anne Clifford, Countess of Dorset, Pembroke, and Montgomery 1590–1627: Her Life, Letters, and Work* (Kendal: Titus Wilson, 1922), pp. 388–89.
60. Cumbria Records Office, Kendal, WD/Hoth/A988/10 [*Great Books of Record, c.1649–1652*], in *The Papers of Lady Anne Clifford, 1590–1676*, vol. III (East Ardsley, UK: Microform Academic Publishers, 1999), p. 164.
61. Richard T. Spence, *Lady Anne Clifford, Countess of Pembroke, Dorset and Montgomery (1590–1676)* (Phoenix Mill: Sutton, 1997), pp. 2–3.

62. New Haven, Beinecke Library, Osborn MS B27 [*Account Book 1600–1602*], fols. 3, 27, 27ᵛ, 29ᵛ, 33, 10ᵛ, 21ᵛ.

63. Anne Clifford, 'Memoir of 1603', in *The Memoir of 1603 and The Diary of 1616–1619*, ed. Katherine O. Acheson (Peterborough: Broadview, 2007), p. 43.

64. Ibid.

65. Osborn MS B27, fols. 12, 5, 7.

66. Osborn MS B27, fols. 5, 5ᵛ, 6ᵛ, 7, 8, 10; Williamson, *Lady Anne Clifford*, pp. 36, 66.

67. Osborn MS B27, fol. 12ᵛ; Williamson, *Lady Anne Clifford*, pp. 69, 70, 73, 85, 154.

68. Clifford, 'Memoir of 1603', p. 49.

69. Osborn MS B27, fol. 29ᵛ.

70. Osborn MS B27, fols. 32, 12ᵛ, 14, 25.

71. Christine Coch, '"Mother of my Contreye": Elizabeth I and Tudor Constructions of Motherhood', *ELR* 26.3 (1996), 423–50 (p. 424).

72. James to Elizabeth, *c.*13 July 1585 and 19 August 1585, in *Elizabeth I: Collected Works*, ed. Leah S. Marcus, Janel Mueller, and Mary Beth Rose (Chicago and London: University of Chicago Press, 2000), pp. 263, 265–66.

73. Pollock, *With Faith and Physick*, p. 31.

6
Letters

Lynne Magnusson

On reading Cicero's newly discovered letters to Atticus, Petrarch exclaimed with pleasure and excitement, 'as I read I seemed to hear your bodily voice, O Marcus Tullius, saying many things, [...] ranging through many phases of thought and feeling'. Similarly, on reading Dorothy Osborne's mid-seventeenth-century letters, Virginia Woolf remarked, 'They make us feel that we have our seat in the depths of Dorothy's mind, at the heart of the pageant': 'we hear men and women talking over the fire'. Sixteenth-century English letters, whether men's or women's, rarely create that sense of an immediate connection to a past world or of an open doorway either into hearts and minds or through which we catch everyday conversation. Woolf claimed that 'in English literature we have to wait till the sixteenth century is over and the seventeenth well on its way before the bare landscape becomes full of stir and quiver and we can fill in the spaces between the great books with the voices of people talking'.[1] Woolf is not alone in suggesting a curious belatedness in England in the appearance of the kind of letters we readily recognize as 'familiar', letters in which we can imagine hearing 'the voices of people talking'. John Donne, writing around 1604 about important models for letter-writing, mentioned classical, biblical, Jesuit, and patristic sources, but nothing in English. He was clearly aware of a disparity between contemporary Continental developments in vernacular letter-writing and English practice, for he commented pointedly on Michel de Montaigne's claim that 'he hath seen (as I remember) 400 volumes of Italian letters'. No one's collected letters had been printed in English, though by this time even printed collections of women's letters were circulating in Italy.[2]

This is all the more surprising given the fact that education of the time apparently placed an insistent focus on achieving just such effects in letters. As their most basic writing practice, grammar-school boys and a few humanist-educated gentlewomen were trained to think of the letter as 'a conversation between two absent persons'.[3] They were set to imitate in Latin Cicero's epistolary ease and fluency and instructed in the rhetorical strategies Cicero used to personalize written interaction and create immediacy. The evident will of humanist educators to effect a kind of 'translatio epistolae', to appropriate the 'bodily voices' heard in classical letters and transfer this articulacy and directness into English contexts, suggests that the sixteenth century was a crucially important period in the formation of English letters. Nonetheless, while this insistent effort to cultivate the casual ease of Latin letters and the theorizing of the rhetoric of familiarity in the works of educational thinkers like Erasmus and Vives had some profound effects one can trace in the English letter-writing of the sixteenth century, it did not produce the transformation or rebirth that might have been expected. Too many things ran interference, tangling English letter-writers in contradictions. First, directness and succinctness in written expression seemed to come less easily in Early Modern English than in classical Latin: writers had to cope with the unstandardized spelling and with graceless syntactic ligatures and cumbersome forms of subordination. Second, the inherited paradigms for English letters – in contrast to the admired Ciceronian paradigm – were heavily formulaic and repetitive; they foregrounded ostentatious markers of status and performances of deference. The hierarchical social order and monarchic government of the sixteenth century encouraged the retention and even elaboration of complicated deference forms, and, in courtly circles and many other contexts, English imitation of classical familiarity could very easily be received as indecorous or even dangerous behavior. Thus, we might expect informal familiarity and casual ease of conversation-like written style to be a 'bottom-up' development, but, paradoxically, it was introduced into the discussion of letters as an elite ideal of humanist education. As such, not only did it represent a form of linguistic capital at odds with elite courtly behavior, but, like Latin learning, it was gendered male. Given women's limited access even to English literacy and fluency in writing – David Cressy estimates that as few as 1 per cent of Englishwomen could sign their names in 1500, rising to 5 per cent by the accession of Queen Elizabeth I, and to 10 per cent by about the 1640s[4] – this contradictory situation affected the production and reception of women's letters in complicated and interesting ways.

It was not just access to education and literacy that posed restrictions on women's letter-writing. In today's world of instant messaging, it is hard to imagine the cumbersome conditions and laborious business of sixteenth-century letter-writing: how, for example, one had to keep a pen knife at the ready to pare (and repair) the nib of one's goose-feather pen; sand or other absorbent material to blot wet ink; candles for light; seal and sealing wax to close up one's folded and addressed sheet of paper. One needed the wherewithal to purchase expensive paper; ink was more often messily prepared in one's own household. Furthermore, because there was no post office, the delivery of a letter meant making demands on a servant or traveling acquaintance as messenger, or, in the case of a few major routes between London and provincial towns, paying (or expecting the recipient to pay) a carrier of goods for bearing the letter.[5]

Still, in terms of the actual numbers of letters written and preserved, in relation to women's writing we can quarrel with Woolf's metaphor for the sixteenth century as a bare landscape without the relief of epistolary shrubbery. James Daybell's invaluable survey turned up over 3,000 extant manuscript letters produced by 650 different women between 1540 and 1603.[6] Compared to the written texts extant by women of this period in all other genres, this is an impressive figure, and strongly suggests that, whether we seek an understanding of women's relation to writing, of the rhetoric of their social relations, or – in the case of highly distinctive letter-writers like Anne Cooke Bacon[7] – of their literary or semi-literary performances, letters of the period should be a chief resource. On the whole, however, Daybell's findings do still lend some support to Woolf's perception, for they suggest that while the number of women's letters gradually increase over much of the sixteenth century, with a sort of 'explosion'[8] in the last three decades and most markedly in the 1590s, the real explosion comes in the seventeenth century, when they become too numerous for rough counting to be practical. Daybell's study excepted, generalizations about early modern women's letters have almost always relied heavily on seventeenth-century examples, and this has had the effect of blurring important distinctions, obscuring our understanding of the jagged and slow development of the genre, and making it difficult to recognize either highly conventional epistolary scripts or performances of particular individuality or accomplishment.

This essay employs two developed case studies and then two briefer samplings in an effort to outline the field and to highlight both normative and distinctive instances of women's epistolary activity in sixteenth-century England. Rather than proceeding in chronological order, I consider women writers belonging to the different social groups most likely to engage in correspondence in this period, including the merchant and professional classes, on the one hand, and the nobility and gentry, on the other. The educational backgrounds or literacy levels vary considerably, from technically illiterate to humanist-educated in Latin and other languages. In the developed case studies of Mary Herrick and Katherine Bertie, I attend to the many diverse elements shaping the contexts of production and reception, to the writer's and other participants' relation to the technology and material culture of letters, to the written text as a nexus of imitation and creativity, to the question of how representative the letters might be, and to the role of gender. One important theme that emerges in these stories is the interplay between skill levels and the controlling power of reception. The two further examples – touching on letters by Mary Sidney Herbert and Juliann Penn – focus on specific struggles between skill and reception, one related to courtly suitors' letters, the other to business letters. Given some of the initial barriers already outlined to our effective hearing of these textualized or materialized voices, these minds 'set down in writing', reading to discern what makes women's letters of the period interesting requires some new forms of attention.

'I wolde have yow sende me worde': Mary Herrick and communal speech acts

The wide range of women's epistolary activity in the period, despite low literacy levels, challenges us to extend the boundaries of what we might mean by women's writing. Consider the case of a Leicestershire mother, Mary Herrick, communicating with her absent son. The boy, William Herrick, had left his large family of ironmongers and shopkeepers to apprentice as a goldsmith to his elder brother Nicholas in London. In 1578, the sixteen-year-old received from Leicester a letter addressed 'To hir lovinge sonne William heryck in London dwellyng with nicolas heryek goldsmith at the syne of the grasshopper in chepeside':

> William, with my hartye commendations and glade to heare of youre good health &c. And this is to geue yow thankes for my povnde garnyte [pomegranate]; and red heayringe yow sent me. willyng yow to geue my daughter hawse thankes for the povnde garnyte, and box of marmalette that she sent me. Furthermore, I have sente yow a payre off knyte hose, and a payre of knyte gersy gloues, I wolde have yow sende me worde howe the[y] serve yowe; for yf the glovffes be to littell for yow, yow sholde geue them to one of youre brother hawesses children, and I wolde sende yow a nother payre. Also I wolde have yow sende me worde yff yow can whither youre sister Lechworth will

come to Lecester betwene this and crismas or no. Thus I leaue for this tyme praying to god to blesse yow, and kepe yow allwayes in his feayre and knowledge: by youre lovinge mother to hir power

Mary Erycke

I praye yow make my commendations to my Sonne hanse and his wyfe, and to my sonne Nicolas Herycke with mary Ableson.[9]

On the back of the single small piece of paper that comprises the unfolded letter, sparing of paper at only six by eight inches, William endorsed it, 'my mothers Leter to me'. He thus identified it as the kind of letter with which we are most familiar: a message written and sent by one person, the letter's 'I', to another, the letter's 'you' – the two persons we regularly associate with correspondence. The distinctive way in which the young man endorses this letter seems to signal how he treasured this letter, the only one 'by' his mother in the vast family correspondence William preserved from the day he left behind his family of ironmongers in Leicester until his death. On this rare occasion, Mary, now a woman in her sixties and the mother of twelve children, seems to have singled out him, her eleventh-born child and youngest son, as the recipient of this special physical token of her affection, sending him not just her utilitarian gift of stockings and gloves, but her own words, 'by your lovinge mother', a textual register of the reciprocity and love between them. Not only does the exchange of 'I' and 'you' in the language testify to a reciprocal loving bond, but the physical letter evokes the sense of an immediate moment – one that her son can, by rereading, reawaken and relive – of special exchange between her and him. Nothing very special, one might think, for almost all letters deploy second-person singular address – and yet this was by no means the regular way that Mary Herrick sent her words to her distant son. The situation is more complex than it at first appears.

If we turn for a moment to a letter of 27 February 1583/4, signed only by William's father, the ironmonger 'John Eyrik' [Herrick], we find its messages or speech acts repeatedly constructed as those of a plural sender, 'your mother and mee'.[10] Addressed to William as the single addressee, the letter nonetheless incorporates messages to a number of older family members who had previously migrated to London: 'I pray yowe have your mother and mee hartely come[n]dyd vnto your m[aster] and mystris And to your brother haues and his wiffe and to Dorothe hawsse. And to your brother holden & his wiffe. and shew them [...].' If we page further through the correspondence, we find, even more frequently, letters signed by William's adolescent brothers Thomas or John, both of them ironmonger's apprentices, communicating Mary Herrick's messages and conflating their own speech acts with speech acts they designate as hers: 'my mother gives yow thankes' or 'my mother wils yow to take it'.[11] Thus, not only do we find ample evidence of Mary's participation in the prolific correspondence penned and signed by male family members, but virtually all the letters between Leicester and London, despite their use of the 'I'/'you' default for personal address, serve as clearing houses for messages to and from various family members, including both women and men.[12] Sometimes it is clear that this function is most important in relation to the particular girls and women who (one infers) cannot pen their own letters, as where the sisters Christian and Mary communicate reciprocally within the letters of their brothers John and William: 'Christian giues yow thankes allso for sending hir word what mari Ablesones mind wear.'[13] This multi-directional family conversation is also incorporated into mother Mary's own personal letter to William.

In this inclusive and solidarity-building communal messaging, we get a sense of one key type of collaborative discourse or social networking featured in the Herrick family letters. Turning back to William's letter from his mother, we can now identify a second communal aspect in the family letter-writing, when we see that the letter unequivocally identified by William as his mother's letter is very likely not in her own handwriting. A comparison with other letters in the correspondence suggests the likelihood that Mary's letter was penned for her by her eighth child, Thomas. Not only the strong resemblance of the handwriting and the clear implication in other letters that Mary cannot write but also Thomas's characteristic habit of abbreviating the standard opening commendation ('youre good health &c') points to a collaboration between the son's pen and the mother's voice.[14] Evidently, for William, his knowledge that his mother did not pen (and most likely did not sign) her letter to him does not nullify his prizing of it as her special gift or missive to him.

Furthermore, there is a third, important sense in which we need to recognize the important role of social invention or communal activity in the production of Mary Herrick's letter. Literary scholars have identified the sixteenth century in England as, above all, an 'era of imitation', with education dominated by the self-conscious theory and practice of classical imitation.[15] English letters of the day are equally the products of imitation, although, for this period, they generally imitate what remain for us virtually invisible models, constructed on rules that do not correspond to those being formulated by humanist scholars for Latin letters and taught to boys in grammar schools. Neither are the formulaic social scripts employed in the first-generation Herrick family letters accurately codified in the English manuals that are just around this time beginning to appear, even though most of their elements (the opening commendation, the health inquiry, the accumulative structure, the sending of 'word') are to be found in only slightly modified form in letters from over a century earlier (for example, in the Paston letters).[16] It will come as no surprise that Mary's simple personal letter to William is almost entirely formulaic as are many other Herrick family letters sent from Leicester to London. Indeed, only if we recognize the background of imitation can we recognize how strongly foregrounded one unusual personalizing element might have seemed: Mary's use of her son's proper name, William, standing alone as her opening greeting. Sixteenth-century English letters characteristically employ a relational term of address such as 'Sir', 'Dearly beloved mother', or 'My good child', and they rarely use a proper name at all. We cannot be certain if the simple contrivance of naming 'William' at the start of the one conventional letter she sent him was Mary's design or the contribution of her scribe, since other family members do at times incorporate the proper name into phrases of greeting. Nonetheless, it adds to the personalization and seeming directness of this special loving message to her absent son.

If Mary Herrick could not readily pen a letter and usually sent and received 'word' through embedded exchanges in the correspondence of her husband or sons, it is interesting to find that she was nonetheless the recipient of letters addressed specifically to her. This is apparent, for example, in a letter by her son John to William concerning correspondence between his 'aunt gilbard' and his mother:

> another cawse of my writing vnto yow is to will yow when yow writ again to send mee word whether yow recevid by Thomas chetle a letter for my [a]unt gilbard I sent yow a letter the same time and with it I sent on for her [...] now my aunt gilbard hath sent a letter for my mother. and shee writs that shee marvils why my mother doth not send her word how she doth. by her letters we perceve she hath not recevid that letter which I writ vnto her.[17]

The implication here seems to be that, in response to a letter by Aunt Gilbard addressed to his mother, John himself had penned the letter back on his mother's behalf, a letter he now fears may have gone undelivered. We cannot tell whether or not Mary might have been able to 'read' letters Aunt Gilbard addressed to her, for skills in reading and writing were acquired separately, and readers with basic skills could likely have read some printed or handwritten scripts but not others. What is clear is that Mary, a Leicester townswoman celebrated on a marble funerary monument when she died in 1611 at the age of ninety-seven as having 142 direct descendants,[18] took an active part in family correspondence, using letters effectively to sustain connections and bonds of affection among her dispersed family members – even though only one conventional letter 'by' her survives in the large collection of Herrick family papers and it seems almost certain that she could not pen letters. Furthermore, however women's 'rude' writing or marginal literacy may have been derogated in many contexts in the early modern period, within this godly and loving family, Mary's epistolary communications were treated with respect, as matters of importance and even as objects of longing. Ironically, in the larger Herrick family correspondence, it is not Mary's epistolary missive that is the object of a derogatory comment by a son but instead a letter by her well-educated daughter-in-law, Lady Herrick, a generation later. William Jr, as a newly arrived Oxford student, demonstrates how gendered distinction-making goes hand in hand with his Latin education when he comments, 'Although my mother's English was well enough, yet her good counsell was very much better.'[19]

If Mary Herrick's example demonstrates that illiteracy (or marginal literacy) was no necessary barrier to active engagement with correspondence, women's education and generally low rate of literacy, together with social and occupational status, were, nonetheless, limiting factors, especially, as James Daybell has suggested, to the development of letters as the vehicle for private interchanges on sensitive topics.[20] As we have seen, in the Herrick family correspondence, separated family members who cannot write have to 'send word' or tell what their 'minds' are on important matters in what are essentially open letters penned by other people and subject to the haphazard delivery practices of acquaintances or town carriers. Even Mary's son, the ironmonger's apprentice and frequent letter-writer John, wanting to discuss his vocational and marital choices with his brother in London, repeatedly expresses frustration with the limitations of letters: 'I wish my self with yow', he writes, 'that I might spack with yow mouth to mouth.'[21]

Katherine Bertie, Duchess of Suffolk: a noblewoman's rhetoric of friendship

Let us turn now to a very different context of letter-writing in the reign of Edward VI in which a young woman in her late twenties and early thirties sustained a remarkable correspondence and succeeded in treating sensitive and confidential matters with stylistic ease and lively wit. Twenty-two letters written by Katherine Bertie (née Willoughby), Duchess of Suffolk, to her friend William Cecil survive from 1549 to 1552, the tense period when they were both close and involved observers of Edward Seymour, Duke of Somerset's fall from grace as Lord Protector, and the correspondence picks up again when the duchess, a Marian exile, returns on Queen Elizabeth's accession. If casual ease of style in letters and a relaxed language of friendship should be regarded not as givens but as rhetorical achievements in this period, her letters deserve special attention. None of them begins with conventional formulae. Brushing aside the usual commendatory greetings and inquiries after health, her letter openings – as if *in medias res* – are refreshingly direct:

> By the late coming of this buck to you, you shall perceive that wild things be not ready at commandment. [be the latte commeng of thes booke to you / you shal persave that wyld thinges be not rede at commandment]

> My good Cecil, But shall I call you so still, now you be master secretary? Choose you if you will not have it so, for till you deny it I will call you so. [My good cyssel / but shale I call you so stell nowe you be master secretare / showes you if you wyll not have it so for tel you deny it I wole call you so]

> I have so wearied myself with the letters that I have written at this session to my Lord's Grace and to my Lady [the Duke and Duchess of Somerset] that there is not so much as one line to be spared for Cecil.

> On horseback going to Master Bucer I received your letters, at the reading of which methought I was mounted a foot higher than before. But I perceive you would but convey me to well doing and to become such a one as you paint me.

> I did never mistrust that you should always live by your change, but at length change for the best and come to a good market.[22]

Katherine's letters are notable for giving voice to very direct opinions, especially when she notes Cecil's willingness to bend and adapt his religion and politics for survival in unfavorable circumstances, but she has the rhetorical finesse to succeed at once in criticizing and sustaining friendship. One of the most forceful examples occurs in the letter of

4 March 1559 she sends from Crossen in Poland at the end of her period of exile, when she accuses him of back-pedaling on religious reform: 'Wherefore I am forced to say with the prophet Elie, how long halt ye between two opinions?' Her long critique concludes with an eloquently articulated reminder of her former trust that Cecil would hear and appreciate 'what I think': 'Thus write I after my old manner, which if I persuade you, take it as thankfully and friendly as I mean it; then I will say to you as my father Latimer was wont to say to me, I will be bold to write to you another time as I hear and what I think; and if not I shall hold my peace and pray God amend it to Him.' This letter she closes not with her usual 'Your assured friend' but with 'So far yours as you are God's'.[23] Clearly, the 'old manner' between them had been such that Cecil not only tolerated but actively sought out the collaborative assistance of her good sense and persuasive force. When his own brief imprisonment as a supporter of Protector Somerset had ended in early 1550, and his still imprisoned former master's fate was as yet undetermined, Cecil had clearly pressed the duchess to return to Court from Grimsthorpe and mediate between Somerset and the Council. Her letter of response demonstrates her complex apprehension of the situation and her ability to use the written letter not just to state bold opinions but also to share ambivalence and explore mental indecision:

The matter between the counsel and my lord, and the state of his cause, seemeth by your letter not much to differ from that which before I heard, but of my greatest fear you have quieted me; for I did never fear so much that wicked tongues should do him harm, in sowing so deep suspects in the council's hearts against my lord, but that God would easily pull them out, whilst they were but only surmises of malice, and no occasion given by any new change in him. Wherefore I trust my journey shall be less needful, for the great good that I could have done for my lord was to have offered him my counsel, in case he had been any thing impatient at their unkind dealings: and, to have wrought so much with him, if need had been, I thought my power somewhat [...]. Howbeit, if I could be any ways persuaded that I might do my lord any good, I would most gladly put myself in any aventure for it: but alas! if I come I am not able to do for him that I would, and as unable to do that which we stuck so long on, then shall I not only do him no good but rather harm, and that I would be most sorry for. Wherefore, in his, I will well bethink me how I can master that froward and crooked mind of mine, before I come, and, if I can bring that to pass, then will I not fail with speed to accomplish your desire and mine own, and till then I shall lament your wrong, and as truly purge you from such slanders, when time shall serve me for it, if the parties [s]hall please to credit me. And so, when I had written my letter, came a letter from a friend of mine, who declared very good news, and great hope of my lord of Somerset's being called to the council very shortly; wherefore I am now the rather determined to stay my coming till their goodness be past, lest, otherwise, if I come up whilst it is moving, they think I come to take away their thanks. I think it were well done to let every honest man have his due, and, therefore, check thanks, but they must not, at this time, be uttered, but thought and laid up till time seemeth better to declare them.[24]

In this letter, as elsewhere, the duchess reflects on the psychology of influence among networks of friends and political allies, calculating when her direct methods will work for persuasion and when others are best left to follow their own dispositions. Not only, then, is writing a means by which the duchess can 'speak' her mind to a friend at a distance; the written articulations of letters to Cecil are also, on the one hand, a means by which she explores and comes to know her own mind and, on the other hand, exercises in rhetorically sophisticated persuasion. One of her most strongly held views, bold for her time and class, is that people – including women and children – should have the opportunity to form their own opinions on matters closely affecting them, like marriage, and make their own choices based on informed understanding. This is a position she elaborates in a long and well-considered letter explaining why she rejects a proposal put forward by the dukes of Northumberland and Somerset to wed her son, the fifteen-year-old Henry Duke of Suffolk, to one of Somerset's daughters (Lady Anne, the eldest, was twelve), since the plan would mean 'that by our power they lost their free choice'.[25]

In Katherine Bertie's letters to Cecil written during Edward's reign, we come close to what Woolf sought and Erasmus theorized – the apparent spontaneity of one-to-one conversation with an absent friend. What – we need to ask – are the conditions in which this apparent spontaneity, this rare stir like 'voices of people talking', arose? One key consideration is the duchess's high rank. In a deference culture, it would have been unthinkable for most women to address a man of Cecil's rising importance with Katherine's directness. Her superior social station gave her an unparalleled degree of latitude in finding a language in which to build up her friendship. Without status, casual ease of address would not have been an option.

Her status also affected the material circumstances of her writing. Whether Katherine wrote to her friend, 'good master Cecil', from her Lincolnshire estate of Grimsthorpe or from another of her residences, she, like Mary Herrick, must usually have been surrounded by other people, for, after her first husband, Charles Brandon, Duke of Suffolk died in 1545, she was licensed to retain forty persons in her livery in addition to her large staff of household servants.[26] When we read her letters of seemingly private friendship and counsel, it is helpful to think of the figurative image she inspired Hugh Latimer, her religious advisor and friend, to paint of Faith as a duchess: 'This faith is a great state, a lady, a duchess, a great woman; and she hath ever a great company and train about her as a noble estate ought to have [...] as the gentleman usher goeth before her, [her] train [...] cometh behind.'[27] It is obvious that the duchess, like other noblewomen, was rarely alone and had access to convenient scribes when she required them. When she received and responded to the letter from Cecil 'on horseback', a letter he sent during the period of imprisonment he suffered as a supporter and employee of Edward Seymour, it is clear that she dictated her lively answer, making the exigencies of her journey the excuse 'why I write not with mine own hand'.[28] However, most of Katherine's letters to Cecil are in her own handwriting, a well-developed version of early Tudor secretary hand. This apparently includes the letter she claimed to write 'at six o'clock in the morning, and, like a sluggard, in my bed'.[29] Even then, her more confidential letter-writing in her own hand is not likely to have been an entirely solitary pursuit: the apparatus of letter-writing – the goose quill, ink bottle, large sheets of paper, pen knife, sand, and sealing wax – were messy and complicated, and some part of the duchess's 'great company' must have been required to assist with managing her writing box and other cumbersome paraphernalia in bed. Whereas the two friends clearly considered writing in one's own hand a requisite to confidentiality, nonetheless, the duchess's command of human resources contributed to the security of their correspondence: for example, she rarely provided a delivery 'address' in the usual manner in her superscriptions to Cecil, since her letters were conveyed by her personal messengers, directly instructed on where to take them, and were not likely to pass, haphazardly, from hand to hand.

If property, manpower, and rank are a part of the context of Katherine's letter-writing, so too is education. While we have to piece together the picture of her early training, there is strong evidence of her later commitment to the spread of education and especially vernacular literacy. Born in 1519, the daughter of a well-educated Spanish lady-in-waiting to Katherine of Aragon and an English lord, her father's death in 1526 left her a wealthy heir, and her wardship was purchased at great expense by King Henry VIII's brother-in-law, Charles Brandon, Duke of Suffolk.[30] When she moved to his country estate at Westhorpe, her education is thought to have been supervised by the duke's third wife, Mary, the French dowager queen. It is difficult to tell to what extent her training emphasized the Latin-based humanist education afforded the King's daughters and other noblewomen of this time and to what extent it accented feminine attainments suitable to Court life. Katherine's background and later connections nonetheless suggest an acquaintance with foreign languages, and the surviving evidence of her English correspondence demonstrates not just her attainment of fluent penmanship and articulate command of English expression but that she felt at home in writing and that it became for her a regular activity, part of her self-definition. When her stepmother died in 1533, the forty-nine-year-old Duke of Suffolk made the fourteen-year-old girl his wife and one of the first peeresses of the realm, and the remarkable young woman demonstrated the ability to make both privileged and challenging life experiences her tutor. Quickly proving herself a charming and influential courtier, she was profoundly influenced by the sermons of Hugh Latimer and, situating herself amidst a network of evangelical Protestant friends and allies, including Katherine Parr's circle, the Seymours, and the Cecils, developed over the next decade into a powerful exponent of religious reform. Religion and the spread of vernacular literacy were, for her and for Parr, intricately connected, for they regarded the capacity to read scripture as essential for all communicants.[31] She worked actively together with Cecil after Henry VIII's death to persuade the Queen to publish her *Lamentacion of a Sinner* in 1547, advocating access to scripture. The duchess founded a grammar school on her family's chantry lands at Spilsby,[32] and she devoted intense energy to the education of her own children, first, until their tragic death while Cambridge students, the two sons and heirs to Charles Brandon and, later, her daughter and son by a later marriage to her gentleman usher, Richard Bertie. Indeed, when Henry Duke of Suffolk and his brother Charles were studying at Cambridge with their tutor Thomas Wilson, she moved to Kingston to be near them and played a role herself in university life, befriending and aiding Martin Bucer, the German theologian who arrived in 1549 in order to take up the regius professorship of divinity and who, at his death in 1551, bequeathed her half of his books.[33] Perhaps it was John Harington, the first (in 1550) to translate the book that articulated the philosophy of friendship informing Latin familiar letters of the period, Cicero's *De amicitia*, who best characterized the duchess's relation to humanist classical learning. Dedicating to her the translation he undertook while imprisoned in the Tower as a supporter of Thomas Seymour, and claiming that her practice of friendship embodied its ideals, he commented: 'This did I not to teach you, but to let you see in learnyng ancient, that you haue by nature vsed.'[34] What he claimed of the quality of her friendship seems also true of her exceptional ability to bring the freshness and immediacy of the familiar epistolary style practiced in Latin by humanist scholars imitating Cicero to life in her English letters.

Virginia Woolf famously proposed that, in order to write, what a woman required was a room of her own. With the Duchess of Suffolk – together with her obvious intelligence – rank, property, prerogative, education, and evangelical piety all contributed to the context that motivated and sustained her high functioning, in this genre of prose letters, as a writing woman. In discussing Mary Herrick's epistolary activity, I have also emphasized the importance of appreciative reception, and this indeed plays an important role at this opposite end of the social and literacy scale. The continuous stream of letters from 1549 to 1552 testifies that the youthful Cecil respected and depended upon the supportive correspondence of the duchess, and there is also evidence that her letters received a favorable and attentive reading among her larger network of important friends and well-placed allies. Patrick Collinson coined the term 'monarchical republic' to characterize the more distributed forms of power coming into play as sixteenth-century England witnessed the reign, first, of a child king and then of three women. Both the influence of the Parr circle on the evolution of English Protestantism and the prominence of various educated gentlewomen in Edward's reign may have been factors contributing to Katherine's confidence that her discourse and counsel could have impact. In his sociolinguistic analysis, Pierre Bourdieu has argued that discourse production is affected by anticipated discourse reception, based on a 'linguistic habitus' or long-term reception history yielding a 'practical expectation [...] of receiving a high or low price for one's discourse'.[35] Katherine Duchess of Suffolk's remarkable facility and inventiveness with letters at mid-century, I would argue, is sustained to an important degree not just by her education and rank but also by a situation of positive reception which is, on the whole, uncharacteristic of women's experience in the early modern period.

Shifting negative reception in the Elizabethan suitor's letter: Mary Sidney Herbert

If confidence about reception is an important part of the context of Katherine Bertie's inventive letters of friendship, one prevalent genre of Elizabethan letters is premised upon an expectation of delayed or even entirely withheld approval: that is, the genre that played a key role in upholding the Elizabethan culture of mediation – the suitor's letter. The petitioning letter is a type that Bertie seems always to have written with reluctance. She is one of only a few women who is sometimes casual enough to make a joke about this kind of letter even when she does feel obliged to undertake the necessary performance of deference and abjection: 'And so I ende my long begging letter', she writes in one case to Cecil in 1567, 'but iff you canne helpe us to these alms, we wol never beg no more; but worke for our lyving, lyke honest poor folke: so as I truste, by God's helpe, the Queene shall have cause to lyke well of us.'[36] Most of her surviving petitioning letters belong to Queen Elizabeth's reign, when she (like many strong-minded women) found herself situated in a more marginal relation to the centers of power than in the period of her youthful ascendancy in Edward's reign. In these letters, it is clear how even this intelligent noblewoman's sense of confidence is eroded as she finds herself obliged to perform the uncomfortable role of humble suitor. In July 1570, when she is petitioning for her second husband's right to use the Willoughby title, she expresses perplexity and debilitating anxiety about this epistolary situation to Cecil. She complains of failing even in trifles and remarks on 'the strangest hap': her sense that she finds gracious and loving responses 'in her Majesty's presence' and, then, her contrary sense reinforced in the conduct of her epistolary suits of being 'neglected, rejected, and forgotten in all things, unless it be for charge and service, as none the meanest in any country the like'.[37] She is by no means the only letter-writer expressing distaste at conforming to the obligatory decorum of self-abasement requisite to Elizabethan request-making or 'courtship' with little expectation of straightforward result. Indeed, this situation leads many women letter-writers to digress from exposition of the complaints for which they seek redress to complaints about the 'work of craving', as Lady Anne Asku puts it in a letter to Lord Burghley in October 1582:

> my letter to you at thys tyme doth make report of my extremytyes whyche I do onlly desier & craue may be helped by your good meanes to her maie[stie]: for I finde that work of crauing so heauy vnto me as neyther can I to you & muche lesse to a greater, finde strength in myselfe to do it, it is now almost halfe a yeare sins it pleased yow to promys me fauor & your furtherance if I could finde one that wold moue my sute to her maiesty, some hath promysed but not done it, & I have often bene in stryfe wyth myselfe & as I sayd finde it wythout my power, so as the tyme still passith away my state growes so ill as to my smart I finde.[38]

Despite the unpropitious terms on which suits were conducted in the Elizabethan court and its satellite institutions, with favorable response almost guaranteed to be deferred, examples of women's suitors' letters are more readily to be found than any other kind of woman's correspondence in the sixteenth century, and hence they demand attention in an account of sixteenth-century women's letters. Perhaps because they are so repetitive, they long escaped serious treatment within literary studies, but their elaborate rhetoric and the hierarchical culture of mediation in which it developed have, in recent years, received ample attention, and I will treat them only briefly here in relation to the theme of anticipated negative reception. As I have suggested elsewhere, the typical script enacts deference or extreme humility in a handful of predictable rhetorical moves that simultaneously lower the self and elevate the other. The suitor's demanding advances are cast as trouble-making to the recipient and attended by apologies for boldness or presumption. This rhetorical script catches the writer up in baroque contradictions, for the underlying requirement that respect be shown by rhetorical *copia* and by trouble-taking on the writer's part is fulfilled by means of elaborate apologies for the troublesome frequency, the extended length, and the 'rude' writing of the letters.[39] The tropes are closely related to those developed in men's suitors' letters, but the feminine version very often adds testimony of womanish weakness and witlessness to the repertoire of self-humbling moves.

Carla Mazzio has recently argued for the need to grapple with 'the "inarticulate" as a central dimension of developing language practices and ideologies' in the sixteenth century. She claims that the generalizations about the Renaissance as an 'age of rhetoric' devoted to 'the pursuit of eloquence' have 'had the power to overwrite an alternative history of involuted speech forms lodged in language practices, textual formations, and cultural phenomena'.[40] Despite the frequent recourse of Elizabethan women's petitioning letters to what seems like pitiful groveling, critics in recent years have legitimately made the positive case that they employ a deliberate rhetoric. Furthermore, in emphasizing the participation of upper-class women in client–patron negotiations, scholars have developed a sound case for women's significant political activity, a case providing a needed corrective to traditional forms of political history that rendered women invisible in politics. It seems important, however, to keep open a double perspective on this genre that is so all-pervasive in this time period, acknowledging as well the extent to which a suitor's rhetoric can be misshaping and dysfunctional as schooling for women in written composition. And the signs are evident that many women were, indeed, 'schooled' or tutored in these involuted epistolary forms of submission. James Daybell argues that women were often supervised in letter-writing, with male relatives or advisors revising or redrafting their efforts.[41] But it is important to recognize that the genre of women's letter-writing that received this studied attention was typically the suitor's letter, for this is the kind most likely to have consequences beyond the woman herself for her husband, her heirs, her family, or a wider network of alliances. Thus, not only did the suitor's genre tend to entangle women in negative stereotypes couched in involuted language – copious inarticulacy – but this tendency was likely to be reinforced by instruction and supervision. It afforded writing practice but in ways that more readily inscribed ideological subjection than promoted individual subjectivity or creativity. As an epistolary genre where many women of the period were encouraged and exercised in rhetorical *copia*, it needs to be regarded as double-edged.

While it is tempting to conclude that the negative conditions of reception associated with such genres were invariably debilitating to women writers, such a generalization fails to take into account how variable are the contingencies that can affect women's composition. It is instructive to see how, in the hands of an expert writer like Mary Sidney Herbert, the extreme demands even of the self-abasing suitor's genre can produce a creative rhetorical performance of a relatively controlled kind:

> Most sacred Soveraigne
> Pardon I humbly beceech yow this first boldnes of yowr humblest Creture, and lett it please that devine goodnes which can thus enlive and comfort my life to vouchsafe to know that not presumption, O no, but the vehement working desire of a thankfull harte so to acknowlidg it selfe for so hygh and presious a favor received hath guided my trembling hand to offer these worthless wordes to yowr exelent eies: [...] I againe, and againe in all reverent humblenes begg pardon for this fearefull boldnes, do end with my never ending praiers. Long Long may that purest light live, [...] who hath made yowr Majesty this worlds wonder and Inglands Bliss.[42]

In this brief sampling from Herbert's long letter, we can see how her artistry works to transform the obligatory self-chastisement for presumption, repetition, and length into a rhetorical gesture at prayerful praise. The stylistic embellishments that turn humility into joyfulness – the exclamatory 'O no' and the verbal repetition 'Long Long' – are reminiscent of devices in her Psalm translations and suggestive of how the writer's apprehension of affinities between Elizabethan courtship and religious worship might have contributed to her artistry across both genres.

Financial assets and epistolary production: Mrs Juliann Penn

In a society where many women had access only to marginal literacy, the suitor's genre is not the only context that encouraged *copia* without articulacy. Let us consider, as a final sampling of epistolary production in the period, the case of the Londoner, Mistress Juliann Penn, whose garrulous prolixity seems to have been encouraged by a pattern of positive reception. After the death of Juliann's first husband, coincidentally an ironmonger, Richard Hickes, the widow gave an account of her possessions that included a lease in a shop in Cheapside called the White Bear and a number of 'wretyngs' registering 'good debts' in excess of £1,800.[43] With these assets and her enterprising spirit, Juliann became a highly successful moneylender, counting among her clients men as important as William Cecil, the Earl of Oxford, and the Earl of Kildare. Not only did she manage such financial instruments as bonds and recognizances, but she sustained her business with curious and often lengthy letters to her debtors. At a time when business relations and social relations were seldom clearly demarcated, many of her letters proceeded in ways that may seem to us baffling, affirming, on the one hand, close and familiar bonds of friendship and demanding or enforcing, on the other hand, payment and harsh penalties. Her letter to Mr Hardwick, a Justice of the Peace housed apparently at her behest in debtors' prison, illustrates the relaxed and self-confident style in which she produces her own curious version of sociability:

> [...] Sir I do very often wishe my self ther with yow, and yow here with me for yow know that I ame butt a prisoner, whersoever I ame, and I know, that your good company with your wise counsell may do me good in my affaires [...]. The sommer came on apiece, hott seasons are contagious especiallie in prisons, & such melancholy places, your self a man brought vp in other sort & vnaquaynted with so hard lodging, and so homlye fare, & to say troth vnfitt, for one of your yeares & calling Besides, the world is geven, to speake loudlye and they that bear yow yll liue ready to raise so sclanderous reportes without your desert. And further, yow are to consider, how by your absence from your owne howse, the state of your thinges will go to wrack & to havock. [...] All which causes layd together, & duly wayed, with a greate many

other which yow in wisdome, can better redlye, call to mynde, then I can, hath moved me, to, as your poor & true freinde to entreat yow, to seke all the good wayes & to use all the beste meanes that yow can, for your spedy delyvuraunce out of trouble.[44]

We do not have Mr Hardwick's reply, but in surviving letters Juliann's male clients, both peers and commoners, address her unctuously as 'good Mrs. Penn' and avouch themselves at length to be her 'loving' friends.[45] It is a strange and fascinating case in which the dependency of debtors seems to have guaranteed their apparently loving letters and warm reception of her missives, licensing her garrulousness and encouraging a style in which, in her own words, 'my mynd ledes my hand neuer to make an ende'.[46]

Large-scale generalizations about women's letter-writing in the sixteenth century can prove to be elusive, since the conditions that encouraged active, prolific, or imaginative letter-writing can be complicated, multi-faceted, and localized. Nor is it always clear by what standard we should measure women's accomplishments in letter-writing, for letters are not in the first instance literary artifacts. We may think we hear the 'stir and quiver' of voices talking when rhetorical style rises to a level of distinction, and yet both the simple and the incompetent can function in significant contexts with entire adequacy. To explore the uneven development of women's letters in the sixteenth century it is fruitful to consider the variable contexts that encouraged epistolary production and to attend to some of the fascinating struggles that emerge between varying levels of skillfulness and the vagaries of gendered reception.

Notes

I am grateful to Paul Stevens for thoughtful comments, to Colleen Shea for research assistance, and to the Killam Foundation and SSHRC of Canada for research support.

1. James Harvey Robinson, *Petrarch: The First Modern Scholar and Man of Letters. A Selection from His Correspondence* (New York: G. P. Putnam's, 1898), p. 240; 'Dorothy Osborne's "Letters"', in *The Common Reader*, Second Series (London: Hogarth Press, 1932), pp. 59–66 (pp. 62, 60, 59).
2. John Donne, *Selected Letters*, ed. P. M. Oliver (Manchester: Fyfield Books, 2002), p. 17; Meredith K. Ray, *Writing Gender in Women's Letter Collections of the Italian Renaissance* (Toronto: University of Toronto Press, 2009).
3. Desiderius Erasmus, 'A Formula for the Composition of Letters' (*Conficiendarum epistolarum formula*), trans. Charles Fantazzi, in *Collected Works of Erasmus*, ed. J. K. Sowards, 86 vols (Toronto, Buffalo, and London: University of Toronto Press, 1985), XXV, 258–67 (p. 258).

4. David Cressy, *Literacy and the Social Order: Reading and Writing in Tudor and Stuart England* (New York: Cambridge University Press, 1980), p. 176.

5. For a detailed account, see Alan Stewart and Heather Wolfe, *Letterwriting in Renaissance England* (Washington: Folger Shakespeare Library, 2004).

6. James Daybell, *Women Letter-Writers in Tudor England* (New York: Oxford University Press, 2006), p. 33. For a thorough bibliography of critical work on English letters of the period by women and by men, see James Daybell, 'Recent Studies in Sixteenth-Century Letters', *English Literary Renaissance* 36 (2005), 331–62.

7. See Lynne Magnusson, 'Widowhood and Linguistic Capital: The Rhetoric and Reception of Anne Bacon's Epistolary Advice', *English Literary Renaissance* 31 (2001), 3–33.

8. Daybell, *Women Letter-Writers*, p. 39.

9. Oxford, Bodleian Library, MS Eng. Hist. c. 474, fol. 68. The Herrick Family Papers, centered on correspondence to William Herrick (1562–1653) and his descendants, are collected in Bodl. MS Eng. Hist. b. 216 and c. 474–84. For history of the family and many letters transcribed and printed, see John Nichols, *The History and Antiquities of the County of Leicester*, 4 vols (London: Nichols, 1795–1815), specifically II, pt. 2 (n.d.), pp. 611–36 and III, pt. 1 (1800), pp. 148–66, with a version of Mary Herrick's letter appearing on II, 2, 622.

10. Bodl. MS Eng. Hist. c. 474, fol. 81.

11. Bodl. MS Eng. Hist. c. 474, fol. 163, John to William Herrick, 18 August [n.y.].

12. On Paston letters incorporating the speech of others, see Valerie Creelman, 'Quotation and Self-Fashioning in Margaret Paston's Household Letters', *English Studies in Canada* 30 (2004), 111–28.

13. Bodl. MS Eng. Hist. c. 474, fol. 160, John to William Herrick, n.d.

14. Compare Thomas's handwriting in Bodl. MS Eng. Hist. c. 474, fol. 152, Thomas to William Herrick, 22 January 1578/9.

15. Thomas M. Greene, *The Light in Troy: Imitation and Discovery in Renaissance Poetry* (New Haven: Yale University Press, 1982), p. 1.

16. Norman Davis, 'The Litera Troili and English Letters', *The Review of English Studies* 16 (1965), 233–44 (p. 236).

17. Bodl. MS Eng. Hist. c. 474, fol. 165, n.d.

18. Nichols, *History and Antiquities*, II, pt. 2, p. 616.

19. Ibid., III, pt. 1, p. 162.

20. Daybell, *Women Letter-Writers*, pp. 86–87.

21. Bodl. MS Eng. Hist. c. 474, fol. 181^v, 12 January 1584/5.

22. National Archives, United Kingdom, Kew, State Papers 10/14/47, June [1552]; SP 10/10/32, 18 Sept. 1550; SP 10/8/35, 24 July [1549]; SP 10/9/58, 28 Dec. 1549; SP 10/10/39, 2 Oct. [1550]. I quote Katherine Bertie's letters in modern spelling for clarity, but in the first two examples here I provide an old-spelling transcription to give a sense of her phonetic spelling. Neither her spelling nor her early Tudor secretary hand would distinguish her writing from that of educated noblemen of her generation. In reading letters of this period, it is important not to make an automatic association of variable spelling with substandard English.

23. SP 12/3/9; quoted from Evelyn Read, *Catherine Duchess of Suffolk: A Portrait* (London: Jonathan Cape, 1962), pp. 134, 135.

24. SP 10/10/2, 25 March [1550]; quoted from Mary A. E. Green (ed.), *Letters of Royal and Illustrious Ladies of Great Britain: From the Commencement of the Twelfth Century to the Close of the Reign of Queen Mary*, 3 vols (London: H. Colburn, 1846), III, 251–53.

25. SP 10/10/6, 9 May 1550. Read (*Catherine Duchess of Suffolk*, p. 76) identifies the proposed bride as Lady Anne Seymour, soon after married to Warwick's eldest son, John Dudley, Viscount Lisle, but the daughter is unnamed in the letter.

26. Read, *Catherine Duchess of Suffolk*, p. 65.

27. Ibid., pp. 89–90.

28. SP 10/9/58, 28 Dec. 1549.

29. SP 10/14/47, June [1552].

30. For details of her life, in addition to Read, see Cecilie Goff, *A Woman of the Tudor Age* (London: John Murray, 1930); Pearl Hogrefe, *Women of Action in Tudor England: Nine Biographical Sketches* (Ames: Iowa State University Press, 1977); Susan Wabuda, 'Bertie [née Willoughby; *other married name* Brandon], Katherine, duchess of Suffolk', *ODNB* (2004); and Melissa Franklin-Harkrider, *Women, Reform and Community in Early Modern England: Katherine Willoughby, Duchess of Suffolk, and Lincolnshire's Godly Aristocracy, 1519–1580* (Woodbridge, Suffolk: Boydell, 2008).

31. Susan E. James, *Kateryn Parr: The Making of a Queen* (Aldershot: Ashgate, 1999), pp. 154–55.

32. Franklin-Harkrider, *Women, Reform and Community*, pp. 93 and 133.

33. N. Scott Amos, 'Bucer, Martin (1491–1551), theologian', *ODNB* (2004).

34. *The booke of freendeship of Marcus Tullie Cicero*, trans. John Harington (London, 1550), sig. A4ᵛ.

35. Pierre Bourdieu, 'The Economics of Linguistic Exchanges', *Social Science Information* 16 (1977), 645–68 (p. 655).

36. SP 12/43/40, 9 Aug. 1567; quoted from John William Burgon, *The Life and Times of Sir Thomas Gresham*, 2 vols (London: Effingham Wilson, [1839]), II, 400–03 (p. 403).

37. HMC, *Cal. Salisbury MSS*, I, 477.

38. British Library, Lansdowne MS 36, item 83, fol. 203, 26 Oct. 1582.

39. Lynne Magnusson, 'A Rhetoric of Requests: Genre and Linguistic Scripts in Elizabethan Women's Suitors' Letters', in *Women and Politics in Early Modern England, 1450–1700*, ed. James Daybell (Aldershot: Ashgate Publishing, 2004), pp. 51–66 (pp. 58–59); and Lynne Magnusson, *Shakespeare and Social Dialogue: Dramatic Language and Elizabethan Letters* (Cambridge: Cambridge University Press, 1999), pp. 100–08.

40. Carla Mazzio, *The Inarticulate Renaissance: Language Trouble in an Age of Eloquence* (Philadelphia: University of Pennsylvania Press, 2009), p. 1.

41. Daybell, *Women Letter-Writers*, pp. 76–79. In addition to suitors' letters, his illustrations include women's letters of submission to estranged husbands, another deferential form with a low expectation of approval.

42. *The Collected Works of Mary Sidney Herbert, Countess of Pembroke*, ed. Margaret P. Hannay, Noel J. Kinnamon, and Michael G. Brennan, 2 vols (Oxford: Clarendon Press, 1998), I, 291–92.

43. BL, Lansd. 108, item 16, fol. 29. On Juliann Penn, see Susan Emily Hicks-Beach, *A Cotswold Family: Hicks and Hicks-Beach* (London: W. Heinemann,

1909), especially pp. 50–79; and Alan G. R. Smith, *Servant of the Cecils: The Life of Sir Michael Hickes, 1543–1612* (London: Jonathan Cape, 1977), pp. 87–88, 98–100.

44. BL, Lansd. 108, item 17, fol. 31 (a copy).
45. Hicks-Beach, *A Cotswold Family*, pp. 70, 73, 76–77.
46. BL, Lansd. 108, item 16, fol. 29.

Playing Spaces

7
The Street

Pamela Allen Brown

Noise. Stench. That's probably what would assail your senses on a busy street in early modern England on a typical market day. Only a few thoroughfares were paved, even in London, and the rest were of dirt and mud. Household trash and effluvia from privies choked the gutters while din filled the air – carts and coaches rattling, bells ringing, voices gabbling and shouting.[1] Over all rose the huckster's relentless cry: *What d'ye lack? What d'ye lack?*

Looking at female textual production from the vantage of this noisy street might seem wrong-headed, even absurd. Not to do so is to overlook a crucial staging ground for writing and reception, especially for non-elite women. All forms of writing express social relations in history inflected by available media, and in this period no one's writing should be mistaken for the private thoughts of a private self in a room of her own. In fact, women wrote in a representational field crowded with jostling bodies and voices. Whether a woman made her home in town, city, or country, or trudged the roads as a vagrant, her daily life was dense with people acting in relation to each other. Just as space was shared by living bodies, writing was shared between people or broadcast to the wider public, whether via texts or the spoken word. Because most written texts were read aloud, and many compositions passed through circuits of handwriting, printing, and speech, writing emerged from a permeable field that continually combined the aural and the written, the spoken and the performed.[2]

As the prime conduit for news and rumor, the street teemed with texts, a rich seedbed for rhetorical *inventio*. All kinds of notices, from royal proclamations to playbills and satiric squibs, were stuck up on cleft sticks and nailed on posts. Alehouses beckoned on every corner, with ballads and broadsides pasted on doors and walls, enticing passersby with images of monstrous births, glamorous fashions, and distant wars. Customers male and female sat outside in good weather, singing catches from penny ballads and trading bawdy quips. While the main pathway to information was overwhelmingly oral – 'What news?' was the standard conversational opener – the growth of cheap print made the urban street itself the indispensable infrastructure for a new mix of media, a phenomenon intensified by the Reformation stress on literacy as the path to godliness. In the latter decades of the sixteenth century, a working woman passing a church might join a crowd listening to an open-air sermon, with the priest reading from the Bible or Foxe's *Book of Martyrs*. On her way home she might browse through book stalls tempting her with religious tracts and devotional manuals, jest books, romances, and advice books. If she had a penny to spare, she might see a play or buy a black-letter ballad. If she couldn't read the penny sheet she could carry it home, parsing out the words with a friend.[3]

Lack of education and low literacy did not bar women from all this verbal commerce. Female literacy, while on the rise in the period, was always lower than men's, with estimates ranging from 10 to 20 per cent depending on the criteria used to measure it. But the existence of partial female literacy – such as the ability to read black-letter type but not handwriting – was far more widespread than was once believed. Many women and girls learned reading in dames' schools or from kin, but writing was taught separately, and generally to boys only.[4] Virtually all women could remember and pass along jokes, stories, verse, and songs they heard, and some could repeat longer texts, such as sermons and speeches, from memory. Some women could compose these forms who could not write.

To gain a sense of this noisier and more inclusive world of female textual invention and dissemination, we must first question the habit of mind that equates authorship with private property, formal schooling, originality, and solitude. For early modern women, most of whom were partially literate, composition and publication could take place by means other than pen and press. 'Publication', for example, could refer to the act of making a text public, and 'composition' could refer to the fashioning of a libel, letter, or song in one's head. Writing occurs in many guises, including crude doggerel and graffiti. Keeping one's writing entirely secreted away in 'private' was probably a rarity – and it must be pointed out that today's concept of privacy was not yet universal. Indeed, according to Lena Cowen Orlin, 'The basic distinction available for early moderns was not that of the public and the individual space but that of the public and the shared.'[5] Some women chose not to publish in print, but many more circulated or printed their writings anonymously. Given the high costs of writing, both in time and materials, few women – no matter how privileged, since almost all women were continually pressed by family and work – indulged in writing for themselves alone or for oblivion. Writing rarely stayed in a cupboard but functioned as a means to traffic with the world outside. That men often criticized women for speaking out and for making their writings public shows that these practices jarred with reigning gender ideology – but not that women fell silent or wrote only for the satisfaction of authorship.[6]

Out of doors, out of place?

The ideal early modern woman was told to guard her speech and sexuality just as avidly as she was to guard her household. Because her mouth, eyes, ears, and vagina were inclined to dangerous looseness and openness, they were to be rigorously policed, just like the doors and windows of her household.[7] To hammer home their point, conduct book writers praised the snail as an emblem of womanly virtue. The timid snail always stays home, and when forced to stir she moves slowly and carries her household on her head. Even inside her house, the chaste woman was still not safe from pernicious outside influences. If she had to read she should limit herself to scripture or edifying histories, not romances or ballads, because 'such books or ballads [...] may make her mind (being of itself very delicate) more feeble and effeminate'.[8]

Few women took this sage advice. Records relating to slander, work, and property, as well as evidence of churchgoing and playgoing, among other activities, show women were mobile, visible, and highly audible in public places that afforded them ample access to profane texts. Women and girls were constantly out and about, running errands, fetching water, carrying messages and letters, doing the washing and marketing, visiting neighbors, going to church or to work. Some public places, such as the bakehouse, riverside laundry, and conduit, were 'patronized mainly by women, and treated by them almost as an extension of their dwellings'.[9] Wealthier women browsed the shops, and gentlewomen clattered through the streets in their coaches.[10] The less well-to-do worked in shops, or ran or worked in alehouses, where ballads and cheap pamphlets were hawked and read aloud. Poor women worked in the street, peddling food, clothing, and household wares or they went begging from door to door. Some trudged miles from outlying villages to urban markets to sell produce at market stalls, and others commuted by water, crowding onto barges. In all these places women swapped tales, songs, and news, spoken forms deeply marked by the circulation of texts and the constant interplay between oral, scribal, and print culture.[11]

The street was never free of tension and risk, however. Some times and places were more dangerous than others. All women were subject to surveillance and vulnerable to sexual harassment and rape, especially at night. Women accused of sexual transgressions or scolding might be forced to stand in a square dressed in a sheet, or undergo a humiliating charivari by neighbors. The unlucky vagrant or whore might be arrested and whipped through the streets at the tail of a cart. Foreign women and prostitutes were subject to abuse by rowdy crowds, especially apprentices in search of rough entertainment. As a result women often traveled in pairs or groups for safety and limited their use of the streets to the daylight hours as much as possible. During the day many women sat outside their doors spinning or standing in their yards, while chatting and keeping an eye on the street, occupying a liminal zone that gained them vital access to the public world while technically 'at home'.[12]

Outside the cities and towns, the open road was an object of fantasy and fear, especially after pilgrimages were banned in 1538. Few women traveled abroad or even to remote parts of England, inspiring desires for mobility that might be safely indulged by enjoying romances and chapbooks featuring bold feats by questing knights, female warriors, and shape-shifting rogues in exotic settings. The most mobile sectors were the very rich and the very poor. Aristocrats moved fairly regularly between great houses, and between country estates and large towns or London. Female vagrants with no home or employment tramped for hundreds of miles across the countryside, and as Patricia Fumerton has shown, some had no firm idea about where they were going or where they had been, living on the road and becoming permanently 'unsettled'. All sorts of people seeking employment and a settled life also shared the road and this experience of placelessness.[13] Gentlewomen and women of the middling sort could also find themselves suddenly rendered homeless. During the dissolution of the monasteries and convents between 1536 and 1540, nearly 2,000 nuns were driven out of their convents, and some became indigent.[14] Both the Protestant Anne Askew and the Catholic Elizabeth Cary, whose lives were so different in terms of status and religion, were pushed out of their homes by husbands who objected to their stubborn professions of faith and refusals to recant.[15] While critics caution against reading Cary's biography into her work, it is unquestioned that *The Tragedy of Mariam* places the politics of women's speech front and center. The play opens with the Queen of Jewry castigating herself for publicly expressing her political views against Herod's express command – 'How oft have I with public voice run on | To censure Rome's last hero for deceit?' – and ends with Mariam beheaded and Herod lamenting his rashness in silencing his wife.[16]

Despite the risks of entering the street, women's basic needs – to make a living, to go to market, to hear the news, and to meet their obligations to church, state, and neighborhood – were always stronger than the ideology of total female enclosure away from the public eye. In a similar way, women's writing shows a drive to satisfy the public needs of authors and readers. Too often women's writing has been misread as a purely domestic or 'inward' pursuit, disconnecting it from the larger spheres of public speech and action. We need to look beyond the walls of the household to understand the linked arenas – social, political, economic, and religious – which gave all writing its place and reason for being.

Via sacra et dolorosa

While the street was a metonym for worldliness, it was never exclusively secular. Religious processions frequently displaced everyday activity. During holidays and funerals long trains of people and clergy jammed the ways, in ceremonies punctuated by chanting, praying, singing, and bell-ringing. For most of the sixteenth century, the major byways of many large towns became the backdrop for annual biblical cycle plays, which transfixed communities for weeks. Women participated in these dramas of the street as spectators, patrons, and players. The Reformation altered but did not purge the street of religious ritual and spectacle. Towns still staged the great cycle plays, albeit in censored forms, until the 1570s. Every official procession still had a religious element – the accession of Queen Elizabeth was punctuated by many prayers and by her pious displays of the English Bible to the crowd, for example. The reformers purged many 'heathenish' festivals from the calendar, but they were unable to root them all out. The street theater of Rogation (in which clergy and citizenry perambulated the parish bounds and celebrated with prayers and toasts) and Hocktide (in which women and men tied up passersby of the opposite sex and demanded ransom to fund parish coffers) persisted in some places despite concerted Puritan onslaughts.[17] Probably the single greatest change in street culture was caused by abrupt reversals in state religion and in policies towards heresy, which led to the bloody street theater of religious reprisal. Whatever the professed beliefs of the condemned, an execution could transform the street into a cosmic site of holy martyrdom for some onlookers, a stern scaffold of righteous justice for others.

Women of all sects communicated their piety and beliefs in a variety of textual performances, such as translating sacred and devotional works, composing prayers, poems, ballads, and saints' lives, and writing marginalia and commentary on the Bible, printed sermons, and tracts. Given the dangers of recording one's religious convictions or translating controversial texts in years of rapid political change, many of these were political and social acts, not private and inward ones. Anne Lock lived her life as a high-profile Protestant activist, promoting the cause by writing poetry and by editing and translating Calvin's sermons, among other works. Lock was unusual among early modern women in her own high mobility, traveling to the Continent and back; she also married three husbands in the course of her long life. Lock arguably forges her activist identity, like her friend and mentor John Knox, from her experiences with the manifold 'playing spaces' of the street, where so many sermons, tracts, and polemical verses were proclaimed aloud or sold, and where so many died on the scaffold. Closely allied with the highest Protestant circles in England, Lock responded to the Smithfield fires by fleeing with her children to Geneva in 1557. In exile she lived with Knox and his family, and returned after Elizabeth came to power. In choosing to radically redeploy the Petrarchan love sonnet, Lock succeeded not only in writing the first English sonnet sequence but in demonstrating her credentials to an international coterie of reform-minded humanists. Modeled on the penitential psalms, and dominated by a narrator who performs a 'mini-drama' of abjection, the sonnets were published in 1560 with her translation of four sermons by John Calvin.[18] Near the end of the sequence the sinner turns from self-flagellation to the larger world, asking for blessing on the walls and streets of London, or England, figured as the new Jerusalem:

> Show mercy, Lord, not unto me alone,
> But stretch Thy favor and Thy pleasèd will,
> To spread they bounty and Thy grace upon
> Sion, for Sion is thy holy hill.
> That with Thy Jerusalem with mighty wall
> May be enclosed under Thy defense,
> And buildèd so that it may never fall
> By mining fraud or mighty violence.[19]

By speaking for 'Sion' as its earthly representative, she arguably takes on the biblical stance of the spiritual leader, prophet, and seer. Bold writing such as this kept her profile high among nonconforming Protestants, and she retained a reputation for passionate engagement in the cause throughout her life.[20]

For pious women of all stripes, reading and listening to sacred and devotional works often took place in public, as did prayer. A devotional aid such as *A Monument of Matrones* was a politically charged publication that retailed prayers written by Protestant queens and martyrs, including Anne Askew and Lady Jane Grey. The massive book could be read and discussed by a mistress instructing her servants and children, by a priest or congregant in the public space of church, or by a woman on the scaffold or deathbed who recited a prayer by memory from its pages. While many Catholic women did read and write religious works (contrary to Protestant caricatures of the Catholic woman as ignorant and credulous), the greatest strides in female literacy occurred among Protestants, a byproduct of the radical elevation of scripture over rituals and good works.[21] The Bible-quoting and hymn-singing Puritan woman became a comic stereotype by the early seventeenth century. John Earle's character of the 'Shee Precise Hypocrite' mocks her overactive mobility and showy piety:

> Her devotion at the Church is much in the turning up of her eye, and turning down the leaf of her Booke, when she heares nam'd Chapter and Verse. When shee comes hom[e] she commends the Sermon for the Scripture, and two houres. Shee loves preaching better than praying, and [...] thinkes the Weekes dayes exercise far more edifying than the Sundayes. Her oftenest Gossiping are Sabbath-day journeys where (though an enemy to superstition) shee will goe in Pilgrimage five mile to a silenc'd Minster, when there is a better sermon in her own Parish. Shee doubts of the Virgin Marie's Salvation, and dare not Saint her, but knowes her own place in heaven perfectly, as the Pew shee ha's a key to.[22]

The idea of a Puritan on pilgrimage is, of course, meant as an insult. Pilgrimage was a Catholic tradition that had been ruthlessly suppressed, beginning in 1538. Until that year, when Henry VIII outlawed pilgrimage and seized the most important shrines, women frequently traveled to pray before relics or holy statues.[23] Perhaps because women pilgrims were temporarily freed from male control they stirred opposition and distrust even when pursuing their pious duty – 'a journeying woman speaks much of all and all of her', one dour proverb had it. Yet women kept venturing out to shrines near and far, often enough to seek relief from sickness in their families and for divine help with childbearing and reproductive problems. After Henry's break with Rome, the faction led by Thomas Cromwell began to attack 'idolatrous' worship, especially by women. They sought to sever the bonds of belief created over centuries between sacred places and objects, attacking miracles, relics, and pilgrimage itself, turning the *via sacra* into a common thoroughfare like any other. Some women actively resisted: in Exeter a group of women were arrested after staging a fierce defense of images in St Nicholas's Priory. Armed with shovels and spikes, they chased out a workman and occupied the church; one assaulted an alderman.[24]

Crushing an ancient social practice entailed doing violence to historical memory as well as to monuments. Pilgrimage stories are vital to the fifteenth-century autobiographic *Book of Margery Kempe*, in which the author tells of many arduous trips to Jerusalem and Rome and to holy places in England, including the cell of Julian of Norwich, Becket's shrine in Canterbury, and the holy house of Our Lady of Walsingham. In the sixteenth century, long after her death, Kempe was editorially enclosed within walls. As Jennifer Summit has shown, Henry Pepwell published a brief extract from Kempe's writing in a devotional anthology in 1521.[25] Pepwell bizarrely refers to Kempe as 'a devout anchoress', as if she had spent all her days in a cell in Lincoln. He omits any mention of her far-flung travels or notorious 'weepings'. An anchoress such as Julian of Norwich was neither removed from the world and religio-political debates, nor free from censure, as Summit demonstrates. But by recasting Kempe as an anchoress, Pepwell does eliminate the need to trouble the reader with Kempe's hyperkinetic, unruly history – and he accomplishes this by taking the open road out of her story. It would take five centuries for Kempe the pilgrim to come to light again, when the manuscript was rediscovered in 1934.[26]

Reformation zeal was an efficient engine for the creation of ghosts: each act of destruction might breed a ghost-memory, and with it writing. No target of iconoclasm was more rued than Our Lady of Walsingham. Founded in 1061 by a woman who had a vision of the Virgin Mary, the shrine was famous not only in England but in Europe for its replica of Mary's house in Nazareth, its sacred statue of Virgin and child, and its relic of her breast milk. For five centuries kings and queens visited 'England's Nazareth', including Henry VII and Elizabeth of York, who sought the Virgin's comfort and help after two of her children died. Women in particular flocked to the shrine along the 'Milky Way', lining up to receive pilgrims' badges and ampullae of water mixed with a drop of the holy milk. Wealthy women showered gifts on the shrine, renowned (and later reviled) for its glittering jewels. Poets praised the Lady of Walsingham, but the shrine also generated practical forms of writing, such as bequests. Propertied women often made provision in their wills to fulfill vows to make pilgrimages in the event of their deaths. One such bequest was made by Katherine of Aragon, who directed the proxy pilgrim to visit Walsingham and to give away 200 gold florins to the poor along the way.[27]

Henry VIII also made devout pilgrimages to Walsingham, going part of the way barefoot. His acts of reverence were forgotten in 1538, when as a first move towards the wholesale confiscation of church properties, he outlawed all pilgrimages and sacked and burned Walsingham. Its Virgin was brought to London, where it too was burned, along with other venerated statues of female saints. In a letter to Thomas Cromwell, Richard Latimer gloated about hauling in a Virgin statue from Worcester: 'She hath been the Devil's instrument, I fear, to bring many to eternal fire; now she herself with her older sister of Walsingham, her younger sister of Ipswich, and their two sisters of Doncaster and Penrhys will make a jolly muster in Smithfield. They would not be all day in burning.'[28]

Even as a charred ruin, Walsingham drew pilgrims. Angry grief marks 'A Lament for our Lady's Shrine at Walsingham', a contemporary ballad by an anonymous Catholic – possibly a woman pilgrim – who contemplates the wreckage.

> In the wrackes of walsingham
>   Whom should I chuse,
> But the Queene of walsingam
>   to be guide to my muse
> [...]
> Levell levell with the ground
>   the towers doe lye
> Which with their golden glittering tops
>   Pearsed once to the skye,
> Where weare gates no gates at nowe,
>   the waies unknowne,
> Wher the presse of peares did passe
>   While her fame far was blowen
> Oules do skrike wher the sweetest himnes
>   lately weer songe
> Toades and serpentes hold ther dennes,
>   Wher the Palmers did thronge
> [...]

> Sin is wher our Ladie sate
> Heaven is turned is to Hell.
> Sathan sittes wher our Lord did swaye
> Walsingam oh farewell.[29]

The song mourns the loss of the 'waies', an allusion to the Walsingham Way leading from London to the shrine, which John Stow named first in his catalogue of major highways in England. An air of tragic loss also pervades Sir Walter Raleigh's 'As you came from the holy land', which ambiguously blends secular and sacred love-lament. A forsaken lover seeks a maid 'lyke a queen' with 'form so divine' and 'Angelyke face', but she has vanished, perhaps to seek a more vigorous love – or a more faithful believer.[30]

The ballad was the most ubiquitous form of printed street literature, sold in city, town, and countryside all over England. As the Walsingham ballads suggest, this medium offers an important source of insight into ordinary people's experience of the Reformation. Costing a penny or halfpenny, the ballad was the quintessential medium of the streets, with copies reaching even the remotest country dwelling via traveling chapmen. While hundreds of thousands circulated in print, a popular song was dispersed far more widely than numbers of copies would indicate, because people quickly memorized and sang it to others.[31] Polemicists on both sides certainly exploited the form: ballads and broadsides were key weapons in the propaganda wars raging in Luther's wake. According to Sandra Clark, the ballad was especially important in reaching non-elites, especially women, because it operated 'between the oral and the written, between commercial transaction and free circulation; it was delivered to its audiences initially in public places such as marketplaces, alehouses, and playhouse entrance, and was thus equally available to men and women'.[32] Though most ballad-writers were male, many ballads are narrated by women and are specifically addressed to them as a target audience. Many are written in dialogue form or as answer ballads, with women taking one point of view, men answering back with another, and vice versa. Some 'women's' ballads show signs of misogynist ventriloquy, but many more are written with no trace of satire. Ballads charge men with flaws ranging from cruelty to drunkenness, lecherous harassment, fortune-hunting, and whoremongering, some of the same charges women brought against men in court. Because so many women knew and sang these songs, shaping them to their own uses and interpreting them through the act of performance, the ballad genre constituted a powerful medium for articulating a female-identified point of view on a wide array of topics, ranging from wife-beating and childbearing to religious controversy.

Fatal professions of faith and spectacular deaths of believers were frequent ballad subjects. The Protestant martyr Anne Askew (*c*.1521–46) is credited with writing two ballads along with her more famous *Examinations* during the months in which she was interrogated and tortured by officials who were probably trying to incriminate Katherine Parr and her circle. Askew was especially vulnerable: she had separated from her husband William Kyme, who objected to her conversion to radical Protestantism. After her arrest her writings were smuggled out of prison, possibly by her maid, who supported her mistress by begging in the streets.[33] One of the ballads was published, along with her *Examinations* and a woodcut of her 1546 execution in Smithfield, in John Foxe's *Actes and Monuments*.[34]

If the *Examinations* were aimed chiefly at godly readers, the ballad and woodcut targeted a much broader group that included the illiterate and partially literate – including women like Askew's nameless servant. 'The Balade whych Anne Askew made and sange while she was in Newgate' is a bold attack on the Henrician regime, which she likens to Satan's court:

> Not oft I use to wryght
> In prose nor yet in ryme,
> Yet wyll I shewe one syght
> That I sawe in my tyme.

> I saw a r[o]yall trone
> Where Justice shuld have sytt,
> But in her stede was one
> Of modye cruell wytt.

> Absorpt was rygtwysnesse
> As of the ragynge floude,
> Sathan in hys excesse,
> Sucte up the gyltlesse bloude.[35]

Note that the Catholic 'Lament for our Lady's Shrine' and the Protestant 'Balade' use the emblem of a throne usurped by Satan.[36] Like most effective ballads, they lean heavily on gesture and inflection and deploy easily grasped tropes for maximum communicative force in delivery on the street.[37] Indeed, the open theater of the streets features large in the eventful history of Askew's life and death, and her afterlife as an author.

In her ballad Askew takes on the serious persona of a poor but righteous prophetess and a female soldier of Christ. This tone is largely absent in the darkly witty *Examinations*, in which Askew takes every opportunity to confound her examiners. She shows her contempt through silences, smiles, and wry queries – 'her proud and presumptuous answers, quips, and nips', in the words of a Catholic detractor in 1605, making what seems to be a disparaging allusion to jest books such as *Quips Upon Questions* and *Tales and Quick Answers*.[38] Playing the plain-spoken wit to the King's doltish straight men, Askew shows herself an adept combatant in the *agon* of Reformation polemic, which labored to capture the vigor of an alehouse jibe or a shout in the street – the rude spirit that filled the diatribes of More and Luther and that would flavor the Marprelate pamphlets decades later.

Askew is more restrained in her diction but just as vigorous in her satire. Propelling her *Examinations* is an intense will to mock those who are racking her and sending her to her death. That it was produced at all, under such duress, shows her desire to inscribe her own meanings on her fate and possibly to inspire resistance in others. John Bale and John Foxe realized the value of her account as propaganda: the first edited it (albeit heavy-handedly) and the second featured it in *Acts and Monuments*, which was placed in church pulpits for all to marvel at. The presentation of Askew's death was unlike the hundreds of others in the volume, for the lurid woodcut people saw was qualified by her own account, in her own words. The pathetic details of her very public end in Smithfield – her body was so broken she had to be carried to the stake in a chair – were overlaid by the powerful textual presence of a woman satirist whose words could sting.[39]

Mocking wills and the will to mock

The will to mock is also a characteristic of female libelers and gossips in the period, who play such an important part in the largely unchronicled history of female participation in early modern popular culture. Sometimes written libels were intended to serve as a form of scandalous entertainment as well as a medium of communication. Women wrote and circulated stories and libels about other men and women, while a few wrote mocking ballads and sang them, spreading them by word of mouth through a neighborhood and even farther afield. In some cases, they composed the verses and dictated them to others. According to Adam Fox, 'the authors of scandal were perfectly capable of rhyming themselves and merely required scribal services in order to commit their work to paper.'[40] One example dates from 1605, when a servant named Elizabeth Maunder instructed apprentice John Parker of Fleet Street 'to write certain libelling verses which [she] could tell him by word of mouth, which he did'.[41] Such actions could lead to slanging matches, cries of slander, and lawsuits. Female mockery and insult generated a slew of legal writing, including court depositions and other statements by women, providing a crucial source for scholars studying the social, cultural, and legal histories of non-elite women. Not coincidentally, a mocking woman is the protagonist of the earliest known *querelle* defense by an Englishwoman: *Jane Anger Her Defense for Women* (1589), a response to the woman-hating *Boke his Surfeit in Love* (1588, now lost). In her preface addressed 'To all Women in generall, and gentle Reader whatsoever', Anger erupts in the passionate, cutting speech of the street harangue and libel, comically tempering her tone in an exasperated apostrophe to the echoing streets – 'O *Paul's steeple* and *Charing Cross'*. Her engaging rant animates the very gutters of the city, bidding them to carry away her enemies in a flood:

> Was there ever any so abused, so slaundred, so railed upon, or so wickedly handeled undeservedly, as are we women? Will the Gods permit it, the Goddesses stay there punishing judgments, and we ourselves not pursue their undoinges for such develish practices. O *Paules steeple* and *Charing Crosse*. A halter hold such persons. Let the streames of the channels in London streates run so swiftly, as they may be able alone to carrie them from that santuarie. [...] Shal surfeiters raile on our kindnes, you stand stil & say nought, and shall not Anger stretch the vaines of her braines, the stringes of her fin-gers, and the listes of her modestie, to answer their Surfeitings? Yes, truely, And herein I conjure all you to aide assist me in defence of my willingness, which shall me rest at your commaundes.[42]

The pamphlet's imagined community is composed of women who gather around as Anger works up a head of steam. She challenges them not to stand idly by, and to help her get revenge on misogynist ex-lovers who 'blaze abroad that they have surfeted with love'. Continuing her street-heavy imagery in the main text, she turns her sarcasm against liars who brag about their conquests of women they barely know: 'true tales come from them, as wild geese flie under London Bridge'.[43]

The comic quips and satiric nips of Jane Anger bear more than a pass-ing resemblance to moments in lowly jest books which, like the plays of Shakespeare that drew on them, were considered 'idle bookes & riffe raffes' unfit for libraries.[44] Another genre filled with mocking women, the 'jest book' is a blanket term that applies to jest collections, jest biographies, and miscellaneous pamphlets filled with popular satire, parodies, bawdy tales, and comic proverbs. Like ballads, jest books were a thoroughly accessible and widespread genre in the period, with a vast combined readership much greater than more staid works of literature.[45] Virtually all women and girls were exposed to jest books because they were shared and read aloud at all levels of society. Even Elizabeth indulged in jest books. In them one could hear men's familiar jokes about women, but one could also hear some women's jokes about men. Jesting women mock and trick ignorant priests, drunken husbands, and leering lechers, or turn the tables on misogynists and teach them a lesson. Whether the jests are set indoors or out in the street, the stories traveled through word of mouth to every street corner and alehouse.

Jest book authors were usually male and always bent on maximum profit for minimum labor. They pilfered freely from old collections of medieval exempla, comic legends, fabliaux, and novellas. Sometimes they fashioned a contemporary setting presided over by hefty viragos like Long Meg of Westminster or Mother Bunch, the jesting alewife from Cornhill, who is so huge her farts can blow down St Paul's steeple.[46] Like John Skelton's Elinor Rumming, Shakespeare's Hostess, and Samuel Rowland's gossips, these comic women play lead roles in fictions of the alehouse, a prime setting for the participation of real women in popular culture. One feature of the subgenre is its geographic specificity. An early example is Robert Copland's *Jyl of Braintford's Testament* (c. 1535), a jest book in the form of a mock will – one of the most familiar tropes of jesting, already old when François Villon used it to bid farewell to Paris a century earlier.[47] In the town of Brainford, popularly identified with lovers' rendezvous and female pleasure, lives a witty alewife. She calls together all her friends, neighbors, and enemies in the local alehouse to announce the terms of her will, with a curate standing by to transcribe her words. During her performance she plays prosecutor, judge, and jury. To every person who has annoyed her in some way, or who has failed to meet her moral code, she bequeaths a fart – making some explode with laughter and others squirm with rage.

Most commentators on Isabella Whitney's *Wyll and Testament* (1573) pay scant attention to jest books such as Copland's *Jyl of Braintford*, possibly out of embarrassment. The latter possesses none of Whitney's literary skill or subtlety. Yet something essential is lost by ignoring the lower sort of mock-testament, with its smell of ale and its rude laughter. We know little about Whitney's life, except that she was of gentle rank, was a member of a large family, and may have worked as a servant in London.[48] The urbanity and unusual specificity of her work engages on many levels, making listening closely for tone and occasion especially important. What is the imaginary 'playing space' of Whitney's testament? Is the speaker a genteel and modest servant between jobs, penning a tribute to London from her desk, witnessed only by 'Paper, pen and Standish'? Or is she a satiric woman-about-town who is amusing her friends and poking fun at people who irritate her, holding forth on the street or in an alehouse, or perhaps a printer's bookstall? Some critics praise her sensible wit and place her outside, walking us through a quick tour of the sights, but most of them fail to sense the more crowded comic situation implied by her chosen genre.[49] The mock testament, like all satire, generally intends to create scandal, to amuse some of its audience and to rile others who (like Jyl's surprised neighbors) won't like what they hear.

Whitney announces her *Wyll* by addressing London and complaining the city is like a hard-hearted, wealthy, and tight-fisted lover she just can't shake off.

> The time is com I must departe
> from thee, ah, famous Citie:
> I never yet, to rue my smart,
> did finde that though hadst pitie,
> Wherfore small cause ther is, that I
> should greeve from thee to go:
> But many women foolyshly,
> lyke me and other moe
> Doe such a fyxed fancy set,
> on those which least desarve,
> That long it is ere wit we get,
> away from them to swarve,
> But time with pittie oft wyl tel
> to those that wil her try:
> Whether it best be more to mell
> or utterly defye.[50]

Tried by London's negligence, she may seem to 'mell', or submit, but under a veneer of self-control she remains defiant. Most critics make much of the end of her poem, in which she names London as sole executor 'because | I lov'd thee best' (ll. 178–79). But a closer reading shows that under the mask of praise her basic attitude is not generous affection, but a more ironic and detached appraisal, tinged with bitterness. Her railing preface loudly signals the reader that her professed love and her oddly superfluous bequests must be taken with a grain of salt:

> And now hath time put me in mind
>   of thy great cruelnes:
> That never once a help wold finde,
>   to ease me in distres.
> Thou never yet, woldst credit geve
>   to boord me for a yeare:
> Nor with Apparell me releve
>   except thou payed weare.
> No, no, thou never dist me good,
>   nor ever wilt I know:
> *Yet am I in no angry moode,*
>   but wyll, or ere I goe
> In perfect love and charytie,
>   My testament here write.[51]

Anyone who firmly claims she is not angry is rarely entirely so – as Whitney goes on to show, with a wink to her friendly auditor. Killing her prey with kindness, she loads London down with increasingly undesirable gifts, from Newgate, Bridewell, Bedlam, and Tyburn to the debtor's prison in Ludgate, all in the name of 'perfect love and charity'. As her catalogue makes plain, not all the city's 'famous' parts are praiseworthy or noble. In fact, many aspects notoriously contribute to the poverty and misery of its inhabitants, including Whitney and her friends.

Satiric complaint drives Whitney's *Wyll*, just as it does her 'Copie of a Letter to a Late Surfeting Lover', which also employs the comic technique of laying a mask of charity over underlying anger. In her mock will she chooses a canny target in calling her beneficiary 'London', which protects her from the charge she targets any particular person. But the lines about being boarded for a year or having her apparel provided for echo the terms of employment often made between masters and servants in the city.[52] As she has announced elsewhere in *A Sweet Nosegay*, the volume in which the *Wyll* appears, she has recently been discharged, and writes as one of the many jobless female servants that filled London streets. She is not only 'very light in purse' but runs the risk of being arrested for vagrancy, under the statute declaring all unemployed women between the ages of fourteen and forty must find work in service or risk jail.[53] All this suggests that the *Wyll and Testament* is playfully aimed at her former employer and her ex-lovers, as well as the tight-fisted mean streets of lickpenny London. By saying she is like other women who can't leave those that don't deserve them, she may well refer to cruel masters and mistresses, as well as surfeiting lovers. After all, she makes her bequests to 'London, and to all those in it'. If the *Wyll* fits, wear it.

As I have tried to show, making the most of Whitney (or for that matter Anonymous, Askew, and Anger) means making an effort to move our own mental theaters back out into the street, whether it is a *via sacra* leading to martyrdom, or a city corner befitting a rough-tongued urban rhetoric. Once there we can listen with a difference to the chapwoman's cry, 'What do you lack?' What has been lacking in many critical studies of women's writing is a sense of the performance occasion and the contribution of the body to texts, whether it involves recruiting laughter or prayer, or speaking through suffering and pain. Without imagining the multiple sacred and secular 'playing spaces' that gave them meaning, the writings of these women are silenced more completely than was ever possible at the early modern moment, when 'to read' also meant to perform – to read aloud – and when to write meant to make one's needs and desires material.

Notes

1. My attention to the urban soundscape is indebted to Bruce Smith's *The Acoustic World of Early Modern England: Attending to the O-factor* (Chicago: University of Chicago Press, 1999). I'd also like to thank Jennifer Summit, Caroline Bicks, Nancy Selleck, Natasha Korda, Julie Crawford, Bianca Calabresi, and Tanya Pollock for helpful comments on this essay.
2. Adam Fox, *Oral and Literate Culture in England, 1500–1700* (Oxford: Oxford University Press, 2000), p. 5.
3. Important works relevant to cheap print and non-elite women include Joy Wiltenburg, *Disorderly Women and Female Power in the Street Literature of Early Modern Germany and England* (Charlottesville: University of Virginia Press, 1992) and Tessa Watt, *Cheap Print and Popular Piety, 1550–1640* (Cambridge: Cambridge University Press, 1991).
4. On reading, writing, and signing ability see Margaret Spufford, *Small Books and Pleasant Histories: Popular Fiction and Its Readership in Seventeenth-Century England* (Athens: University of Georgia Press, 1982); Eve Rachele Sanders, *Gender and Literacy on Stage in Early Modern England* (Cambridge: Cambridge University Press, 1998); and Heidi Brayman Hackel, *Reading Material in Early Modern England: Print, Gender, and Literacy* (Cambridge: Cambridge University Press, 2005). On partial literacies see Margaret Ferguson, *Dido's Daughters: Literacy, Gender, and Empire in Early Modern England and France* (Chicago: University of Chicago Press, 2003).
5. Lena Cowen Orlin, *Private Matters and Public Culture in Post-Reformation England* (Ithaca: Cornell University Press, 1994), p. 185.

6. I owe to this point to Julie Crawford, whose important work argues that early modern women wrote for material, social, and political ends, not in order to become authors per se. I am grateful to her for sharing her ideas with me.

7. Peter Stallybrass, 'Patriarchal Territories: The Body Enclosed', in *Rewriting the Renaissance: The Discourse of Sexual Difference in Early Modern Europe*, ed. Margaret W. Ferguson, Maureen Quilligan, and Nancy J. Vickers (Chicago: University of Chicago Press, 1986), pp. 123–44, esp. pp. 126–27.

8. Thomas Salter, *A mirror meet for all mothers, matrons, and maidens* (1581), quoted in Jacqueline Eales, *Women in Early Modern England, 1500–1700* (London: UCL Press, 1998), p. 37.

9. Sara Mendelson and Patricia Crawford, *Women in Early Modern England* (Oxford: Clarendon Press, 1998), p. 207; see pp. 207–10 for an overview on women's use of space.

10. On women as workers and customers in new sites of consumption such as the theaters and the Royal Exchange, see Jean E. Howard, *Theater of a City: The Places of London Comedy, 1598–1642* (Philadelphia: University of Pennsylvania Press, 2007), esp. pp. 37–38, 60–67.

11. Fox, *Oral and Literate Culture*, p. 5.

12. Mendelson and Crawford, *Women in Early Modern England*, p. 208.

13. Patricia Fumerton, *Unsettled: The Culture of Mobility and the Working Poor in Early Modern England* (Chicago: University of Chicago Press, 2006). Also see Linda Woodbridge, *Vagrancy and Homelessness and English Renaissance Literature* (Urbana: University of Illinois Press, 2001).

14. In 1534 about 142 English convents housed 2,000 nuns. Nearly all were closed by 1540 (Eales, *Women in Early Modern England*, p. 89).

15. John Foxe labored to show that Askew's rebellion against her husband was in no way comparable to the similar acts of female saints (Jennifer Summit, *Lost Property: The Woman Writer and English Literary History, 1380–1589* [Chicago: University of Chicago Press, 2000], p. 155).

16. Elizabeth Cary, *The Tragedy of Mariam*, in *William Shakespeare and Elizabeth Cary, Othello and The Tragedy of Mariam*, ed. Clare Carroll (New York: Longman, 2003), p. 145.

17. Ronald Hutton, *The Rise and Fall of Merry England: The Ritual Year, 1400–1700* (Oxford: Oxford University Press, 1994), pp. 34–35, 59–60, 119, 142–43.

18. Susan M. Felch, 'Anne Vaughan Lock', in *Teaching Tudor and Stuart Women Writers*, ed. Susanne Woods and Margaret P. Hannay (New York: Modern Language Association, 2000), pp. 127–34 (p. 132).

19. *Female and Male Voices in Early Modern England: An Anthology of Renaissance Writing*, ed. Betty Travitsky and Anne Lake Prescott (New York: Columbia University Press, 2000), p. 125.

20. Felch, 'Anne Vaughan Lock', pp. 128–29, 131.

21. Frances Dolan, 'Religion: Roman Catholic Women', in *Teaching Tudor and Stuart Women Writers*, ed. Woods and Hannay, p. 90.

22. John Earle, *Microcosmographie, or, a Peece of the World Discoevred*, in *Essayes and Characters* (London, 1629), sigs. K2ᵛ–5ᵛ.

23. Susan Signe Morrison, *Women Pilgrims in Late Medieval England: Private Piety as Public Performance* (New York: Routledge, 2000), pp. 17–25.

24. Eales, *Women in Early Modern England*, p. 88.

25. Wynkyn de Worde had printed the same excerpt two decades earlier as *A shorte treatyse of contemplacyon taught by our lord Iehesu Cryste, or taken out of the boke of Margerie Kempe of Lynne* (Summit, *Lost Property*, p. 126).
26. Ibid., pp. 126–38.
27. Morrison, *Women Pilgrims*, pp. 17–18.
28. Latimer quoted in Eamon Duffy, *The Stripping of the Altars: Traditional Religion in England c.1400–c.1850* (New Haven: Yale University Press, 1992), p. 404. On the destruction of shrines of female saints, including the exhumation and burning of their bones, see Carole Levin, 'St. Frideswide and St. Uncumber', in *Women, Writing and the Reproduction of Culture in Tudor and Stuart Britain*, ed. Mary E. Burke, Jane Donawerth, Linda L. Dove, and Karen Nelson (Syracuse: Syracuse University Press, 2000), pp. 223–37.
29. *The Penguin Book of Renaissance Verse*, ed. R. H. Woudhuysen (London: Penguin, 1992), pp. 531–32. 'The MS of this possibly unique text contains other Catholic works and may date from about 1600', p. 820 n. 250.
30. Ibid., p. 248.
31. By 1600 as many as three to four million ballads were circulating in England. Watt, *Cheap Print*, pp. 11, 42.
32. Sandra Clark, quoted in Pamela Allen Brown, *Better a Shrew than a Sheep: Women, Drama and the Culture of Jest* (Ithaca: Cornell University Press, 2003), p. 24. Also see Clark's essay 'The Broadside Ballad and the Woman's Voice', in *Debating Gender in Early Modern England, 1500–1700*, ed. Cristina Malcolmson and Mihoko Suzuki (New York: Palgrave Macmillan, 2002), pp. 102–20.
33. Elaine Beilin, 'Introduction' to *The Examinations of Anne Askew*, ed. Elaine Beilin (New York: Oxford University Press, 1996), esp. p. xix, and Betty Travitsky, *The Paradise of Women: Writings by Englishwomen of the Renaissance* (New York: Columbia University Press, 1989), p. 170.
34. The second ballad, 'I am a woman poore and blind', was not printed until the early seventeenth century and may be by another writer (Beilin, 'Introduction' to *The Examinations of Anne Askew*, p. xxxix).
35. Beilin (ed.), *The Examinations of Anne Askew*, p. 150.
36. Ecclesiastes seems to be the source for both, and Askew may have imitated a paraphrase of Ecclesiastes by Henry Howard, Earl of Surrey. Beilin, 'Introduction' to *The Examinations of Anne Askew*, p. xxxii, esp. n. 50.
37. Natascha Würzbach, *The Rise of the English Street Ballad, 1550–1650* (Cambridge: Cambridge University Press, 1990), pp. 54, 74–80.
38. The quotation is from Robert Parsons, a Jesuit who attacked Askew's writings in 1605 as part of his campaign to discredit Foxe. Beilin, 'Introduction' to *The Examinations of Anne Askew*, pp. xxxviii–xxxix.
39. Travitsky, *Paradise of Women*, p. 169.
40. Fox, *Oral and Literate Culture*, p. 313.
41. Ibid., p. 313. Also see pp. 302, 305, 310, 312.
42. Ferguson, *Dido's Daughters*, p. 59.
43. Ibid., pp. 60, 68.
44. Thomas Bodley, quoted in Brown, *Better a Shrew*, p. 218.
45. Ibid., pp. 21–22, 22 n. 56.
46. Epistle to *Pasquils Jests. With the merriments of Mother Bunch* (London, 1629), quoted and discussed along with other alehouse jests in Brown, *Better a*

Shrew, pp. 56–82. On Rowlands's gossip pamphlets see Susan O'Malley, *Custom Is an Idiot: Jacobean Pamphlet Literature on Women* (Urbana: University of Illinois Press, 2004), pp. 13–108.

47. Jill P. Ingram, 'A Case for Credit: Isabella Whitney's "Wyll and Testament" and the Mock Testament Tradition', *Early Modern Culture Online* (2006), http://emc.eserver.org/1-5/ingram.html (accessed 28 March 2009) (para. 1 of 28).
48. *The Early Modern Englishwoman: A Facsimile Library of Essential Works. Series I. Printed Writings, 1500–1642*, ed. Betty S. Travitsky and Patrick Cullen, 10 vols (Aldershot: Ashgate, 2002), part 2, X, p. ix.
49. Some place Whitney's will within the female legacy genre. Ingram disagrees, calling her a Piers Plowman-type satirist whose 'rollicking and outlandish bequests of the indebted, the insane, the indigent, and the widowed' has the effect of moving 'the mock-testament into a credit age' ('A Case for Credit', para. 1, 27 of 29).
50. Isabella Whitney, *Will and Testament*, http://rpo.library.utoronto.ca/poem/2947.html (accessed 27 March 2009) (ll. 1–13).
51. Ibid., ll. 17–30; italics added.
52. Ann Rosalind Jones, 'Apostrophes to Cities: Urban Rhetorics in Isabella Whitney and Moderata Fonte', in *Attending to Early Modern Women*, ed. Susan D. Amussen and Adele Seeff (Newark: University of Delaware Press/London: Associated University Presses, 1998), pp. 154–75 (p. 158). Also see Wendy Wall, *The Imprint of Gender: Authorship and Publication in the English Renaissance* (Ithaca: Cornell University Press, 1993).
53. Ann Rosalind Jones, 'Maidservants of London: Sisterhoods of Kinship and Labor', in *Maids and Mistresses, Cousin and Queens: Women's Alliances in Early Modern England*, ed. Susan Frye and Karen Robertson (New York: Oxford University Press, 1999), p. 22.

8
The Theater

Marion Wynne-Davies

Introduction: questions and theories

The dates that define this essay, 1500–1610, must appear to limit a history of Englishwomen's writing classified under 'Theater' since during this time no women wrote plays for public performance, no women acted on stage, and very few attended theatrical productions. What then could theater possibly have meant to these women and how could they engage with contemporary dramatic discourses? This essay begins, therefore, with an interrogation of our assumptions about drama and theater as genre and space.

Theater has traditionally been defined as requiring a performance, an audience, and a playing space, although present-day plays often undermine these so-called necessities. Just as contemporary dramatists and theorists of the theater question what would happen if any or all of these elements were removed, so sixteenth-century Englishwomen found that they too had to develop innovative and, often, subversive ways of circumventing the requirements of performance, audience, and stage. It is essential, therefore, when analyzing dramatic texts and fragments, that we think beyond the public stage and develop an understanding of alternative playing spaces. Recent studies have begun to redefine the ways in which early modern women negotiated the concept of performance space. In 2005 two important scholarly interventions demonstrated that, while the Restoration had traditionally been accepted as a watershed for women's active participation in the theater, such a development could not have occurred in isolation and without foundations. Sophie Tomlinson, in *Women on Stage in Stuart Drama*, argues that 'female performance in Stuart masques' necessitates a revisionist history of 'a variety of stages', while Pamela Allen Brown and Peter Parolin in their introduction to *Women Players in England, 1500–1660* identify these 'alternative playing areas [...] [as] the street, alehouse, market square, parish green, manor house and court'.[1] More recently, Alison Findlay, in *Playing Spaces in Early Women's Drama,* demonstrated that women dramatists 'confront[ed] the dangers of exposure, in order to chart new possibilities [...] [in] home, garden, court, city, convent, and female academy', and this focus on confrontation is echoed by Mary Ellen Lamb in the Introduction to *Oral Traditions and Gender in Early Modern Literary Texts* where she points out that the common denigration of women's oral performances, such as 'the ballads sung by household maids [and the] lacemakers' work chants', was used in a gender binary 'to valorize an emergent model of individual male authorship'.[2] This essay engages with both the revisionist agenda to trace the ways in which early modern women accessed alternative discursive spaces and the need to reassess how this recovery of the female voice confronts and undermines conventional gender binaries.

There are four known extant dramatic pieces composed and/or translated by women during this period: Jane Lumley's *Iphigeneia,* Mary Sidney Herbert's *The Tragedy of Antonie,* Elizabeth I's fragment *Hercules Oetaeus,* and Elizabeth Cary's *The Tragedy of Mariam.* This essay considers Elizabeth I's translation only briefly since her *oeuvre* as a whole is considered elsewhere in this collection; however, it will include Margaret Roper's *Letter to Alice Alington,* which provokes questions about audience and performance allowing it to be analyzed as participating in dramatic discourses. This essay sets out to explore these works in order to uncover the ways in which women negotiated the constraints upon their access to and use of playing space. But, while we know and accept that women were prohibited from involvement in public theater, it is important to recognize that they were not the only group to be so excluded. As such, the essay integrates the dramatic writing by sixteenth-century Englishwomen with a range of sixteenth-century discourses – faith, self-fashioning, sexual identity, and autocracy – that, in turn, relied upon upholding a dominant hierarchy and forced those marginalized by such ideologies to resort to imaginative substitutions for performance, audience, and stage. Consequently, the imagined or actual playing spaces investigated are similarly marginal: Margaret Roper's representation of martyrdom necessitates a visualized scaffold; Jane Lumley's familial fashioning used a banqueting house; Mary Sidney Herbert's interrogation of female sexual identity invoked an off-stage brothel or bed-chamber; while Elizabeth Cary's scrutiny of tyrannical power envisions a negation of space and a radical revision of the audience/reader expectations. But while constructed as marginal by the dominant hierarchies, the impact achieved by articulating rebellion from these alternative sites suggests that the public theater was not necessarily the only influential playing space.

Margaret Roper: *Letter to Alice Alington* (1534)

One of the most provocative and powerful alternative playing spaces of the early modern period was the scaffold, and this was particularly true if the speaker was female. Frances E. Dolan highlights 'the theatricality of public executions and [...] the relationships between the scaffold and the stage', going on to demonstrate that the 'scripts' available to women were 'strikingly different from those available to men'.[3] Similarly, Catherine Belsey argues that, 'the supreme opportunity to speak was the moment of execution. The requirement for confessions from the scaffold [...] paradoxically [...] offered women a place from which to speak in public with a hitherto unimagined authority.'[4] One of the most famous of all female gallows speeches – and one mentioned by Dolan – may be found in John Foxe's description of Jane Grey's execution in *Acts and Monuments* (1554).

Foxe begins in good Protestant form: 'she mounted the scaffold [and] [...] said to the people standing thereabout, "Good people, I am come hither to die, and by a law I am condemned to the same" asking them to "assist me with your prayers"'. The most powerful part of the description occurs as Foxe allows the reader to imagine the scene in graphic detail. It commences with Jane Grey as she 'gave her maiden, mistress Ellen, her gloves and handkerchief, and her book to master Bruges. And then she untied her gown.' The hangman tried to help Grey disrobe but she, with suitable propriety, 'turned towards her two gentlewomen' for aid; he then 'willed her to stand upon the straw; which doing, she saw the block'; she was then given 'a fair handkerchief to knit about her eyes' so that, kneeling she had to 'feel [...] for the block', asking, 'What shall I do? Where is it? Where is it?'[5] The words of the stalwart martyr become mingled with the compelling image of a young woman who is alone, fearful, and defenseless.

Jane Grey's execution occurred in private, partly to offer the privacy her status required, but also because a closed and regulated group of attendees were less likely to be inflamed by a powerful or poignant scaffold speech. For her execution to become effective as Protestant propaganda Foxe had, therefore, to ensure that her words became linked to an imagined performance. If the state denied the martyr an arena for their final inspirational pronouncements then the stage for their 'Act' had, perforce, to be recreated in a text that could be circulated amongst the faithful.

It was precisely this dramatic martyrological discourse that Margaret Roper participated in when describing the events that led to her father's death in her letter to Alice Alington. Margaret Roper is best known as the daughter of the English Catholic martyr, Thomas More, although before her father became engaged in the religious controversies surrounding Henry VIII's divorce from his first wife, she had embarked upon her own independent scholarly work, translating Erasmus's *Precatio Dominica* (1523) as *A deuout treatise vpon the Pater noster* (1524). Since Roper's name did not appear in the published version it is possible to detect a careful balancing of humanist enterprise – the translation – with the expected proprieties for early modern women – the work is prefaced or 'allowed' by her male tutor, Richard Hyrde. This quasi-anonymity lost its relevance when More refused to swear the Oath of Supremacy, was imprisoned in the Tower of London, and faced certain execution. From this point on, anything Roper wrote, published, or 'acted' would become part of a wider discourse in which the familial became inextricably bound to religious conviction and the preservation of the Catholic faith. In effect, when her father's voice was silenced by the King, Roper's texts served to rehearse and perpetuate his words as part of early counter-Reformation propaganda in which martyrdom was used as a tool to elicit pity and inspire courage. In order to comply with this agenda, which was no doubt bulwarked by the strong affection she felt for her father, Roper abandoned scholarly reasoning in Latin and began to employ an evocative vernacular style embedded as much in the visual as the textual. This is particularly apparent in the *Letter to Alice Alington*.

In this work Roper recounts how she tried to persuade her father to comply with the King's demands. The most significant critical debate about the letter, however, from its first publication to the present day, is how much was authored by More and how much by Roper. I have argued elsewhere that the powerful impetus of the familial discourse demands mutuality rather than independent authorship, but here I would like to concentrate on how visual the letter is even as it evokes the more formal disputation of Plato's *Crito*.[6] It begins with a description of how Margaret 'came next' to More, how they decided 'to sit and talke, and be mery', and how when she began to challenge his decision he 'smiled [...] [and] loked sadly'.[7] The scene is set by Roper through a depiction of actions and a static description of her father's demeanor, so that the images of his facial expressions are interleaved with the detail of what they did. More is described as reading over the letter from Alice 'ouer again [...] [with] no maner hast' (p. 517) and laughing when she continued to persuade him, while Roper noted that she sat 'very sadde' (p. 529) because of the refutation of her arguments. Dialogue is frequently noted with 'quod I' and 'quod my father' or 'quod he', allowing Alice and subsequently the wider group of Catholic readers for whom the letter was intended to imagine the discourse in the form of an actual conversation.

Roper even includes a quasi 'play within the play' as she recounts 'a tale' that she can 'skant tell' in More's words since 'it hangeth upon some tearmes and ceremonies of the law', and so translates it into a more readily accessible account. She tells the story of a Northern trader who, because he was 'outelawed', was arrested at Bartholomew Fair by an 'eschetour' or officer of the law (pp. 521–22). In retaliation the trader's fellow Northerners brought a counter-claim against the officer and arranged that the 'quest' or jury would consist of their associates. When the jury rapidly agrees to find the officer guilty, one of them, a man called 'Cumpany' refuses to accept the verdict until 'they tell hym such reason therin' (p. 522). At first Cumpany is ignored because he was 'but a foule and sate still and said nothing' but when he refused to be persuaded they scorn his punctiliousness and joke about his name:

> 'Cumpany,' quod they, 'now by thy trouth good fellow, playe than the gude companion, come theron furth with vs, and passe euen for gude company.' (pp. 522–23)

But Cumpany is a wise man and refuses to be coerced; he adheres to true justice since 'the passage of my pore soule passeth all good company' (p. 523). The moral of the tale for More is that he also trusts to his conscience and will not succumb to the persuasions of the 'cumpany' of his family. But the letter allows Roper to devise a lively and comic fable that is presented in her own words; she even begins with a feigned ignorance of the court's name, 'But, tut, let the name of the courte go for this once, or call it if ye will a court of pye' and when referring to the jury she pretends not to know the correct name of 'quest' calling it instead a 'periury', which indicates the false evidence accepted by the men (p. 521). The final key to the tale must be, of course, in the verdict, since More is identified with that 'foule' man, Cumpany. But neither More nor Roper provides the court's final decision; it is sufficient to assert the power of conscience, so that the fate of the lone protester in the tale merges into More's own end and the 'court of pye' becomes a timely reminder that worldly justice must always be superseded by heavenly judgment.

The *Letter to Alice Alington* accomplishes what would have been impossible for More himself to do, since he had been ordered by the King, 'at your execution you shall not vse many wordes'.[8] Denied the right to speak of his conscience, More allowed his words to be translated by his daughter into an imaginative tale that could be circulated amongst his family and his fellow Catholics constructing them as viewers of a drama in which he and Cumpany elicit sympathy and demand that conscience and truth be upheld. Ironically, when Roper describes Cumpany refusing to accept the majority decision, she is not, as her overt reason for the letter suggests, trying to persuade her father to forgo his decision to reject the King's demands, but rather to encourage others to join More's 'cumpany' of those who put their faith in spiritual justice. While Roper never mentions the scaffold in her letter (indeed, it would have been dangerous to do so), she adopts a position of agency, using More's execution (in Belsey's words) as 'a place from which to speak in public with a hitherto unimagined authority'.

Letters, accounts, and biographies were essential tools in the distribution of a martyr's last words, so that Roper's contribution to the perpetuation of her father's memory and his faith should be set alongside scaffold speeches that encompassed Protestant and Catholic martyrs alike. As such, Roper and Foxe locate their texts within a discourse of martyrdom that allowed them to recreate a tragic death on the imagined scaffold, thereby providing a stage for the protagonist's final dramatic speech. Placed in the context of dramatic writing by early sixteenth-century Englishwomen the consanguinities extend further since the right to open speech on any stage, be it in the theater or on a scaffold, was not only denied to women, but to all those irrespective of gender who challenged the dominant power structures of their time. When Margaret Roper chose to invoke the visual and verbal tools of the stage in her letter, she evaded both the strictures upon her as a woman to remain silent and the King's command that her father should 'not vse many wordes' on the scaffold and in so doing she placed herself not only amongst the 'cumpany' of faithful Catholics but in a company of performers whose words could never be acted on the public stage, but whose 'acts' conjured up a dramatic production for all those who read them.

Jane Lumley *Iphigeneia* (*c.*1557)

If Margaret Roper was enmeshed in the discourse of faith, adopting an imagined scaffold for performance, Jane Lumley's use of a banqueting house may be linked to the self-fashioning of the Tudor nobility.

Therefore, in order to understand why Jane Lumley decided to translate Euripides's tragedy *Iphigenia at Aulis* using political allegory to represent the execution of Jane Grey, it is necessary to understand her own position within the political strategies of her day and how she became familiar with a playing space. Although Lumley was first cousin to Grey on her mother's side, her father was Henry Fitzalan, 12th Earl of Arundel, a man who had been involved in deposing the young Protestant Queen and the consequent ascent to the throne of Mary Tudor. Although he had appeared to support Jane's accession, even accompanying her on her ceremonial progress to the Tower of London, Arundel had simultaneously started to plot the young Queen's downfall. Critically, it was Arundel's eloquent speech to an assembled group of nobles at Baynard's Castle that persuaded them to support Mary's claim to the throne and that finally facilitated the Catholic Queen's victory. Arundel and his family were duly rewarded: Jane Lumley sat in the third chariot of state in the coronation procession, while Arundel was granted, among other prizes, the royal palace of Nonsuch. Lumley's husband, John, acted for Arundel in the acquisition of the property and it subsequently became the Lumleys' primary residence. The building itself was certainly spectacular; however, in terms of playing spaces the most interesting feature of Nonsuch was its banqueting house.

Tudor banqueting houses had initially been temporary constructions that could be used for a number of purposes, including suppers, formal banquets, and performances of various kinds. The designs were not uniform but often included either an internal performance space or viewing balconies from which the diners could watch an outdoor play or spectacle. They were primarily built by monarchs because of the expense and, as such, to own and use a banqueting house became a significant indicator of wealth and power. The one at Nonsuch was set on a small hill and approached from the palace through the gardens and the Grove of Diana with its fountain in the form of the goddess. It was a square wooden construct with a viewing balcony at each corner to allow guests to watch the various entertainments provided by Arundel and Lumley. The first recorded use of the banqueting house was during Elizabeth I's visit to Nonsuch in 1559 when the young Queen was provided with a diverse series of shows including a play written by John Heywood and performed by the children of St Paul's. It is highly likely, however, that Arundel had begun to use the banqueting house soon after he acquired the palace in 1557; not only would such displays have been an important statement of his status, but his family were conversant with drama – Jane Lumley's translation of *Iphigeneia* – and performance – both John

Lumley and Arundel's son, Henry Maltravers had been involved in producing a court masque. The presence of a banqueting house designed for dramatic performance at Nonsuch signifies that Lumley's translation should be excavated for the possibility of an imagined or actual performance.

The most recent criticism of the play concludes that the text facilitates acting: Stephanie Hodgson-Wright argues that internal evidence 'points to the likelihood of an envisaged, if not actual, performance'; Marta Straznicky points out that 'readerly and performative devices [...] [suggest that] the play was designed for performance'; and Alison Findlay notes that 'the outdoor setting of this play [...] has close affinities with the "Wildernes" or outer garden at [...] Nonsuch.'9 For example, evidence for a projected performance may be elicited from the final scene in which the Nuncius describes what happened at Iphigeneia's execution, 'the whole hooste began to desier the goddes Diana, that she wolde accepte the sacrifice of the virgins blode [...] [but she] vanisshed sodenlye awaye [and a] [...] white harte' was found lying in her place.10 The logical route for actors to leave the playing space before the banqueting house would have been down the hill to the wooded Grove of Diana, which would have been visually off-stage for those sitting in the viewing balconies.11 With textual evidence that the play was envisaged for performance, the strong possibility of a familial audience, and the ready availability of a playing space, it is essential to ask why Lumley, one of the Catholic nobility, would choose a play that may be identified as representing the execution of the Protestant Queen, Jane Grey.

The political allegory rests on the understanding that Jane Grey had to be executed, like Iphigeneia, in order to allow the Catholics (Greeks) to defeat the Protestants (Trojans). The similarity between the events of the classical play and early modern political concerns has been repeatedly noted by critics of Lumley's play: Stephanie Hodgson-Wright comments that, 'the contemporary resonances of Jane Lumley's text become [...] apparent'; Barry Weller and Margaret W. Ferguson argue that the plot 'bore striking resemblance to dilemmas in her own aristocratic patriarchal family'; and Betty S. Travitsky suggests that the characters in the play 'related to some of the principal actors in the contemporary debacle [of Lady Jane Grey's rule and execution]'.12 Lumley would have found the use of political allegory in stately-house dramas commonplace, although it would be wrong to interpret this engagement as a challenge, covert or otherwise, to the dominant discourse of court or noble household. Greg Walker argues effectively that these domestic 'plays represent [...] a message from the household playwright to the patron'.[13] Tudor household theater was intrinsic to the self-fashioning of the most powerful nobles in the land and its political import demanded a careful balancing of persuasion and ostentatious show.

Returning to the final scene of the play it becomes apparent that while Lumley presents Iphigeneia in a sympathetic light, she never criticizes the decision to sacrifice the young woman. In a final speech to her mother Iphigeneia claims that,

> I muste nedes die, and will suffer it willingelye. Consider, I praie you mother, for what a lawfull cause I shalbe slaine. Dothe not bothe the destruction of Troie, and also the welthe of grece, whiche is the mooste frutefull country of the worlde, hange upon my deathe? (p. 30)

Iphigeneia goes willingly to a death that she recognizes as 'lawfull', in order to preserve 'grece'. Within the political allegory this may be translated into the acceptance of Grey's execution as lawful and necessary for the good of England. Such a conclusion would have been perfectly acceptable to Arundel who had been instrumental in Jane Grey's death and who would certainly have seen the security of England as commensurate with the preservation of the Catholic faith. The almost Christ-like sacrifice of Iphigeneia and the Marian associations of Diana serve, therefore, not as religious propaganda, but as a way in which the Arundel family chose to justify its actions, rewriting the spiritual narrative in a distinctly political form. The use of household theater in the mid-sixteenth century as a means of facilitating the self-fashioning of the patron elides perfectly with Lumley's careful reworking of both original text and political events, evidencing her familiarity with the dominant dramatic discourses of her period. For example, John Heywood, the dramatist invited by Arundel to write a play for Elizabeth I's visit to Nonsuch, was involved in similar dramatic productions; as Greg Walker argues, 'his dissent was expressed not in factional infighting or secret conspiracy, but in the more public forum created by the production of courtly drama'.[14]

By comparing Lumley's play with those of Heywood and other writers of household theater, it becomes possible to identify the constraints imposed upon them, since they often relied upon the goodwill and financial reward of their patron. Heywood, like Lumley, used political allegory carefully, balancing the desire of his customer to fashion him or herself as powerful and wealthy together with a message that sought to engender virtue. Read within the tortuous combination of praise and moral lessoning that characterized Tudor household theater, *Iphigeneia* must be identified as a text that exonerates Arundel but at the same time offers him and his family a narrative of selfless uprightness. Lumley's adoption of this dramatic discourse allowed her to display the power and cultural sophistication of her father, while simultaneously presenting his actions as part of a wider necessity, perhaps even encouraging him to adopt such a stance as a new Protestant queen ascended the throne. As a daughter within a household dominated by Arundel, as a woman within a society that prevented her access to public performance, and as a Catholic in a newly Protestant England, Jane Lumley wisely chose to employ the cautious dramatic form of household theater, the subtlety of political allegory, and the secluded space of a banqueting house.

Mary Sidney Herbert, *The Tragedy of Antonie* (1590)

More than thirty years after Jane Lumley translated a tragedy by Euripides for an envisaged country house performance, Mary Sidney Herbert translated Robert Garnier's *Marc Antoine* in the form of a closet drama meant to be read aloud rather than acted, suggesting that women's play-writing had advanced little in content or form. Indeed, an examination of Elizabeth I's translation of a dramatic fragment from Seneca's *Hercules Oetaeus* suggests that if anything more than a private exercise, the piece with its long declamatory speech was more suited to closet drama than the public stage. As such, there can be no question that at the end of the sixteenth century women were still not permitted to write texts destined for the public stage, but Mary Sidney Herbert's *The Tragedy of Antonie* is a more radical work than is generally assumed and the key to under-standing the extent of its subversive discourse is through the character of Cleopatra. Indeed, by reimagining the use of a private and concealed space within the play, Mary Sidney Herbert challenges the supposition that closet dramas – and the women who wrote them – were contained by the patriarchal discourses of the public theater.

Mary Sidney Herbert's literary productivity primarily suggests a writer who carefully avoided original works, sustaining an appropriate pro-priety through editing and translating. She edited her brother's (Philip Sidney) *Arcadia* and continued his translations of the Psalms, and, in addition to Garnier's play, translated Petrarch's *The Triumph of Death* and Philippe de Mornay's *A Discourse of Life and Death*. As Margaret Hannay sums up:

> Mary Sidney [...] by remaining within the established limits, became the most important woman writer and patron of the Elizabethan

period, one who demonstrated what could and what could not be accomplished in the margins.[15]

Nevertheless, writing from 'the margins' can be a potent mechanism for challenging preconceptions and undermining social and political practice. And by choosing to translate Garnier's tragedy, Sidney Herbert engaged directly with the construction of gender identity, in particular the question of chastity and sexual promiscuity, in other words, that central dialectic of the *querelle des femmes* – Mary versus Eve and virgin versus whore. Moreover, while the generic form of closet drama might initially appear to be constricting, its very secrecy and containment facilitated an exploration of female subjectivity that was associated with the power of desire and the danger of allurement.

Critics have consistently noted that Sidney Herbert alters the traditional view of Cleopatra as a seductress; as Tina Krontiris notes, '*Antonie* offers a sympathetic view of the adulterous lovers, and especially of Cleopatra.'[16] Although such interpretations align easily with the feminist agenda to reclaim women authors, Sidney Herbert's Cleopatra cannot be so easily pigeon-holed. First, the play undoubtedly corroborates the representation of Cleopatra as a fickle seductress whose relationship with Antonie is based on erotic desire. Act I consists entirely of a 148-line monologue by the Roman general that presents women as unreliable sexual predators. Although Antonie accepts that Cleopatra is the 'idol of [...] [his] heart',[17] he asserts that she has trapped him with 'allurements', 'sweet baits', 'amorous delights' (p. 21), and 'wanton love' (p. 22). As such, he claims that she has made him a 'slave' and 'servile' (p. 21), forcing him to 'wrong' (p. 19) his wife and abandon 'honour' (p. 21), so that he has become 'low, dishonored, [and] despised' (p. 22). Cleopatra is a 'fair soceress' (p. 21) who has 'poisoned' (p. 21) him and 'infected' (p. 22) his heart so that, instead of martial feats he has succumbed to wanton play, giving up 'field tents to courtly bowers' (p. 21). This accusation is repeated in Act III where Antonie compares Cleopatra to the witch Circe who transforms Odysseus's men into swine, 'in filthy mire / With glutted heart I wallowed in delights' and himself to Hercules who also undertook 'base unseemly service [...] [while dressed] in maid's attire' (p. 33). The danger of Cleopatra's sexual allure is further underlined in Act III by Antonie's comrade, Lucilius, who argues that 'Venus' sweet delights [...] over-cloud our sprights [...] [and] [...] from our hearts out chase all holy virtues [...] [making] our souls [...] too lickerish' (p. 33). The shift to a spiritual discourse serves to associate Cleopatra with Eve, a point made explicit by Sidney Herbert in her choice of the word 'lickerish' since it is not used by Garnier (who instead refers to 'friande' or a small delicate cake).[18] Sidney Herbert thus allows the greed for rare food to merge with erotic desire, thereby compounding the 'lickerish'/lecherous feelings Eve arouses in Adam when she tempts him to eat the forbidden fruit. Finally, in Act IV Caesar castigates Antonie's relationship with Cleopatra as 'lewd delights' (p. 35) and 'unchaste love' (p. 39). However much Cleopatra might assert that she loves Antonie, the play is dominated by the description of her as a dangerous seductress, a witch, an Eve-like figure, and a whore.

But if Cleopatra is vilified and constructed as on the margins of acceptable female behavior where does that place Antonie? Intriguingly, he describes himself as a 'chamberer' (p. 33) who has been 'sunk in foul sink' (p. 22). Sidney Herbert's choice of these two terms, 'chamberer' and 'sink', is particularly interesting since Garnier uses 'casanier' (p. 141) and 'croupissant en ta fange' (p. 112). A 'casanier' was someone who preferred to stay at home rather than go out, in Antonie's case, to fight battles. On the other hand, a 'chamberer' in Elizabethan English was a man who frequented ladies' bedrooms or their inner chambers, with the inevitable sexual pun upon such illicit intrusion. In parallel, 'croupissant en ta fange' in French suggests stagnating in the mud or gutter whereas for an Elizabethan, 'sink' was a slang term used for a place of vice or a brothel with a similar sexual innuendo on degeneration (sinking) and intercourse (penetration). Therefore, if Cleopatra is a whore, then Antonie becomes one of her customers, a frequenter of those illicit spaces, the bed-chamber and the brothel. *The Tragedy of Antonie* begins by setting out the traditional patriarchal construction of bifurcated female identity into virgin and whore, but it shifts into a representation of how marginal women, such as Cleopatra, through their potent erotic power cannot be excluded from the dominant male ideology. Sidney Herbert challenges the construction of female sexuality as dangerous and therefore of necessity to be excluded, by demonstrating that the female 'other' inheres within male discourses of power and desire. Therefore, just as Rome seeks to conquer Egypt, so Antonie cannot help but desire Cleopatra, and Adam must take the apple from Eve. Moreover, by exposing the dialectic, the play calls into question the very boundaries by which men, imperial power, the church, and society seek to contain women. Through this process the sites of bed-chamber and brothel become playing spaces in which supposed containment and marginality are revealed instead as the loci for a deconstruction of traditional gender roles.

Mary Sidney Herbert is not often associated with the public theater of the sixteenth century; however, her focus on female sexual identity in the play evidences her engagement with contemporary male-authored plays' fascination with the dialectic of virgin/whore. For example, the character of Zenocrate in Christopher Marlowe's *Tamburlaine* is particularly relevant to Sidney Herbert's character, Cleopatra, both being defined by their eastern, or oriental otherness, and by the fact that they are described as whores. While, however, Zenocrate is originally described as a 'base concubine', by the end of the play she is reinvented as a chaste maiden: Tamburlaine states that '[from] all blot of foul in chastity, I record heaven, her heavenly self is clear', and their subsequent marriage ensures Zenocrate's reinstatement in social convention.[19] Through the focus upon illicit female sexual activity Marlowe, like Sidney Herbert, exposes the weaknesses of patriarchal ideology and thereby destabilizes its claim to be timeless, natural, and immutable. However, one of the key differences between the plays is in the nature of their performance: in *Tamburlaine* Zenocrate's disgrace and reinstatement are public acts viewed on a public stage, whereas in *The Tragedy of Antonie* sexual acts, Antonie's 'amorous delights', are all imagined as occurring within the confines of an illicit space, a bed-chamber or a brothel. Given the sex of the dramatists and the generic demands of the forms they employed, it might be expected that Marlowe would parade a concubine across the stage, whereas Sidney Herbert demands that we imagine a private space for sexual passion. At the same time, it should be recalled that Zenocrate's reputation is restored at the end of the play, while Cleopatra remains a dangerous seductress, and that Tamburlaine conquers Egypt and the eastern world in stark contrast to Antonie's defeat in the Egyptian Queen's bed-chamber. For, if world and public stage may be seen as patriarchal domains, then the private room or closet may be identified as female playing spaces. Late-sixteenth-century restrictions on women dramatists placed them on the margins of acceptable female behavior and they, like the unchaste woman or courtesan, had perforce to ply their trade within a closed and carefully policed environment. Nevertheless, the allurements and delights of the texts produced within these confines had the power to elicit male engagement, in turn, demanding that the distinctions between male/female, public/private, and visible/closeted are undermined. So that, just as Antonie resides with Cleopatra in her chamber, so male and female audiences gather in the 'closet' to read the play, and the readers of *The Tragedy of Antonie* enter the closed world of the text. In a particularly bold and deft maneuver, Sidney Herbert allies these illicit sexual and dramatic acts and, by constructing the reader/audience as a 'bedchamberer', undermines the dialectical construction of female identity into virgin or whore.

Elizabeth Cary, *The Tragedy of Mariam* (*c*.1602–04)

Elizabeth Cary is the most important woman writer to be considered in this essay since she is the first early modern Englishwoman to write an original play. Indeed, although there is no evidence that the work was written for performance, let alone performed, when produced on the public stage today it is powerful, imaginative, and overpoweringly relevant. Moreover, the play is packed with excellent parts for women, so that a cast-list might be edited in the following manner:

Mariam, Herod's second wife	ideal but independent
Alexandra, Mariam's mother	an embittered matriarch
Salome, Herod's sister	makes Cleopatra's sexual activities look chaste
Doris, Herod's first wife	a vengeful harpy
Graphina, a maid	incurable romantic, in love with Herod's brother

In contrast, the male characters are weak, boring, or duplicitous, although Herod's vacillation, barbed relationship with Salome, and genuine, but jealous, love for Mariam make him more than a stereotypical villain. *The Tragedy of Mariam* is, therefore, a conundrum: a performable play that was not written for performance – on stage, scaffold, or banqueting house. In addition, while several early critics assumed that the play was a closet drama – perhaps taking the lead from Sidney Herbert's clearly defined use of that genre – recent analyses of *Mariam* have presented a more complex interpretation. For example, Marta Straznicky points out that,

> [the] conjunction of theatrical and literary effect produced by the typographic arrangement of *Mariam* suggests that the play is 'private' in a unique sense: its format resembles the most classical of closet dramas, but its accommodation of stage business links it equally with some of the elite dramatic publications emerging from the 'private' theatre.[20]

Similarly, Alison Findlay refers to the play's representation as necessitating the concept of a 'floating stage' that encompasses its household and political frames.[21]

The most pressing questions about Cary's play must be, therefore, why she created a work that was so powerfully vocal while at the same time silencing it, why she chose drama when a prose or poetic text would have been more readily published, and what issues did she hope to explore that made such choices seem apt? What we know of Elizabeth Cary confirms that she was a highly individualistic woman who was both independent and innovative. In addition to composing the first original drama by an Englishwoman, she was precociously intelligent, translating a number of works and authoring a hybrid text – *Edward II* – that, with its mixture of prose, poetry, and drama, looks surprisingly postmodern. She challenged her husband's authority by leaving him and converting to Catholicism and she arranged for a swashbuckling abduction of her younger children from their Protestant elder brother so that they could be sent to religious houses on the Continent. *The Tragedy of Mariam* was written *c.*1602–04 when Elizabeth was about eighteen and shortly after her marriage to Henry Cary, although during the period of the play's composition her husband was a prisoner in Spain.[22] At this stage Cary cannot have envisaged her future rebellion – as wife and convert – but the play returns repeatedly to the idea of mutiny and its suppression, in particular how language and silence are powerful operatives in these processes.

The importance of open speech within an autocratic society is made clear in the first line of the play when Mariam confesses, 'How oft have I with public voice run on', describing her outspoken criticism of her – supposedly – dead husband, Herod.[23] In the subsequent two Acts all the other characters in the play note how they too have revealed or concealed secrets with explicit regard to the impact these words and/or silences would have on Herod when he was alive. Alexandra is now able to castigate Herod openly, her tongue freed by knowledge of 'the tyrant's end' – as Salome points out,

> You durst not thus have given your tongue the rein
> If noble Herod still remained in life. (p. 52)

Salome gleefully recounts that she has told Herod 'infamy [...] [and] slander[s]' (p. 52) about Mariam, but with her brother dead she acknowledges that she cannot rid herself of her husband Constabarus in order to marry Silleus since, her 'tongue / To Contstabarus by itself is tied' (p. 53). Herod's brother, Pheroras, has concealed his love for Graphina since it was against the King's wishes, while Constabarus, in turn, has 'concealed [...] from the tyrant's sword' (p. 56) the two sons of one of Herod's enemies, Babus. Finally, Doris and her son, Antipater, realize that because 'Each mouth within the city loudly cries [...] Herod's death' (p. 58), they must plot to kill Mariam and her children secretly.

Perhaps the only character in the play not to be revealing or concealing something is Ananell, the high priest, and so it is perfectly fitting that he will 'fill [...] the temple with my thankful voice' (p. 61), announcing that Herod lives.

At the news of Herod's survival, Salome and Pheroras plan how to use their brother's return to their advantage, using the power of language to betray Constabarus – 'I'll go from hence / In Herod's ear the Hebrew to deface' – and malign Mariam – 'Now tongue of mine with scandal load her name' (p. 61). In sharp contrast Mariam begs, 'tell me not that Herod is returned', although she knows that her 'gentle word' could overcome Salome's 'wind' (p. 62). But as Sohemus (Herod's counselor) notes, 'unbridled speech is Mariam's worst disgrace' (p. 62), a judgment emphasized by the chorus:

> When any ears but one therewith they [the words of a wife] fill,
> Doth in a sort her pureness overthrow. (p. 63)

On his return Herod, in wonderful tyrant-mode, castigates his brother for marrying Graphina against his orders, commands the execution of Constabarus and Babus's sons because they are 'traitors' (p. 65), has Sohemus killed because he believes the counselor was Mariam's lover, and imprisons Mariam for living 'too wantonly' (p. 66). Later, Salome encourages Herod to put Mariam to death because 'she speaks a beauteous language [...] [that] doth [...] allure the auditors to sin' and the King finally agrees that 'her mouth will ope to every stranger's ear' (p. 68). The play persistently links women's public speech with lack of chastity, disobedience, and female rebellion. In Mariam's case, the refusal to remain silent and/or to lie about her feelings for Herod results in her death, the ultimate repression of the independent subject's voice. Yet this rebellion is echoed by the other women in the play: Alexandra, Salome, Doris, and Graphina all use language to challenge dominant ideologies by carping against the sovereign, defying husbands, and refusing to accept arranged marriages. Cary's engagement with rebellion, however, extends beyond gender roles, for the men in the play fare little better in a totalitarian state where any questioning of the ruler's will is interpreted as treachery and must be punished with death.

Although Mariam does not appear in the play's final act, news of her execution and her last words are recounted to Herod by the messenger:

> Tell thou my lord, thou saw'st me lose my breath
> [...]

If guiltily, eternal be my death
[...]
By three days hence, if wishes could revive,
I know himself would make me oft alive. (p. 72)

These lines are commonly read as presenting Mariam as a Christian martyr, the 'three days' referring to the description of Christ's resurrection in Matthew (27:63–64); indeed, given Cary's later conversion to Catholicism, it is often argued that Mariam's execution shadows that of Mary Queen of Scots. As Margaret W. Ferguson notes, Mary 'was in the eyes of many English Catholics a victim of Protestant tyranny'.[24] At the conclusion of the play, therefore, Cary invokes the discourse of martyrdom that was so effectively manipulated by Roper and Foxe so that the suggestion of Catholic sympathies cannot be ignored. At the same time, the repetition and circulation of the last words of any man or woman who was considered, by a faction and/or themselves, to be executed unjustly was essential for both cause and reputation. In this manner, Walter Raleigh's scaffold speech in which he proclaimed his innocence is equally indicative of how the powerless individual is unjustly condemned by the tyrant. Mariam, therefore, serves as a reminder not only of Catholic martyrdom, but more widely of prejudice based on faith and the repression of women. Moreover, the play actively projects this challenge to dominant hierarchies through language and provides a stringent warning against all those – men and women – who speak out against a tyrannical sovereign. Cary's play needs, therefore, to be understood as part of the wider early modern discourses of power, rebellion, and freedom of speech.

One of the central arguments of this essay has been that women's dramatic writing cannot be divorced from its male counterpart and that to avoid such ghettoization it is essential to explore a mutuality of discursive enterprise. This is, perhaps, more important for Cary's play than with any of the other works considered here; for example, *The Tragedy of Mariam* is most commonly compared to Shakespeare's *Othello* since both plays focus upon a jealous husband, an unjustly executed wife, betrayal, and the problems of racial difference. However, I would like to suggest that Cary's engagement with the way in which language relates to power might well offer consanguinities with other Shakespearian plays, in particular *King Lear*. In Shakespeare's tragedy it is Cordelia's decision to say 'nothing' that alienates her from the King and allows her sisters, who conceal their true thoughts behind false words, to obtain sovereign power. The play is, of course, rife with concealment and the lack of accurate perception, from Edgar's disguise as Tom to Gloucester's blinding. Jan Kott, one of the most acute postwar critics of *Lear*, identified the work's thematic focus upon the mechanisms of power but also argued that by the end of the play, 'all bonds, all laws, whether divine, natural or human, are broken. Social order, from the kingdom to the family, will crumble into dust.'[25] This assessment is particularly resonant for an interpretation of *The Tragedy of Mariam* for Cary's play concludes with a similarly nihilistic view of humankind's situation. The 'bonds' of marriage, faith, love, justice, and truth have all been 'broken' and Herod's kingdom, his authority, and even his sanity have 'crumble[d]'. As the chorus concludes:

> This day's events were certainly ordained,
> To be the warning to posterity;
> So many changes are therein contained,
> So admirable strange variety. (p. 75)

This consanguinity with what we recognize as theater of the absurd offers an unexpected insight into Cary's radical forms of textual production and goes some way towards answering the questions of why she wrote a play that was never intended for performance and what that implies for the idea of a playing space. But I would like to suggest that an understanding of how to manipulate a marginalized position extends beyond Cary to the other women dramatists considered in this essay.

Conclusion: to exist and not exist

This essay began by questioning the need for performance, audience, and playing space, arguing that early modern women dramatists had perforce to work beyond these traditional definitions. In parallel, the theater of the absurd undertook the same interrogative processes, challenging the audience in its presuppositions about the constituents of dramatic production. In his essay on *Lear* Kott analyzes the scene in which Gloucester jumps from the cliff pointing out that in order to have a tragic impact 'as a parable of universal human fate' the 'stage must be empty' thereby constructing a playing space that simultaneously 'exists and does not exist'.[26] If we return to the question of performance, Cary develops a similar dilemma: the playing space for *Mariam* must exist as part of the imaginative processes of the reader, but at the same time the stage must be empty because women are denied access to the public vocalization of their writing. This contradiction is underscored by the play's persistent foregrounding of the female voice at exactly the moment that it is silenced or repressed, a point emblematized by the recounting of Mariam's last words after her death. In this sense, the speech's biblical allusions serve to turn Mariam's fate into a 'parable' of human experience, an interpretation further evidenced by the deaths of the play's male characters.

Of all the women dramatists considered in this essay it is Cary who most acknowledged the limitations that constrained a sixteenth-century Englishwoman writing a dramatic text, namely: that they could hardly hope for a performance of their work, that propriety and convention ensured that they would have no audience, and that they had no access to a public stage. Each writer considered here did, however, find ways to manipulate these restrictions in order to produce a dramatic text. Margaret Roper immersed herself within the discourses of faith and martyrdom, projecting a scaffold as stage for the final words of her father. Jane Lumley used the conventions of household drama to fashion her family's political aspirations and, of all the writers here, is the most likely to have had her play performed in the banqueting hall at Nonsuch. Mary Sidney Herbert, by focusing on female sexual identity was able to recreate an illicit and intimate performance space that rewrites closet drama as the theater of the bed-chamber or brothel. And, finally, Elizabeth Cary who took the negation of voice, action, and space to its absurd conclusion, produced not only a stringent condemnation of the repression of women, but also an early modern parable of tyranny, rebellion, and subjugation. This essay posited the question of what theater could possibly have meant to sixteenth-century English women writers of dramatic texts. The response must be as multi-faceted as the discourses and playing spaces engaged with by Roper, Lumley, Sidney Herbert, and Cary. In their specific contexts each woman produced a revisionist work that exploited the space between voice and silence, what is concealed and what revealed, and, finally, between existence and negation.

Notes

1. Sophie Tomlinson, *Women on Stage in Stuart Drama* (Cambridge: Cambridge University Press, 2005), pp. 3 and 1; *Women Players in England, 1550–1660: Beyond the All-Male Stage*, ed. Pamela Allen Brown and Peter Parolin (Aldershot and Burlington: Ashgate, 2005), p. 1.
2. Alison Findlay, *Playing Spaces in Early Women's Drama* (Cambridge: Cambridge University Press, 2007), p. 224; *Oral Traditions and Gender in Early Modern Literary Texts*, ed. Mary Ellen Lamb and Karen Bamford (Aldershot: Ashgate, 2008), p. xviii.

3. Frances E. Dolan, '"Gentlemen. I Have One More Thing to Say": Women on Scaffolds in England, 1563–1880', *Modern Philology* 92 (1994), 157–78 (pp. 157–59).

4. Catherine Belsey, The *Subject of Tragedy. Identity and Difference in Renaissance Drama* (London: Methuen, 1985), p. 190.

5. John Foxe, *The Church Historians of England: The Acts and Monuments of John Foxe*, 8 vols (London: Seeleys, 1858), II, p. 424.

6. Marion Wynne-Davies, *Women Writers and Familial Discourse in the English Renaissance* (London: Palgrave Macmillan, 2007), pp. 17–21.

7. Margaret More Roper, *The Correspondence of Sir Thomas More*, ed. Elizabeth Frances Rogers (Princeton: Princeton University Press, 1947), pp. 514–15. Subsequent references are cited parenthetically in the text.

8. Nicholas Harpsfield, *The life and death of Sr Thomas Moore, knight, sometymes Lord high Chancellor of England*, ed. Elsie Vaughan Hitchcock (London: Early English Text Society, Oxford University Press, 1932), p. 202.

9. Stephanie Hodgson-Wright, 'Jane Lumley's *Iphigenia at Aulis: multum in parvo*, or, less is more', in *Readings in Renaissance Women's Drama: Criticism, History, and Performance, 1594–1998*, ed. S. P. Cerasano and M. Wynne-Davies (London: Routledge, 1998), p. 137. Marta Straznicky, *Privacy, Playreading, and Women's Closet Drama, 1550–1700* (Cambridge: Cambridge University Press, 2004), p. 44. Findlay, *Playing Spaces*, p. 74.

10. Jane Lumley, *Iphigeneia*, in *Three Tragedies by Renaissance Women*, ed. Diane Purkiss (Harmondsworth: Penguin Books, 1998), p. 34. Subsequent references are cited parenthetically in the text.

11. Wynne-Davies, *Women Writers*, p. 79.

12. Hodgson-Wright, 'Jane Lumley's *Iphigenia at Aulis*', p. 133. Barry Weller and Margaret W. Ferguson (eds), *The Tragedy of Mariam* in *The Tragedy of Mariam, The Fair Queen of Jewry with the Lady Falkland: Her Life* (London: University of California Press, 1994), p. 27. Betty S. Travitsky, 'The Possibilities of Prose', in *Women and Literature in Britain, 1500–1700*, ed. Helen Wilcox (Cambridge: Cambridge University Press, 1996), p. 240.

13. Greg Walker, *The Politics of Performance in Early Renaissance Drama* (Cambridge: Cambridge University Press, 1998), p. 71.

14. Ibid., p. 76.

15. Margaret P. Hannay, *Philip's Phoenix: Mary Sidney, Countess of Pembroke* (Oxford: Oxford University Press, 1990), p. x.

16. Tina Krontiris, *Oppositional Voices: Women as Writers and Translators of Literature in the English Renaissance* (London: Routledge, 1992), p. 69.

17. Mary Sidney Herbert, *The Tragedy of Antonie*, in *Renaissance Drama by Women: Texts and Documents*, ed. S. P. Cerasano and Marion Wynne-Davies (London: Routledge, 1995), p. 19. Subsequent references are cited parenthetically in the text.

18. Robert Garnier, *Two Tragedies. Hippolyte and Marc Antoine*, ed. Christine M. Hill and Margaret G. Morrison (London: Athlone Press, 1975), p. 141.

19. Christopher Marlowe, *The Complete Plays*, ed. J. B. Steane (Harmondsworth: Penguin Books, 1969), pp. 145 and 177.

20. Straznicky, *Privacy, Playreading, and Women's Closet Drama*, p. 59.

21. Findlay, *Playing Spaces*, p. 31.

22. The compositional date of Mariam has proved problematic. It is generally dated at *c.*1602–04 because of internal evidence from the dedicatory poem, addressed to Cary's sister-in-law, 'Mistress Elizabeth Cary'. The Elizabeth Cary of the dedication could only have been referred to as 'Mistress' before 1605, when her husband, Philip Cary, Henry's brother, was knighted, after which she would have been referred to as 'Lady'. In addition, the author refers to her husband as the absent 'sun', whose 'absence makes it night, / Whilst to the Antipodes his beams do bend', which suggests the period when Henry Cary was abroad on military activity between 1602 and 1606.

23. Elizabeth Cary, *The Tragedy of Mariam*, in *Renaissance Drama by Women*, ed. Cerasano and Wynne-Davies, p. 50. Subsequent references are cited parenthetically in the text.

24. Margaret W. Ferguson, 'The Spectre of Resistance: *The Tragedy of Mariam* (1613)', in *Staging the Renaissance: Reinterpretation of Elizabethan and Jacobean Drama*, ed. David Scott Kastan and Peter Stallybrass (London: Routledge, 1991), pp. 244–45.

25. Jan Kott, '*King Lear* or *Endgame*', in *Shakespeare: An Anthology of Criticism and Theory, 1945–2000*, ed. Russ McDonald (Oxford: Blackwell Publishing, 2004), p. 185.

26. Ibid., p. 181.

Tudor Courts

9
The Courts

Carolyn Sale

This chapter presents the work of four early modern English women writers who engaged in one way or another with the courts: Anne Askew (*c.*1521–46), who was tried for heresy in the 1540s before bishops, the Privy Council, and possibly a 'quest' (a grand jury of twelve men);[1] Isabella Whitney (fl. 1566–73), who represents, in verse, the legal culture of London in the 1560s and 1570s; Elizabeth Cary (1586–1639), the daughter of a lawyer who rose to be a chief justice, Lawrence Tanfield; and Arbella Stuart (1575–1615), a descendant, along with her first cousin, James VI of Scotland and I of England, of Henry VIII's elder sister Margaret. Their writing, which engages with the issues arising from, events within, and phenomena of early modern English courts, reflects the range of courts in early modern England, which ran the gamut from the humble market court known as the 'pie powder', at which disputes over purchases and any actions that took place within market fairs were adjudicated, to Parliament, the highest court in the land, whose sense of itself as court deepened across the sixteenth century. In the vast terrain in between the 'pie powder' and Parliament, we find all of the sovereign's central courts at Westminster (the King's Bench, the Common Pleas, the Exchequer, and the Chancery) as well as the more humble but extremely popular Court of Requests, to which anyone, even the poorest of subjects, could bring his or her 'Bill of Complaint'. We also find at Westminster the notorious Star Chamber, manned by the justices of the central courts along with the Privy Council sitting in a judicial capacity. The most popular venues for women in which to bring legal action were the consistory courts, the busiest of which were at London and Canterbury, where wills were proved and women defended themselves against various onslaughts against their reputation, including the utterance of slanderous words by neighbors.[2] For women charged with felonies, both the Assize courts, scattered across the country, and the King's Bench and Star Chamber were particularly dangerous places: women could defend themselves therein, but they could not have anyone to assist in their defense in criminal trials.

As they contributed to English literary history by offering it one or another important 'first' – Isabella Whitney, for example, published the first book of secular verse by an Englishwoman and Elizabeth Cary, the first original play by a woman in English – these writers innovated within the genres in which they chose to work, Askew and Whitney doing so in radical ways to offer their readers books that were unique entities. But whether they were furnishing a virtuoso contribution to an established literary genre, as Cary did with her play *The Tragedy of Mariam* (composed *c.*1602–04, published 1613), making a playful use of a legal genre as Whitney did with her 'Wyll' to London (1573), or engaging in an unusual act of writing that we are only able to trace through surviving records in the legal archives (as is the case with Arbella Stuart's intervention into *Att.-Gen.* v. *Chatterton* in 1609), each of these writers makes an incursion into the 'legal' by which she expands the sense of what a woman's writing 'hand' may do in sixteenth-century and early seventeenth-century England. These texts show women writers using their writing to do the kind of work that women in early modern England, who could not train as lawyers and who could only in the rarest of instances serve in any judicial capacity, could *not* do in the courts. In the case of Isabella Whitney the recourse to legal forms may be playful and in the case of Anne Askew, deadly earnest, but this writing coheres as a body around the idea of the literary as a domain and a resource to which women writers might turn not simply to negotiate particular legal matters, and larger ideas of law, but also to create innovative literary texts that expanded, for early modern culture, the sense of what one might do with literature.

'I answered I was no heretik': *The Examinations* (1546)

In 1603, the Catholic writer Robert Parsons complained in print that Anne Askew should be counted 'among the famous wryters of her age' for writing what he dismissed as 'some 4. or 5. sheets of paper in priuate letters'.[3] These '4. or 5. sheets', were, however, hardly 'priuate letters'. They were the self-representation ('by me Anne Askewe' [p. 191]) of several encounters with the courts by a woman charged with heresy under a series of statutes issued in the decade between 1534 and 1544.[4] Testimony, on the one hand, accusation and condemnation, on the other, the *Examinations* constitutes a seminal text for the 'author' in early modern England, one predicated on Askew's rejection of the 'courts' within which she was examined and the authorities who examined her as places and persons without proper jurisdiction.

As testimony, the *Examinations* counters the official narrative of Askew's prosecution, especially as that was shaped by Edmund Bonner, the Bishop of London, who examined her in the spring of 1545. At the climax of this examination, Bonner had Askew sign a recantation that he had penned for her, a recantation that she signed (she claims) with wording that undid its effect: 'I writte after this maner. I Anne Askew do beleve all manner thinges conteined in the faith of the Catholike church' (p. 175). Askew's syntax created ambiguity: she might have been claiming that she subscribed to all of the beliefs that Bonner did, or simply that she understood that these were the beliefs propounded as the beliefs of 'the Catholike church'. More slyly, given the position of Reformers that it was they, not their opposition, who represented the true 'Catholike church', she may have been claiming the direct opposite of what he wished her to. Askew's sleight was clear to Bonner, who, after reading her equivocal wording, purportedly 'flung into his Chambre in a great fury' (p. 178). The document nevertheless resulted in Askew's release. Sometime, however, on or around the date of Askew's execution thirteen months later, Bonner had a copy of the supposed recantation, without Askew's equivocal signature, entered into the Bishop's Register. The purpose of this was clear: Bonner wanted the official court records to help make the case against Askew. Askew had recanted, he could claim, but then she had lapsed, and the lapse permitted legal authorities to move towards a final condemnation.

Askew reveals some concern with Bonner's attempts to shape public opinion against her, by noting (for example) in the 'lattre' examination that she had read the document that Bonner had put into print and assuring her readers (the lawyer John Lassels in the first instance) that she 'never ment thing les than to recant' (p. 188). Foxe follows Askew's text lead in challenging Bonner's narrative by interrupting his presentation of Askew's text to provide in full the record as published by Bonner after her execution. The reader 'might the better understand therby', Foxe wrote, 'what credit is to be geven hereafter to such bishops and to such regesters' (p. 175). Intervening into the text only this once, to provide the official record and comment briefly upon it, Foxe underscores the importance of Askew's writing as counter-testimony – that is, as a set of texts that not only challenged but contradicted official legal records.

Askew's text is, however, important as far more than documentation that challenges institutional narratives. The unique character of the *Examinations* is clearer when we set Askew's writing in relation to the one earlier English book that might have served her as a model, the *Boke Made by John Frith Prisoner in the Tower of London* (1533). Frith's *Boke* includes his account of his final examination by all the bishops of England. Frith's and Askew's principal doctrinal point was the same: they both denied the doctrine of Real Presence, that is, the belief that 'in the most blessed Sacrament of the Aulter, by the strenghe and efficacy of Christe myghtie worde, it beinge spoken by the prest, is p[re]sent really, under the forme of bread and wyne, the naturall bodye and bloode of our Saviour Jesu Criste'.[5] 'To this belefe of theirs saye I naye', Askew wrote in her final 'confession' from Newgate before being burnt at the stake in July 1546 (p. 190). Frith also, in his own way, said 'naye', taking the position that one might 'without danger of damnation, either beleeve it, or thinke the contrarie'.[6] Askew and Frith differed radically, however, in how they responded to the ostensible authority of those examining them. Believing (tragically) that he could – indeed, should – share his views with his examiners in full on the assumption that as long as his examiners heard him 'indifferently' they could not reasonably put him to death, Frith responded to his examiners' questions without reservation, at no time challenging or making any attempt to subvert the premises of the examination. Although it is quite clear that those prosecuting her assumed a connection between her and Frith (an archdeacon, for example, confronts her over holding what he believes to be one of Frith's books in her hand), Askew's position was that the true letter of the law, scripture, was 'shut up' or 'closed' within her heart, and that she was under no moral or legal obligation to share her interpretation of that law with anyone.

Askew's text also differs radically from Frith's in its handling of the genre of the 'examination'. Frith's *Boke* shows him conceding to the form and authority of the examination even after the fact of the event: his examiners put a question, he furnishes an answer, and he does not deviate from this form when supplying his written account, which includes no contextual detail whatsoever. Askew, in contrast, shatters the institutional form. She notes some of the questions put to her, as well as her responses, but never in a programmatic way, and in addition to turning back at least one question upon her examiners (and being informed by them that 'it was against the order of scoles that he which asked the question should aunswere it' [p. 168]), one of her most common techniques, as writer, is to suggest that her answers consistently rendered her examiners speechless. She also consistently refuses to show them her mind, using various circumlocutions – 'I beleve as the scripture doth teach me' (p. 172), 'I holde no opinions contrarie to his mooste holye worde' (p. 189), 'I beleve all those scriptures to be true, whome he hath confyrmed with his most precious bloud' (p. 190), and 'That I had said, I had said' (p. 168) – to foreground the person that believes and that speaks before them in the courtroom even as she withholds from her examiners the precise contents of her belief. Askew expresses herself, in short, in precisely the right form, a form that simultaneously asserts that scripture is the letter of the law, and that she is under no legal obligation to disclose her constructions of that letter to them. She bolsters these rhetorical tactics with regular recourse to irony, which is not simply the tool by which she manifests to her readers her distance from and disdain for the proceedings against her, but more importantly the means by which she manifests, both in the legal event of the examination and her writing of her account of it afterwards, a person and a personality beyond their jurisdiction.

With Edmund Bonner, in 1545, Askew's rhetorical tactics proved legally unassailable. Despite the ambiguous character of the words that she appended to the recantation that he drafted for her, Bonner had to release Askew, for he was unable to compel any incriminating statement from her. That Askew was subsequently condemned to death the following year in no way suggests that she had somehow lost her ability to handle herself adroitly in the kind of court in which heretics were tried. Elaine Beilin is almost certainly right when she adduces from the various records relating to the proceedings against her that Askew must have been brought before legal authorities in an examination, for whatever reason, not recounted in the *Examinations*.[7] That would have made the outcome of her third prosecution in the spring of 1546 inevitable: under the provisions of *34 & 35 Henry 8 c. 1* (1543), the Act for the Advancement of True Religion, alleged heretics were permitted to recant or be acquitted only twice. If her prosecution in the spring of 1546 did indeed represent the third occasion on which she was brought before the courts, there was virtually no chance of Askew walking away from the encounter alive. She could only have avoided death at the stake with a recantation that was, unlike the document of 1545, unquestionably sincere.

This goes a long way to explaining the entirely different character and way of proceeding that Askew presents in the 'lattre' examination. She is now not only openly scornful of her examiners, but also openly condemnatory. When Stephen Gardiner, the Bishop of Winchester, informs her, for example, that she is to be burnt at the stake, she responds, 'God will laugh your threatninges to skorne' (pp. 181–82). In this climactic exchange with Gardiner, she also makes the text over whose interpretation they have been fighting the authority for delivering her indictment of all those prepared to put her to death for her beliefs. For while she can find, in scripture, statements that support her idea of law, she cannot, she informs them, find statements that support theirs: 'I answered that I had searched all the scryptures, yet coulde I never find, that eyther Christe or his Apostles putte anye creature to death' (p. 181). John Bale may deny that Askew had any worldly cause,[8] but Askew here makes scripture speak directly to the issue of the legality of the proceedings against heretics. She articulates precisely the same position at the scene of her condemnation at the Guildhall: 'They said to me there that I was an heretic and condemned by the law if I would stand in mine opinion. I answered that I was no heretik, neither yet deserved I any death by the law of God' (p. 184). Over the course of the exchange, her declaration that she is 'no heretik' is tied to a final plain answer to the crucial matter of the doctrine of Real Presence:

> Then they demaunded. Wil you plainly deny Christ to be in the Sacrament? I answeared that I beleve faithfully the eternall sonne of God not to dwell there. In witnesse whereof I recited again the history of Bel, and the xix. chapter of Daniell, the vii and xvii. of the Actes, and xxiii. of Mathew, concluding thus. (pp. 184–85)

The Guildhall thus serves her as the venue in which, even as she makes an unequivocal declaration of her position on the crucial doctrinal matter, a declaration that facilitates their final condemnation of her, she delivers her indictment of them with a statement that undermines the very legal category according to which they would define her. She also asserts the authority that will render their seeming jurisdiction in the courtroom ultimately nothing more than a fantasy. In the Guildhall, 'there can be no right judgement' (p. 183), but right judgment will come, in another court.

Gathered together in Bale's 1546 edition, Askew's texts (which included subsequent letters of petition to the Lord Chancellor and the King) did all kinds of work for her after her death at the stake. While it is true that Askew was, in the final analysis, condemned to death for her denial of the doctrine of Real Presence ('this is the heresye whiche they reporte me to holde, that after the priest hath spoken the wordes of consecration, there remayneth bread styll' [p. 189]), she was also prosecuted for her engagement in a set of practices, practices that she engaged in up until the moment of her death, for the scene of her execution was, Foxe reports, a scene at which she died preaching. These practices included unauthorized acts of reading, which the *Examinations* draws attention to by recounting the appearance in Lincoln Cathedral in which Askew flagrantly broke the law by reading one of the two bibles on display there in contravention of *31 Henry 8 c. 14*. (The statute prohibited the reading of scripture in public by women.) We would not know about these acts of defiance, however, if Askew had not engaged in a greater act of law-breaking by writing an account of her examinations. Under the 1539 and 1543 heresy acts, according to which Askew was disseminating her 'pvers fantasies' to others with her writing, Askew broke the law with greater enduring effect than she did with her appearance in Lincoln Cathedral.[9] Under those acts, everyone who played a role in getting her '4. or 5. sheets' out of prison and into print joined her in her act of law-breaking.

When Askew's text went into public circulation in the illicit edition published by John Bale, it also furnished others with a rhetorical primer. Here was a text that other women might use in their attempts to keep themselves from being condemned to death in other courts. And in the form of a 1550 octavo that survives in a sole copy at the Pierpont Morgan Library in New York, it came in a small enough incarnation that, unbound, it might have been carried about with them (and possibly to their own examinations), perhaps as Anne Askew's friend Joan Burcher purportedly carried banned books, under her skirts tied with strings.[10]

The later incarnation of Askew's writings in John Foxe's *Acts and Monuments* invites us to situate Askew's text within larger historical narratives about women's engagements with the law in sixteenth-century England. We might, for example, read Askew's examinations for their possible influence upon the examinations of two later women, Elizabeth Young and Alice Driver, the accounts of which (furnished by others) bear suggestive connections to the *Examinations*.[11] And by presenting Elizabeth I as the figure in whom all of the bloodshed of the English Reformation triumphs when she, unlike Askew, managed to escape death at Gardiner's hands, *Acts and Monuments* also encourages us to set Elizabeth's writings in relation to Askew's. We cannot doubt that Elizabeth, who was part of the circle of ladies at Court that Bathsua Makin claimed were 'seasoned [...] by [Askew's] Precepts and Examples', was, after Askew's death, one of her readers.[12] It is therefore worth reading Elizabeth's texts for the possibility of Askew's influence upon her relationship with language. We might, for example, see in the surviving drafts of her speeches to Parliament, on the matter of whether she would authorize the execution of Mary Queen of Scots, the possibility that, even though she was *lex loquens* or the voice of the law, she benefited from rhetorical techniques learned from one of the 'famous wryters of her age'. For in that matter she famously left the highest court in the land, which was demanding of her, as Gardiner had demanded of Askew, a 'direct answer' (p. 180), an 'answer answerless'.[13]

Willing trials: Isabella Whitney's *Copy of a Letter* (1567) and *Sweet Nosgay* (1573)

Two decades after Anne Askew was burnt to death at Smithfield, we find a mid-sixteenth-century female poet doing with her texts what Askew, writing from places of incarceration and writing out of dire circumstances, could not do: make playful use of legal forms. The religious strife of the previous three decades put to rest, partly with Elizabeth's Act of Uniformity (1559), Whitney was in little danger of finding herself before a court compelled to defend herself over contentious religious beliefs. She could devote herself to entirely different – indeed, everyday – legal concerns. In her two known books, each of which survives in only a single copy, Isabella Whitney yokes 'trew' legal matter to the 'fained' as she appropriates legal genres, and turns them to inventive ends, to expand, for her readers in the 1560s and 1570s, the possibilities of what one might do with 'letters'.

Whitney's first book *The Copy of a Letter* (1567) advertises its blending of the 'trew' and the 'fained' in its opening epistle, which appeals to the reader to buy the book on the basis that it serves both the readerly desire for 'some trifle that is trew' as well as the desire for 'some Fables that be fained'.[14] Whether the 'matter of it selfe | Is true' because Whitney was representing her own situation, one which 'many know', or because it was the situation of many, is unclear, but the fact is that Whitney chose for her 'matter' one of the most common issues that drove sixteenth-century English women into the ecclesiastical courts, breach of a marriage pre-contract. With the 'letter' proper, 'I.W. | To her vnconstant | Louer', Whitney accomplishes one of the ends behind such litigation by holding up the 'vnconstant Louer' for a representative berating and shaming. By displaying her wit and graciousness, she accomplishes another end, for the letter demonstrates that the lover cannot have jilted her for 'wants that rest in [her]' (sig. A4ʳ). The letter thus protects the thing most damaged when a man reneged on a contract to marry, the woman's reputation. For women in the sixteenth century, Laura Gowing notes, 'reputation' was 'an issue worth going to court over', even if, as Martin Ingram suggests, the success rate in such litigation, in the form of compensatory 'payment in money or goods', was low.[15]

As a substitute for legal action, Whitney's 'letter' is in fact a superior form of action to any that she could have taken in the courts. While, as Gowing has suggested, these suits were important opportunities for self-representation for women, and the depositions left in such litigation (about thirty cases a year in the London Consistory Court in the 1570s) are unusual for recording 'a vast amount of detail about both typical behavior and deviations from it',[16] in print, 'I.W.'s' 'letter' had the power to circulate to many more people than may ever have heard a word spoken by 'I.W.' in the Consistory Court or a report of her appearance there second-hand in gossip between neighbors. The printed letter also accomplishes its goals in a more subtle way than Whitney or any other woman could have done in any courtroom. Charting a psychological trajectory in which she moves from declaring herself content to be the lover's 'refuse' to bestowing upon him more than one blessing, the letter serves her affective needs in a way that the Consistory Court could not have, for there, to secure redress, she would have had to insist on her sense of injury. The claim in the penultimate stanza that the letter is something that the lover must keep 'in store' (sig. A5ʳ) suggests that it outdoes institutional forms of action in yet another way: it may continue to unsettle the lover with its sense of her virtue and his folly in a way that no deposition filed away in the Consistory Court could possibly do.

As it went into public circulation as print artifact, the letter may also have shown women in 1560s London one of the things that 'letters' could be made to do – take their case to a court other than the London Consistory Court for another kind of judgment and another form of 'redresse' (sig. A5ᵛ). The letter makes its principal case not against the lover but rather against the literary tradition, which furnishes too many narratives in which men who have wronged women are not only not blamed for their deeds, but held up as models for imitation. Arguing that the 'fame' of such characters ought really to be their 'shame' (sig. A3ᵛ), Whitney implicitly holds those who have created and valorized such characters accountable for the dynamics between the sexes in 1560s London. The 'trew' or the factual (the predicament or case of real women, who may include herself) is thus fashioned into a literary 'trifle' that makes its case against ways of reading and writing from Virgil onwards that Whitney finds damaging to the members of her sex. But Whitney's book does not end there. Concluding with a question to the unconstant lover, who may be puzzled, she notes, as to 'why at large | [her] mind is here exprest' (sig. A6^v), the letter suggests that ultimately the book is neither about nor for him, and not about or for her. Her 'mind is here exprest' for another constituency entirely, that of 'all yong Gentilwomen: And to al other Maids being in Loue' for whom 'I.W.' proceeds to offer an 'Admonicion'.

With the change of text, Whitney changes tactics. The letter constitutes a kind of accusation, and it swiftly makes its case against the lover and the literary tradition. The 'Admonicion', on the other hand, offers counsel, and within it 'I.W.' herself constitutes the principal proof: she is evidence of a wrong that her female readers must not let be done to them. The 'Admonicion' calls a certain readership into being, and requires of that newly constituted readership a particular kind of action. A form of public address, from a woman to women, the 'Admonicion' adjures its female readers to put their prospective lovers to 'triall':

> Trust not a man at the fyrst sight,
>   but trye him well before:
> I wish al Maids within their brests
>   to kepe this thing in store
> For triall shal declare his trueth
>   and show what he doth think:
> Whether he be a Louer true,
>   or do intend to shrink. (A6^v)

The idea of 'counsell' here is not moral, but rather legal: the 'Admonicion' does not advocate a mode of behavior, or promote any particular virtue, but rather offers a warning meant to 'redresse' legal cares before they can properly arise. Well and widely read by young single women who took its cautions seriously, the book would help prevent the kind of affair that would compel wronged women to seek redress in the courts. We thus might see its function in regard to the courts as pre-emptive, or the text itself as a kind of prophylactic. The 'Admonicion' would render certain recourses to the courts unnecessary by making women devise and engage in their own pre-emptive forms of 'triall'.

At the same time, the 'Admonicion', like the 'Letter', counters the literary tradition, for the stanzas following Whitney's appeal to women to subject men to a 'triall' offer Scylla and Oenone as literary examples of female characters who failed to do what the writer of the 'Admonicion' recommends. Culminating, however, with a positive example, that of Hero – 'Hero did trie Leanders truth | before that she did trust' (A7^v) – the poem promotes literature (and by extension itself) as model. Even, then, while literature is held culpable in the 'Letter' for promoting as acceptable male behavior that is injurious to women, it is also shown to be the source of models of female behavior worth imitating (and indeed in Leander it suggests that it may also furnish worthy models of imitation to men). Literature, a category that includes I.W.'s 'Letter', includes 'things' worth keeping 'in store'. Whitney's own literary text thus fulfills a double advocacy function: it stands up for women as readers who might be duped by a literary tradition that valorizes as heroes male characters who have wronged women. But it also stands up for and asserts the capacity of women as writers to speak up in a figurative court of their own making, one that can be invented through the forum of print, not only for themselves but also for others. Together, the 'Letter' and the 'Admonicion' assert an idea of the literary in relation to the law: with 'letters', women, by 'faining', may invent their own forms for dealing with 'matter' that might otherwise take them to the courts.

Its very inventiveness, which made Whitney's *Copy of a Letter* (from what we know) a unique commodity in the English print market of the late 1560s, may account for the text's survival despite the fact that it has been characterized as ephemera. Bound by its first owner into a leather cover along with several other literary texts published between 1566 and 1571, and subsequently preserved in the library of one of the early seventeenth century's most famous lawyers, John Selden, Bodleian H 44(6) testifies to the fact that at least one sixteenth-century reader (most likely a justice of the peace from the handwritten notes on the opening leaves) regarded Whitney's *Letter*, along with texts such as Seneca's *Agamemnon*, as literature worth saving.[17]

With her second book, *A Sweet Nosgay* (1573), Whitney offered a less direct yet more sophisticated instance of engagement with the courts. The legal facets of the book have received little attention, however, in part because the book has been treated as of principal interest for its depiction of Whitney's economic situation, and in part because it has been regarded as a 'poetic miscellany' with no overarching design or thematic around which its parts might be understood to cohere. But its parts do cohere, strikingly, around ideas of law and imagined legal action both in and outside the courts, and taken together offer the reader not only a vision of distributive justice, but a representation of the possible place of the book within circuits of exchange in 1570s London. The *Sweet Nosgay* is more conspicuously concerned with the place and function of the literary in relation to the legal in early modern London than the *Copy of a Letter*, for it imagines itself as placed not in the 'store' of one man, but rather within the 'store' of books that Whitney leaves for her 'Friends' to buy at her printer's bookstall 'by Paulles' (sigs. Ev^v–Evi^r). The principal readerly constituency with which the book appears to be concerned and which it attempts to reach through its placement there is not, however, that of 'Gentlewomen' or 'Maids in loue', but rather that of young men at the Inns of Court.

The *Nosgay* reflects Whitney's interest in this constituency in several ways. Its opening letter dedicates the book to Sir George Mainwaring, who was, in 1573, a student at Gray's Inn.[18] The 'nosgay' proper consists of a hundred 'floures' or *sententiae* taken from a book published the year before by Hugh Plat, who was at that time a student at Lincoln's Inn.[19] And in the section entitled 'familier Epistles and friendly Letters', Whitney publishes correspondence with her brothers, at least one of whom (Geoffrey) was, in the early 1570s, a student at either Thavies' or Furnivall's Inn.[20] The 'friendly Letters' include, moreover, her correspondence with three male friends; and while these male friends are identified only by their initials (T.B., C.B., and T.L.), one of their letters suggests, with its declaration that the writer will help Whitney with a 'quarrel' in which he would die (Dvi^r), that he too was either a law student or already a lawyer, for the only 'quarrel' or cause to which Whitney refers (in addition, that is, to her general quarrel with Fortune) is a legal one: she fears that Hugh Plat may want to 'leave her worth a rag' for daring to 'brag' with his 'Flowers' (Ev^v). But even as her 'friendly Letters' publicly advertise her filiations with young men at the Inns of Court, the *Nosgay* suggests that the Inns may constitute both real and discursive terrain that Whitney is discouraged from entering.

In the topographical tropes in which Whitney talks of both Plat's book and her own acts of reading and writing in 'The Auctor to the Reader', the 'Lane' that a young male friend declares hazardous to her health – 'yf you regard your healthe | out of this Lane you get' (Avi^v) – may very well be Chancery Lane, that lane on or immediately off which so many of the Inns were situated. Estranged from certain places and certain roles, Whitney nevertheless indicates at the end of her dedicatory letter to Mainwaring that there is another lane from which she may write, Abchurch (which is east of the Inns of Court, running south off Elizabethan London's most important thoroughfare, Cheapside). In that lane, Whitney turns from the act of reading 'crimes' in 'Histories' (sig. Av^v) to the act of writing a fictional will, her testament to London. And with that 'Wyll', Whitney may find one way into the lane from which she had always already been estranged before any warning from a male friend, simply by virtue of her sex.

With the 'Wyll', Whitney appropriates the only legal genre that she had the authority to write to assert a particular kind of 'Auctor'. In the course of its fantasy of redistribution, in which she gives back to 'London' what it already possesses, the 'Wyll' disrupts the city's standing economics and the political philosophy by which it operates, for Whitney pointedly gives with one hand ('I [...] | Did write this Wyll with mine own hand | and it to London gaue' [sig. Eviii^r]) while refusing to take with the other ('For there it is: I little brought | but no thyng from thee toke' [sig. Ev^r]). Giving to London even as she declines to take anything from it, Whitney makes her authorial signature, not that of one who claims, but one who disposes. With this double gesture – the book wills in order to give, gives in order to will – the *Nosgay* expresses desire for performative power within a discursive domain in relation to which Whitney could play no institutional role.[21] But more importantly with the 'Wyll' Whitney leaves for those men of the Inns of Court whom it depicts as already her readers, a book that challenges the ethos behind the very kind of work that they were being trained to do in the courts as the 'Lawyers' who help those who 'cannot quiet bee, | but must striue for House or Land' (sig. Evi^r). For the vision of distributive justice she offers is one that depends not on an endless supply of money at the Mint ('Yf they that keepe what I you leaue, | aske Mony: when they sell it: | At mint, there is such store, it is | unpossible to tell it [sig. Cv^r]), but rather on a political philosophy that encourages everyone to give more to the *polis* than one takes from it. Only when everyone does not 'strive for House or Land' can 'needfull things' be 'dispearsed round' (sig. Evi^v) to those who would otherwise have nothing (or little) to their 'share'. Its concern is with matters, in short, for which her friends at the Inns of Court may have not had the time in the midst of their 'Actiuytie', but to which their 'brused brayne[s]' (sig. Av^v) needed to turn in order that they might (re)orient themselves in relation to law and the work that they were being trained to do, as the lawyers who fought for and presided over the circulation of goods in Elizabeth's courts. But the *Nosgay* may also have been seeking another, more influential reader.

In the dedicatory letter, Whitney associates her gift to Mainwaring with the legendary gift of a poor man to the Persian Prince, Darius. With the allusion, Whitney suggests that the book's greatest fantasy involves not the fantasy of an endless supply of money at the Mint, but rather the fantasy of its own potential reach, or its own possible distribution, one in which the book passes not only, as humble gift, to Mainwaring, but also either from him directly or through one pair of hands or another, on to a Prince. The fantasy may very well have found encouragement in the historical fact that the streets that Whitney depicts are streets through which Elizabeth had passed as she had made her coronation progress up Cheapside (and past Abchurch Lane), on west to 'Paulles' and the Inns of Court, and then on to Westminster, receiving, as she went, the humble gifts of nosegays from her subjects, several of them from 'poore womens handes'.[22] She purportedly responded to one of these with a speech that 'melt[ed] heartes [that] heard the same' by claiming that there was no 'more famous thing' to 'read in auncient histories of olde tyme, then that mightye prynces haue gentlye receyud presentes offered them by base and lowe personages'.[23] Whitney's choice of genre for her book may also have been encouraged by the fact that a small literary nosegay, *The Treasure of Gladnesse* (1563), had been published several times across the previous decade at the Queen's injunction. The *Nosgay* may, in short, have been a 'soueraigne receypt' (sig. Cv^v) for sovereign reception: a prescription for the health of the commonwealth, or a dream of distributive justice, that makes a journey from the solitary scene of writing at Abchurch Lane, where the only 'standers by' are 'Paper, Pen and Standish' (sig. A7^v), to a scene of reading beyond the bounds of the place that the 'Wyll' represents. (The 'Wyll' makes no mention of Westminster.) There, it would have found itself in the hands of the most important legal reader in the land, its ultimate law-maker, the Prince, the person best positioned to will things for the common good.

'What she sayd for herself': Elizabeth Cary's *The Tragedy of Mariam* (*c.*1602–04)

With Elizabeth Cary's play *The Tragedy of Mariam* we have another 'first' in English literary history – the first original play in English by a woman. We may also have, in its incarnation in print, another book for lawyers. *The Tragedy of Mariam* was published, in 1613, by Thomas Creede for the bookseller Richard Hawkins, whose shop was in Chancery Lane, next to Serjeants' Inn. As Marta Straznicky notes, Hawkins's 'list' was not a literary one, and the location of his shop suggests that law students, lawyers, and judges may very well have furnished most of his custom.[24] If Hawkins was banking on the fact that the same book-buyer who would want to purchase copies of the King's letters patent or the literary work of the Attorney General for Ireland John Davies would also be tempted to buy *The Tragedy of Mariam*, he was making a good bet: as a book for lawyers, Cary's play is a rich one. With the rapid case-putting of its characters, Cary is indeed 'like a lawyer presenting ambiguous fact statements to a judge', one who is exercising her readers' capacities to judge.[25] But the play also invites its readers to consider the dynamics of courts, and the other roles that they might play in relation to them. The play's legal character comes into sharp relief when we set the play in relation to an account of an episode from Cary's childhood as recounted in *The Lady Faulkland Her Life*, a biography written by one of Cary's daughters in the mid-seventeenth century. This is not to say that we should read the play for its relation to Cary's life or her psychology, a way of reading that has proved a problem and a source of contention in scholarship on the play to date,[26] but rather that the episode from the *Life* and the play matter for the psychology that they represent, a psychology tied to the predicaments of Englishwomen on trial in early modern courtrooms.

The episode shows Cary, at the age of ten, intervening into events in her father Lawrence Tanfield's courtroom.[27] While the account, crafted by one of the daughters, is clearly designed to present the mother as a prodigy capable of discerning, as a child, what adults around her could not, it is nevertheless important as evidence of a cultural phenomenon of considerable importance to Cary's play, whose tragedy turns on its protagonist's feeble self-defense in the face of an accusation of attempted murder. Cary's intervention, which depended crucially on her theory of the psychology that might have been disabling a woman accused of witchcraft, suggests the ways in which women could fall into the trap of colluding with the production of their guilt in early modern courtrooms.

Despite the fact that the witness brought into speak against the accused woman (who is nameless in the *Life*'s account) was 'not [...] found convincing', when asked by Tanfield 'what she sayd for herself', the woman dropped to her knees 'trembling and weeping' and 'confest all to be true'.[28] In so doing, the woman gave false testimony against herself. Although it is entirely unclear from the account whether Tanfield was capable of discerning the psychology that was driving the false confession and its attendant fictions, or whether he would have done anything to prevent the woman's false claims about her actions from leading to her condemnation (and presumably her execution), the *Life*'s narrative presents everyone else present not only as taken in by it, but urging judgment: 'then the standers by sayd; what would they have more than her owne confession?' (p. 107). Analysis and action were left, in the *Life*'s account, to the ten-year-old Cary:

The child, seeing the poore woman in so terrible a feare, and in so simple a maner confesse all, thought feare had made her idle, so she w^h^ispered her father and desired him to aske her, whether she had bewitched to death mr John Symondes of such a place (her uncle that was one of the standers by). (p. 107)

The writer of the *Life* would have her readers believe that Cary comprehended that fear – of institutional authorities and the judicial process – was so thoroughly dominating the woman's sensibility and thought that she could be 'idle' on her own behalf: that is, speak in ways that were utterly self-destructive. This sense of fear was produced, it appears, by others, possibly some of the 'standers by', for when Tanfield eventually demanded to know why she had made false statements about herself, the woman claimed that an indefinite 'they had threatened her if she would not confess; and sayd, if she would, she should have mer[c]y shewed her' (p. 107). The psychology driving her does not get unpacked any further than this within the brevity of the *Life*'s account, but it presumably involved a certain propensity to judge herself guilty simply for the fact of being accused. This was a way of thinking long encouraged by ecclesiastical authorities in England. Working according to the presumption, inculcated by the indefinite 'they', that she had to help produce her guilt if she were to have any hope of escaping punishment (or drastically mitigating it), the woman simply supplied whatever the questions seemed to demand of her as an answer. When asked, for example, by Tanfield why she had responded in the affirmative to the question of whether she had killed John Symondes she declared 'I sayd so because you asked me' (p. 107). This was a phenomenon only 'too too common'[29] in early modern criminal trials in England, especially those for witchcraft, in which the accused could generally hope to escape punishment only by conceding to her guilt.[30]

Cary's comprehension of part or all of the psychology at work permitted a potentially tragic event to be converted into comedy. When the accused responded to the question about how precisely she had bewitched Symondes to death with 'one of her former storys', she transformed the standers-by who had been, only minutes before, urging her condemnation into a 'company laughing' (p. 107). The daughter's word choices, which witness 'accusers' and 'standers by' turned into a 'company' united in laughter, suggest how powerful Cary's intervention was in changing the character of those gathered in the courtroom that day; but more importantly Cary's intervention changed the character of the accused's engagement with the juridical environment and processes, for the woman moved from fearful complicity in the production of her guilt to an emphatic declaration of her innocence. When Tanfield asked, 'are you no witch then', she responded, 'no God knows [...] I know no more what belongs to it then the child new borne.' The *Life* claims that she uttered this with 'such simplicity' that she 'was easyly beleeved innocent, and qvitted' (p. 107). The daughter's account thus concludes with the implicit claim that the quality of certain utterances can be sufficient to generate certainty in an adjudicating body, and produce the right judgment, a claim that Cary's play, which is greatly concerned with the dangers of hearing a tale with 'ears prejudicate' (p. 60) and in which every character but one proves themselves taxed by the challenge of self-representation, puts seriously into doubt. The account is nevertheless important for suggesting Cary's interest, even as a child, in judicial dynamics and her own capacity to act, albeit indirectly, on another's behalf. Coming as it does immediately before the account of Cary's reading and writing as a young woman, the account suggests that Cary's writerly character must be construed, at least in part, in relation to her interest in legal matters and events, and the dynamics in the discursive spaces of courtrooms that resulted in a party being judged guilty or 'qvitted'.

The *Life* notes that Cary appeared in other courtrooms, and was, extraordinarily, permitted to sit in on the examination, by bishops, of those 'esteemed Hereticks' (p. 112). *Mariam*, however, seems most concerned with the kind of problem that arose in the trial in her father's courtroom: the problem of a woman not knowing how to speak in self-preserving ways in a legal venue, when accused of a crime. The play generally represents the accusatory dynamic of early modern criminal trials, which entailed a rapid back-and-forth between accusers and accused in which the accused was expected to furnish crucial evidence of character, and to do so without any assistance.[31] In this regard, the play constitutes a superlative use of its genre, Senecan-inspired 'closet drama', for the fact that the play is all talk is entirely to the point: the play constitutes a mimetic representation of the dynamics of early modern courtrooms, with its Chorus functioning as an important dramatic counterpart for the cohort of 'standers by' in early modern criminal trials who could exert sufficient force, with their oral commentary, to determine a trial's outcome.[32] Cary's adherence to the dramatic unities permits the play also to simulate the pressured atmosphere of an early modern criminal trial in England, where amidst the verbal chaos, judgments were reached with great rapidity.[33] The capacity of any person to provide adequate self-representation in such an environment would have been highly taxed. Cary's play focuses on the psychological forces that might have rendered it particularly difficult for women to do so.

From the opening lines of the play, Mariam is presented as a character who interrogates and sits in judgment upon herself. In this sense, the accusation that she directs at herself after Herod has imprisoned her for the alleged crimes of conspiring to kill him and committing adultery with Sohemus is apt: 'Had not myself against myself conspired', she says, 'No plot, no adversary from without, | Could Herod's love from Mariam have retired' (p. 70). The sources of this self-critique and self-condemnation are, however, brilliantly withheld: the character's references to her thoughts suggest that she is motivated by psychological forces that she does not understand. Mariam's grave unreliability as witness to her own character intensifies the sense that the audience is required to penetrate its mystery for her.

The little that Mariam does say at the scene of her accusation becomes, within the larger psychological profile that the play presents, telling. In response to the Butler's claim that she asked him to deliver the poisoned drink Mariam responds 'Did I?' (p. 65); and in relation to Herod's charge that she has tried to murder him, 'Is this a dream?' (p. 65). The scene of Mariam's accusation thus unfolds as a scene of impotence in which she helps to produce the sense that she is guilty – both for herself and for others – by asking a question that should be unaskable. Although it is charged with a certain irony, 'Did I?' suggests that Mariam has too acute a sense of how she might in fact be held culpable of the charge that she has attempted to murder Herod. She is here representative, and importantly so: she represents members of a culture who were encouraged to think of themselves as 'guilty' if there were any part of them that experienced the urge to defy one or another social construct, especially those that would put off limit to them the very discursive entity ('mind' or 'conscience') that motivates (and would justify) their opposition.

It is to the point, in this regard, not only that the Chorus should accuse Mariam of having 'a common mind' (p. 63) – that is, one indiscriminately shared with others – but also that the act of which Mariam is accused, that of plotting Herod's death by poison, would have been construed in early modern culture as an act of imagination. (The real crime here is that of treason, imagining and/or attempting to bring about the death of the king.) Ultimately, it would not have mattered that Mariam had not in fact arranged for the cup to be brought in: if she had at any time imagined Herod's death, she could be held guilty of the desire to have brought it about. In this regard, she has, in effect, with the opening speech of the play, already given in evidence against herself: she has, she tells us, imagined Herod's death many a time ('Oft have I wished that I from him were free, | Oft have I wished that he might lose his breath, | Oft have I wished his carcass dead to see' [p. 50]). That she has not imagined this particular means for him to die, or herself as the agent of death, does not matter. Too willing, perhaps, to condemn herself for one 'crime' – what Margaret Ferguson refers to as the 'property crime' of withholding her mind and body from her husband[34] – she is predisposed to think of herself as somehow also already guilty of another (the treason of the attempt to murder Herod), and the sense of being already rightly condemned for one 'crime' makes possible the self-condemnation for the other. Mariam's 'soul' is not, as she claims, 'free from adversary's power' (p. 70). The adversary lies within.

Inasmuch as the character's troubled psychology stands in metonymically for troubled ways of thinking within the culture, the play constitutes for its audiences and/or readers a 'school of wisdom' (p. 75) in which they may learn to resist, for themselves and for others, the discursive mechanisms that produce women's 'guilt' not only within the culture but within the specific space of courtrooms. Reduplicating the psychology at play, however, with the Butler, who chooses to hang himself rather than 'enforce [his] tongue' the 'tale' against Mariam to 'control' (p. 66), Cary suggests that women are hardly alone in their willingness to rush to their own condemnation. The play thus offers a radically different idea of the function of revenge tragedy from that offered in the most famous revenge tragedy of the period. 'Guilty creatures' sitting at a play may find themselves provoked to an act of public confession that makes possible their trial and execution (whether legally or extra-legally); but plays may also work not to produce 'guilty creatures' but to challenge the institutional mechanisms, cultural discourses, and social forces that produce them.[35] As a 'school of wisdom' widely disseminated as a book, the play performs an important surrogate function for its writer, who could not, after all, have been in every courtroom in the land, preventing self-destructive acts of speaking by women, even if she had been a figure of legal authority. But the play, as print artifact, could do all kinds of legal work for her and others, including but not limited to challenging women to question the extent to which their culture shapes them into 'guilty creatures'.

Ultimately, however, the play makes its most provocative sally against institutional legal thinking in early modern England through Salome. In Act IV, when Salome leaps into the verbal vacuum that Mariam creates with her lack of a self-defense, the play yokes its tragedy of inadequate self-representation to the tragedy of non-representation. Pretending to rush to Mariam's defense only so that she may ensure that Herod will order her execution, the 'custom-breaker' who claims that she wishes to 'show [her] sex the way to freedom's door' (p. 53) actually helps usher another member of her sex to death's instead. That Salome should also be the character who offers the most powerful legal critique in the play (in her complaint about Mosaic law, which permits husbands to divorce their wives, but not wives to divorce their husbands) suggests just what is lost when she chooses to act not for Mariam, but against her. The play's great uncontained force, Salome is the means by which Cary challenges the premise of the accusatorial dynamic of the criminal trial in early modern England, to point, quite urgently, to what was missing from it.[36] Criminal trials in England supplied accused women on trial with adversaries, but no champions. A literary advocate for legal advocacy, the play begs the question of why it is that women could not be trained to be lawyers, and be placed in a position to do what Salome so conspicuously refuses to do for Mariam, turn to Herod, as the nation's law-maker and ultimate judge, and say 'Mistake [her] not' (p. 56). But even as it suggests the need for advocates in another forum, the play itself acts as advocate for a constituency not limited to any one courtroom, as it manages what Cary had achieved, as a child in her father's courtroom in 1595, when 'she wₐhₐispered her father' and got him to question what a woman 'sayd for herself'.

Subversive hands: *Att.-Gen.* v. *Chatterton* and *Hole* v. *White*

The Tragedy of Mariam leaves open the question of how or to what extent women might successfully function as advocates for one another in a legal system that did not formally allow anyone, no matter their gender, to act as an advocate for another in a criminal trial. It was, however, possible for at least one woman in early seventeenth-century England to use her legal literacy to act for another – not directly, as an advocate, but indirectly, by shaping the outcome of a trial from behind the scenes.

The case, which I have laid out in some detail elsewhere, is an important one for any account of women writers' engagements with the courts in early modern England for it shows the Lady Arbella Stuart intervening into the information-gathering phase of a Star Chamber trial, *Att.-Gen v. Chatterton* (1609), by appropriating a legal genre, that to which *The Merchant of Venice*'s Portia refers as 'inter'gatories'.[37] *Att.-Gen.* v. *Chatterton* was an unusual case in that the defendant, Margaret Chatterton, a gentlewoman in service to Elizabeth Cavendish, the Dowager Countess of Shrewsbury, was accused of 'ravishing' Sir William Cavendish, the countess's grandson, who was several years Chatterton's junior.[38] The surviving records show that Stuart gathered her own set of depositions in order to contradict the Attorney General Henry Hobart's prosecutorial narrative and bring the legal machinery that was acting against Chatterton to a halt. Showing us just how subversive Stuart's act of writing her own interrogatories was perceived to be, the records suggest that the legal archives may ironically supply, not only with this case but with others, the materials by which we may contribute to the history of British women writers' engagements with the courts, by tracing or tracking women's resistance to cultural constructions of the period through the very records that the courts have left in their attempt to prosecute the women as 'guilty' subjects. The records for *Att.-Gen. v. Chatterton* are also more generally tantalizing, for they offer concrete proof that, as of the beginning of the twenty-first century, there is still material within the legal archives to which we may turn in order to contribute to the history of women's writing in Britain. I located the records for the trial with the aid of a manuscript index at the National Archives at Kew. The rapid digitization of the records that is now taking place there, along with the cataloging of their contents, means, however, that social and literary historians are about to be in a better position than they have ever been to plumb the legal archives for other evidence they may hold of other acts of writing by women in the period.

That there is other such evidence to be found is clear. The records for another Star Chamber trial, *Hole v. White* (1607), suggest that a woman acted as the chief orchestrator, or from the law's perspective, the 'author', of a series of slanderous street spectacles in Wells – and this despite the fact that she may have been illiterate.[39] The legal constructions of Thomasine White's activities in the interrogatories for the case suggest that as scholars search the legal archives for any other evidence about women's engagements with the courts they may wish to do so with as capacious a definition of 'writing' as was in use in early modern courts. As far as the Star Chamber justices who presided over *Hole v. White* were concerned, one could function as 'author' without producing a written text, and act as a dramatist without necessarily holding a pen. White, who may very well have been illiterate, could, as far as the court was concerned, act as an 'author', whether or not she could write, by supplying another with words to utter in performance.

White may not have left us with texts to turn to as we turn from the legal records, but Stuart did. The surviving records for *Att.-Gen. v. Chatterton*, in addition to throwing direct light upon certain matters in Stuart's letters, encourage us more generally to ask where Stuart's letters (and indeed the work of other women writers in the period) may be about legal matters and ideas even where they seem to be about other things. Stuart's surviving letters, which include several petition letters that she wrote after she was imprisoned for her secret marriage to William Seymour came to light in 1610, also remind us that early modern courts were not simply places where women could be prosecuted. They were also places for the assertion and protection of rights, and in Stuart's case, places that she was desperate to get into: her letters include letters of petition to Thomas Fleming, the Lord Chief Justice, and Edward Coke, then the Chief Justice of the Common Pleas, in which she pled for their assistance in securing a writ of habeas corpus.[40]

As acts of self-representation, Stuart's letters of petition are terse and legally astute, and in their careful commixture of audacity and restraint, masterful. Her tragedy was that she found, in James I, an intractable and negligent reader, one apparently so fearful of the authority that she had demonstrated in her intervention into the *Chatterton* case and continued to demonstrate in her letters of petition, that he refused to let her out of the 'few little and hott roomes' in which she died at the age of forty.[41] Available to us in a way that they were not to her contemporaries, these letters cultivate a longing for everything that they – written from incarceration, in a desperate attempt to secure justice in the face of an implacable sovereign authority – could not be: literary confections in which the writer might simply display her wit, or her talent for writing verse, or her cleverness at plotting. They cultivate a longing, that is, for the literature that she (like Askew) might have written if the force of personal and historical circumstances had not required her to write for herself, in regard to a matter of law – that is, if she could simply have written for her pleasure and the pleasure of sharing verbal works of imagination with others. In Stuart's case, we need only turn back to the letters written before 1610, available to us in a modern edition by Sara Jayne Steen, for instances of that kind of writing. The tantalizing references that we have from Whitney, Cary, Stuart, or their contemporaries, to other work by them, which include Whitney's reference to the 'dayntier thing' that she planned to write after the *Nosgay* and John Davies of Hereford's reference to a play by Cary set in Syracuse, hold out some hope that we may still recover more writing by them to take account of for the history of women's writing in Britain. In the meantime, we have plenty to do in reading the work of early modern women writers for a fuller sense of how their work, in its engagement with the shaping power of the courts, shaped the literature of early modern Britain.

Notes

1. In her modern edition, Elaine Beilin follows Bale's edition in assuming that Askew 'was not given the lawful benefit of a "quest"' in the final court in which she was examined, the Guildhall, on 28 June 1546. It is, however, almost certainly the small surviving octavos of Askew's text and its incarnation

in Foxe's *Acts and Monuments* which are correct with their version of Askew's (ironic) statement that she was condemned with a quest. See Elaine Beilin, *The Examinations of Anne Askew* (Oxford and New York: Oxford University Press, 1996), pp. xxxii, 112, and 184. Subsequent references are cited parenthetically in the text.

2. For the best account to date of women's engagements with the courts in early modern England, see Timothy Stretton, *Women Waging Law in Elizabethan England* (Cambridge: Cambridge University Press, 1998).

3. For Parsons's discussion of Anne Askew, see *A Treatise of Three Conversions of England from Paganism to Christian Religion*, 3 vols (Ilkley: Scolar Press, 1976), III, pp. 491–97.

4. On Foxe as 'author' of the *Examinations*, see Thomas Freeman and Sarah Wall, 'Racking the Body, Shaping the Text: The Account of Anne Askew in Foxe's *Book of Martyrs*', *Renaissance Quarterly* 54 (2001), 1165–96. For the argument that Bale not only had sufficient knowledge of hagiographical texts by women but was also sufficiently adept at 'the art of inventing fake sources for female lives' that the *Examinations* may be largely his work, see Oliver Wort, 'The Double Life of Anne: John Bale's *Examinations* and *Diue Anne Vitam* (sic)', *Review of English Studies* 58 (2007), 633–56 (p. 645).

5. *Statutes of the Realm*, vol. 3 (1509–45), p. 739, http://heinonline.org (accessed 19 April 2009).

6. John Frith, *A Boke Made by John Frith Prisoner in the Tower of London* (1533), L7ʳ.

7. For the date problems surrounding the examinations, their most likely chronology, and the possibility of an arraignment and examination for which we have no surviving account, see Beilin, *Examinations*, pp. xx–xxii.

8. In 1546, Bale's denial appears as 'The onlye true honoure of God was it, and no wordlye cause, that Anne Askew and her companye dyed for' (Beilin, *Examinations*, p. 81). The misprinting of 'wordlye' for 'worldly' has its own delightful irony in relation to a speaker and writer who made such careful use of words in the course of her worldly cause.

9. *Statutes of the Realm*, vol. 3 (1509–45), pp. 740 and 894 respectively, http://heinonline.org (accessed 19 April 2009). The principal objective of the 1543 Act was 'to take awaie purge and clense this his Highnes Realme territoryes confynes domynons and Countreys, of all suche bokes wrytings sermons disputacons arguments balades playes rymes songes teaching and instruccons'.

10. Robert Parsons, *A Temperate Ward-Word* (1599), fol. 16, sig. B5ᵛ.

11. See Carolyn Sale, 'Contested Acts: Legal Performances and Literary Authority in Early Modern England' (unpublished doctoral dissertation, Stanford University, 2002), pp. 46–52.

12. Bathsua Makin, *An Essay to Revive the Antient Education of Gentlewomen* (London, 1673), p. 28.

13. For a transcription of BL MS Lansdowne 94, the draft speech for 'Queen Elizabeth's second reply to the parliamentary petitions urging the execution of Mary, Queen of Scots, November 24, 1586', see *Elizabeth I: Autograph Compositions and Foreign Language Originals*, ed. Janel Mueller and Leah Marcus (Chicago and London: University of Chicago Press, 2003), pp. 73–78.

14. Isabella Whitney, *The Copy of a letter, lately written in meter, by a younge Gentilwoman: to her vnconstant Louer* (1567), A1ᵛ.

15. Laura Gowing, *Domestic Dangers: Women, Words and Sex in Early Modern London* (Oxford and New York: Oxford University Press, 1996), p. 267. Martin Ingram, *Church Courts, Sex and Marriage* (Cambridge: Cambridge University Press, 1990), pp. 207–08.
16. See chapter 5 of Gowing's *Domestic Dangers*, esp. pp. 141–42.
17. On the provenance of the sole surviving copy of Whitney's *Copy of a Letter*, and for a listing of the other texts with which it is bound, see Michael David Felker, 'The Poems of Isabella Whitney: A Critical Edition' (unpublished doctoral dissertation, Texas Tech University, 1990), pp. 40–41. Selden's library was acquired by the Bodleian after his death in 1654.
18. *Students Admitted to the Inner Temple, 1547–1660* (London: W. Clowes and Sons, 1878), p. 58.
19. *Lincoln's Inn Black Books*, vol. 1 (1422–1586), (London: Lincoln's Inn, 1897–2001) notes that in 1574 Plat served as the Master of the Revels for the Inn (p. 395).
20. Andrew King, 'Whitney, Geoffrey (1548?–1600/01)', *ODNB*, http://oxforddnb.com (accessed 12 January 2008).
21. For another perspective on the ways in which and ends to which Whitney's 'Wyll' represents the dispossessed of London, see Crystal Bartolovich, '"Optimism of the Will": Isabella Whitney and Utopia', *Journal of Medieval and Early Modern Studies* 39 (2009), 407–32.
22. See *The Passage of our most drad Soueraigne Lady Quene Elyzabeth through the citie of London to westmisnter the daye before her coronacion* (1558), Aii^v. The *Passage*, which is attributed to Richard Mulcaster, states that Elizabeth's gracious receipt of these nosegays 'emplanted a wonderfull hope in' Londoners 'touchying her worthy gouernement in the reste of her reygne'.
23. Ibid., sig. Eiii^v.
24. See chapter 3 of Marta Straznicky's *Privacy, Playreading, and Women's Closet Drama, 1550–1700* (Cambridge: Cambridge University Press, 2004), esp. p. 62. Straznicky's principal contention is that Hawkins, in conjunction with the printer Thomas Creede, was purveying a play for an 'elite readership', but not necessarily a legal one.
25. See Margaret Ferguson, 'Running On with Almost Public Voice', in *Tradition and the Talents of Women*, ed. Florence Howe (Urbana: University of Illinois Press, 1991), pp. 37–67 (p. 48), and William Hamlin, 'Elizabeth Cary's *Mariam* and the Critique of Pure Reason', *Early Modern Literary Studies: A Journal of Sixteenth- and Seventeenth-Century English Literature* 9 (2003), 2.1–22, http://purl.oclc.org/emls/09-1/hamlcary.html (accessed 23 April 2009).
26. In 'Running On', for example, Ferguson suggested that *Mariam* be read not only as a text through which she was taking revenge on the family into which she had married by representing Mariam (with whom she 'identified') as uttering 'open or veiled insults about base birth' at other women (p. 59), but also as a text that betrays Cary's anxieties about writing and publishing, and as a result one or another form of self-censorship (see especially pp. 46–49). In 'The Canonization of Elizabeth Cary', Stephanie Hodgson-Wright objected to biographical readings of Cary's work, especially where critics read backwards from Cary's later conversion to Catholicism to find in her work a religious writer who might be 'venerated'. Hodgson-Wright's essay is in *Voicing Women: Gender and Sexuality in Early Modern Writing*, ed. Kate

Chedgzoy, Melanie Hansen, and Suzanne Trill (Keele: Keele University Press, 1996), pp. 55–68.

27. It is not clear from the account where the trial was taking place or precisely what Tanfield's judicial status was. It was only in 1595 that his legal career truly started to soar, with his appointment as a Reader to the Middle Temple. As a local judge in New Woodstock, Oxfordshire, Tanfield had a terrible reputation, however, for being unjust. See E. I. Carlyle, 'Tanfield, Sir Lawrence (*c*.1551–1625)', rev. David Ibbetson, *ODNB*, http://oxforddnb.com (accessed 3 April 2009).

28. *Elizabeth Cary: Life and Letters*, ed. Heather Wolfe (Cambridge, England and Tempe, AZ: RTM Publications and the Arizona Center for Medieval and Renaissance Studies, 2001), p. 106. All further references to the *Life* will be cited parenthetically in the text.

29. *The Tragedy of Mariam*, in *Renaissance Drama by Women, Texts and Documents*, ed. S. P. Cerasano and Marion Wynne-Davies (London: Routledge, 1996), p. 50. All further references to *Mariam* will be cited parenthetically in the text.

30. Alan Macfarlane, *Witchcraft in Tudor and Stuart England: A Regional and Comparative Study* (London: Routledge, 1999), p. 20. Conversely, accused witches might be set free if they could find three or four persons who would swear that their denial of guilt was true (p. 68).

31. Cynthia Herrup, *The Common Peace: Participation and the Criminal Law in Early Modern England* (Cambridge: Cambridge University Press, 1987), p. 141.

32. As Jim Sharpe notes, this was especially true of trials for witchcraft: 'Sometimes the throng in the court during a witchcraft trial might be so oppressive, and demonstrate its hostility to the accused so forcefully [...] the judge might be pressured into convicting against his inclinations.' See 'Women, Witchcraft and the Legal Process', in *Women, Crime and the Courts in Early Modern England*, ed. Jennifer Kermode and Garthine Walker (London: University College of London Press, 1994; 2nd edn, 2005), pp. 106–24 (p. 113).

33. Herrup, *Common Peace*, p. 142.

34. Ferguson, 'Running On', p. 53.

35. William Shakespeare, *Hamlet* in *The Riverside Shakespeare* (Boston: Houghton Mifflin, 1997), II.2.589.

36. Curiously, most of those scholars who have considered the play's legal character have discussed this character in relation to one or another notion of absence. See Jonathan Goldberg, *Desiring Women Writing: English Renaissance Examples* (Stanford: Stanford University Press, 1997), pp. 180–81; Hamlin, 'Critique', esp. para. 22; and Laurie Shannon, 'The Tragedie of Mariam: Cary's Critique of the Terms of Founding Social Discourses', *English Literary Renaissance* 24 (1994), 135–53. Shannon finds what is absent from the play in its dedication, in which Cary calls her sister-in-law her 'next belov'd', her 'second Friend' (p. 153).

37. William Shakespeare, *The Merchant of Venice* in *The Riverside Shakespeare* (Boston: Houghton Mifflin, 1997), V.1.298. For Lanyer's reference to Stuart as the 'rare Phoenix' see *Salve Deus Rex Judaeorum* (London, 1611), C^r.

38. For my original, detailed account of the case, see 'The "Roman Hand": Women, Writing and the Law in the Att.-Gen. v. Chatterton and the Letters of the Lady Arbella Stuart', *ELH* 70 (2003), 929–61 (esp. pp. 931–42).

39. For a full discussion of the importance of *Hole* v. *White* to the history of British women's writing, see my 'Slanderous Aesthetics and the Woman Writer: The

Case of *Hole* v. *White'*, in *From Script to Stage in Early Modern England*, ed. Peter Holland and Stephen Orgel (New York: Palgrave Macmillan, 2004), pp. 181–94.

40. For a fuller discussion of Stuart's letters of petition, see Sale, '"Roman Hand"', pp. 952–56.

41. *The Letters of Lady Arbella Stuart*, ed. Sara Jayne Steen (New York and Oxford: Oxford University Press, 1994), p. 259.

10
Elizabeth I

Christine Coch

> And though I be a woman, yet I have as good a courage
> answerable to my place as ever my father had. I am your
> anointed queen. I will never be by violence constrained to
> do anything. I thank God I am indeed endued with such
> qualities that if I were turned out of the realm in my pet-
> ticoat, I were able to live in any place of Christendom.[1]

Elizabeth Tudor was in many respects the most anomalous of early modern women writers. Although as a female she was inevitably subject to
her culture's gender expectations, as an unmarried queen and the only
woman in England wielding official government power she defied all
gender bounds, laying claim to authority that surpassed every man's in
her realm. In contrast to her sister, Mary Tudor, and her kinswoman,
Mary Queen of Scots, Elizabeth did not hesitate to channel this authority
into a bold public voice, addressing even Parliament and the universities in her own words and in person.[2]

The 'qualities' empowering this voice developed out of a sharp native
intelligence and a humanist education of the sort normally reserved
for boys. Thanks in part to the influence of her learned stepmother
Katherine Parr, from the age of ten Elizabeth was tutored alongside her
brother Edward by prominent Cambridge humanists. William Grindal
and later Roger Ascham found her an avid student of Latin and Greek.
She studied, translated, and – when employing Ascham's favored method
of double translation – retranslated texts that ranged from the Greek
New Testament to writings of St Cyprian and Melanchthon to Sophocles,
Cicero, and Livy. She also mastered French, Italian, and in later years
some Spanish. Although no one at the time could have predicted that
Elizabeth would become queen, and her training did not include the

instruction in government that Edward received, the breadth of her education prepared her for the challenges that lay ahead. Facility with languages would become a practical skill for one called on to negotiate with ambassadors from across Europe. A humanist curriculum gave her a store of wisdom to draw on with an ideal of civic service rooted in classical and modern learning. And the rhetorical sensitivity she honed through linguistic exercises like Ascham's double translation taught her to understand writing as action in the world, eloquence as power.

Elizabeth's approach to writing was also shaped by her early experience navigating the treacherous waters of Tudor family politics. Many of the earliest writings we have of hers are letters to members of the royal family and the Court seeking to demonstrate fidelity on occasions of various uncertainty. Letters are by nature interactive, but even as Elizabeth matured and took up other genres her writing retained this sense of immediacy, of addressing a particular audience in response to a situation familiar to both writer and reader. Very often she reflected, as she wrote, on how a situation constrained her, at times deploring the exigencies of fortune and necessity, at other moments embracing what she saw to be the duties before her.

In all instances her writing centers on self-representation. The 'I' and the relationship between the 'I' and the reader are as important as any situation she addresses. Even her translations beg the question of how her 'I' relates to the text at hand. In a larger sense this is true for all her writings. Even where the 'I' is forcefully characterized, as Janel Mueller observes, 'a scholar can make no assured claim to some unmediated truth of the woman's mind or heart'.[3] 'The letters do not reveal her innermost secrets, for she never surrendered the key of her mystery', affirms an early editor.[4] Biographer Wallace MacCaffrey laments that 'the inner woman remains locked away from us'.[5] This elusiveness intrigues and frustrates. Much of the delight of Shekhar Kapur's 1998 award-winning film *Elizabeth* derives from the imaginary access it grants to the 'real Elizabeth' behind the rhetorical polish, in all her passionate intensity. The transformation at the film's end from headstrong young woman to icon elicits the wonder and the shudder that it does only because of our fascination with all that lies under the elaborately crafted surface. Nor is this interest merely anachronistic. It is built into much of Elizabeth's writing.

The marvel (some said horror) of a female ruler lay in the distance perceived between her feminine private self, naturally inferior to men in mind and body, and her public role. How could a woman rule a nation of men? Legally, English administrators resolved the paradox through the notion of the King's two bodies, already invoked for Mary Tudor. Elizabeth's 'body natural', it was conceded, was just what it seemed to be: female, fallible, and mortal. Yet when she took the throne, her body natural mystically melded with a second body, her 'body politic', eternal and legally male. In the process the body politic perfected the body natural.[6] Elizabeth could and did point to her body politic to justify her rule and remind her subjects that she was to be reverenced like any king of England. Yet even in moments of crisis she also foregrounded her body natural, as when in the same breath that she defies Parliament's attempts to force her to action in 1566, claiming 'as good a courage answerable to my place as ever my father had', she also, startlingly, asks her listeners to imagine her as a woman in her underclothes, 'turned out of the realm in [her] petticoat'. In part this strategy compensated for facts that were already on everyone's mind. There was Elizabeth at the front of the hall, quite clearly a woman in woman's clothing. Any argument for her authority needed to acknowledge this condition. Whether purposefully or inadvertently, her habit of drawing attention to her private self even as she affirmed her public power accomplished more, however. In an age increasingly interested in interiority – the Protestant's conscience, the sonnet-speaker's agonies, the self-conception of a character like Hamlet – Elizabeth's gestures towards a private side of her character sustained the wonder of a selfhood riven with contradictions.

One of Elizabeth's notable talents as a ruler and a writer was her ability to transform liabilities, especially gendered liabilities, into rhetorical strengths. Her failure to marry, for instance, allowed her to claim England as her spouse, to play the unattainable Petrarchan beloved for her courtiers, and ultimately to take on the iconography of the Virgin Queen. Her childlessness opened the way for her to declare herself mother of her country. By offering tantalizing glimpses of a private, specifically feminine self she addresses the fears of those who cannot forget that she is a member of the weaker sex, on some occasions by asserting that this self is capable in its own right (hence her claim about thriving were she cast out of England); more usually by insisting that it be perceived as a subordinate component of a more complex and complexly gendered royal selfhood in which public duty trumps private preference. Simultaneously she creates an illusion of intimacy between herself and her audience, granting a privileged view of what is normally withheld from full public gaze (like a petticoat). Jennifer Summit aptly describes Elizabeth's 'poetics of covertness', by which she 'continually stages matters of public policy as the stuff of secrets'. Summit relates this strategy

to the contemporary 'vogue for the "secret" arts of miniatures and sonnets [in which] Patricia Fumerton discerns the effort to create a private
self both within and beyond the artifice of public display'.[7] As both
Summit and Fumerton observe, secrets generate desire. In a world where
'the power of the crown and state depended largely upon its representation of authority',[8] and on subjects' willingness to cooperate with that
representation, Elizabeth's ability to evoke intimacy and curiosity at the
same time as awe helped ensure 'the loving conservation of [her] subjects' hearts', than which nothing was 'more dear to [her]'.[9] Her need to
sustain her readers' interest in herself as an individual helps to explain
the interactive and personal nature of much of Elizabeth's writing. The
more effective the illusion of intimacy, however, the more vexing it can
be for modern readers to come to terms with the fact that much of the
writing we have of hers is a product of collaboration rather than single
authorship, as Marcus, Mueller, and Rose discuss in their introduction
to her *Collected Works* (pp. xii–xiii). A letter signed by Elizabeth may
have been written in part or in whole by a secretary or an advisor like
William Cecil. Speeches are often memorial reconstructions by one or
more auditors. In a broader sense even generic conventions might be
understood as co-producers of her texts. The contingency underlying
the composition and transmission of the texts resonates with many of
the texts' own meditations on how the individual 'I' relates to larger
forces in the world. Each genre Elizabeth wrote in – translation, epistle,
prayer, poetry, speech – offered unique possibilities and limitations for
exploring this issue and for self-representation in courtly, national, and
international contexts.

Translation may seem the most limited of the genres for these purposes. After selecting a text, a translator like Elizabeth who followed her
sources closely was restricted by the author's ends. When Elizabeth was a
child, she may not have even chosen her texts herself, following instead
the guidance of a tutor or someone like Katherine Parr. That person and
others might have assisted with her translation and compounded the
collaborative constraints.[10] Yet translation afforded the young princess
a safer mode of self-expression than others in an era of political uncertainty. For a student and especially for a female, it was more decorous
to defer to the authority of an established writer than to compose from
scratch, allowing her to display her learning without the risk of unseemly
self-assertion. Moreover, blame for anything in a text could be deflected
from a translator, at least in part.

The example of the earliest translation we have from Elizabeth shows
her seizing full advantage of the genre's expressive potential. For her

1545 New Year's gift to Queen Katherine, the eleven-year-old princess prepared an English translation of Marguerite of Navarre's verse meditation
Le Miroir de l'âme pécheresse (1531) titled 'The Glass of the Sinful Soul'.
An apt present for a learned, pious queen, the 'Glass' testifies to Elizabeth's
devotional commitments and implicitly celebrates the work of religious
women writers like Marguerite and later Katherine. Marguerite's original
was temporarily banned after publication due to what were perceived to
be reformist sympathies, so Elizabeth's choice would have appealed to
Katherine's Protestant interests while also allowing Elizabeth to demonstrate respect for a Roman Catholic writer, essential for a princess who
might yet need to marry a Catholic.[11] The soul in the text '(beholding
and contempling what she is) doth perceive how of herself and of her
own strength she can do nothing that good is, or prevaileth for her salvation, unless it be through the grace of God, whose mother, daughter,
sister, and wife by the Scriptures she proveth herself to be'.[12] Family
relationships were no simple matter for Elizabeth. One purpose of her
translation was doubtless to retain the sympathy of her influential stepmother, a critical counterbalance to the mercurial Henry VIII who had
only recently restored Elizabeth to the succession. Modern commentators have speculated on how the familial metaphors for spiritual relationships in the 'Glass' may have allowed her to recast kinship in more
congenial terms.[13] Some have seen in the metaphors early patterns of
thought that would eventuate in her royal self-representations as wife
and mother of the realm.[14]

The 'Glass' communicated still more about the princess through its
material form as an italic manuscript bound in an ornate embroidered
cover. 'In the sixteenth century, roman and italic hands, associated with
Humanism, came to England, where they became fashionable and served
as an indicator of learning and class status', notes Frances Teague. 'Roger
Ascham would later praise Princess Elizabeth's handwriting in terms that
suggest an equivalence between hand and head, between characters and
character.'[15] Although Elizabeth's everyday handwriting changed as she
adapted it to the business of queenship, developing into a 'much more
informal cursive mixed italic and secretary hand', she was well aware that
hands conveyed much about a writer and her relation to her material
and her intended reader.[16] Even in her maturity she retained what her
editors call her 'inscriptional italic' hand 'whenever she took special care
in writing out a text', its 'beauty and legibility' suiting 'expressions of
affection, familiarity, and gratitude'.[17] Her needlework on the binding of
the 'Glass' demonstrated that her learning had not displaced more conventionally feminine accomplishments. The embroidered initials 'KP'

personalize the volume for her stepmother, while a surrounding cross may symbolize piety, an elaborately entwined knot virginity, and pansies in each corner 'love and thought'.[18]

Like some of Elizabeth's other writings, the 'Glass' later appeared in a new form for a different audience. Whereas for Katherine the text was an intimate hand-wrought gift testifying to the values she shared with her stepdaughter, in the hands of Protestant polemicist John Bale it became a public window into the 'godly occupied heart' of the king's sister, a book printed and distributed 'to the intent that many hungry souls by the inestimable treasure contained therein may be sweetly refreshed'.[19] Bale's 1548 edition was followed by others in 1568–70, 1582, and 1590, implying that Elizabeth was pleased with the publicity and her readers with the view into their then-sovereign's character, its aura of authenticity enhanced by the translator's tender age.[20] Elizabeth continued translating throughout her life. Although none of her other translations saw print, some were 'deliberately circulated in manuscript by the court' and others advertised even if reserved from wide public view. 'The primary reason she translated', suggests Leah Marcus, 'was in order to be publicly known to be translating. For Elizabeth I, translation was not the virtuous womanly service it might have been for some others, but a form of political assertion'. In some instances her audience interpreted her choice of texts as a response to particular challenges, as when William Camden connects her 1593 translation of part of Boethius's *The Consolation of Philosophy* with 'the cataclysmic news of her ally Henry of Navarre's conversion to Catholicism so that he could accept the French crown as Henry IV'.[21] Boethius's themes of patience and devotion helped Elizabeth to 'reinforce her own devout nature' and her policy of pacifism in the face of Protestant criticism.[22] Any translation of a respected text could generate this kind of speculative interest and ally Elizabeth with ancient and modern authorities. From young adulthood to old age she worked on selections from Parr, Calvin, Petrarch, Horace, Plutarch, Sallust, Seneca, Isocrates, and others.[23] When her translations were not made directly available to readers, 'their function as royal propaganda concerned intellectual rather than artistic accomplishment [...] [I]t became well known that she had written them and, above all, in a very short time at that'.[24] Though such translations remained rough and literal, few saw them to judge, and her practice reminded her subjects of her learning and attested to an inner life of intellectual exercise and deliberation informing her rule. If those educated enough to know the texts in question were enticed to puzzle over what the selections revealed about her mind, all the better. The practice of translating likely had cognitive benefits as well for an intellect trained by humanist tutors to associate eloquent expression with clear thinking.

Accompanying her youthful translation of the 'Glass' for Katherine Parr was a letter, exemplifying a second genre Elizabeth wrote in from youth through maturity. The Parr letter is one of the earliest we have. Janel Mueller estimates that there are at least a thousand extant letters that are 'known to [have been] signed and sent' by Elizabeth up to the month before she died.[25] Many of these conduct routine business and are of scant literary interest. But like translation, the personal epistle was a respected form of writing in the period, with 'letters by eminent persons' read with interest in manuscript and print anthologies.[26] The epistle was also considered an appropriate form for women, affording further opportunity for the young Elizabeth to showcase her learning without incurring gendered censure.[27]

In the letter accompanying the 'Glass' we can see the princess following guidelines that would have been imparted by her humanist tutors, based on 'a composite epistolary theory made up of three interrelated traditions: (1) the medieval *ars dictaminis*, (2) early modern rhetorical theory; and (3) the revived theory of the "familiar letter"'. These traditions were in key respects contradictory, the first two emphasizing rhetorical structure and the 'hierarchical relationship' between writer and reader and the third instead 'reviv[ing] [...] the classical idea that letters should be [...] loosely structured, free of strict rhetorical rules and inspired by selfless *amicitia*'.[28] In addressing her 'noble and virtuous' stepmother and 'most gracious and sovereign princess' Elizabeth takes pains to prove herself both 'humble daughter' and dutiful subject. She opens and closes with formal prayers for Katherine's 'felicity', defers to her 'excellent wit and godly learning', and justifies the translation project by citing a classical maxim. At the same time she appeals to Katherine at a more personal level, asking that she keep the translation private until it can be refined, '[lest] my faults be known of many'. Much like the 'Sinful Soul' in Marguerite's meditation that 'can do nothing that good is or prevaileth for her salvation, unless it be through the grace of God', the dependent princess, knowing her work not 'worthy to come in your grace's hands, but rather all unperfect and uncorrect' yet 'hope[s] that after to have been in your grace's hands, there shall be nothing in it worthy of reprehension', the hierarchic gap between stepmother and stepdaughter bridged by faith and love.[29]

Thanks to the competing priorities of formality and familiarity in letter-writing, the genre was well suited to experimenting with characterizations of a personal 'I' accompanying a public self. As queen, even when she was not foregrounding the division, Elizabeth strove in her letters to sustain the impression of intimate correspondence between individuals, despite routine collaboration with or outright composition by members of her staff and, frequently, the preservation of ostensibly personal letters among state records. Her modern editors observe that 'it is often impossible to separate the queen's "authentic" voice from an official style that she developed in conjunction with her secretaries and principal ministers and that was used with equal facility by all of them'.[30] She 'personally composed much of [the correspondence] sent to foreign rulers', however, and 'sometimes attached personal notes in her own handwriting to secretarial letters at the time of dispatch'.[31]

For a ruler who never traveled beyond the south-east portion of her realm, letters were an indispensable means of self-representation on a national and international scale, and Elizabeth developed a range of prose styles to suit her varied needs. 'When she was writing coyly, or for effect, or to hide her thoughts and intentions, she was diffuse and affected, hunting the metaphor tediously, and indulging in sententious conceits and flourishes of wit', remarks Harrison. 'On the other hand, when she wished, she could be terse and direct in all her moods'.[32] Mueller sees in her more labored style 'a set of linguistic constructions that render authoritativeness concretely textual in writing'. 'Constant engagement with [these] suspensive and strung-out constructions [ensures] that any expenditure of the reader's energy, beyond that demanded by the intricate and ceremonious workings of the labyrinthine sentence structure, is merely and sheerly ruled out'.[33] May argues further that the 'figurative language, allusions, and emotion-charged expression' which Harrison at times laments are what 'enliven [Elizabeth's] discourse in ways all but unknown in the direct, formal, and circumspect letters turned out by her secretaries', giving it much of its force and appeal.[34]

Consider her letters to François Hercule, the Duke of Alençon and later, on the crowning of his elder brother Henry III of France, the Duke of Anjou. 'Monsieur', as the *Collected Works* editors call him, was the likeliest prospective husband for Elizabeth in the 1570s and early 1580s. She seems to have felt genuinely affectionate towards him, fondly addressing him as her 'very dear Frog' and 'commending [herself] a thousand times to the little fingers'.[35] Towards the end of their failing marriage negotiations she begs him not to 'forget my heart, which I risk a little for you in this matter – more than you will be able to imagine but not more than I already feel. And it rejoices me to have tasted of it, more than a fine liquor'. Her emotional investment, conveyed in the vivid language May praises, she finally sets counter to her duty as queen, 'entreating [Monsieur] to believe that if our marriage were made, I would not take away from it any good for England'.[36] Here in the straightforward syntax, the simple monosyllables, and the mostly iambic regularity of the final clause we encounter the force of her terseness when she wishes to be direct, as Harrison notes. Quite another matter is the style she can assume when, during the years of negotiations, she leverages the emotional charge of their personal relationship for political advantage, or at least attempts to. 'You will forgive me the curiosity that holds me to your actions, to whom I wish all the honor and glory that can accrue to the perpetual renown of a prince', she flatters as she tries to persuade him to support Henry of Navarre and the Huguenots in the French civil wars.[37] Later she chides him for not sending her recent news 'of France or of the Low Countries or of any other parts', in her annoyance tipping her hand and revealing his use value to her as an intelligence source on the Continent.[38] The more frustrated she becomes with his military and political actions in the Netherlands, the less willing she is to continue exchanging all manner of support for the opportunity to influence him, and her style becomes more 'diffuse and affected', in Harrison's words, as she works to extricate herself without seeming to do so. Pointing to the King of France's objections to the marriage in 1582, she protests:

> if I do not dare to justify myself before everybody that it has never been owing to me that he himself did not conclude after my last promise – which I made you under such conditions as you alone know and admit as well as I myself to be very difficult ones – notwithstanding, in keeping with your contentment, I accorded myself with a very good will.[39]

Her opening 'if' initially would seem to be half of one of the 'clausal connectives' ('if [...] then [...]') that Mueller identifies as a construction 'directive in its force because it relays attention from one to the next element of a pair [...] while withholding the closure that would make meaning complete'. Its 'suspensive' effect, 'monopolizing short-term memory and attention', is further intensified by the insertion of the parenthetical.[40] Worse, the expected 'then' never actually comes. The reader is left dangling, with only Elizabeth's reiteration of her good faith to comfort him.

As intensely as she could assert her autonomy, Elizabeth often dwelled on the factors that limited it: providence, chance, weakness, responsibility, trust, public perception. This concern is nowhere more evident than in her prayers. Like letters to God, her prayers are at once intimate addresses from an individual soul to its creator and communications from the nation to its protector. In them the humble poignancy of Protestant supplication balances the confidence of divine-right sovereignty. A monarch's declaration of abject dependence on God had the paradoxical effect of reaffirming her special status as His chosen ruler, particularly when her successes seemed unlikely to have derived from her own abilities. Her 'weakest sex' attested to God's 'strongest help'.[41] From the very beginning of her reign Elizabeth was sensitive to the interest this paired relationship of human to God and earthly ruler to heavenly ruler would have for her people, perhaps perceiving its similarity to the relationship in the Psalms, so popular in her day. As early as her coronation procession we find her staging moments when her subjects can overhear her speaking to God. At the Tower, where the procession began, she was reported to have

> lifted up her eyes to heaven and said:
> O Lord, almighty and everlasting God, I give Thee most hearty thanks that Thou hast been so merciful unto me as to spare me to behold this joyful day. And I acknowledge that Thou hast dealt as wonderfully and as mercifully with me as Thou didst with Thy true and faithful servant Daniel, Thy prophet, whom Thou deliveredst out of the den from the cruelty of the greedy and raging lions. Even so was I overwhelmed and only by Thee delivered. To Thee (therefore) only be thanks, honor, and praise forever, amen.[42]

With the audience who witnesses this prayer, Elizabeth is a beholder of 'this joyful day', a helpless human who owes her salvation entirely to God's mercy. Yet she is also the recipient of a miracle, a wonder that lifts her out of her weakness to a position of divine favor and authority comparable to those of a biblical male prophet. Part of the appeal of the prayer as a performance lies in the audience's voyeuristic pleasure at being privy to an intimacy at once familiar and strange.

It is perhaps Elizabeth's desire to maintain this atmosphere of privacy that complicates the textual history of her prayers. Although the editors of her *Collected Works* attribute thirty-nine prayers to her authorship, Steven May observes that 'no official publication of any prayer unquestionably by Elizabeth is known to have taken place during her reign', and he and others suggest that some of the printed and manuscript prayers purporting to be in the Queen's voice may have been composed by other writers.[43] May points to Elizabeth's recall of one of her prayers printed anonymously by John Whitgift in 1597 as evidence that she 'resented any public dissemination of her prayers', considering them 'personal and private forms of expression'. Such actions, no matter their motivation, would of course have intensified public interest, and May notes the irony that Elizabeth's 'private devotions became her most widely disseminated writings in the century and a half after her death', an irony that might have come as no surprise to a canny monarch.[44] Fittingly, Elizabeth opens the prayer that 'ranks as the best-known and most influential of her writings' in the seventeenth and early eighteenth centuries, if judged by the 'number of extant copies of any of her works',[45] with an image of secrets revealed. 'Most omnipotent Maker and Guider of all our world's mass, that only searchest and fathomest the bottom of all our hearts' conceits and in them seest the true original of all our actions intended', she begins. The 'conceits' thus brought to light are not hers alone, but the nation's, manifested in 'the resolution of our now-set-out army' en route to attack Cádiz in May 1596.[46] This petition for God's help is the very prayer that Elizabeth later orders Whitgift to remove from his volume, even though '[a]ccording to Camden and Stow, [she] ordered this prayer to be distributed among the departing fleet; it was also apparently issued in a printed version for use in parish churches, perhaps against the queen's wishes'.[47] The prayer's secrets are at once communal and performatively private.

Assisted by generic convention and shifting literary tastes, Elizabeth was even more successful at creating beguiling intimacy in poems. Although she wrote relatively few (the *Collected Works* includes just fifteen – most in English, several in Latin or French – and her authorship of some of these is uncertain), and her poetry was the least widely circulated of all her writing, it powerfully influenced her contemporary reputation as a writer. Edmund Spenser praised her as a 'most peereless Poëtesse', as did George Puttenham, Francis Meres, and Edmund Bolton.[48] Jennifer Summit argues in a seminal essay that 'the covert terms and restricted circulation associated with coterie manuscript poetry offered [Elizabeth] a means of manipulating the privacy that humanism famously demanded of women in order to produce the public effects on which [her] authority as a monarch depended', effects that included 'an aura of "privileged insidedness" around the text and its readers'.[49] As Leah Marcus has shown, most of Elizabeth's poems 'circulated anonymously', or with an attribution that has been 'heavily scored through', registering 'a violation of secrecy. When it came to the writing of love poetry and other ephemeral occasional verse, Queen Elizabeth I took care never to acknowledge authorship'.[50] Poesy could be seen as a trivial distraction for a queen, although a number of English monarchs before her wrote verse, including her father.[51] That she was concerned about this risk is suggested by John Harington's account of how one of her poems first circulated in manuscript. 'The Doubt of Future Foes' (*c.*1571), about the problems posed by Mary Queen of Scots, Puttenham particularly admired and eventually printed with attribution in his *The Art of English Poesie* (1589). Yet originally, Harington reports:

> My lady Willoughby did covertly get it on her majesty's [writing] tablet and had much hazard in so doing, for the queen did find out the thief and chid for spreading evil bruit of her writing such toys when other matters did so occupy her employment at this time, and was fearful of being thought too lightly of for so doing.[52]

One wonders, however, whether any Court lady would have dared such a stunt without knowing that Elizabeth would not mind overmuch, might even be secretly pleased. Offering more expressive freedom than translations, letters, or prayers, ostensibly private verse allowed the Queen to engage a reader's senses, emotions, and intellect together, the dynamic further heightened by the air of transgression.

Following Wyatt, the sixteenth-century courtly lyric centers on the internal experience of the speaker, seeming to reveal what is ordinarily hidden from view. Poesy was artful play, and a means of reflection, but it was also an increasingly important mode for the serious political business of self-representation. Even Elizabeth's earliest poems show a sensitivity to the usefulness of the genre's characteristic compression and ambiguity. The first we have date from a period in her childhood when Henry and Catherine were dead and her brother Edward's Lord Protector suspected her of conspiring in traitorous designs on the throne. He forbade her to leave her household at Woodstock to come and speak in her own defense at court. The shorter of the two poems she wrote in response is an epigram said to have been etched by the princess '*with her diamond in a glass window*' of her chamber:

> Much suspected by me,
> Nothing proved can be.
> *Quod* [said] Elizabeth the prisoner[53]

The medium of a window nicely epitomizes the transparency poetry was supposed to afford into a speaker's mind, and also the genre's protective surface. Those who could read the poem from outside saw through the constraints of public duty that imprisoned the princess, but only obliquely, only as clearly as the poem's problematic material trace and ambiguous language allowed. Presumably the original writing would have appeared in reverse to an outdoor reader, though later the couplet was widely printed. Janel Mueller points to the uncertainty of the word 'by', meaning either simply 'by' or 'to have been done by', the suspicions being Elizabeth's in the first reading, her enemies' in the second. Mueller further notes that 'antithesis and irony' are 'the undergirding staples of [Elizabeth's] verse composition' more generally.[54] If the final subscription to the couplet is Elizabeth's and not a later addition, it highlights the poem's function as a tool of self-characterization at a moment when few other means were available, depicting her as intelligent, confident, and victimized.

When Elizabeth composed poetry during her reign, as she did until the end of her life, she wrote from a position of power. Yet at times she used lyric conventions to portray a doubting, vulnerable, private side of herself subordinate to the stable strength of her queenship. Feeding readers' natural curiosity about how two such inconsistent selfhoods could coexist in one person, she could demonstrate how her rule resolved her internal divide – for readers and perhaps for herself – in the process of dramatizing it. Her subjects' continuing interest in her self-division is visible in other poets' work as well. Witness Spenser's decision to 'shadow her' in multiple characters in *The Faerie Queene*, 'considering she beareth two persons, the one of a most royall Queene or Empresse, the other of a most vertuous and beautifull Lady'.[55] Stylistically, like many courtly poets of the period, Elizabeth did not employ 'the advances in English verse made by Sidney and his friends', building instead on models from earlier in the century, although her 'style [did evolve] in keeping with broad trends in poetic form and prosody during her lifetime'.[56] Petrarchan tropes were her starting-point for 'On Monsieur's Departure', three iambic pentameter stanzas likely written around 1582 in reaction to her failed marriage negotiations.

> I grieve and dare not show my discontent;
> I love, and yet am forced to seem to hate;
> [...]
> I am, and not; I freeze and yet am burned,
> Since from myself another self I turned.[57]

The usual Petrarchan paradoxes expressing simultaneous despair and ecstasy are here adapted to the unique experience of a queen in love.

No matter what her body natural desires, she must respect the exigencies of her body politic by resisting a match that could be harmful to England. Neither passive beloved nor rejected lover, she controls the relationship, regendering the traditional Petrarchan speaker and redefining the conditions of love even as she agonizes. The other 'self' she turns away is both Monsieur and her own private persona – the 'Elizabetha' half of the *'Elizabetha Regina'* subscription that follows the poem's final line. No sixteenth-century manuscripts of 'On Monsieur's Departure' survive, leading some scholars to speculate that Elizabeth 'kept [it] truly private during her lifetime'.[58] It is doubtful that a queen constantly surrounded by ladies-in-waiting and other courtly staff would have considered anything she did or wrote 'truly private', but it is possible that she composed the poem primarily for herself, suggesting that her divided self-representation may have been at least as reflective and expressive as it was strategic.

At the opposite end of the spectrum from potentially private poetry were her speeches. Designed for public performance, and 'widely available in print and manuscript [even] generations after her death', they are often considered 'her greatest literary achievement'.[59] Like her poems, however, most survive in manuscripts written by others, and the usual textual uncertainties of scribal copies are compounded by the problem of auditors attempting memorially to reconstruct what they have heard. Where we do find speeches in the Queen's own hand, still more difficulties arise. The editors of the *Collected Works* argue that Elizabeth typically composed and delivered speeches before writing them down. She might then write or dictate a version to her secretaries or even revise an auditor's transcription. Her ministers added further revisions. The written versions of the speeches could vary considerably from her oral delivery, then, even when she penned them, particularly if she wished to modify what she had said. Existing evidence suggests that she frequently 'ton[ed] down the original vividness of her language and replac[ed] it with more measured, abstract, often (to us) windy and convoluted, but more formal and politically neutral wording and syntax'.[60] For modern readers, and especially modern editors, this poses a question that resonates with the doubleness of Elizabeth's self-representations. Which is the 'real' Elizabeth: the impassioned speaker, whose words are usually available to us only second-hand, or the considered writer? The answer the *Collected Works* editors propose is that the real Elizabeth composes to her situation. Her speeches, like her other writings, are occasional and interactive, adapted to varied audiences and shifting conditions.

Many address the vexed issues of marriage and succession. Elizabeth used the theory of the monarch's two bodies to validate her authority from her Coronation speech onwards, most famously in addressing her troops amassed at Tilbury to repulse the attack of the Spanish Armada in 1588. Here she is reported to have declared, 'I know I have the body but of a weak and feeble woman, but I have the heart and stomach of a king and of a king of England too'.[61] Earlier in her reign, in parrying Parliament's relentless requests for a husband and an heir, she added personal dimensions to her body natural by vividly depicting the desires she was sacrificing to political duty. In 1563, she countered rumors that she was resolved to remain a virgin by telling the House of Lords that 'though I can think [that kind of life] best for a private woman, yet do I strive with myself to think it not meet for a prince'.[62] Compensating for the origination of these rumors in her own dramatic 1559 avowal that 'in the end this shall be for me sufficient: that a marble stone shall declare that a queen, having reigned such a time, lived and died a virgin',[63] in 1576 she boosts the rhetorical charge of her defense with two vital images:

> though I must confess mine own mislike so much to strive against the matter [of marriage] as, if I were a milkmaid with a pail on mine arm, whereby my private person might be little set by, I would not forsake that single state to match myself with the greatest monarch. [...] Yet for your behoof there is no way so difficile that may touch my private, which I could not well content myself to take, and in this case as willingly to spoil myself quite of myself as if I should put off my upper garment when it wearies me.[64]

Through its association with the figure of the milkmaid, her 'private person' is rendered feminine, humble, familiar, and sympathetic. Analogized to an 'upper garment', in contrast to the petticoat that earlier revealed her sexual difference, it is also inessential, something that can be donned and 'put off' at will.

And put it off she did, though in a different sense than she promised. She never married, of course, but in later speeches she seems largely to have given up the figure of her 'private person', exchanging her self-division for a more capacious, unified royal identity. Perhaps more confidence and political stability allowed her to turn her attention away from defending her rule and gaining support. Perhaps the end of marriage negotiations marked an end as well of the central conflict between duty and personal desire. The parliamentary address that would come to be known as her Golden Speech, delivered in 1601 and copied and printed in multiple editions, portrays a queen thoroughly comfortable in her royal role. In a 'summary' version of the speech 'printed with the royal arms as its frontispiece', likely 'published under the auspices of the court', when Elizabeth acknowledges mistakes she has made, there is no defensive gesture to the weakness of her body natural, no blunt reminder of her authority over Parliament.[65] She thanks her audience as a 'loving king' for 'keep[ing] their sovereign from the lapse of error' and makes no move to counter anticipated objections to her gender. She even goes so far as to envisage her deposition, declaring, '[f]or were it not for conscience' and for your sake, I would willingly yield another my place, so great is my pride in reigning as she that wisheth no longer to be than best and most would have me so'.[66] No desire for a private life, but duty itself would draw her from the throne, except for her certainty that God's will and her people's love sustain her there.

In the end, did Elizabeth influence the cultural status of women? Scholars disagree. Some argue that she acted as an 'honorary male' and consequently reinforced the structures of 'patriarchal governance'.[67] Others counter that by successfully modeling female authority and will she destabilized gender norms, at least for later generations looking back at her example.[68] Still more difficult to assess is the role her writing played in her legacy. Judging from how few of her texts were in circulation after her death as compared with 'apocrypha' and 'third-person remembrances of the Queen', Steven May 'conclude[s] that her seventeenth-century myth owes little of substance to her skills as a writer'.[69] In 1630 Diana Primrose does praise her eloquence in *A Chaine of Pearl*.[70] Bathsua Makin follows suit in *An Essay to Revive the Antient Education of Gentlewomen* (1673), noting further that '[t]hose ingenious Fancies, and pleasant Poems, bearing [Elizabeth's] Name, shews she was a good Poet'.[71] Yet other seventeenth-century women writers who celebrate her, like Anne Bradstreet, do not address her authorship. Even in Elizabeth's lifetime, Mary Sidney Herbert, who wrote about Elizabeth's role as patroness of English 'Wit' and 'Art' in a dedicatory poem prefacing her psalm translations, did not directly salute the Queen as a fellow female writer.[72]

The recent proliferation of new editions and analyses of Elizabeth's writings both reflects and effects a change in how they inform contemporary interest in the Queen. When I show my students Kapur's *Elizabeth*, they often single out a scene of composition as curiously striking. In it, the young Queen agonizes over a speech she is preparing. Stopping and starting, she tests phrases, diction, tones. For my students, the chance to witness even a fictionalized version of the process behind the self-assured texts we have been reading all term feeds an appetite generated by the texts themselves. In contrast with her iconic portraits, Elizabeth's writings offer repeated, tantalizing glimpses of a conflicted human selfhood coexisting with her sovereignty. At a moment when readers face ever-increasing public demands on their time and their privacy, the writings of an admired leader who so vividly represented herself as choosing duty over other forms of personal satisfaction have disquieting relevance.

Notes

1. Elizabeth Tudor, *Elizabeth I: Collected Works*, ed. Leah S. Marcus, Janel Mueller, and Mary Beth Rose (Chicago: University of Chicago Press, 2000), speech 9, version 2, p. 97. All subsequent quotations of Elizabeth's writings, unless indicated otherwise, are taken from this edition.
2. Mary Thomas Crane, '"Video et Taceo": Elizabeth I and the Rhetoric of Counsel', *Studies in English Literature* 28 (1988), 1–15 (p. 4).
3. Janel Mueller, 'Virtue and Virtuality: Gender in the Self-Representations of Queen Elizabeth I', in *Form and Reform in Renaissance England: Essays in Honor of Barbara Kiefer Lewalski*, ed. Amy Boesky and Mary Thomas Crane (Newark: University of Delaware Press, 2000), pp. 220–46 (p. 221).
4. *The Letters of Queen Elizabeth I*, ed. G. B. Harrison (New York: Funk & Wagnalls, 1968), pp. xv–xvi.
5. Wallace MacCaffrey, *Elizabeth I* (London: Edward Arnold, 1993), p. 7.
6. See especially Ernst H. Kantorowicz, *The King's Two Bodies: A Study in Mediaeval Political Theory* (Princeton: Princeton University Press, 1957) and Marie Axton, *The Queen's Two Bodies: Drama and the Elizabethan Succession* (London: Humanities Press, 1977).
7. Jennifer Summit, '"The Arte of a Ladies Penne": Elizabeth I and the Poetics of Queenship', in *Reading Monarch's Writing: The Poetry of Henry VIII, Mary Stuart, Elizabeth I, and James VI/I*, ed. Peter C. Herman (Tempe: Arizona Center for Medieval and Renaissance Studies, 2002), pp. 79–108 (pp. 92, 91) (first published in *English Literary Renaissance*, 26 [1995], 395–422). Patricia Fumerton, *Cultural Aesthetics: Renaissance Literature and the Practice of Social Ornament* (Chicago: University of Chicago Press, 1991).
8. Kevin Sharpe, *Remapping Early Modern England: The Culture of Seventeenth-Century Politics* (Cambridge: Cambridge University Press, 2000), p. 127.
9. Speech 23, version 3, p. 343.
10. Anne Lake Prescott, 'The Pearl of the Valois and Elizabeth I: Marguerite de Navarre's *Miroir* and Tudor England', in *Silent But for the Word: Tudor Women as Patrons, Translators, and Writers of Religious Works*, ed. Margaret P. Hannay (Kent, OH: Kent State University Press, 1985), pp. 61–76 (p. 64).
11. Frances Teague, 'Princess Elizabeth's Hand in *The Glass of the Sinful Soul*', in *Writings by Early Modern Women*, ed. Peter Beal and Margaret J. M. Ezell, English Manuscript Studies, 9 (London: British Library, 2003), pp. 33–48 (p. 38).
12. Letter 2, p. 7.
13. Prescott, 'The Pearl of the Valois and Elizabeth I'; also Marc Shell, *Elizabeth's Glass: With 'The Glass of the Sinful Soul' (1544) by Elizabeth I and 'Epistle*

Dedicatory' and 'Conclusion' (1548) by John Bale (Lincoln: University of Nebraska Press, 1993).

14. Shell, *Elizabeth's Glass*, pp. 7 and 64–73; Louis Montrose, *The Subject of Elizabeth: Authority, Gender, Representation* (Chicago: University of Chicago Press, 2006), p. 34.
15. Teague, 'Princess Elizabeth's Hand', p. 40.
16. H. R. Woudhuysen, 'The Queen's Own Hand: A Preliminary Account', in *Elizabeth I and the Culture of Writing*, ed. Peter Beal and Grace Ioppolo (London: British Library, 2007), pp. 1–27 (p. 13).
17. *Elizabeth I: Autograph Compositions and Foreign Language Originals*, ed. Janel Mueller and Leah S. Marcus (Chicago: University of Chicago Press, 2003), p. xviii.
18. Teague, 'Princess Elizabeth's Hand', p. 43.
19. John Bale, 'Epistle Dedicatory', in Shell, *Elizabeth's Glass*, p. 91.
20. Shell, *Elizabeth's Glass*, p. 4.
21. Leah Marcus, 'Queen Elizabeth as Public and Private Poet: Notes Toward a New Edition', in *Reading Monarch's Writing*, ed. Herman, pp. 135–53 (pp. 142, 143).
22. Lysbeth Benkert, 'Translation as Image-Making: Elizabeth I's Translation of Boethius's *Consolation of Philosophy*', *Early Modern Literary Studies* 6.3 (January 2001), http://purl.oclc.org/emls/06-3/benkboet.htm (accessed 20 August 2008), 2.1–20 (2.18, 2.15–16).
23. Caroline Pemberton, *Queen Elizabeth's Englishings* (London: Kegan Paul, 1899).
24. Steven W. May, *The Elizabethan Courtier Poets: The Poems and Their Contexts* (Asheville: Pegasus Press, 1999), p. 135.
25. Janel Mueller, 'Queen Elizabeth I', in *Teaching Tudor and Stuart Women Writers*, ed. Susanne Woods and Margaret P. Hannay (New York: MLA, 2000), pp. 119–26 (p. 121).
26. Steven W. May, 'Queen Elizabeth Prays for the Living and the Dead', in *Elizabeth I and the Culture of Writing*, ed. Peter Beal and Grace Ioppolo, pp. 201–11 (pp. 206–07).
27. See Lynn Magnusson's essay on women's letter-writing in this volume.
28. Jonathan Gibson, 'Letters', in *A Companion to English Renaissance Literature and Culture*, ed. Michael Hattaway (Malden: Blackwell Publishing, 2003), pp. 615–19 (pp. 615, 616).
29. Letter 2, pp. 6–7.
30. *Elizabeth I: Collected Works*, ed. Marcus, Mueller, and Rose, p. xiii.
31. *Queen Elizabeth I: Selected Works*, ed. Steven W. May (New York: Washington Square Press, 2004), p. xviii.
32. Harrison (ed.), *Letters of Queen Elixabeth I*, p. xv.
33. Janel Mueller, 'Textualism, Contextualism, and the Writings of Queen Elizabeth I', in *English Studies and History*, ed. David Robertson (Tampere: University of Tampere, 1994), pp. 11–38 (pp. 29, 28).
34. Steven W. May, '"Tongue-tied our Queen?": Queen Elizabeth's Voice in the Seventeenth Century', in *Resurrecting Elizabeth I in Seventeenth-Century England*, ed. Elizabeth H. Hageman and Katherine Conway (Madison: Fairleigh Dickinson University Press, 2007), pp. 48–67 (p. 63).
35. Letters 46 and 50, pp. 244 and 251.
36. Letter 52, p. 256.

37. Letter 45, p. 238.
38. Letter 46, p. 244.
39. Letter 51, p. 252.
40. Mueller, 'Textualism', pp. 28, 29.
41. Prayer 37, p. 424.
42. Speech 2, pp. 54–55.
43. May, *Selected Works*, pp. xxx, xxviii and 'Queen Elizabeth Prays', p. 206; Woudhuysen, 'The Queen's Own Hand', p. 19.
44. May, 'Queen Elizabeth Prays', pp. 203, 206.
45. Ibid., p. 205.
46. Prayer 38, pp. 425–26.
47. Prayer 38, n. 1, p. 425.
48. Summit, '"The Arte of a Ladies Penne"', pp. 82, 79.
49. Ibid., p. 108 and p. 94, quoting Jonathan Crewe, *Hidden Designs: The Critical Profession and Renaissance Literature* (New York: Methuen, 1986), p. 78.
50. Marcus, 'Queen Elizabeth as Public and Private Poet', pp. 148, 149.
51. Peter C. Herman and Ray G. Siemens, 'Introduction' to *Reading Monarch's Writing*, ed. Herman, pp. 1–10 (p. 2).
52. *Nugae Antiquae*, quoted by Janel Mueller in 'Elizabeth I: Poet of Danger', in *Approaches to Teaching Shorter Elizabethan Poetry*, ed. Patrick Cheney and Anne Lake Prescott (New York: MLA, 2000), pp. 202–09 (p. 208).
53. Poem 2, p. 46.
54. Mueller, 'Poet of Danger', pp. 204, 207–08.
55. Edmund Spenser, 'A Letter of the Authors', appended to *The Faerie Queene*, ed. A. C. Hamilton (London: Longman, 1977), pp. 737–38 (p. 737).
56. May, *Courtier Poets*, p. 138; May, *Selected Works*, p. xxi.
57. Poem 9, ll. 1–2 and 5–6, pp. 302–03.
58. Marcus, 'Queen Elizabeth as Public and Private Poet', p. 146; May, *Selected Works*, p. 13.
59. May, *Selected Works*, p. xxv; *Elizabeth I: Collected Works*, ed. Marcus, Mueller, and Rose, p. xi.
60. *Elizabeth I: Collected Works*, ed. Marcus, Mueller, and Rose, pp. xxi, xii; Leah S. Marcus, 'From Oral Delivery to Print in the Speeches of Elizabeth I', in *Print, Manuscript, and Performance: The Changing Relations of the Media in Early Modern England*, ed. Arthur F. Marotti and Michael D. Bristol (Columbus: Ohio State University Press, 2000), pp. 33–48 (pp. 35, 37–38).
61. Speech 19, p. 326.
62. Speech 6, p. 79.
63. Speech 3, p. 58.
64. Speech 13, p. 170.
65. *Elizabeth I: Collected Works*, ed. Marcus, Mueller, and Rose, pp. 342–43, n. 1.
66. Speech 23, version 3, pp. 343, 344.
67. Allison Heisch, 'Queen Elizabeth I and the Persistence of Patriarchy', *Feminist Review* 4 (1980), 45–56 (p. 45).
68. Mary Beth Rose, 'The Gendering of Authority in the Public Speeches of Elizabeth I', *PMLA* 115.5 (2000), 1077–82 (p. 1080); Lisa Hopkins, *Writing Renaissance Queens: Texts by and about Elizabeth I and Mary, Queen of Scots* (Newark: University of Delaware Press, 2002); Ilona Bell, 'Elizabeth I – Always Her Own Free Woman', in *Political Rhetoric, Power, and Renaissance*

Women, ed. Carole Levin and Patricia A. Sullivan (Albany: State University of New York Press, 1995), pp. 57–82; Mueller, 'Textualism', p. 33.

69. May, '"Tongue-tied"', p. 48.

70. Lisa Gim, '"Faire *Eliza's* Chaine": Two Female Writers' Literary Links to Queen Elizabeth I', in *Maids and Mistresses, Cousins and Queens: Women's Alliances in Early Modern England*, ed. Susan Frye and Karen Robertson (New York: Oxford University Press, 1999), pp. 183–98 (p. 191).

71. Bathsua Makin, *An Essay to Revive the Antient Education of Gentlewomen* (1673), intro. by Paula L. Barbour (Los Angeles: Augustan Reprint Society, 1980), p. 20.

72. Mary Sidney Herbert, Countess of Pembroke, Dedicatory Poem in the Tixall Manuscript of the *Psalmes*, in *The Collected Works*, ed. Margaret P. Hannay, Noel J. Kinnamon, and Michael G. Brennan, 2 vols (Oxford: Clarendon Press, 1998), I, 51 (ll. 45–48, 51).

Part III Developing Histories

11
Religious Writing and Reformation

Nancy Bradley Warren

I want to begin by changing the last word of this essay's title from 'Reformation' to 'reformations'. The plural signifies my agreement with the views of scholars who argue that there was not one Protestant Reformation in England, but many. The Protestant Reformation is an extended, multi-layered process, not a unified, momentous event; it unfolded episodically, locally, even piecemeal. Such a view of the development of English Protestant religion makes its history a more hospitable environment for considering women's religious writing, since such writing is often not monumental or officially institutional (though exceptions exist, as we shall see). This is not to say, though, that women's religious writings are not culturally influential. Women's writings, even when unofficial and local – even domestic – in scope, do vital work shaping the processes of Protestant reforms in England.

The plural 'reformations' matters, furthermore, because engagement with religious reformations overlaps in women's writings with other reformist aims. Women writers of religious works are also concerned with the reform of political institutions and literary ideologies, aims that go hand-in-hand with their efforts to reform ecclesiastical institutions and devotional practices. Important strands of women's religious writing in the period under consideration deal with revisions of the body politic, while other female-authored texts contest religiously inflected antifeminist views.

The plural 'reformations' also signals the need to pay attention to reforms occurring beyond the Protestant sphere. Protestant religious institutions were not the only ones engaging in reform in the period between 1500 and 1610, and English Catholic women participated in the international phenomenon of the Counter-Reformation (which might also simply be called the Catholic Reformation). Though English

Catholic women's writings from this period are generally less well known than those of Protestant women, there has been a recent upturn in scholarly interest in recusant women's writings. Thus, I focus here specifically on early modern English monastic women's writings, which are still very little studied, in dialogue with Protestant women's writings.[1] English monastic women's writings both recount and participate in reform efforts involving their monastic institutions as English foundations – quite literally acts of re-formation – and efforts involving the English body politic.

It is particularly important to consider early modern English Protestant and monastic women's writings together because, even though the Protestant wife and the cloistered nun are frequently juxtaposed as binary opposites, such texts share important dimensions. In addition to exhibiting harmonies with each other, texts written by women from both confessional camps also manifest continuities with the writings of English women of earlier generations. Alexandra Walsham argues that 'sharp polarities in church and society indicated by labels like "Catholic" and "Protestant" are, in many respects, invalid in the early modern environment.'[2] One might, I would suggest, extend Walsham's argument about such labels for church and society to ways of classifying devotional and textual practices as well. In this essay I aim, therefore, to undertake some work of reformation myself in rethinking such categories as confessional orientations, historical periods, and literary genres.[3]

In her fascinating recent book *Patterns of Piety: Women, Gender, and Religion in Late Medieval and Reformation England*, Christine Peters gives us one of the very few studies that engages in sustained comparison of medieval and early modern female spirituality. At the heart of her argument is a claim that 'Evolving Christocentric devotion offered a bridge to the Reformation in terms of religious understanding.'[4] One of the trends that Peters notes in exploring this evolution is what she terms 'a growing realisation of the gulf between mankind and the incarnate Christ' that appeared in the fifteenth century in 'Christocentric parish piety'. She sees parish piety as quite different from the piety of the mystics and of the cloistered religious. Additionally, she sees the evolution of Christocentric devotion among people of the parish as having had the effect of 'reduc[ing] the significance of gendered patterns of devotion' as an emphasis on striving toward union with Christ gave way to less gendered, decorporealized forms of *imitatio Christi*.[5]

English Protestant and monastic women's religious writings engaged in various processes of reformation between 1500 and 1610 confirm Peters's argument concerning the ways in which Christocentric devotion forms a bridge between later medieval and post-Reformation religion. In the women's writings explored in this essay, Christocentric devotion features quite prominently indeed. These same women's writings, however, complicate Peters's claim about the emergence of a gulf between humans and the incarnate Christ, particularly the crucified Christ. Union with and imitation of Christ are modes of devotion that are not always clearly separable in women's writings, and both remain important spiritually and textually for women writers of diverse confessional orientations. The writings of monastic and Protestant women alike reveal, furthermore, strong commitments to incarnational piety (by which I mean devotion centered on the human body and embodied experiences of Christ), incarnational modes of knowing the self and the divine (by which I mean epistemological processes grounded in embodied experience), and incarnational paradigms of textuality (by which I mean understandings of textuality in which porous borders between embodied readers and the textual corpus obtain). The shared presence of these incarnational paradigms in Protestant and monastic women's writings suggests continuing emphasis on intimate relations between women as gendered subjects and the incarnate, and crucified, Christ.

The presence of these features in women's religious writings, I argue, does not constitute evidence that women's textual or devotional cultures are somehow 'backward'.[6] Rather, these incarnationally inflected elements represent living, dynamic parts of Catholic and Protestant textual and devotional traditions. The interplay of incarnational elements is, perhaps, particularly characteristic of certain kinds of religious texts by women precisely because later medieval and early modern women are excluded from official participation in the institutional bodies – particularly the ecclesiastical hierarchy and the universities – where hard categorical boundaries are forged. This is not to say that women writers could not adopt positions of certainty or engage in religious polemic; they readily did both. But, because even the most politically prominent women, like Queen Katherine Parr discussed below, always occupy as a result of their sex positions that are, in Michel de Certeau's formulation, tactical rather than strategic vis-à-vis ecclesiastical and political institutions, their writings too can occupy, and make the most of, the spaces in between, so to speak.[7] Women writers make virtues of necessity and, through bricolage, through productive consumption, create something hybrid, using the individual and the non-institutional to craft texts that might aptly be characterized as 'both and' rather than 'either or'.[8]

Women's religious writings from the period between 1500 and 1610 are numerous, diverse, and the subject of extensive scholarly attention.

To treat either the women's writings themselves or the critical conversation concerning them with anything approaching systematic thoroughness is far beyond the scope of this essay. Thus, in what follows, I proceed by a series of snapshots. I examine both print and manuscript texts, focusing on well-known and much lesser-known women writers. I quite deliberately do not focus on the best-known examples of particular types of religious writing (for instance, Mary Sidney Herbert's versions of the Psalms). My aim in such omissions is to call attention to the widespread participation of women from a range of social and political circumstances in important types of textual production. By examining texts and figures with thematic, historical, and intertextual links to each other, I seek to illuminate the landscape of English reformations and the cultural, political, and spiritual work performed by women's religious writings in it. This landscape will, I hope, look in some ways familiar yet in other ways perhaps a bit unfamiliar, to students both literary and historical of 'the English Reformation'.

Complexities, ambiguities, and continuities: Protestant reform as dynamic process and the writings of Katherine Parr

Henry VIII's desire to divorce Katherine of Aragon (mother of the future Mary I) in order to marry Anne Boleyn (mother of the future Elizabeth I) is often marked as the beginning of Protestant reforms in England. It thus seems appropriate to begin this essay with a consideration of the religious writings that flowed from the pen of Henry's final wife, Katherine Parr, who served as stepmother to both of these future Tudor queens, whose reigns would be characterized by so much political and ecclesiastical tumult. Parr's personal history, including her relationships with her confessionally opposed stepdaughters, resonates with the complexities and ambiguities that characterize her religious writings. As her biographer Susan James indicates, Katherine was named for Katherine of Aragon, who may have served as her godmother, and she spent much time in the Princess Mary's household after Anne Boleyn replaced Katherine of Aragon at Henry VIII's side.[9] Indeed, Katherine Parr seems to have caught Henry's eye – rather to her dismay – through her position in Mary's household.[10] Katherine had, however, close ties with both stepdaughters, something that might be, from our historical vantage point, difficult to comprehend, given the animosities that came to exist between Mary and Elizabeth and their respective Catholic and Protestant supporters. Katherine played an influential role in Princess

Elizabeth's education, and Elizabeth, at age eleven, presented Katherine with a significant piece of religious writing of her own – a translation of Marguerite of Navarre's *Le Miroir de l'âme pécheresse*. Katherine did a great deal to help restore both daughters to Henry's favor late in his life and to ensure their places alongside their half-brother in the royal succession. Her success in these efforts testifies to her intellectual and diplomatic abilities.[11]

Katherine Parr's religious writings in a sense mirror her relationship to the Catholic Mary and the Protestant Elizabeth; they illustrate her affinities with both faiths, even as her religious views change over the course of her career as a writer. Though she would narrowly escape Henry VIII's disfavor late in his life for embracing religious views that were, in the King's view, too far towards the Lutheran and Calvinist end of the spectrum of Protestant reforms, there are elements in her religious writings that harmonize closely with devotional writings from earlier generations. In recent work on Katherine Parr's religious writings, Kimberly Coles describes Parr's spirituality as 'transitional', arguing, 'While we too often think in terms of the separation of Protestant and Catholic devotional attitudes, the writing of Katherine Parr shows us that effective reform of devotion in England depended upon cultural and religious integration.'[12] While I agree with Coles's point concerning the importance of integration in the processes of reformation, I would prefer to characterize Parr's spirituality as 'hybrid', a term which does not imply a linear, teleological relationship between the medieval and the Catholic and the early modern and the Protestant. This distinction is particularly important given that, as I will argue, there are important similarities between Parr's earlier and later religious writings, even as there is also clear evidence of change in her religious thought.

Katherine Parr's first published piece of religious writing may have been an English translation entitled *Psalms or Prayers taken out of Holy Scripture*, a text 'originally published in Cologne in Latin about 1525 and attributed to John Fisher, Bishop of Rochester, whom the king had executed in 1535'.[13] The English version for which Parr is perhaps responsible was published on 25 April 1544, by Thomas Berthelet, the King's printer, and it was preceded a week earlier by a Latin version, 'which was likely the queen's first patronage project, her connection to it evidenced by the appendage of her "Prayer for the King" in English at its conclusion'.[14] The *Psalms or Prayers* appeared anonymously, and Katherine Parr has 'never received credit as translator' for the text.[15] James makes a strong case based both on comparisons of verbal parallels with other texts definitely attributed to Parr and on the text's print history for Parr's authorship. Coles likewise sets out evidence supporting Parr as the translator of the *Psalms or Prayers*, though she admits, 'All of the evidence that might identify Parr as a translator of the *Psalms* can equally be applied in support of an argument for her patronage.'[16]

Even if it cannot definitively be assigned to Katherine Parr, the *Psalms or Prayers* serves as a fitting point of departure for considering women's religious writing, since its anonymity is quite characteristic of women's textual production (especially the production of religious texts). It introduces us to three fundamentally important forms of religious writing for women in the period under consideration. Many of the women whose texts participated in the work of reformation were translators. Many also produced versions and interpretations of psalms, with particular attention being paid to the penitential psalms (especially Psalm 51), as well as collections of prayers. In doing so, early modern female writers took up genres that are also found among the religious writings of later medieval English women. For instance, Dame Eleanor Hull (*c.*1394–1460) translated from French under the title *The Seven Psalms* 'an elaborate thirteenth-century French commentary on the Latin text of the Penitential Psalms', a text that 'demonstrates the level of theological and linguistic competence that could be achieved by women'.[17] She also translated a collection of prayers and meditations from Old French under the title *Meditations upon the Seven Days of the Week*. Similarly, Eleanor Percy, whose husband Edward Stafford, third Duke of Buckingham, had been Margaret Beaufort's ward and was in due course executed for treason by Margaret's grandson Henry VIII, wrote a macaronic verse prayer (which is a version of the Latin hymn 'Gaude virgo, mater Christi') on the final page of a Book of Hours.[18]

Eleanor Hull's *Meditations upon the Seven Days of the Week* incorporates representative examples of the incarnationally focused, emotionally driven forms of devotion characteristic of much later medieval female piety. Hull focuses in detail on the bodies of Christ and the Virgin Mary, and particularly on the corporeal processes and experiences of Christ's birth and passion. For example, in a section treating the Annunciation and Christ's conception, Hull describes Christ's immediate, fully formed and ensouled presence in Mary's womb (contrary to medieval understandings of normal fetal gestation) at the moment of her affirmative response to the angel Gabriel's salutation. Hull writes:

> And than none conceyvyd she Goddys sone in flesshe and blode in
> here vergynes wombe, a quyke childe, God and Manne. For also sone
> as she assentyd to the angelle, all the Holyte Trynyte, Fader and Sone

and Holy Goste, made and formyd of noght the soule of Jhesu Chryste and in the wombe of that purist vyrgyne clothyd it with her most puryst flesshe and bloode with alle the parfyt membrys parfytly of his body. At one tyme was that blessyd soule made and that blessyd body formyd and everyche of hem, both God and man, joynyd ino persone, wherfor ther was never so lytylle a childe quykke. (pp. 227–28)

Hull also mobilizes another frequent aspect of later medieval affective devotion in her account of Christ's conception, the language of nuptial union, though her use of the language is somewhat unusual. Hull frames Christ's conception as a marriage between Christ and humanity conducted in the chamber of the Virgin Mary's womb; the conception is at the same time a wedding between Christ and the Church (the mystical body of Christ). She says:

Who may thynke the joy and the feste that was at that hevynly and erthely maryage, where the Sone of God, kyng of hevyn [...] humbled hymselfe to that noble and gloryous lady as forto wedde in her our kynde, the whiche he toke to hym in that chambre that was most clene and pure. [...] What hert myght thynk the joy that there was where alle the Trynyte helde the fest of this weddyng bytwene the Sone of God and of Holy Chirche? (pp. 228–29)

Whether Parr translated the *Psalms or Prayers* or served as its patron, we see in it her extensive interest in similarly detailed devotional attention to the place of the body in salvation history. It also emphasizes corporeal experiences and their emotional corollaries in devotional practice. In a variation on the Ecce Homo trope characteristic of so much medieval passion piety, the speaker of the *Psalms or Prayers* weaves into a version of Psalm 51 a plea for divine mercy in which the speaker addresses God the Father and asks him to behold his son. The speaker first calls to God the Father's attention the Christ of his adult ministry, preaching, healing, comforting, and giving 'syght to the blynde', and then asks God to consider Christ of the Nativity, saying, 'Behold thy littell one, which was borne for vs.'[19] In the very next sentence, the focus shifts to Christ's passion, which is recounted at length and in minute physical detail. The speaker repeatedly directs God's gaze upon the suffering body of his incarnate son who 'toke vpon him in his body our infirmities, and he bare our peines' to prompt God to be merciful to the sinful human speaker whose nature Christ shares (sig. Bvib). The scene of the passion is every bit as blood-soaked as that set out by the medieval anchoress

Julian of Norwich in her famous description of her vision of Christ's suffering on the cross. The speaker of the *Psalms or Prayers* tells God to 'Loke vpon al the partes of his body, from the crowne of the head vnto the sole of the fote', whereupon the account proceeds, blazon fashion, from 'the blessed head [...] crowned with sharpe thornes, & the blood runnyng downe vpon his godly visage' to the marks of the scourge on 'his tender bodie' to 'his sinewes bestretched fourthe' to his arms 'blewe and wanne' to his 'beautifull legges [...] feble and weake', and finally to his feet upon which 'stremes of bloud issuynge out of his bodye, runne downe apace' (sigs. Cia–Cib).

In addition to bearing witness to the vibrant presence of medieval affective piety in the text, the dynamics of the extended interlude on Christ's passion serve to align the speaker of the *Psalms* with the suffering Christ. As the text reiterates, the speaker and Christ share the same human body and both stand under the scrutiny of God the Father. These aspects suggest a closeness rather than a gulf between the speaker and the incarnate, suffering Christ. They also suggest, at least potentially, a shared feminization for both the speaker and Christ. That is to say, the bleeding, suffering Christ on display before God the Father shares something with the feminized, maternal, suffering Christ of medieval female spirituality about which Caroline Walker Bynum has written so eloquently.[20] One might speculate that the presence of this material in the source text for the translation might have been particularly familiar, and attractive, to a female translator, particularly one whose youth was spent in a later medieval Catholic devotional culture.

The *Prayers or Meditations*, which appeared in 1545, is the first text published with Katherine Parr's name attached.[21] With this text, Parr engages in a relatively unusual activity for a female writer, but an activity that she as a reigning queen was particularly well situated to accomplish – that is, she writes with the aim of shaping devotional practices on a large scale.[22] Janel Mueller describes the *Prayers or Meditations* as an undertaking 'to complement the vernacular service books for public church worship being advocated to Henry VIII by archbishop Thomas Cranmer. She would assemble a vernacular manual for the private devotion of individuals in the new national Church of England.'[23] To this end, Parr creates a textual self that balances the individual with the communal, a balance that requires blending the personal with the collective and the feminine with the masculine. These revisionary processes sometimes overlap, since the general and universal was in Parr's time, and in some cases still is, gendered masculine either implicitly or explicitly. As Mueller observes, though, Parr, through subtle adaptations of her sources, engages at the same time in 'degendering from masculinst norms' in ways that 'resul[t] not just in universalizing but in articulations that are identifiably feminine'.[24]

One of the main sources with which Parr works is Thomas à Kempis's *Imitation of Christ*; her redaction of Book 3 of the *Imitation* is followed by a series of five prayers headed 'A prayer for the kinge', 'A praier for men to saie entering in to battayle', 'A deuoute praier to be daiely saied', 'An other praier', and 'A deuoute praier'. Scholars have offered varying perspectives on the quality and religious orientation of the *Prayers or Meditations*. C. Fenno Hoffman dismisses it as 'a piece of schoolboy plagiarism', an assessment of a piece with his generally negative evaluation of Parr's writings.[25] He also finds the *Prayers or Meditations* to lack a 'Protestant tone'.[26] Mueller, in contrast, calls *Prayers or Meditations* 'a sensitive and discerning contribution to a Cranmerian literary program'.[27] James argues that the text 'must be seen in the context of the queen's ongoing programme of vernacular translations of primarily humanist-inspired religious works for popular consumption', denying that it should be considered 'a work of conservative Catholic piety rather than part of the new vernacular reform canon', and asserting, 'In a medieval work, the clarion call of the Reformation can now be heard.' In her assessment, both the *Psalms* and the *Prayers or Meditations* take 'an essentially Catholic text and give it a subtle Protestant coloration and emphasis'.[28] Coles, alternatively, sees significant differences emerge between the *Psalms* and the *Prayers or Meditations*, stating, 'One might attribute the revision of late medieval Catholic mysticism found in the *Prayers or meditacions* – in contrast to the wholesale adoption of Catholic-inflected dogma in the *Psalmes* – to the change in Parr's personal faith that occurred between 1544 and 1545. While such an attribution of cause is pure conjecture, the devotional transitionality of the *Prayers* does correspond to the spiritual transformation of its author.'[29] I agree with those who assert that the *Prayers or Meditations* is a work to be taken seriously and one that does important work in the processes of Protestant reformation; I would also argue that it offers us an opportunity to rethink the binaries of 'medieval' and 'early modern', of 'Catholic' and 'Reformed' or 'Protestant' that underpin the critical assessments outlined above.

That Katherine Parr was interested in *The Imitation of Christ* is not surprising; this text was popular with Catholic and Protestant readers alike through the early modern period. Henry VIII's grandmother Margaret Beaufort, mother of the Tudor dynasty, translated the fourth book of the *Imitation* and was the patron for Richard Pynson's 1504 printing of the version that included her translation along with William Atkynson's translation of the first three books. Barratt points out that Eleanor Hull, whose *Meditations* I discuss above, may 'have acted as a model' for Margaret Beaufort, since she was 'another laywoman from the ruling class who translated devotional texts from the French'.[30] The Protestant Northamptonshire gentry woman Grace Mildmay (*c*.1552–1620), whose autobiography and meditations I discuss in the final section of this essay, read *The Imitation of Christ* extensively, and it helped to shape her religious views and devotional practices. As she reports, her mother

> thought it ever dangerous to suffer young people to read or study books wherein was good and evil mingled together, for that by nature we are inclined rather to learn and retain the evil than the good. The Bible, Musculus's *Common Places*, *The Imitation of Christ*, Mr. Foxe's *Books of Martyrs* were the only books she laid before me, which gave me the first taste of Christ Jesus and his truth whereby I have found myself the better established in the whole course of my life.[31]

Equally, entries for copies of this work and other devotional writings by Thomas à Kempis appear in the library catalogue of the English Benedictine nuns of Our Lady of Good Hope Priory in Paris, a daughter house of the English Benedictine nunnery at Cambrai, which was founded by women who were near contemporaries of Grace Mildmay.[32]

What might be more surprising than Parr's interest in the *Imitation* is that in producing her version of the third book of Thomas à Kempis's text, she worked with an earlier English version that has been attributed to the Brigittine monk of Syon Richard Whitford (who strenuously resisted Henry VIII's efforts to dissolve the house), published in 1530 under the title *The Folowynge of Christ*.[33] Parr thus not only chooses a late medieval monastic text with which to work, but she chooses a version that at least possibly originates in a monastic environment. The lines demarcating the piety of the cloister and the piety of the parish are thus very permeable indeed in this case. Parr does, as Mueller argues, remove many markers of the monastic, the affective, and the mystical from Thomas à Kempis's original. However, she also uses language of affective devotion that resonates not only with religious writings by medieval women but also, as we shall see, with writings by women religious from Whitford's community of Syon.

For instance, in the *Prayers or Meditations*, Parr adopts nuptial language, drawing on the devotional register that Hull uses in her *Meditations* and that, as we shall see, features significantly in the Brigittine nuns' writings.

In the *Prayers or Meditations*, Parr prays, for example, that God will 'Quicken my soul and all the powers thereof, that it may cleave fast and be joined to thee in joyful gladness of ghostly ravishing' (sig. Bvb). James, noting that such language 'echo[es] through Parr's early works', denigrates it as 'pseudo-religious, sexual images'.[34] She perceives in the *Lamentacion* a move away from this form of spirituality, a move that helps, in her view, mark the *Lamentacion* as Parr's most truly 'reformed' work. I see no reason to label such language as 'pseudo-religious', given its long-established presence in Judeo-Christian devotion. Furthermore, it is by no means inconsistent with doing the work of reformation. Indeed, at times precisely such intimate unions with the incarnate Christ catalyze the work of reformation.

Again invoking nuptial language, Parr, emphasizing her desire for union with Christ, says, 'O Lorde Jesu, most louing spouse, who shall gyve me wynges of perfect loue, that I may flye up frome these worldly miseries, and rest in thee. O, whan shal I ascend to the and see, and feele how swete thou arte?' (sigs. Aviiia–Aviiib). The sense-oriented dimensions of this passage emphasize seeing and feeling, experiencing sweetness, providing evidence of incarnational devotional and epistemological paradigms focusing on embodied experience of the incarnate Christ. Such paradigms seem contrary to the idea Peters posits of a growing gap between the individual and Christ in early modern English Protestantism. Furthermore, Parr maintains an idea of an emotional connection between her and Christ through which her sighs and longings, her affective and embodied devotional responses, will stir a similar affective response in him. Echoing the affective dynamics of the passion sequence in the *Psalms*, in which the speaker, united with Christ in human nature, holds Christ's sufferings before the gaze of God the Father to move him to be merciful, here Parr prays that her longings will move Christ: 'I beseche the lorde Jesu that the syghynges and inwarde desires of my hert maie moue and incline the to here me' (sig. Bib).

Parr enhances the significance of the incarnational in her substantial discussions of suffering in the *Prayers or Meditations*. Earthly suffering is a mainstay of Catholic and Protestant devotional writings both medieval and early modern, going hand in hand with what James calls 'the always viable themes of vanity [...] and the impotence of men' that pervade the *Prayers or Meditations*.[35] In Eleanor Hull's *Meditations*, for instance, in a section devoted to the name of Mary, she writes, 'Alle this world is a grete see, fulle of cloudys and of tempestys. Ther-in is no stabilnes nor no suerte, no more than in the wild see. For now we be hole, now syke, now glad, now sory, or angry, or wel plesyd, upon this see that is so fulle of perillys' (p. 224). For Parr, suffering in the world is not, though, simply part of the human condition and an appropriate prompt to prayer and devotion. She additionally interprets suffering and affliction as a means to union with and, correspondingly, better knowledge of, Christ. Earthly, and especially bodily, suffering has spiritual and epistemological value, value that goes beyond encouraging an attitude of *contemptus mundi*, though such encouragement is abundantly present in the text.

In light of the attention given to turning away from the fleshly, one might read the *Prayers or Meditations* as participating in a reformed Protestant move away from the materiality of Catholic piety (though the *contemptus mundi* tradition is firmly established therein as well). Such a turn away from the material world and the material bodies that inhabit it also aligns with understandings of early modern reformed Protestantism that insist on the development of a strong separation between bodies and souls, between the exterior and the interior. Even in passages that may well be informed by such developments, however, the *Prayers or Meditations* also includes indications that body and spirit continue to have a fundamentally important, positive relationship with each other. The text also makes clear that the imitation of Christ as an embodied practice continues to have devotional value. Parr writes, for instance:

> Blessed is that man, that for the loue of the lorde, setteth not by the pleasures of this worlde, & lerneth truely to ouercome hym selfe, *and with the feruour of spirite crucifyeth his fleshe*, so that in a cleane and a pure conscience, he maie offer his prayers to the, and be accepted to haue company of thy blessed angelles, all erthly thynges excluded from his herte. (sig. Cviiib)

As Coles points out, this passage directs the reader 'in an act of affective devotion' to 'suffe[r] with Christ [...] in an attempt to set his or her mind above material existence'. She argues, 'It is the orientation of late medieval religious practice, rather than a Lutheran point of reference, which is activated in the devotional mechanism of Parr's meditation for private prayer.'[36]

Parr additionally writes of the woes of earthly life, 'I am poore, and haue been in trouble and peyne euer from my youthe, and my soule hath ben in great heauinesse throughe manyfolde passions, that come of the worlde, and of the fleshe.'[37] The passions of the flesh affect as well as effect the soul, prompting the author to seek Christ's presence, a state characterized through sensual, corporeal experiences involving the senses of taste and hearing. She continues:

> I aske of the, to come to that rest whiche is ordeined for thy chosen children, that be *fedde and nourished* with the lighte of heauenly comfortes: for without thy helpe, I can not come to the. Lorde geue me peace, geue me inwarde ioye, and then my soule *shalbe full of heauenly melody*, and be deuoute and feruente in thy laudes and praisynges.[38]

Parr combines language resonant with Protestant ideas of election, as when she speaks of rest ordained 'for thy chosen children', with affective language oriented toward sensually experienced union with the divine.[39] The spiritual manifests itself corporeally; through the process of feeding and nourishing, the speaker incorporates divine knowledge (the light of heavenly comforts). That knowledge leads the speaker to Christ, and the experience of being with Christ is itself sensual (being filled with heavenly music). The language Parr uses elsewhere to describe Christ's role as a comforter, though traditional, also reveals the persistent presence of the corporeal in and with the spiritual. She writes, 'No creature under Heaven may comfort me, but thou lord God, the hevenly leache and mans soule, which strikest and healest, which bringest a man nighe unto death, and after restorest him to life againe, that he may therby learne to know his owne weakenesse and imbecilitie, and the more fully to truste in the (Lord)' (sig. Cviia). Not only does this passage align the corporeal and the spiritual, but it again imbricates corporeal experience – this time of pain rather than nourishment – in the process of acquiring knowledge of the self and the divine.[40]

Katherine Parr's last published work is the *Lamentacion of a Sinner* (1547), which as a spiritual autobiography or conversion narrative represents another important genre for women's religious writing between 1500 and 1610.[41] The *Lamentacion* has been labeled her most fully 'reformed' – that is to say, her most Lutheran and Calvinist influenced – work.[42] James calls it, for instance, 'Kateryn's open testament to her reformed faith'. There is no doubt that Lutheran and Calvinist influences shape this text, especially in the attention given to 'the sin of the speaker, the universality of sin, remission and salvation through the free grace of God embodied in the life and death of His Son'. The text also sounds notes characteristic of the Lutheran and Calvinist traditions in expressing '[b]elief in justification by faith alone, salvation by God's grace, given as a divine gift and not earned by the merits of the receiver of the gift'.[43]

Parr's open espousal of such ideas in the *Lamentacion* does much to explain why the text was not published until after Henry VIII's death; indeed, it was not published until after her own death. These beliefs would have been a bridge, if not several bridges, too far in the process of Protestant reformation for Henry VIII and his religious officials, particularly Stephen Gardiner. Katherine's diplomatic and intellectual prowess was put greatly to the test late in Henry VIII's reign, when she ran afoul of the King and his ecclesiastical officials for directions in which her reformed religious views had evolved. In Anne Askew's account of her imprisonment and torture for heresy in 1546, she reports that she was put on the rack in order to attempt to extract from her the names of ladies at court who shared her views, in hopes of implicating the Queen.[44]

Askew went to her execution tight-lipped, however, and Katherine, according to John Foxe's version of events, returned herself to Henry VIII's good graces through a dramatic scene of submission. Foxe indicates that Henry accused Katherine not only of religious heresy but also of wifely insubordination, domestic rebellion that in this case is of the highest political magnitude, given the household in question. Foxe reports that the King said, 'You are become a Doctor, Kate, to instruct vs (as we take it) and not to be instructed, or directed by vs.' Katherine's response quickly restores gendered spiritual and political hierarchies. She situates herself as a good wife attempting to aid her husband and positions herself entirely subject to his authority both spiritual and monarchical. She indicates that she engaged in religious arguments with the King 'not so much to maintaine opinion' but 'rather to minister talke, not onely to the end that your Maiestie might with less griefe pass over this paynfull time of your infirmitie, being intentiue to our talke, & hoping that your Maiestie should reape some ease therby: but also that I hearing you Maiesties learned discourse, might receaue to my self some profit thereof'.[45]

Though the *Lamentacion* clearly participates in Continental trends in Protestant reform to which Katherine Parr was deeply committed, even this 'most reformed' of her texts incorporates affective, incarnational elements resonant with earlier Catholic women's writings and with texts associated with contemporary Catholic reformist movements.[46] Parr picks up, for instance, language that echoes the *Prayers or Meditations* in uniting soul and body, speaking of the 'passions of the flesche [as] medicines of ye soule' (sig. D). Most strikingly, when she contemplates Christ's passion in the *Lamentacion*, she writes:

> We may see also in Christ, vpon the crosse, howe greate the paynes of hell, and howe blessed the Joyes of heauen be: and what a sharpe,

paynfull thyng it shalbe to them that from that swete, happye, & glorious Joye, Christ, shalbe depriued. Then this crucifix is the booke, wherin God hath included all thinges, & hath most compendiously written therein, all truth, profitable and necessary for our saluacion. (sig. Ciia)

That Parr uses the term 'crucifix' rather than 'cross' is highly significant, because the choice of term places particular emphasis on the presence, rather than the absence, of Christ's suffering body in the scene. Parr points to Christ's human body, and his embodied experience on the cross, as the locus of truth, of all the knowledge that is necessary for salvation. In this respect, the *Lamentacion* again returns us to incarnational devotional and epistemological paradigms. Interestingly, the *Psalms and Prayers* for which Parr may be the translator includes in the extended account of Christ's passion discussed above, language that anticipates this conceit of the book of the crucifix. The speaker, addressing God the Father, says that Christ, submitting 'to the deth of the crosse, [...] put oute the handwrityng that was agaynst vs, conteyned in the lawe wrytten, and takyng it oute of the waie, fastned it to his crosse' (sig. Bviiib). The cross becomes a book as the writing of the law, fastened on the cross, is rewritten through the suffering of the divine Word made flesh. Parr understands, furthermore, the divine Word to have a presence within her as an embodied subject. In the *Prayers or Meditations* she petitions, 'Open my hert lorde, that I maie beholde thy lawes'.[47] The 'book of the crucifix', in addition to being the corpus itself (the technical term for the figure of Christ on the cross, the presence of which differentiates the crucifix from the plain cross) and the textual corpus of scripture, is also a written corpus inscribed in and on her body. For all that reformed Protestants are said to privilege the word of scripture – and there is plenty of scripture to be found in the *Lamentacion* as well as in Parr's other religious writings – the divine Word in its incarnate, fleshly form has a central place for Parr as well.[48]

'The Book of the Crucifix' and English monastic reformations: the Brigittine nuns of Syon

Texts associated with the Brigittine nuns of Syon represent a component of reformation that is often ignored, and that is worth considering in dialogue with both Protestant women's religious writings.[49] After Henry VIII dissolved the monasteries, many of the nuns of Syon fled England together for the Continent, seeking to continue their distinctive form of monastic life while remaining an entirely English community despite their residence in foreign realms. Following their brief return home during the reign of Mary I, the nuns went again en masse into exile during the reign of Elizabeth I. During this second exile, the women religious produced extensive records of their experiences.

In these texts the Brigittine nuns produced during their years of exile, we see versions of 'the book of the crucifix' being read, interpreted, lived, and rewritten as the nuns recount the re-formation of their monastic community and record their participation in efforts to re-form (quite literally) the English body politic by remaking it as a Catholic realm. In this section, I will focus on two of the texts produced by the Syon community, *The Life and Good End of Sister Marie*, and a collective account of their troubles in France and their flight to Lisbon, which was translated into Spanish and published in Madrid in 1594 under the title *Relacion que Embiaron Las Religiosas Del Monasterio de Sion de Inglaterra, que estaban en Roan de Francia, al padre Roberto Personio de la Compañia de Iesus, de su salida de aquella ciudad, y llegada à Lisboa de Portugal* (hereafter *Relacion*).[50]

While Syon was residing in Malines after fleeing England for the second time, they endured great poverty due both to Protestant hostilities and to the fact that their pension from the Spanish Crown was paid only irregularly. Accordingly, the abbess and sisters decided to send a group of nuns covertly back into England to raise alms, including Marie Champney. Marie, who died in England, is primarily known through the anonymous account of her life and her community presented in the *Life*, a generically hybrid text that blends third-person biography with accounts of events presented as first-person narratives. Though the *Life*'s author is not known, and it cannot be precisely dated, Ann Hutchison offers convincing arguments for the text's having been written 'very shortly' after Marie's death on 27 April 1580, by someone who was 'in all probability a lay person' living 'near London' and who was an eyewitness to Marie's death.[51] She also speculates that the author 'might, in fact, be a woman'.[52] That the *Life* exists as a manuscript, not as a printed text, is a detail worth highlighting. Manuscript textual transmission has particular significance in English Catholic circles, since access to printing presses was for Catholics difficult and dangerous to achieve.[53]

Like the *Life and Good End of Sister Marie*, the *Relacion*, with its long 'Prembulo' by Syon's confessor general Seth Foster setting out the history of the foundation from its fifteenth-century establishment, combines what might be called communal biography with collective autobiography. The complexities of generic identity and authorship evident in this text and in the *Life and Good End of Sister Marie* highlight another characteristic common to women's religious writing, whether Catholic or Protestant, one that some of Katherine Parr's texts also exhibit – that is, they are collaborative endeavors involving women and men working together, a quality that later medieval women's religious writings also frequently exhibit. It remains worth reiterating that men's involvement does not preclude women's independent contributions, nor does the participation of male collaborators render women's contributions necessarily of secondary importance.

The *Life and Good End of Sister Marie* and the *Relacion* are in parts accounts of women's reliving past holy lives, and particularly the *vita Christi*, that simultaneously offer themselves to others as what Christopher Abbott in his work on Julian of Norwich calls 'shareable religious autobiography'.[54] This is a textual tradition accordingly possessed of a strongly performative imperative. Though the two Brigittine texts upon which I am focusing can be construed as forms of life-writing, these works, like those of Katherine Parr and Grace Mildmay, move beyond the private, the personal, and the domestic spheres. Perhaps even more significantly, they make the personal, the private, and the domestic the very material with which they do public and political reformist work. That the *Relacion* circulates in Spanish calls attention to the fact that this political and spiritual reformist work takes place on an international stage. Like Katherine Parr's *Lamentacion*, individual experiences made textually available seek to reform the lives of individual others as well as of institutions. In fact, I contend that a major component of the *Life*'s and the *Relacion*'s *raison d'être* is to encourage precisely such re-embodying and reliving of holy lives by members of the monastic community of Syon and by other English Catholics with the aim of channeling textual performance into the creation of a transformed Catholic England.

The *Life and Good End of Sister Marie* first recounts Marie Champney's departure from England as a young woman and the sequence of events leading up to her monastic profession with the Brigittines in exile. In these early experiences, Marie's processes of coming to self-knowledge depend on corporeal experiences of the incarnate Christ. While Marie is on the Continent, she experiences conflict and spiritual turmoil about what course she should pursue. At one point she is filled with longing to return home to England, and a 'father of the Jesuites' advises her to pray 'with as much quietnes of minde as she coulde'. He also directs her the next morning to 'heare Masse with as much devocyon as she coulde' (fol. 2ᵛ). During Mass, at the elevation of the Host, she has a visionary experience of the sort that characterizes the Eucharistic piety of many later medieval holy women. At the moment in the Mass when Christ's body present in the transubstantiated Host is displayed to the gathered members of the congregation, that body is made manifest in its human form to Marie:

> When the preiste came to the blessed Elevation, this most comfortable vision, God shewed her, that our Saviour Christ appeared to her in visible shape over the Chalice (belike to confirme her in trewe beleefe of those dreadfull misteries, besides the woing of her, as it were to further perferccion, lookinge most graciouslye towardes her, and with his twoo fingers (as the vse if the Byshopps is) blessinge her. (fols. 2ᵛ–3ʳ)

These 'livelie pictures', as Marie describes the visionary experience, provide divine confirmation of the Catholic doctrine of transubstantiation, simultaneously legitimating the Catholic office of bishop as a vicar of Christ (fol. 3ʳ). They also, in 'woing [...] her [...] to further perfeccion', reinforce Marie's religious vocation.

Ultimately, the 'livelie pictures' have a physical effect on Marie, somaticizing her vocation and uniting body, mind, and spirit. Upon perceiving the incarnate Christ over the chalice, 'her hart seemed to be ravished halfe from her, and her fleshe also felte a kinde of tremlinge for Reverence of so heavenlye a sighte' (fol. 3ʳ). As if to mark the change in her identity that her religious vocation demands, Marie's visionary experience leaves a lasting corporeal legacy, a form of somatic inscription. Though Marie's vision 'vanished againe from her eyes' the 'perfecte shape & printe of his gracious countenaunce (as she woulde saye) coulde never while she liued out of her hartes remembraunce' (fol. 3ʳ). Her heart, like Katherine Parr's, becomes a version of the book of the crucifix, marked with the divine word through her experience of the divine word made flesh.

Subsequently, when Marie first glimpses the Brigittine abbess's 'blacke veyle on her heade lyned with pure white, and the white crowne withall spotted with five spotts of redd, which that order weareth, and no other sorte of nunnes but they', she is 'astonyed' at the sight of this distinctive element of the Brigittine habit, which commemorates Christ's wounds (fol. 3ʳ). Her further reaction to the habit is an appropriately embodied one as she recalls having prophetically dreamed in her youth of being clothed by a bishop in just such a habit. The author says that Marie's eyes brim with tears and that 'her harte presently melted, as the spowses very worde is in the Canticles' (fol. 3ʳ). The author's reference to the

Spouse of the Song of Songs calls to mind the identity of Christ's bride that Marie will have once professed as a Brigittine nun, even as it recalls the nuptial language Katherine Parr adopts in her religious writings.

In an episode recounting Marie's reaction to news of her community's fate at the hands of Protestant forces in Malines in February 1578, the *Life* becomes itself a book of the crucifix that highlights the roles of incarnational piety in the English Brigittines' agenda for political reform. Learning that the Protestants have captured the city, Marie believes the convent may have been totally lost among the many religious houses that were destroyed in the violence. The author of the *Life* recounts that when Marie hears 'of the losse of Machline, and of the captiuytye at leaste of her systers there remaynynge' her 'harte' is 'perced [...] with marveylous compassyon of their calamyte' (fol. 12ᵛ). The account's details suggest that Marie not only identifies with her community's troubles, suffering along with her fellow women religious, but that her suffering, like theirs, is also a simultaneous reiteration of Christ's and Mary's linked experiences of suffering at the crucifixion. For instance, the language of Marie's heart being pierced with compassion recalls the common medieval representation of Mary's heart being pierced by the sword of sorrow when Christ is on the cross. The author of the *Life* underlines this linkage of Marie's and Syon's experiences with those of Christ and Mary alike at the Passion, saying, 'Belike she both felte & perceaued the *nayle* of both theire sorrowes' (fol. 12ᵛ; emphasis added). The implication, of course, is that the Protestant forces who cause Syon's, and by extension Marie's, pain are re-enacting the deeds of those who inflict pain on Christ at the crucifixion. The women religious, in re-embodying Christ's agony, become martyrs for a holy cause, one which, they hope, will end with their suffering effecting a resurrection of a Catholic England.

As in the *Life and Good End of Sister Marie*, where Marie's life is presented as a reincarnation of past holy lives and is offered as an experience open to being relived by others, so too in the *Relacion* the collective life and sufferings of Syon are construed both as sacred lives (and especially Christ's life) re-enacted and as a form of potentially shareable religious (auto)biography in which bodies signify powerfully on the political stage. A large portion of the *Relacion* is devoted to the nuns' discussion of their flight from Rouen to Lisbon, a flight necessitated by the rise to power in Rouen of hostile Protestant forces. The nuns recount their somewhat fraught preparations for departure from the city and their eventual embarkation, events that correspond with Holy Week. Writing another iteration of the book of the crucifix, the nuns foreground this coincidence of timing to align their experiences with

Christ's life and death. For instance, they recall that on Palm Sunday ('el Domingo de Ramos') their confessor general, having said Mass, went to the Governor of Rouen's house ('à casa del Gouernador de Roan'), where he undertook complicated negotiations to obtain passports and passage (sig. 32^r). They report packing up their belongings on Wednesday of Holy Week ('Miercoles de la Semana Santa'), and, significantly, they finally depart from Rouen to begin their perilous sea voyage on Good Friday: 'dos dias despues, que fue el Viernes Santo, nos embarcamos todos [...] y començamos à hazer nuestro camino' (sig. 35^r).

The nuns' description of an encounter between their vessel and hostile English ships on their way to Lisbon further enhances the *Relacion*'s connection of their experiences and Christ's sufferings on the cross. When they meet the English ships, the brethren dress as soldiers to attempt to scare off their adversaries by fooling them into thinking the ship on which the religious of Syon are traveling is a warship. Meanwhile, 'la señora Abadessa' and 'las damas religiosas', becoming aware of their dangerous situation ('el peligro en que estauamos') go below deck to seek divine aid through prayer ('al socorro diuino poniendose en oracion') (sig. 51^v). Specifically, they undertake 'el exercicio espiritual dela Cruz', which, they say, has been practiced in their order since its beginnings with great advantage and consolation to the nuns ('que [...] ha sido vsado en nuestra orden desde su principio, con singular prouecho y consuelo de las religiosas della') (sig. 51^v). The 'exercicio espiritual dela Cruz' is, according to the current Lady Abbess of Syon, almost certainly the Stations of the Cross, which is written into some Syon nuns' prayer books of a later date. This devotional exercise focusing on Christ's body and on embodied acts of devotion brings past into present as the practitioners relive the events of Christ's passion step by step in their journey to re-form their monastic community and to continue to strive – in no small part by publishing their experiences – for the re-formation of a Catholic English realm.

The ongoing complexities of reform: the 'Autobiography' and 'Meditations' of Grace Sharington Mildmay

Grace Sharington Mildmay, the relatively little known gentry woman mentioned above whose faith was also shaped by reading *The Imitation of Christ*, is perhaps not the obvious choice of an early modern female writer to pair with an English queen and English Brigittine nuns as a means to explore women's religious writings and the work of reformation. However, Grace Mildmay, who lived from 1552 to 1620 and so

could far less readily than Parr be assigned to a 'transitional' generation in the unfolding of the Protestant reformation, produced religious
writings that exhibit, like Parr's, continuities with both medieval and
contemporary Catholic women's religious writings. Grace Mildmay's
spirituality too has hybrid, multi-dimensional qualities.

Linda Pollock, the editor of the brief excerpts of Grace Mildmay's
writing that have been published, states, 'Catholics employed more
imagination, visualizing time and place, and strove to achieve raptur-
ous union with Christ', while Protestants 'were more literary and scriptural in their meditative technique' (p. 51). She thus draws a sharp line
between devotional practices that, as the writings of Katherine Parr have
begun to demonstrate, actually is far more blurry. There is no doubt
some truth in Pollock's assessment; the literary and scriptural qualities
that she cites as hallmarks of Protestant meditations are indeed readily
evident in Grace Mildmay's writings. Bible reading features prominently
in Grace's devotional life. She revealingly calls the Bible 'the book of
God, which above all earthly things is to be embraced, to be believed,
obeyed, feared, loved, and praised; with continual delight, exercise and
meditations therein whereby a good and virtuous life may be framed
from youth to old age' (p. 70). Furthermore, her writings are filled with
echoes and quotations of biblical language from the Old and New Testament alike. However, such biblicism is by no means the exclusive prov-
ince of Protestant writers; texts associated with the Syon nuns discussed
above are similarly filled with biblical language, and as we have seen,
Eleanor Hull readily engages with scripture in her writings.

For the sake of brevity, I will focus in what follows on illustrating the
ways in which Grace Mildmay's meditations exhibit a commitment to
purportedly 'Catholic' practices, especially those connected with Christ
and affective, corporeally focused devotional practices – including imagination and visualization. I will also argue that joint consideration of
Grace Mildmay's writings with those of Katherine Parr and the Syon nuns,
all of which are profoundly personal texts but all of which attribute to
the personal much larger spiritual and political significances, complicates
ideas about selfhood, means of knowing God, and the nature of Christian
community often marked out across the boundary of the Reformation as
basic components of religious change.

It is true that Grace Mildmay upholds the importance of imitating
Christ in what Peters calls the Protestant mode of *imitatio Christi* – that
is, a decorporealized mode of imitation centered on adopting Christ's
virtues. However, when Mildmay describes the 'sympathy and union'
that exist 'betwixt God and us in Christ Jesus', it becomes clear that

no large gulf separates her from the incarnate Christ (p. 80). Further suggesting that she shares with Parr, and with both earlier and contemporary female monastic writers, a desire to unite with Christ, Mildmay writes, 'Oh, glorious Lord, which way so ever I turn me let me turn unto thee, from this world and all mortal vanities thereof. Let me open mine eyes, lift up my hands and my heart unto thee. Let me sit up and arise, walk, live and die unto thee. Let me continually taste, feel and find thee, retain, hold and keep thee, in all things and above all things' (p. 74). The emphasis on senses and sensations in this passage highlights that for Mildmay, as for Katherine Parr and for members of the English monastic community of Syon, in order to know God and to know herself, more is necessary than following Christ's examples. Imitation of Christ's virtues is not enough. Knowledge of Christ has to be embodied knowledge; Grace Mildmay accordingly seeks to experience Christ the Word made flesh in her own flesh.

In other words, Grace Mildmay shares with medieval affective devotional writers, with Katherine Parr, and with the Syon nuns, a commitment to incarnational spirituality and incarnational epistemology. These commitments become quite clear in her engagements with Christ's passion. Mildmay indicates that she 'think[s] often of the death of Christ and of his suffering', and, as in Parr's writings, Christ's suffering and her own suffering are prominent, linked, themes (p. 71). She states that she endeavors 'patiently and thankfully to embrace his cross, for as much as I find it not a means to drive me from him but rather to draw me unto him' (p. 82). Grace Mildmay describes an experience of spiritual and physical torment during which, as she lies in her 'bed of sorrow', she says:

> then ugly shapes and a fearful view of hellish figures and monstrous apparitions presented themselves unto my mind. [...] And in the instant thereof there was the figure of the face of a man exulted and lifted up. Whereupon I settled the eye of my mind most fixedly, beholding well the countenance of that face which was so dolorous and sorrowful as no heart can imagine. [...] And in the very same instant of my beholding that face my heart was stirred up to apprehend with a deep impression, the sorrows of Christ's death, hanging upon the cross, sweating water and blood in the garden, his stripes, buffets and spittings in his face, with a meditation thereupon. And immediately in the same instant all the said fearful shapes vanished away to the great consolation of my mind. For I was most assuredly persuaded in my heart that Jesus Christ together with God his

heavenly father and the Holy Ghost [...] did vouchsafe to visit me in this my bed of sorrow. (pp. 87–88)

Mildmay's suffering catalyzes her experience of Christ's passion, and meditation on the passion concomitantly involves transformative bodily experiences and, indeed, even a merging of herself with the suffering Christ.

To add further weight to the case for the persistence of affective devotional traditions, as well as of gendered modes of union with Christ in early modern Protestant female spirituality, it is worth noting that accounts of nuptial union with Christ feature prominently in Grace Mildmay's devotional writing. She describes her intimate relationship with Christ in language even more closely aligned with traditions of bridal mysticism than that used most frequently by Parr. Grace Mildmay includes in her meditations extensive passages of sensual language drawn from the Song of Songs, situating herself through this discourse as Christ's spouse, just as Parr and Marie Champney do. For instance, Mildmay writes:

Let me be so open to my welbeloved that my hands may drop down myrrh and my fingers pore myrrh upon the handles of the bars. Oh, let my welbeloved put his hand by the hole of the door and let my heart be affectioned unto him. Oh, let my welbeloved lay his left hand under my head and with his right hand embrace me. (pp. 74–75)

Christ responds, 'I am come into my garden, my sister, my spouse. I gathered my myrrh with my spice, I ate my honeycomb with my honey, I have drunk my wine with my milk' (p. 75). She then continues, '[L]et my sanctified soul continually and wholly love and be in love with him' (p. 75).

For Grace Mildmay, as for Katherine Parr and the Syon nuns, the individual experience of the divine has spiritual and social significance reaching beyond the merely personal. Mildmay strongly posits the value available to others through her individual experiences of God presented textually. Mildmay's writings exist in manuscript rather than in print, a fact that highlights the ongoing importance of this textual technology for Protestant as well as Catholic women. Though she seems not to have designs towards print herself, she intended her writings to be read by her daughter and grandson, and manuscript markings show that she revised them. Furthermore, a later reader seems to have considered the writings worthy of a wider audience, since the manuscripts contain revisions other than Mildmay's own that may have been made with a view to editing her writings for publication. Both Katherine Parr's and Grace Mildmay's texts thus bear witness to a Protestant view of the nature of textuality contrary to the 'distrust' of writing 'as a diluted, secondary and dangerous medium' characteristic of some of the godly.[55] As Tom Webster points out, Daniel Rogers, in his 1642 *Naaman the Syrian*, claims, 'You know no pencil can fully reach a living face: The Presse cannot comprehend the Pulpit, and writing of a Booke is but as the picture of a dead man.'[56] Grace Mildmay, in contrast, sees her writings as offering ready access to herself and to the divine. She says:

> [T]he book of my meditations written which book hath been to me as Jacob's ladder and as Jacob's pillar. [...] Thus have I given my mind unto my offspring as my chief and only gift unto them. And unto such of them [...] as shall receive and put the same in practice [...] I dare pronounce an everlasting blessing from God. (p. 71)

Though Katherine Parr, the Syon nuns, and Grace Mildmay do not participate in it directly, the larger social or communal values that their texts place on their personal, gendered experiences as women interacting with the divine resonate with views expressed in one of the most influential, sustained debates in early modern textual culture – that is, the fraught exchanges concerning the nature of women. This dimension of their religious writings represents another aspect of women's work to reform textual culture as well as larger ideological paradigms of gender relations. As Patricia Demers observes, 'Questions of women's rationality and constancy, responsibilities and conduct, worthiness and specific virtues, were embedded in the cultural and educational contexts in which early modern women writers lived and worked.'[57] This early modern debate picks up many questions and attitudes articulated in the medieval *querelle des femmes*, and it is worth noting that Christine de Pizan's important contributions to that debate in her *Cité des dames* circulated in early modern England via Brian Anslay's English translation printed in 1521 by Henry Pepwell. Many early modern women's contributions to this debate also share with Katherine Parr's, the Syon nuns', and Grace Mildmay's writings skilful mobilization of scriptural writings for their own reformist projects, as Rachel Speght's extensive use of biblical citations in *A Mouzell for Melastomus* (1617) and Esther Sowernam's use of the story of Esther in *Ester Hath Hang'd Haman* (1617) illustrate. Just beyond the end of the period considered in this essay, the poet Aemilia Lanyer would write her own book of the crucifix, the *Salve Deus Rex Judaeorum* (published in 1611, the same year as the King James Bible). *Salve Deus Rex Judaeorum* juxtaposes a defense of Eve with an affective account of Christ's passion that presents a feminized Christ in the company of women who share his suffering. Surrounding Lanyer's devotional material and highly personal interpretation (or, better, rewriting) of scripture are patronage poems and a country-house poem that appeal to shared female experience and idealized visions of female community.

Interestingly, like Parr's *Lamentacion*, Grace Mildmay's meditations, in spite of their clear sympathies with Continental Protestant ideas from Lutheran and Calvinist schools, do not hew towards a stringent reformed doctrine. Mildmay's commitment to the communal, and the value she places on female experience within larger communities, seem to shape her understanding of salvation. Mildmay's writings do not manifest strict interpretations of Calvinist beliefs concerning predestination and election; as Pollock states, Grace Mildmay's writings exhibit 'applied rather than theoretical Calvinism' (p. 60). In spite of her emphasis on the primacy of God's word, Mildmay's take on soteriology does not follow what is often considered the expected Calvinist path. In many 'godly' Protestant writings, when the authors use the word 'all' in referring to the recipients of divine grace and salvation, they simply mean all of the godly or elect. When Mildmay refers to the elect, she uses 'such terms as the saints, the elect, God's chosen people and the faithfull' (p. 60). But in understanding salvation, she has something different in mind. When Grace Mildmay says all in the context of the availability of salvation, she means *all*. She exhibits what I would call a paradoxically optimistic Calvinism. Her belief system suggests a kind of irenicism or at least a very broad view of what constitutes adiaphora, and she exhibits a toleration with important political ramifications, given that she witnessed the dramatic, official hardening of the line against recusancy in the later sixteenth century. I contend that Grace Mildmay's spirituality, along with its theological and political corollaries, owe some of their optimism and toleration to her ties with the 'old religion's' understanding of Christ's corporeal availability, not in this case through consuming the transubstantiated Host in the Eucharist, but through consuming texts, imitating Christ, and uniting with Christ – through the processes of incarnational piety, epistemology, and textuality. Thus the body of Christ that is the church is for Mildmay a rather more capacious, commodious body than it is for some of her co-religionists. Like Katherine Parr's texts, Grace Mildmay's writings reveal that supposedly medieval and supposedly Catholic practices centering on the senses, the human body, and the body of Christ are, rather, catholic in the more general sense of the term. They are embraced by early modern Protestant women as readily as by early modern nuns, and for both groups of women, they are a vital component of performing various sorts of reforming work.

Notes

1. Two excellent studies of early modern English nuns and their writings are Claire Walker, *Gender and Politics in Early Modern Europe: English Convents in France and the Low Countries* (New York: Palgrave Macmillan, 2003) and Nicky Hallett, *Lives of Spirit: English Carmelite Self-Writing of the Early Modern Period* (Aldershot: Ashgate, 2007).
2. Alexandra Walsham, *Church Papists: Catholic Conformity and Confessional Polemic in Early Modern England* (Woodbridge: Boydell, 1993), p. 8.
3. Kimberly Coles clearly formulates the need for this sort of rethinking of categories. She notes, 'While the ample critical work concerning the revisions or redactions of medieval literature in early modern English poetics has tried to appreciate change by first observing residual likeness, it has frequently been assumed that the doctrinal disruptions of the early Tudor period resist this kind of comparison' (*Religion, Reform, and Women's Writing in Early Modern England* [Cambridge: Cambridge University Press, 2008], p. 46). She further observes that as a result critics have tended to locate religious writings 'in the frame of either antecedent or emergent forms of religious thought, or to try to tease out the elements of one or the other within a particular writer's output. This approach hinders our understandings of the complicated forms that straddle the fault line of literary and religious change' (p. 46). Many scholars are now engaged in such revisions. See, for instance, historical studies by Alexandra Walsham and Michael Questier as well as David Wallace, 'Periodizing Women: Mary Ward (1585–1645) and the Premodern Canon', *Journal of Medieval and Early Modern Studies* 36 (2006), 397–43, and Jennifer Summit, *Memory's Library: Medieval Books in Early Modern England* (Chicago: University of Chicago Press, 2008).
4. Christine Peters, *Patterns of Piety: Women, Gender, and Religion in Late Medieval and Reformation England* (Cambridge: Cambridge University Press, 2003), p. 4.
5. Ibid., p. 347.
6. See Frances Dolan, 'Reading, Work, and Catholic Women's Biographies', *English Literary Renaissance* 33 (2003), 328–57.
7. Michel de Certeau writes, 'I call a "strategy" the calculus of force-relationships which becomes possible when a subject of will and power (a proprietor, an enterprise, a city, a scientific institution) can be isolated from an "environment". A strategy assumes a place that can be circumscribed as *proper (propre)* and thus serve as the basis for generating relations with an exterior distinct from it (competitors, adversaries, "clientèles", "targets", or "objects" of research. [...] I call a "tactic", on the other hand, a calculus which cannot count on the "proper" (a spatial or institutional localization), nor thus on a borderline distinguishing the other as a visible totality. The place of the tactic belongs to the other. A tactic insinuates itself into the other's place, fragmentarily, without taking it over in its entirety, without being able to keep it at a distance. [...] [A] tactic depends on time – it is always on the watch for opportunities

that must be seized "on the wing". [...] It must constantly manipulate events in order to turn them into "opportunities"' (*The Practice of Everyday Life*, trans. Steven Rendell [Berkeley and Los Angeles: University of California Press, 1984], p. xix).

8. Michel de Certeau considers reading as an act of productive consumption. He writes, 'Reading (an image or a text), moreover, seems to constitute the maximal development of the passivity assumed to characterize the consumer. [...] In reality, the activity of reading has on the contrary all the characteristics of a silent production.' The reader 'insinuates into another person's text the ruses of pleasure and appropriation: he poaches on it, is transported into it, pluralizes himself in it like the internal rumblings of one's body' (ibid., p. xxi).

9. Susan James, *Kateryn Parr: The Making of a Queen* (Aldershot: Ashgate, 1999), p. 71.

10. Ibid., p. 91.

11. On Parr's work to ensure that Mary and Elizabeth were both included, along with Edward, in the line of succession, see James, ibid., pp. 135–36. On her involvement with Elizabeth's education, see pp. 136–37.

12. Coles, *Religion, Reform, and Women's Writing*, pp. 45–47.

13. James, *Kateryn Parr*, p. 200.

14. Ibid., p. 204. James also points out that the Latin text appeared 'with no reference to Fisher and although his name remained connected with the book on the Continent, it was conveniently forgotten in England'.

15. Ibid., p. 204.

16. Coles, *Religion, Reform, and Women's Writing*, p. 57.

17. Alexandra Barratt (ed.), *Women's Writing in Middle English* (London: Longman, 1992), p. 219. Hereafter I quote Eleanor Hull's *The Seven Psalms* and *Meditations upon the Seven Days of the Week* from the excerpts included in this volume.

18. London, British Library, MS Arundel 318, fol. 152r–152v. Eleanor Percy's son Henry 'became a leading Protestant and also translated Erasmus into English' (Barratt, note to editorially assigned title 'Eleanor Percy's Prayer', *Women's Writing in Middle English*, p. 279).

19. Katherine Parr, *Psalms or Prayers taken out of Holy Scripture* (London, 1545), Bvia. Quotations are from the copy in the Bodleian Library (STC 2nd edn. 3002.7), accessed via Early English Books Online, http://eebo.chadwyck.com/ (accessed 11 June 2009).

20. See Caroline Walker Bynum, *Jesus as Mother: Studies in the Spirituality of the High Middle Ages* (Berkeley and Los Angeles: University of California Press, 1984), and Caroline Walker Bynum, *Fragmentation and Redemption: Essays on Gender and the Human Body in Medieval Religion* (New York: Zone, 1992).

21. Katherine Parr, *Prayers or Meditations* (1545); quotations are taken from the Bodleian Library copy (STC 2nd edn. 4818.5) accessed via Early English Books Online, http://eebo.chadwyck.com/ (accessed 11 June 2009).

22. The *Psalms*, whether or not Parr was the translator, had a similarly important role. As Coles points out, '[E]vidence concerning the circulation of the *Psalms* puts it in proximity (both physical and doctrinal) to the new English *Litany* – and judging from this history, it appears to have been part of the reforming scheme began in the spring and early summer of 1544' (*Religion, Reform, and Women's Writing*, p. 49).

23. Janel Mueller, 'Devotion as Difference: Intertextuality in Queen Katherine Parr's *Prayers or Meditations* (1545)', *The Huntington Library Quarterly* 53 (1990), 171–97 (p. 174).
24. Ibid., p. 178.
25. C. Fenno Hoffman, Jr., 'Catherine Parr as a Woman of Letters', *The Huntington Library Quarterly* 23 (1960), 349–67 (p. 355 n. 21). One of Hoffman's closing remarks gives a clear sense of his overall assessment of Parr's writings; he asserts that Parr 'Certainly [...] has no place among English authors' (p. 357).
26. Ibid., p. 355.
27. Mueller, 'Devotion as Difference', p. 177.
28. James, *Kateryn Parr*, pp. 215–18, 201.
29. Coles, *Religion, Reform, and Women's Writing*, p. 53.
30. Barratt (ed.), *Women's Writing in Middle English*, p. 220.
31. Linda Pollock, *With Faith and Physic: The Life of a Tudor Gentlewoman Lady Grace Mildmay, 1552–1620* (New York: St. Martin's Press, 1993), p. 28. Hereafter I quote Grace Mildmay's writings from the excerpts included in Pollock's volume.
32. Paris, Bibliothèque Mazarine, MS 1062.
33. In his entry for Richard Whitford in the *ODNB*, J. T. Rhodes doubts the attribution of the *Folowynge* to Whitford. See J. T. Rhodes, 'Whitford, Richard (d. *c*.1543)', *ODNB*, Oxford University Press, 2004, http://www.oxforddnb.com/view/article/29308 (accessed 11 June 2009).
    The claim that Katherine Parr used the *Folowynge* as the basis for her version of book 3 is first made by Fenno Hoffman in 'Katherine Parr as Woman of Letters', and is taken up and developed extensively by Janel Mueller in 'Devotion as Difference'. Both Hoffman and Mueller accept the attribution of the *Folowynge* to Whitford, as does Susan James.
34. James, *Kateryn Parr*, p. 237.
35. Ibid., p. 217.
36. Coles, *Religion, Reform, and Women's Writing*, p. 60.
37. *Prayers or Meditations*, sig. Dia.
38. Ibid., sig. Dib, emphasis added.
39. In an even clearer example of Parr's embrace of the Protestant idea of election, she describes God's kingdom as 'ordeined for thine electe people from the beginning' (sig. Civb).
40. Significantly, Grace Mildmay also writes of Christ as a physician, and in her meditations too this understanding of Christ's role is part of a set of devotional practices and a mode of epistemology that insists on the interrelatedness of the spiritual and the corporeal.
41. Katherine Parr, *Lamentacion of a Sinner* (1547); quotations are taken from the Cambridge University Library copy (STC 2nd edn. 4827) accessed via Early English Books Online, http://eebo.chadwyck.com/ (accessed 11 June 2009).
42. Patricia Demers somewhat oddly calls the *Lamentacion* 'the first original prose composition by an Englishwoman' (Patricia Demers, *Women's Writing in English: Early Modern England* [Toronto: University of Toronto Press, 2005], p. 103), a claim that sounds very strange to scholars of medieval women's writing, who might immediately think of such counterexamples as Julian of Norwich's *Showings* or *The Book of Margery Kempe*.
43. James, *Kateryn Parr*, p. 242.

44. See James Gairdner, *Lollardy and the Reformation in England: A Historical Survey* (London: Macmillan, 1908), p. 453, and also James, *Kateryn Parr*, pp. 269–74.
45. John Foxe, *Acts and Monuments*, 1570 edition, Book 8, pp. 1424–25; accessed via Humanities Research Institute Online, http://www.hrionline.ac.uk/johnfoxe (accessed 11 June 2009).
46. James observes, for example, 'She enthusiastically embraces the Lutheran position on predestination and the kingdom of God's elect, yet remarks: "Christ hath made us free, setting us in godly liberty. I mean not license to sin, as many be glad to interpret the same, when as Christian liberty is godly entreated of." This owes far more to Erasmus than to Luther and illustrates the tangled skein of religious ideas with which the queen was trying to weave a web of truth' (*Kateryn Parr*, p. 247; quoted from *Lamentacion*, sig. Eiiib).
47. Sig. Biia. Coles's analysis of this passage is quite relevant to my argument. Building on the work of Eric Jager, she notes that Parr 'returns us to the conception of the heart as a devotional text. The meanings that remain elusive to the reader of the material text are discernible when the penitent examines the book of her heart. Early reformers alter this interpretive model, so that the reader absorbs scripture through the heart (or soul, as these are almost indistinguishable terms at this time), but they make an important distinction between the heart and text as readable matter. The material codex has primacy. [...] By contrast [...] Parr's "book of the crucifix" relies upon pre-reform ideas of scriptural sufficiency; the picture of the Crucifixion is contained in the heart where the devotee can "read" it – a practice very similar to that of *imitatio*' (*Religion, Reform, and Women's Writing*, p. 66).
48. Janel Mueller describes the *Lamentacion* as '[l]avishly interspersed with Biblical citations' ('Literature and the Church', in *The Cambridge History of Early Modern English Literature*, ed. David Lowenstein and Janel Mueller [Cambridge: Cambridge University Press], pp. 257–310, p. 289). As Patricia Demers observes, the 'principle of study' advocated in this passage is a 'creative blend of the textual and the iconic [...]: personal reading of the Bible, presumably in the vernacular, along with contemplation of the crucifix as a devotional object, a sacramental. Reformation and Romanist ideas are joined in this salient trope' (*Women's Writing in English*, p. 105). Coles includes an extensive analysis of this image, including the possibility that Katherine Parr takes up the concept of the book of the crucifix from John Fisher (*Religion, Reform, and Women's Writing*, pp. 65–67). She argues that Parr's deployment of the image 'reveals the mixture of old and new faith that ground her belief' (p. 67).
49. This community, founded by Henry V in 1415, quickly became the wealthiest nunnery in England, and it was renowned for its learning and its sophisticated textual culture.
50. *The Life and Good End of Sister Marie*, London, British Library, MS 18650.
51. Ann M. Hutchison, 'Mary Champney, a Bridgettine Nun under the Rule of Queen Elizabeth I', *Bridgettiana* 13 (2002), p. 6.
52. Ibid., p. 8.
53. Elizabeth Sanders, one of Marie Champney's religious sisters who accompanied her back to England, was intimately involved in circulating a famous, or notorious, illegal Catholic text, Edmund Campion's *Brag*. See Nancy

Bradley Warren, *Women of God and Arms: Female Spirituality and Political Conflict, 1380–1600* (Philadelphia: University of Pennsylvania Press, 2005), pp. 142–49.

54. Christopher Abbott, *Julian of Norwich: Autobiography and Theology* (Woodbridge: Brewer, 1999), p. 140.

55. Tom Webster, 'Writing to Redundancy: Approaches to Spiritual Journals and Early Modern Spirituality', *The Historical Journal* 39 (1996), 33–56 (p. 41).

56. From 'To the Reader', *Naaman the Syrian*, quoted in Webster, ibid., p. 41.

57. Demers, *Women's Writing in English*, p. 37.

12
Race and Skin Color in Early Modern Women's Writing

Sujata Iyengar

Early modern mythologies of race

Early modern women found themselves at the intersection of multiple, competing beliefs about sexual reproduction, physical health, morality, and work, beliefs that often manifested themselves culturally as 'race'.[1] As Margo Hendricks points out, the most common use of the word 'race' in the early modern period refers to lineage or bloodline, but early modern writers also use it in our contemporary sense of perceived bodily differences between groups of persons associated with a particular part of the world.[2] Women, the guarantors of legitimacy, became surrogates for discussions of racial purity. Debates about female health and beauty also engaged with theories of race through heliotropic beliefs which considered the sun (through its tanning rays) to turn 'the More black, and the Europaæn white, | Th'American tawnie, and th'East Indian red'.[3] But since exposure to the sun was known to tan skin, the outdoor labor of rural women marked them racially as a different group from the upper-class women who protected their faces from the sun indoors and behind veils or masks; race among women became a proxy for rank. Climate-theory extended heliotropism to take account of features in addition to the sun, and also integrated humoral theory, connecting dark skin with melancholy or black bile; brown or 'yellow' skin with choler or yellow bile; fair, blushing skin with blood, the sanguine humor; and each with its associated temperament. Women, cold and moist, were constitutionally phlegmatic – pale and listless – and men, hot and moist, were sanguine – ruddy and vigorous. Within this system, however, dark-skinned 'Southerners' were generally malicious, highly civilized, and subtle; fair-skinned 'Northerners' docile, barbaric, and gullible; and 'yellow' Equatorial peoples hot-tempered. Climate-theory's foremost proponent, Jean Bodin, carefully observes, however, that since temperaments depend upon heat, humidity, longitude, latitude, elevation, winds, upbringing, and systems of rule, all personalities can be found in any given region.[4]

Some early modern origin stories explaining variations in physical features (including skin color) recast reproduction (sexual and asexual) as catastrophe, removing parental influence from children's appearance. Two frequently cited tales, Ovid's account in *The Metamorphoses* and sailor George Best's retelling of Genesis, fantasize that all human beings were created with white skins until some accident blackened or burned them. The Ovidian fable imagines that Phaethon, the son of the sun-god, stole his father's chariot and, unable to control the fiery horses, careered wildly across the heavens, burning the Ethiopians 'blacke and swart' and crisping their hair in the process.[5] Discourses of catastrophe and contamination overlap in sailor George Best's 1578 gloss on the story of the great flood, which suggests that God condemned Noah's son Cham to beget a black-skinned son, Chus, as a punishment for fornication in the Ark: 'from this blacke and cursed Chus came all these blacke Moores which are in Africa'.[6] An 'infection of the blood' transmitted by 'lineall descent' from parent to child, Chus's blackness (the supposed result of God's curse) becomes an acquired characteristic, heritable by future generations.[7] In other words, sexual immorality becomes both visible and permanent, a habit or practice that becomes naturalized.

Proto-Lamarckian theories blamed women's creative or medical work for physical distinctions between peoples (Jean Baptiste de Lamarck would argue in 1800 that acquired characteristics could be inherited, a now-discredited theory known as Lamarckian evolution). Anti-cosmetic pamphleteers accused women of 'cosmesis' (Frances Dolan's useful term), of using cosmetics to create a new, female art that deceived men's eyes.[8] Such treatises argued that women's use of make-up threatened to infect or pollute them and, ultimately, the people among whom they lived: 'th'Blush which Art makes is adulterate' or corrupted, and made-up women are mixed-up hermaphrodites, 'a feminine as well consorting with a masculine'.[9] John Bulwer explains that the Scythians of Phasis have heads shaped like a 'sugar loaf' to this day because long-ago midwives swaddled the babies' heads and so 'Nature [...] began to conspire with Custome, and so left them to their own vain invention, that there was no need of any Artificiall compultion.'[10]

Sir Thomas Browne uses comparative standards of female beauty to frame his well-known discussion of race. He identifies black skin as an inborn, unchanging attribute bestowed from God for reasons unknown, perhaps in order to inspire awe and wonder. Concluding that pulchritude depends upon symmetry, rather than color, he argues that standards of beauty are culturally determined, social decisions rather than objective truths: 'if we seriously consult the definitions of beauty [...] we shall not apprehend a curse, or any deformity in dark skin, nor in any particular nose- or eye-shape'.[11] Following a tradition of praise of blackness established by the third-century commentator Origen, Browne singles out the bride called 'black' in the Canticles (often identified by patristic and early modern commentators with the Queen of Sheba) as evidence of the coexistence of beauty and blackness, despite their seeming contradiction in seventeenth-century England.[12] (Kim Hall observes, however, that Browne's well-meaning analysis nonetheless fetishizes blackness.[13]) Finally, one of the earliest statements of polygenesis (the proto-racialist belief that bodily differences marked groups of persons constituting a separate species, not descended from Adam and Eve like other human beings but remaining from a prior creation or even descended from apes) has long been attributed to the seventeenth-century writer and natural philosopher Margaret Cavendish, who writes: 'Blackmoors [are] a kind or race of men different from the White', belonging to species as distinct as 'A Cow and a Lyon'.[14] (The opposite belief, monogenesis, maintains that all peoples belong to a single species or race from the shared biblical ancestor Adam.)

Traces of racial or proto-racialized language and tropes appear in different genres of early modern women's writing such as the metrical translations of the Psalms (probably composed in the 1590s, circulated widely in manuscript, but unpublished until 1823) by Mary Sidney Herbert, Countess of Pembroke; the Senecan closet drama *The Tragedy of Mariam, The Fair Queen of Jewry* (composed *c.*1602–04, published 1613) by Elizabeth Cary, Lady Falkland; and the anthology *Salve Deus Rex Judaeorum* (probably composed in 1609–10, published in 1611) by Aemilia Lanyer.[15] Sidney's Psalms demonstrate how early modern culture imagines the imprint of sin upon flesh as a physical stain, troping such markings as darkness or infection; they also turn race into religious election. Cary's *Tragedy of Mariam* ranges across multiple mythologies of color in order to distinguish between women and to figure personal or domestic choices as cosmic chaos. Lanyer mobilizes Italianate literary convention (Petrarchism), generic mixing (a modified *contaminatio*, the Terentian practice of cannibalizing Greek texts for plots, characters, and scenes), and biblical allegory (the figure of the black bride in Canticles) in order to account for herself as a poet in a culture that multiply 'others' her as a woman attempting to control her erotic life; a working woman who never fully gained access to the aristocratic literary circles of other well-known women authors; and a 'black' woman of Italo-Jewish ancestry.[16]

Race as divine (s)election: Mary Sidney Herbert's Psalms

Mary Sidney Herbert's 107 Psalms are metrically brilliant; including manuscript variations, note her current editors, she generated 118 different verse forms. Lyn Bennett attends closely to Sidney's skill as *rhetor*, identifying her metrical variation not as the formal pedantry some prior critics thought it but as a mark of her innovative, ongoing demonstration that women could master this highly educated idiom. Sidney's editors note her skillful, erudite collation of multiple sources (the Geneva and Bishops' Bibles; the Parker Psalter; the religious lyrics of Anne Lock and the secular sonnets of Philip Sidney; Theodore Beza's French *Psaumes* and his Latin commentary; Calvin's commentary on the Psalms).[17]

Mary Sidney Herbert's choices in synthesizing these sources for her Psalms engage both mythologies of skin color and ideologies of race. As did her brother, Sir Philip Sidney, Mary adds 'the idea of blushing where shame occurs in her Biblical sources', equating the consciousness of sin, and the possibility of remorse, with the embodied sign most visible to English people.[18] Blushing in women is particularly loaded for early modern writers: the polemicist Richard Braithwait complains, 'How can [women] begge pardon, when their sinne cleaves unto their faces, and when they are not able for to blush?'[19] A few commentators in the period do realize that all peoples experience and manifest shame, even if it is not visible to early modern eyes as a rosy blush; Richard Jobson comments that Fulani women in West Africa veil themselves or hang their heads when ashamed, and Thomas Underdowne's white-skinned African princess displays shame and erotic prostration through both blushes and 'grete swette'.[20]

For Mary Sidney Herbert, however, blushing and paling are physical correlatives to shame, guilt, and pride. Psalm 44 reads 'the shame of my face couereth me' in the Bishops' Bible (44.6) and 'hath couered me' in Geneva (44.15), and Parker reads 'confusion, | standth full to daunt myne eye: | My face all shame' (44.15), but Sidney's translation adds 'Soe Confusion on mee groweth, | that my face I blush to show' (ll. 59–60). Similarly, where Psalm 69.3 gives 'Let not them that trust in thee O Lorde God of hoastes, be for my cause ashamed', and Parker gives 'My face hyd: for infamy' (69.7), Sidney writes:

> Mighty lord, lett not my case
> Blank the rest that hope on thee:

Lett not Jacobs god deface
All his frends in blush of me.
Thyne it is, thyne only quarrell
Dightes me thus in shames apparrell:
Note, nor spott, nor least disgrace,
But for thee, could taint my face. (ll. 19–24)

Typically, Sidney expands two lines in the Psalm to a stanza of extended, revitalized metaphor. Establishing the semiotics of color that I have elsewhere characterized as blanching, blushing, and blacking, Sidney contrasts the 'blank' or white faces of those who love God (who are literally ap*pall*ed, made pale, by God's anger) to God's own face blushing for shame at his worshiper's sin, and to the speaker's own spotted or tainted face. The spot or stain is, however, like 'apparrell', clothing, something that can be shed to reveal the underlying purity or homogeneity of the devotee. 'Note' exists here in its most common early modern usage, something of note, a mark, but it also follows on from 'blank' as a space to be filled out, a line to be written. Blank faces await the spots or notes of God; since the lyricist has suffered these marks in God's own 'quarrell', a 'blank' or unmarked face would, paradoxically, be a face 'defaced', a sign of divine abandonment. In contrast, one of Sidney's best-known translations, Psalm 51 (the 'Miserere', or 'Misericordia'), contrasts the blank 'whiteness' of virtue with the spots or stains of leprosy or of 'filth'. The lyric voice exhorts God to 'Cleanse still my spots, still wash away my stainings, | Till stains and spots in me leave no remainings' (ll. 6–7) and to wash away 'my filthie fault, my faultie filthiness' (l. 9).

In Psalm 78, Sidney deals directly with the word 'race' in three ways: its traditional sense of lineage or ancestry; its emergent sense of a nation distinguished from others by specific physical features; and in a way very specific to Sidney and her own faith: as a group (s)elected by God. The Psalm exhorts the people of Israel *not* to follow their forefathers' example in disobeying Jehovah's word, retelling two stories of Exodus and Numbers, first the Israelites' escape from Egyptian slavery and their exile in the desert, and then going back in time to recount events leading up to their departure. After Jehovah's division of the Red Sea, he appears as a 'flaming piller' (l. 47) at night or as 'a cloud' (l. 45) to guide the Israelites through the desert away from Egypt. Although the people of Israel, 'a wayward, stubborn, stailesse, faithlesse race' (l. 27), constantly disobey his word and blame him for their hunger, thirst, and fatigue, God does not punish them at first but offers them water gushing from 'rift Rocks' (l. 49), rocks riven just as the Red Sea was cleft in twain.

The rocks are allegorized, with their upper-case letter and their 'perced sides' (l. 49) as prefigurations of Christ on the cross. 'Jacobs race [God] did so so dearly love' (l. 66) that he sent 'Ambrosian Manna rain' (l. 74) from the sky and quail when even the pure bread of the angels is not enough to silence the Israelites' grumbling. When 'gluttons' (l. 99) gorge on the 'feathred rain' (l. 90), God kills their leaders. The second story the Psalm retells includes the 'filthy' plagues of Egypt, God's protection of 'the Race, | the twelv-fold race of godly Israell' (ll. 174–5) and the Israelites' nonetheless falling 'to their fathers crooked by-pathes' (l. 180). This time, redemption appears in the person of David, whom God chooses to 'shield | his people which of Jacob did descend | and feed the flock his heritage did yeld' (ll. 212–14).

The Psalm has a double narrative structure, but one underlying, cumulative argument about race, presented as a process of further and further refinement. The Bishops' and Geneva Bibles describe the tribes' ancestors as their 'generation'; Matthew Parker's *Whole Psalter* (1567), often cited as a model for Sidney's own more varied, robust, and polished metrical paraphrases, uses the words 'kynde', or 'linage', and the Coverdale Psalter gives 'posterity'. But Sidney chooses to call the people of Israel a 'race', a 'Race', and finally, a 'people', translating Geneva's 'generation' as 'race' (lower-case) until its last usage in the poem, where Geneva has God casting out the 'heathen'. Sidney represents this distinction among the peoples of Israel by signaling this purer or newer tribe by a capital letter, giving us 'Race', for the first time in the psalm (l. 174). In other words, Sidney distinguishes *Race* from 'generation'. Generation is a matter of inheritance and bloodline, but 'race' signifies selection, both selection by God and the choice of individual group members or of a group of people to adhere to or to disobey God's will. Sidney's editors observe that she emphasizes from Calvin's commentaries on the Psalms the doctrine of election, God's predestined choice of those to whom he will extend 'grace', the power to come to God and to be saved; she would have precedent in doing this from Parker, who writes 'David meke: he dyd *elect*' (78.70, italics mine) to talk about God's choosing David, of the tribe of Judah, over the other tribes of Israel and subsequently only his 'folke' or his 'heyres' (78.71). Sidney ends, however, with a Christianized reading of the Old Testament that emphasizes that this kind of divine election extends beyond the bloodline of Israel to those of all ancestries who are called by God. David is charged 'to shield | his people which of Jacob did descend, | and feede the flock his heritage did yeld' (ll. 213–14). David's folk are not the 'Race' that forsook God in the desert, nor yet the 'twelve-fold race' identified by

Jewish blood, but a 'people', a people comprising both Jacob's offspring and the yieldings or gifts of God, understood in Protestant terms as the followers of the English Reformed Church.

This Protestant identity that Sidney has cast in terms of race both incorporates and transcends class distinctions, too; her God in Psalm 78 is a sleeping 'knight' 'roused at the noise' of 'alarm' (ll. 197–78), and his sanctuary rises 'Castle-like' upon a mountain (l. 205). In this sense the shepherd David is God's feudal 'servant' (l. 209) and when God 'converts his cares' to a 'nobler end' it is as though he has been dubbed God's knight, complete with duties to 'shield' the weaker (ll. 212–13). Feudalism and Calvinism share a belief in predestination before birth, but God's Calvinist devotees cannot be detected from their birth – only through their conversion. Thus one may *elect* to be God's servant where one cannot choose one's social rank in early modern England. Mary Sidney Herbert thus plays two notions of race against each other, one inherited and unchanging (genetic inheritance or bloodline, such as the lineage of the Israelites or the rank of the Sidneys), the other situational and contingent (skin that changes color with blushing or pallor; spots that God can wash away; election by God). The double narrative structure of Psalm 78 (in which the same story is told twice) re-presents race as both inflexible and fluid: through the grace of Sidney's Protestant God, the biological race of rank and nationality can be transformed into the mystical race of election.

Race as cosm(et)ic catastrophe: Cary's *Tragedy of Mariam*

Mary Sidney Herbert engages the racialized religious discourse of English Protestantism, but Elizabeth Cary's Senecan closet drama interweaves early modern beliefs about color, Jewishness, and English nationalism to pit women against each other, as Dympna Callaghan has observed.[21] Here I focus upon two of King Herod's speeches at the end of the play in order to demonstrate the range of racialized reference deployed within even a few lines. We will see that Cary's text additionally mobilizes the language of catastrophe, cosmetics, and comeliness in order to turn domestic tragedy not just into political commentary on royal or religious tyranny (as other critics have suggested) but into a cosmic cataclysm with world-changing consequences.

The play establishes the raced underpinnings of sexual difference from its beginning, when Mariam, Herod's beautiful and chaste wife, and Salome, his wicked sister, castigate one another in terms that explicitly link social class, what the play calls 'race' (Jewish blood-heritage), and skin color.[22] When Salome taunts Mariam for her 'base' birth, Mariam retorts that her pure Jewish blood makes her nobler than Salome, a 'parti-Jew, and parti-Edomite', a 'mongrel [...] issu'd from rejected race' (I.3.230, 231, 235–36). Salome has complained about Mariam's hot temper or 'choler' and her 'fumish' words, and now defends herself with a monogenetic argument for racial unity: 'What odds betwixt your ancestors and mine? | Both born of Adam, both were made of Earth, | And both did come from holy Abrahams line' (I.3.240–2). Mariam concludes that she will speak no further, because even to speak of Salome's crimes would corrupt her by association: 'With thy black acts I'll not pollute my breath' (I.3.244). Racialization is overdetermined in the play not only by class, lineage, and pigmentation but also through the discourses of contamination or 'pollut[ion]', of religious election ('holy Abraham's line') and geohumoralism, in the pun on color/choler lost in modernized spelling (recall Jean Bodin's assertion that Equatorial peoples find themselves prone to choleric anger and perhaps to 'yellow'-toned skin).

Salome plans to urge her brother to execute Mariam for alleged adultery, denying Mariam's virtue or beauty for two reasons. First, claims Salome, Mariam duplicitously covers her dark complexion with paint, 'A crimson bush [sic], that ever limes | The soul', to simulate the genuine 'blush' of fairness, because she is too dark to blush naturally (IV.7.401–02, 405). Because dark-skinned peoples were thought to be unable to blush, they were thought to be likewise unable to experience shame or remorse. Mariam's red cheek, suggests Salome, presents a grotesque parody of the burning bush that Moses encounters in the book of Exodus (3:2); Mariam's 'crimson bush' is smeared with 'lime' to catch the soul in sin just as farmers smeared lime upon the branches of trees to catch birds. 'Lime' evokes the stickiness and the pallor of fucus or face-paint. Salome similarly turns Mariam's blush into paint, her remonstrances into evidence of her guilt. Second, argues Salome, 'A sable star hath been but seldom seen'; since Mariam is 'ebon-hued' in both her eyes and her face, she cannot exhibit the stellar beauty that Herod believes she possesses (IV.7.455, 454). 'Sable' is the term for black in heraldry, and also for the black garments worn by mourners. Here Salome reverses the underlying racial logic of her previous statement to emphasize what she sees as Mariam's duplicity; having argued that Mariam's blush is artificial, her fairness painted on to a dark or plain surface, she then claims that Mariam's blackness itself is a cover, her 'hue' the external appearance of something different inside.

Cary's King Herod, however, responds by accusing Salome herself of ugliness, activating heliotropic and polygenetic theories of blackness in tandem by comparing Salome to 'an ape', 'a sun-burnt blackamoor' (IV.7.460, 462). Herod's speech associates sunburn with blackness and blackness with a geographical origin in Africa, in the standard helio-tropic move, but also equates the ape and the 'blackamoor', compar-ing the differences between human beings and apes to those between Europeans and black Africans in a rhetorical gesture that would become increasingly popular during the seventeenth century.[23] At the same time, 'Salome's exotic beauty [...] is produced as comically subhuman not against the beauty of an Anglo-Saxon princess, but against that of a black-eyed, Jewish queen. [...] The conventions of "race" here are [...] displaced.'[24]

After Mariam's death, Herod continues to code differences between his dead wife and his living sister as displaced racial conventions. Demand-ing an eclipse from the sun as a sign of mourning, he complains, 'You could but shine, if some Egyptian blowse, | Or Æthiopian dowdy lose her life', but if his 'fair and spotless wife' is dead, no one should be able to 'distinguish which is day and night' (V.1.192–93, 198, 201). Cary establishes in these references to an imagined 'Egyptian blowse' or slat-tern (later in the speech called a 'black Egyptian') another distinction between women that the play codes as racial: the difference between Mariam, Fair Queen of Jewry, and Cleopatra, (black) Queen of Egypt. Mariam also contrasts to the biblical Queen of Sheba (a proverbial figure for black-skinned beauty), who in comparison to her is a mere 'Æthiopian dowdy', a dark-complected, slatternly woman.[25] 'Dowd' or 'dowdy' appear from their earliest uses in opposition to that which is fair; Shakespeare equates the 'dowdy' woman with the dark-skinned 'Gipsy' explicitly in *Romeo and Juliet* (II.4.42).[26] 'Blowse' adds an ele-ment of sexual promiscuity to skin color by comparing women to fallen ('blown') blossoms. The ruddiness of a blowse's complexion marks not her shamefast blushing but her outdoor travail (both labor or travel); the term is first applied to beggar women, tinkers, milkmaids, and outlaws.[27] In Herod's formulation women from Egypt or from Ethiopia appear both sexually promiscuous and sexually unattractive; Mariam, in contrast, is both chaste and desirable.

Cultural associations of blackness with mourning overlap with the language of cosmic catastrophe when Herod blames 'fond idolaters, the men of Greece' (V.1.203) for claiming that their deities rule the planets when, if there were any intelligence guiding them, 'They all would put their mourning garments on: | Not one of them would yield a light to me [...] the cause that Mariam's gone' (V.1.208–10). Pre-Copernican cosmology held that the sun, moon, and planets each circled the earth on solid, crystalline spheres. By the sixteenth century, Christian theologians had suggested that each of these 'orbs' was moved by an angel or divine force, each of which was subject to the will of the Prime Mover, understood as God.[28] Were each Ptolemaic sphere truly spun by subordinate, angelic spirits or by the Greek divinities, Herod argues, adherent to moral 'just[ice]' as well as to the 'steadfast' astronomical course of the heavens (V.1.206), angels or gods would push the moon, stars, sun, and planets away from Herod, Mariam's murderer, who would see only darkened spheres, as punishment for his crime.

The implicit association of darkness with black bile or the melancholy humor takes Herod in his next lines further to question Greek cosmology:

> For though they feign their Saturn melancholy,
> Of sour behaviours, and of angry mood,
> They feign him likewise to be just and holy,
> And justice needs must seek revenge for blood. (V.1.211–14)

The invocation of Saturn introduces geohumoral elements into his myth of cosmic disaster. Saturn, the planet associated with blackness, melancholy, and anger, and both 'sour' behavior and taste, ought to have sought revenge for Mariam's death, because he is 'just and holy'; his failure to cover the heavens in 'mourning garments', that is, to blacken the entire sky, proves that the learned men of Greece are merely 'fond Idolaters', rather than philosophers. Such an eclipse of the heavens would not, however, be a sign of 'sour behavior' or 'ang[er]', but of 'justice', since Mariam's death is so egregious.

The sun is thus, paradoxically, both the source of light and also the source of darkening (the tanning of skin). Herod makes the collapse of the categories, dark coloring and dark night, explicit and further explains Mariam's death as a paradoxical consequence of her fairness:

> If she had been like an Egyptian black,
> And not so fair, she had bene longer liv'd:
> Her overflow of beauty turnèd back,
> And drown'd the spring from whence it was deriv'd. (V.1.239–42)

Cary's Mariam is choked by her own pallor, imagined as water or a river, perhaps to evoke the associations of water and religious purification and the implicit parallel between the binary pair of *sin* and *virtue* and the opposites *dark* and *fair*. In this way, Cary turns the seemingly private and personal topics of female beauty and eroticism into figures for a general chaos and a moral collapse, the end of a world order. Herod's fury and its consequences 'overflow' the domestic realm and threaten to submerge worldly institutions such as marriage and male authority. Insisting upon the rights of men alone to determine fidelity, purity, and beauty in women leads only to the concepts themselves becoming muddied or racially contaminated. Like a river that has burst a dam, female expressiveness (in beauty, in love, in eroticism) cannot or ought not, Cary suggests, to be subject to male control, lest it 'overflow' the bounds between male and female, Jew and Edomite, black Egyptian and fair queen, altogether. Female self-expression is one of Lanyer's major concerns, too, but we shall see that she removes men from the hierarchy of power only to reinstitute nobly born women as the bestowers and arbiters of freedom and beauty.

Race as *contaminatio*: Aemilia Lanyer

Born in 1569, the daughter of Margaret Johnson and Baptista Bassano, a member of the well-known Italian and probably Jewish musical family, Aemilia Lanyer grew up in modest circumstances, although she may have spent some time at the houses of the noble ladies to whom she dedicated her major work.[29] Almost certainly a former mistress of Lord Hunsdon, Lanyer married the Court musician Alphonso Lanyer in 1592 while pregnant with her son Henry (named after his putative father). The astrologer Simon Forman, whom she visited in 1597, claimed to have enjoyed a sexual affair with her, but there is no way to distinguish fantasy from fact in his rather lurid journal entries. At forty-two, Lanyer published her major work, *Salve Deus Rex Judaeorum*, dedicating it to female patrons and asserting the right of women to testify at and to Christ's passion and to speak in a range of lyric voices and genres. After her husband's death in 1613, Lanyer briefly ran a school and sued her brother-in-law for her share of the hay-weighing monopoly that her husband had been awarded by Queen Elizabeth. Although she ultimately won her suit, it is unclear whether she successfully claimed the money; some accounts maintain Lanyer died in poverty, but Woods notes that '[t]he parish record lists her as a "pensioner", a term which designated a steady income'.[30]

Woods rightly questions A. L. Rowse's identification of Lanyer with Shakespeare's 'Dark Lady' and Roger Prior's emphasis on the possibility that her family was Jewish.[31] We do not need, however, to identify Lanyer as Shakespeare's Dark Lady or her ancestors as Jews or crypto-Jews in order to analyze her responses to and engagement with proto-racialized discourses of early modern England. Barbara Bowen complains that Rowse's 'misogynistic' analysis 'poisoned' discussion of Lanyer's ethnicity, but argues that Lanyer's text deliberately deploys blackness and abasement in tandem with regard to her aristocratic patronesses in her dedications (so that she is, for example, the 'blacke foyle' beneath the 'diamond' that is the Dowager Countess of Cumberland). In other words, Lanyer's documented, though slight, Jewish and Italian ancestry makes her culturally and aesthetically 'black' to the English. Bowen argues that a full analysis of the racial poetics in Lanyer's work would need to account for her Jewishness, her Italian ancestry, her class status and her femininity in dialogue with one another and in historical context.[32] Such a reading is beyond my scope here, but I can pause to unpack perhaps the best-known sections of the volume, Lanyer's invective against Beauty (ll. 185–248), and her paean to Christ the divine bridegroom (ll. 1305–20). First, we can consider the form of the volume itself: as Lewalski comprehensively described, *Salve Deus* demonstrates Lanyer's command of many traditionally male-authored literary genres, moving from sonnet to complaint to ode to elegy, and so on with impressive skill.[33] The invective ventriloquizes a traditionally male form, the anti-cosmetic tract, in its complaints against 'outward beuty unaccompanied with virtue' (marginal gloss, l. 185).[34]

Anti-cosmetic tracts warned readers of the physical and moral perils of beauty, of its duplicity and its subordination to time. Lanyer similarly singles out inward beauty for praise. Having described the physical depredations of beauty in terms that recall the anti-cosmetic debate's emphasis upon 'poyson' (a salient point given that the same toxic paints used on canvas also served as make-up), she borrows some of the same examples of famous women doomed by beauty, such as King John's victim Matilda Fitzwalter (voiced by the poet Richard Barnfield), or King Henry II's mistress Rosamund (ventriloquized by Samuel Daniel).[35] In literary terms, Lanyer deliberately employs *contaminatio* – the Renaissance practice of mixing genres, sources, and forms – to create a hybrid form for her anthology.[36] An exercise in the development of voice and formal inventiveness, it recreates the self in literary and social terms (through its bold address to female patrons and its invocation of female authorship and readership, suggests Woods). This self is also feminist, Jewish, and Italianate. Responding to Elaine Beilin's argument that Lanyer cannot be considered a feminist because her work is literary, rather than political, Janel Mueller reads *Salve Deus Rex Judaeorum* as a 'locution' that by its very nature is political, in that it establishes Lanyer in opposition to 'the people of her own descent', the Jews, and aligns her instead with a community of women.[37]

Just as Lanyer deploys her Jewish ancestry to break down the category of 'woman', so, Pamela Benson suggests, she adapts and adopts Italian publishing conventions and social mores and 'turned the stigma of Italy into the allure of Italy'.[38] Benson, Michele Marrapodi, and Lara Bovilsky independently suggest that the Elizabethan representation 'of Italy in particular [...] [w]as a fundamentally double-faced vision of allurement and bias'.[39] Benson reads Lanyer's self-presentation in the published form of her volume as self-consciously Italian, arguing that through Lanyer's comportment as the Italian 'honest courtesan' in her personal life and the use of the dream-vision as genre in the final address to the reader, Lanyer attempts to overcome her class status and to evoke the Italy of storied high culture rather than of intrigue. The marks of this feminist Italianate self include Lanyer's 'name [...] on the title page, common enough in Italy but rare in England', and her dedications to non-family members and exclusively to women, typical (Benson argues) of Italian women writers but not of English ones.[40]

Lanyer addresses her invective against traditional standards of female beauty to the Dowager Duchess of Cumberland, who is, as Woods has argued, a 'suffering [...] figure for the perfect church for whom Christ the bridegroom has performed his sacrifice and translation of suffering into triumph'.[41] But however poetically apt the focus upon the Duchess of Cumberland, Leeds Barroll notes that this dedication was a tactical error that praised a woman who had little influence at Court and who could not help Lanyer to the patronage she desired.[42] Lanyer's attempt at self-sufficiency and her invention of a female circle of patrons thus ended up marking her exclusion from rather than her entry into the halls of power. After the invective against outward beauty, *Salve Deus* takes us through Christ's passion before returning to beauty again, this time in the person of Christ (ll. 1305–28). Earlier, as we have seen, Lanyer employed the language and generic form of (usually male) anti-cosmetic writers in an 'Invective' against Beauty, but in this much-discussed passage, she deploys the important early modern counter-Petrarchan poetic discourse in praise of black beauty in her paean on the beauty of Christ. Red and white in women is tainted; red and white in Christ can still exemplify beauty, just as blackness in him, too, can be 'gold', shining and brilliant. His blackness is paradoxically 'milke'-white, sustaining and nourishing as milk and pure and sacrificial as the 'doves' washed in it, yet nonetheless dark enough to be 'Raven'-like in its depth.

Several critics suggest that Lanyer uses the diction of Canticles to describe Christ in order to break down existing structures of gendered authority, first by rewriting the story of Solomon and the Queen of Sheba, identified with the black bride in Canticles, in order to remove Sheba from her traditionally subservient position and place her 'in a love that transcends hierarchy'.[43] Second, since Lanyer's poem is structured around woman's experience of and erotic response to Christ, and Christ himself is feminized both in the conventional terms of early modern love lyric (as the erotic object of poetry) and 'endowed with feminine characteristics [...] the gender relationships between Christ and his female followers are sexually complex'.[44] The stanzas evoke erotic liquefaction – river water, milk, honey, dew, and myrrh. The lyric speaker pleads for mercy from her imagined female interlocutor in an apostrophe that includes an antanaclasis, the repetition of a word in one sense at the beginning of the phrase and in a different one at the end: 'Ah! give me leave (good lady) now to leave | This taske of Beauty which I tooke in hand, | I cannot wade so deepe' (ll.1321–22). She asks for permission ('leave') to depart from ('leave') the description of true beauty, which threatens to drown the poet 'wad[ing]' in an ocean of worshipful desire, and to 'leave' (antanaclasis again) behind Christ's 'perfect picture' in her heart, 'Deepely engraved' (ll. 1326–27). 'Engraved' suggests the technical process of etching of a picture on metal (as a frontispiece), the scratching of a pen on paper, and the carving of an epitaph on a gravestone; it would seem to reassert Christ's masculinity in conventional terms once more by turning him into the impression placed upon the Countess's heart, were it not that the female poet wields the implement. Lanyer's treatment of the Passion also anglicizes and Christianizes the poet, so that Lanyer effects not only a figuration of Christ as divine bridegroom but herself as the black bride washed white, the Jew converted, the Italian anglified, the woman-object the woman-subject.

Note, however, the class differential between the lyric speaker and her hearer. The Countess is still the speaker's 'good Lady' and later 'good Madame', one who has set her a 'task' or feudal duty that she needs 'leave' to abandon. We can contrast Lanyer's Protestantism usefully here with Sidney's, and with Cary's secret (later open) Catholicism. For Sidney, election supersedes rank (both called 'race') through the aristocrat's willingness to become God's vassal or servant. For Cary, to use rank as an excuse to control women's self-expression (through the racialized language of religion and skin color) is inexcusable, no matter how august a personage is attempting to rule. But for Lanyer, the barrier of class remains intact when distinctions of religion (as she hails 'the Jews' in her title, with herself in implicit opposition to them) and national origin (as she presents herself as an anglicized bride of Christ) and even gender (as she publishes work under her own name and blames men, not Jews, for Christ's murder) break down. And it is tempting to speculate that Lanyer cannot imagine a world free from rank because she is lower-middle class, unlike the aristocratic Sidney and Cary, and her Italo-Jewish ancestry races her as 'black' in early modern England, regardless of her physical appearance.

Conclusion

As we have seen, women take on immense importance in early modern culture as the guarantors of bloodlines, icons of shamefast beauty, and professors of religious belief. Each of these three functions can be (and often is) expressed in women's writing in racialized terms, particularly through skin tone. Some critics have recently argued that the coupling of race with skin color in scholarship on early modern race can restrict our understanding of early modern bodies. Mary Floyd-Wilson argues that focusing on skin color ignores corporeal attributes notable to early moderns but largely invisible to us today, such as humoral regulation; Lara Bovilsky argues that by overemphasizing 'black' and 'dark' as modifiers of skin tone and surrogates for geographical origin we subordinate their associations with, say, hair and eye color, religion, social class, and so on. Ranging across the genres and decades of early modern women's writing as I have done here, however, suggests that although 'race' in the early modern period is most commonly understood as the inheritance of qualities and features from parent to child, we must continue to consider skin color in tandem with race in the accounts of early modern women. I speculate that early modern women privilege skin tone in their discussions of race for several reasons: the early modern 'beauty myth' so ably identified and analyzed by Kim Hall (the cultural emphasis placed upon 'fair', red-and-white skin); the ubiquitous biblical trope used to structure early modern femininity, the figure of the biblical 'black' Bride in Canticles who is 'washed white' by God; and the expectation of visible 'shamefastness', manifested as a blush, on the faces of women, blushes thought to be invisible and thus non-existent on the faces of dark, black, or made-up women. Skin color also functions as a proxy for class through the association of tanned skin with outdoor labor, and spots or stains as surrogates for moral pollution; race clearly overlaps with distinctions of rank through the idea of blood purity in the aristocracy. In other words, we cannot consider gender alone in women's writing without also engaging emergent and existing early modern concepts of race and physical appearance, as we continue the difficult, ongoing, elusive process of discovering what it means to be a 'woman' or to have a woman's body in early modern England.

Notes

1. The rich and varied scholarship on early modern race includes: Peter Fryer, *Staying Power: The History of Black People in Britain* (London: Pluto, 1984); David Dabydeen (ed.), *The Black Presence in English Literature* (Manchester: Manchester University Press, 1985); Virginia Mason Vaughan, *Performing Blackness on English Stages, 1500–1800* (Cambridge: Cambridge University Press, 2005); Alden T. Vaughan and Virginia Mason Vaughan, *Shakespeare's Caliban: A Cultural History* (Cambridge: Cambridge University Press, 1991); Francesca Royster, '"White-Limed Walls": Whiteness and Gothic Extremism in Shakespeare's *Titus Andronicus'*, *Shakespeare Quarterly* 51 (2000), 432–55; Arthur B. Little, *Shakespeare Jungle Fever: National-imperial Re-visions of Race, Rape, and Sacrifice* (Stanford: Stanford University Press, 2000); Mary Floyd-Wilson, *English Ethnicity and Race in Early Modern Drama* (Cambridge: Cambridge University Press, 2003); Lara Bovilsky, *Barbarous Play* (Minneapolis: University of Minnesota Press, 2008). On early modern race and gender, see Ania Loomba, *Gender, Race, Renaissance Drama* (Manchester: Manchester University Press, 1989); Margo Hendricks and Patricia Parker (eds), *Women, 'Race' and Writing in the Early Modern Period* (London: Routledge, 1993); Kim F. Hall, *Things of Darkness: Economies of Race and Gender in Early Modern England* (Ithaca: Cornell University Press, 1996); Joyce Green MacDonald, *Women and Race in Early Modern Texts* (Cambridge: Cambridge University Press, 2002).
2. Margo Hendricks, '"Obscured by dreams": Race, Empire, and Shakespeare's *A Midsummer Night's Dream'*, *Shakespeare Quarterly* 47 (1996), 37–60 (p. 42); Hall, *Things of Darkness*, pp. 107–15; Sujata Iyengar, *Shades of Difference: Mythologies of Race and Skin-Color in Early Modern England* (Philadelphia: University of Pennsylvania Press, 2005), p. 106.
3. Sir John Davies, '*Nosce Teipsum*: A Critical Edition' (1599), ed. Clarence Simpson (unpublished doctoral dissertation, Stanford University, 1951), p. 257.
4. *The Six Bookes of a Common-Weale*, trans. Richard Knolles (London, 1606), in EEBO, http://eebo.chadwyck.com/ (accessed 30 May 2009).
5. Ovid, *Metamorphoses*, trans. Arthur Golding (London, 1575), Book 2, fol. 20.
6. 'Experiences and reasons of the Sphere [...] to confute the position of the fiue Zones', in *The Principal Navigations, Voyages, Traffiques and Discoveries of the English Nation*, ed. Richard Hakluyt (London, 1598), vol. 3, sigs. D6ᵛ–E3ᵛ, sig. E2ᵛ.
7. Ibid., sig. E2ᵛ.
8. Frances Dolan, '"Taking the Pencil out of God's Hand": Art, Nature, and the Face-painting Debate in Early Modern England', *PMLA* 108 (1993), 224–39.
9. Richard Braithwait, *The Good Wife, or a Rare One Amongst Women*, B8ᵛ; Thomas Tuke, *A Treatise of Painting and Tincturing*, Kʳ.
10. Sig. C3ʳ. On early modern midwives' imagined power to shape a baby's appearance, see Caroline Bicks, *Midwiving Subjects in Shakespeare's England* (London: Ashgate, 2003), pp. 94–126.
11. *Pseudodoxia Epidemica* (1646), ed. Geoffrey Keynes, in *The Complete Works of Sir Thomas Browne* (London: Faber, 1928), III, p. 245.
12. On this tradition, see Hall, *Things of Darkness*, esp. pp. 107–11, and Linda Van Norden, *The Black Feet of the Peacock: The Color-concept 'Black' from the Greeks to the Renaissance*, ed. John Pollack (Lanham: University Presses of America, 1985), esp. pp. 45–60.

13. Hall, *Things of Darkness*, pp. 12–13.
14. See Rosemary Kegl, ' "This World I have made": Margaret Cavendish, Feminism and *The Blazing World*', in *Feminist Readings of Early Modern Culture: Emerging Subjects*, ed. Valerie Traub, M. Lindsay Kaplan, and Dympna Callaghan (Cambridge: Cambridge University Press, 1996), p. 135, and Sujata Iyengar, 'Royalist, Romancist, Racialist: Rank, Gender, and Race in the Science and Fiction of Margaret Cavendish', *ELH* 69.3 (Fall 2002), 649–72.
15. References to Mary Sidney Herbert come from *Collected Works*, ed. Margaret P. Hannay, Noel J. Kinnamon, and Michael G. Brennan, 2 vols (Oxford: Clarendon Press, 1998), II (hereafter Hannay). References to Cary come from *The Tragedie of Mariam, the Fair Queen of Jewry*, ed. Margaret Ferguson and Barry Weller (Berkeley: University of California Press, 1994) (hereafter Ferguson and Weller). References to Lanyer come from *The Poems of Aemilia Lanyer*, ed. Susanne Woods (Oxford: Oxford University Press, 1993) (hereafter Woods). All references henceforth appear within the text. For the textual history and transmission of Mary Sidney Herbert, see Hannay, I, pp. 21–55 and II, pp. 308–57; of Cary, see Ferguson and Weller, pp. 43–47; of Lanyer, see Woods, pp. xlvii–li. I can here only gesture towards the burgeoning scholarship on the lives and works of these women. See Margaret Hannay, *Philip's Phoenix: Mary Sidney, Countess of Pembroke* (Oxford: Oxford University Press, 1990); Heather Wolfe (ed. and introd.), *Elizabeth Cary, Lady Falkland: Life and Letters* (Tempe: Arizona Center for Medieval and Renaissance Studies, 2001); Susanne Woods, *Lanyer: A Renaissance Woman Poet* (Oxford: Oxford University Press, 1999); Mary Ellen Lamb, *Gender and Authorship in the Sidney Circle* (Madison: University of Wisconsin Press, 1990); Elaine Beilin, *Redeeming Eve: Women Writers of the English Renaissance* (Princeton: Princeton University Press, 1987); Lynn Bennett, *Women Writing of Divinest Things: Rhetoric and the Poetry of Pembroke, Wroth and Lanyer* (Pittsburgh: Duquesne University Press, 2004); Patricia Demers, *Women's Writing in English: Early Modern England* (Toronto: University of Toronto Press, 2005); Theresa M. DiPasquale, *Refiguring the Sacred Feminine: The Poems of John Donne, Aemilia Lanyer, and John Milton* (Pittsburgh: Duquesne University Press, 2008); Marshall Grossman (ed.), *Aemilia Lanyer: Gender, Genre, and the Canon* (Kentucky: University of Kentucky Press, 1998); Tina Krontiris, *Oppositional Voices: Women as Writers and Translators of Literature in the English Renaissance* (London: Routledge, 1992); Barbara Lewalski, *Writing Women in Jacobean England* (Cambridge, MA: Harvard University Press, 1993); Anita Pacheco (ed.), *A Companion to Early Modern Women's Writing* (Oxford: Blackwell, 2002); Kim Walker, *Women Writers of the English Renaissance* (New York: Twayne, 1996); Heather Wolfe (ed.), *The Literary Career and Legacy of Elizabeth Cary, 1613–1680* (Basingstoke: Palgrave Macmillan, 2007).
16. On Lanyer's imputed sexuality and class aspirations, see Susanne Woods, 'Aemilia Lanyer's *Salve Deus Rex Judaeorum*', in *Companion to Early Modern Women's Writing*, ed. Pacheco, pp. 125–26; on her ethnicity, see Roger Prior, 'Jewish Musicians at the Tudor Court', *Musical Quarterly* 69 (1983), 253–65, and Barbara Bowen, 'Aemilia Lanyer and the Invention of White Womanhood', in *Maids and Mistresses, Cousins and Queens: Women's Alliances in Early Modern England*, ed. Susan Frye and Karen Robertson (Oxford: Oxford University Press, 1999), pp. 274–305.

17. References to the biblical Psalms come from the Geneva Bible (Geneva, 1560) and henceforth are cited parenthetically by biblical chapter and verse within the text; to the Coverdale Psalter from Miles Coverdale, *The Psalter or Boke of the Psalmes* (London, 1548) and appear within the text; to *The Whole Psalter* from Matthew Parker, *The Whole Psalter translated into English Metre* (London, 1567), and appear within the text. For others, see Hannay.

18. Hannay, 'Introduction', I, p. 70.

19. Richard Braithwait, *The English Gentleman* (London, 1630), Eᵛ.

20. *The Golden Trade*, sig. F2ᵛ, and *An Aethiopian Historie*, sig. O2ᵛ, quoted in Iyengar, *Shades of Difference*, p. 107, p. 39.

21. Dympna Callaghan, 'Re-Reading Elizabeth Cary's *The Tragedie of Mariam, Faire Queene of Jewry*', in *Women, 'Race' and Writing*, ed. Hendricks and Parker, pp. 163–77.

22. Ibid., p. 173.

23. On apes/Africa, see esp. Fryer, *Staying Power*, pp. 133–46; Winthrop Jordan, *White over Black: American Attitudes towards the Negro, 1550–1812* (Chapel Hill: University of North Carolina Press, 1968), pp. 24–36; Kim Hall, 'Troubling Doubles: Apes, Africans and Blackface in "Mr Moore's Revels"', in *Race, Ethnicity and Power in the Renaissance*, ed. Joyce Green MacDonald (Lanham, NJ: Association of University Presses, 1997), pp. 120–44.

24. Callaghan, 'Re-Reading Elizabeth Cary's *The Tragedie of Mariam*', p. 175.

25. Ferguson and Weller read 'Aethiopian' as another reference to Cleopatra's dark complexion, p. 175 n. 196.

26. *OED*, dowd, n. 1 and dowdy, n. 1 and adj. 1.

27. *OED*, blowse, n. 1 and 2. Ferguson and Weller gloss *blowse* as a 'coarse-complexioned woman', but the implication of red or pink coloring, from the idea of the blown blossom, is telling.

28. On early modern angelology, see Peter Marshall and Alexandra Walsham (eds), *Angels in the Early Modern World* (Cambridge: Cambridge University Press, 2006), and J. L. E. Dreyer, *A History of Astronomy from Thales to Kepler*, 2nd edn (New York: Dover, 1953), pp. 230–31.

29. Leeds Barroll, 'Looking for Patrons', in *Aemilia Lanyer*, ed. Grossman, pp. 29–48, p. 38.

30. 'Introduction', *The Poems of Aemilia Lanyer*, p. xxx.

31. For the Bassanos' Jewish ancestry, see Prior, 'Jewish Musicians at the Tudor Court'. For the almost certainly false identification of Lanyer with 'Shakespeare's Dark Lady', see A. L. Rowse (ed. and introd.), *The Poems of Shakespeare's Dark Lady: Salve Deus Rex Judaeorum, by Emilia Lanier* (London: Cape, 1978).

32. Bowen, 'Aemilia Lanyer and the Invention of White Womanhood'. 'To the Ladie *Margaret* Countesse Dowager of Cumberland', ll. 19–20, quoted in ibid., p. 284.

33. Barbara Lewalski, 'Seizing Discourses and Reinventing Genres', in *Aemilia Lanyer*, ed. Grossman, pp. 51–54.

34. For a full reading of Lanyer in the context of the anti-cosmetic debate, see Patricia Berrahou Phillippy, *Painting Women: Cosmetics, Canvases, and Early Modern Culture* (Baltimore: Johns Hopkins University Press, 2006), pp. 138–61.

35. 'The Complaint of [...] Matilda Fitzwalter', in *The Complete Poems of Richard Barnfield*, ed. George Klawitter (Selinsgrove: Susquehanna University Press),

pp. 107–09; 'The Complaint of Rosamund', in *The Complete Poems of Samuel Daniel*, ed. Alexander Grosart (n.p.: Hazell, Watson and Viney, 1885), I, pp. 79–113.

36. For *contaminatio* as the combination of two or more different early modern sources, see Alastair Fox, *The English Renaissance: Identity and Representation in Elizabethan England* (Oxford: Blackwell, 1997), p. 186; and Michele Marrapodi, *Italian Culture in the Drama of Shakespeare and his Contemporaries: Rewriting, Remaking, Refashioning* (London: Ashgate, 2007), pp. 51–53.

37. Beilin, *Redeeming Eve*, chapter 4; Janel Mueller, 'The Feminist Poetics of *Salve Deus Rex Judaeorum*', in *Aemilia Lanyer*, ed. Grossman, p. 114, p. 116.

38. Pamela Joseph Benson, 'The Stigma of Italy Undone: Aemilia Lanyer's Canonization of Lady Mary Sidney', in *Strong Voices, Weak History: Early Women Writers and Canons in England, France and Italy*, ed. Pamela Joseph Benson and Victoria Kirkham (Ann Arbor: University of Michigan Press, 2005), p. 153.

39. Marrapodi, *Italian Culture*, p. 1.

40. Benson, 'The Stigma of Italy', p. 154.

41. Woods, 'Aemilia Lanyer's *Salve Deus Rex Judaeorum*', p. 131.

42. Barroll, 'Looking for Patrons', p. 40.

43. DiPasquale, *Refiguring the Sacred Feminine*, p. 191, p. 188.

44. Lynette McGrath, *Subjectivity and Women's Poetry in Early Modern England: 'Why on the ridge should she desire to go?'* (Aldershot: Ashgate, 2002), p. 230.

13
Translation/Historical Writing
Chris Laoutaris

Women who translated a work from one particular language or local context into another were manipulating histories: sacred, social, national. The extent to which their appropriation and transformation of such texts could have a lasting impact on their own and successive cultures is still relatively little understood. In this chapter I hope to recuperate the immediate intellectual, theological, and political pressures that influenced women's engagement with acts of translation and historical inscription and to reveal how their works, published or privately circulated, helped in turn to shape the worlds in which they lived and wrote.

The women we will be exploring were all passionate activists for the particular causes they espoused and the ambitious political reach of their endeavors challenges the preconception that translation was a 'degraded activity'.[1] The 'interventionist power' and 'performative role' of the translator, in the words of Luise von Flotow, are only now being recognized by historians and critics, but within this newly acquired understanding is imbedded the kinetic root of terms used to designate translational acts in their earliest uses: *transferre, transposer, translatio,* and *metaphrasis* in the Greek, indicate the translator's ability to render texts 'active' – transferable, malleable – and ultimately responsive to new and urgent contexts.[2] We might therefore approach with caution Joan Kelly's insistence that the advent of humanism made women subservient to a 'patriarchal and misogynous' past.[3] The authors we will encounter were able to commandeer the textual histories and, one might add, the history of textualities, with which the new humanist curriculum brought them into contact, both for their own and their country's benefit. These women were not merely the dutiful disciples of the controversial divines, charismatic pedagogues, and intelligencing statesmen with whom they forged pathways into international political arenas. As we will see, their writings actually helped define the agendas and set the terms for the rhetorical arsenal upon which their male co-activists depended.

Operating at the heart of a Europe-wide community of intellectuals, Margaret More Roper was more than the humanists' show-piece. Their co-equal, she collaborated with them in the propagandist reproduction of her public image in ways which facilitated the dissemination of their shared social vision. For the Cooke sisters, Anne Lock (Dering), Dorcas Martin, and Mary Sidney Herbert, religious translation was not a second-best alternative to secular or 'original' composition,[4] nor a means of softening the provocative edge of their forays into print and manuscript circulation.[5] It was rather the most effective medium for their participation in the politics of nation-building during pivotal phases in the international struggle for radical reform. Women's appropriation of secular texts also afforded them opportunities for intervening critically in English military histories and policies. Mary Sidney Herbert's role as her brother's memorializer authorized her daring reinterpretation of royal emblemature in ways which may have been intended to strengthen the Queen's commitment to the Protestant cause. Anne Dowriche sought, more explicitly, to influence the Elizabethan anti-Catholic initiative. Standing virtually alone as a published female historical writer in this period, Dowriche's isolation in this generic category has obscured the sophisticated strategies of historiographical selection and political commentary which both she and her fellow translators channeled in highly goal-directed ways; an understanding of which, it is hoped, her inclusion in this chapter will help restore.

Whether they were adapting narratives from the distant past, such as the works of the Church Fathers, or texts which looked back to the sufferings of communities closer to home, like the Marian Exiles or the Huguenots in 1570s France, women who translated – literally transferred or transposed – these histories to new cultural, geographical, and political contexts intended their writings to be suasive rather than static. They saw their undertakings as one half of a transaction for which they expected reciprocation from their readers in the form of an anticipated change in belief, behavior, or political outlook; and sometimes the covert bargain they hoped to strike was with no less a personage than their monarch. Their, often radical, textual interventions made them the agents rather than the passive subjects of historical change.

Making a woman of letters: Margaret More Roper among the humanists

In July 1978 a team of archaeologists opened the burial vault of the Roper family in the Church of St Dunstan in Canterbury. What they discovered there would lend flesh to the bones of a national legend: a relationship between father and daughter which stood at the heart of the development of humane letters in Europe exactly five centuries before. Clearing away half a millennium's accumulation of dust and debris, they exposed an iron grate at the northern end of the vault-wall. Behind this was a niche in which there remained fragments of a human skull.[6]

'As St Augustine had his Adeodatus, whose admirable talents he could never sufficiently admire', wrote one of Thomas More's early biographers in 1588, 'so had More his Margaret'.[7] While St Augustine provided the humanists with one of their primary models for scholarly emulation, Stapleton radically overturned the tightly scripted hierarchical order of this pedagogic relationship in his appraisal of Margaret.[8] Though starting life as a devoted pupil of her father's 'school', she grew to become the shrewd political advisor who engaged him in a passionate debate over his decision to refuse the oath ratifying the 1534 Act of Succession.[9] Margaret's subsequent role as a transmitter of More's memory, following his execution on 6 July 1535, so concerned the authorities that she was 'brought before the King's Council, and charged with keeping her father's head as a sacred relic, and retaining possession of his books and his writings'.[10] It is probable that Margaret was buried in Chelsea then re-interred at St Dunstan's, following the death of her husband, William Roper, in 1578, where a niche was made to house in perpetuity the head of England's greatest scholar.[11] The unity of Margaret and her father, even in death, bears testimony to a collaboration which was recognized and memorialized by her immediate descendants. Providing the template for the woman of letters upon which later generations of female scholars would build, the career of Margaret More Roper offers one of the earliest examples of the potential cultural and political reach of women's translation.

In 1529 Erasmus addressed Margaret as the 'ornament of Britain', one of 'that most dear company to which I owe a great part of whatever little fortune or glory I possess'. The plaudit came in recompense for a unique gift which had been sent to him: Holbein's preparatory sketch for what would eventually become the grand portrait of the More family, which survives in a copy made by Rowland Lockey in 1593 (Figure 13.1). In her reply, Margaret scripted herself into a pattern of scholarly reciprocation

299

Figure 13.1 Sir Thomas More and his family, by Rowland Lockey after Holbein. Nostell Priory (The National Trust), ©NTPL/John Hammond.

established by a literary community at whose center stood one of Europe's most productive intellectual partnerships:

> As often as I show it [Erasmus's letter] to anyone, I realize that from it no small praise will accrue to my reputation [...] We pray for nothing more ardently than that we may some time be able to speak face to face with and see our teacher, by whose learned labors we have received whatever of good letters we have imbibed, and one who is the old and faithful friend of our father.[12]

Margaret's reference to her addressee as her teacher is borne out by Lockey's rendering of the Holbein group-portrait in which she reads from Seneca's *Oedipus*, a text issued by the Venetian Aldine Press in a version corrected by Erasmus. The pages to which she points warn against the pitfalls of public service, adapting Plato's metaphor of the ship of state, delineated in his *Republic*, in order to affirm the importance of navigating a reasoned middle course free from the vagaries of over-reaching ambition.[13] More returned to Plato's image in his *Utopia* in which his fictionalized namesake stresses the necessity of influencing 'politics and life at Court' by working 'indirectly' on reforming the prejudices of kings and statesmen through a 'civilized form of philosophy'. Rather than abandoning the 'ship' of 'public life' entirely, the scholar wishing to improve society should use his learning in a manner which is relevant to the 'dramatic context' of 'current' social dilemmas.[14]

Margaret's orchestration of this epistolary and iconographical exchange may have been modeled on an earlier, well-publicized, correspondence involving a double-portrait: the diptych of Erasmus and Peter Gilles commissioned from Quentin Metsys in 1517 as a gift for Thomas More (Figures 13.2 and 13.3). Presented as a diligent student of Erasmus, Gilles is surrounded by works composed or edited by his mentor, including editions of Seneca, Plutarch, and Suetonius. In recompense More produced a laudatory poem identifying the sitters as 'friends as dear to each other as were Castor and Pollux of old'. This exchange, which found a wider readership in the 1518 edition of Erasmus's *Auctarium selectarum epistolarum*, elevated the amicable alliance from which grew the *Utopia*.[15] Margaret's correspondence with Erasmus completes – reciprocates – his first act of gift-giving to More. Revealing her own attempts at managing her public image, the painting and letters stage her role in the transformation of the humanist conception of *bonae litterae*. By the time Holbein's sketch reached Erasmus's desk, the vision of a scholarly community structured primarily around models of masculine friendship, or *amicitia*, had given

Figure 13.2 Quentin Metsys's portrait of Peter Gilles. Photographic Survey, The Courtauld Institute of Art, London. Private Collection.

way to a more expansive notion of male–female relations within the enclave of the family. That Margaret was conscious of, and actively sought to facilitate, the radical change which I am suggesting, can be gleaned from her translation of Erasmus's *Precatio Dominica* (Basel, 1523).[16]

Margaret's *Devout Treatise upon the Pater Noster* was first published in a now lost 1524 edition. The surviving second printing (*c.*1526) carried a frontispiece which presented the female scholar as Erasmian student,

Figure 13.3   Quentyn Metsys's portrait of Erasmus. The Royal Collection ©2010, Her Majesty Queen Elizabeth II.

feminizing the posture of masculine academic discipline which Metsys had established in the humanist imagination (Figure 13.4). While the nineteen-year-old translator was not named in print, both More and Erasmus had been laying the groundwork for the easy identification of Margaret among a Europe-wide humanist community. More had shown Margaret's letters to men 'of the widest attainments in literature' including Reginald Pole, kinsman to Henry VIII, and John Veysey, Bishop of Exeter, who praised her writing 'for its pure Latinity'.[17] Noted for being as skilled a translator as her father, Margaret would go on to earn respect

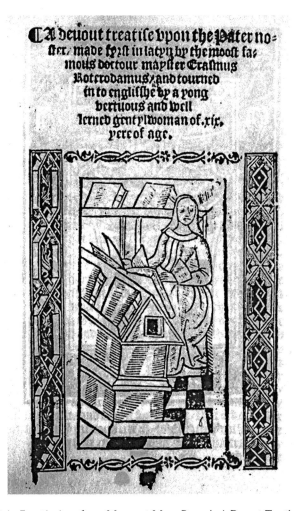

Figure 13.4 Frontispiece from Margaret More Roper's *A Devout Treatise upon the Pater Noster* (*c*.1526). ©The British Library Board. Shelfmark C.37.e.6.

as an editor after correcting a 'corrupted' text of St Cyprian which had been misinterpreted by less competent scholars.[18] By 1521 Erasmus acknowledged that the example of More's daughters had opened his eyes to the moral value of education for women,[19] and within two years Juan Luis Vives publicly praised Margaret and her sisters in the treatise which Richard Hyrde would later go on to translate as the *Instruction of a Christian Woman* before 1528.[20] It was Hyrde, one-time tutor in the

More household, who provided the introductory epistle to Margaret's translation, in which he maintained that 'profe evydente ynough/what good lernyng doth' is to be found in the female translator's own 'pruden[n]t/ humble/and wifely behauor'.[21] This praise of female learning for its domestic utility appears to complement the restrictions More placed on his daughters' education, particularly his injunction that Margaret shun 'the praise of the public'.[22] While this view has defined subsequent critical evaluations of Margaret's impact,[23] we should look to the Senecan compromise which Lockey's painting places directly in her hands for a window into the indirect means with which she served the interests of the Christian humanist vision for public reform.

In 1523, in the shadow of the Zurich council's adoption of wide-scale Zwinglianism, Erasmus completed his *Precatio* and was working on his edition of Prudentius's Christmas hymns which he dedicated to Margaret. A public gesture of reciprocation, Margaret's translation was, perhaps not coincidentally, produced in the very same year in which Erasmus penned his only formal anti-Lutheran statement, the *De Libero Arbitrio Diatribe*. Erasmus's appeal for a reasoned, decidedly non-apocalyptic, approach to social change would shortly be swept away by the beginnings of the Peasants' War which, erupting in parts of Germany in 1524, would end with the slaughter of 70–100,000 people.[24] These ruptures were perhaps forefront in Erasmus's mind when he composed his Colloquy, *The New Mother*, in which the abominations of a Europe in 'anarchy', where 'the Church is shaken to its very foundations by menacing factions', are attributed to 'tyrant [...] custom'. The breast-feeding mother who eschews the custom of employing a wet-nurse is not only brought into metaphorical alignment with the ideal ruler who nurtures his subjects, but becomes the biological foundation for a reformed society because 'she molds' her child in readiness for the 'learning process [...] between teacher and pupil' which underpins the civil order.[25] Similarly, in *The Abbot and the Learned Lady* the witty Magdalia, popularly believed to represent Margaret herself, lauds a Europe-wide community of learned women, among whom are 'the daughters of the More family'. Responding to the Abbot's insistence that women should reject the paraphernalia of education in favor of 'the distaff and the knitting needle', she laments that 'princes and emperors' are no longer 'remarkable for their learning' and condemns those who, embracing 'popular customs, which authorize evil of every sort', refuse to 'accustom' themselves to 'the highest standards' through which 'what used to be unusual will become common'.[26] Female learning occupies the same semantic space as an uncorrupted hierarchical system: both are rare yet, through the discarding of the prejudices of custom, both can become 'common'.

In those *Colloquies* composed after his acquaintance with the talents of More's daughters, Erasmus developed the ideological potential of female pedagogical practice in ways which turned gender-specific familial roles – those of wife, daughter, and mother – into legitimate models for the ideal social and sacred constitution.[27] Learned femininity becomes politically active, capable of furthering the humanists' shared goals: the cultivation of irenic community and the application of human reason against the prejudices arising from a blind adherence to custom.[28] These values tapped a seam of Stoic philosophy descended from the sect's founder Zeno, whose *Republic* demonstrated, according to Plutarch, 'that we should consider all men to be of one community and one polity, and that we should have a common life and an order common to us all'.[29] Margaret's translation urged Christians to reject self-directed appeals to the godhead and instead 'praye in commen' as 'members of one body [...] for that whiche indifferently shalbe expedient and necessary for us all'.[30] This must have acquired further urgency in an English context in which the collapse of the European Peace Treaty of 1518 culminated, less than a year before Margaret took up her pen, in Wolsey's shipping of an army to Calais in readiness for war.[31] Demonstrating a willingness to convey core principles at the heart of the humanist social agenda to a wider audience, Margaret introduces words which, to an English reader, resonated with familiar political connotations. Her frequent use of 'sclaundre', 'bac[k]bytinge', and their variants (e.g. pp. 17, 19, 21, 41), would have evoked corruptions specifically associated with court factionalism.[32] The danger that 'ambicious desire of worldely promocion' (p. 15) poses to a harmonious community is deftly augmented through her use of amplifications; Erasmus's concise 'quo/ties rejecto mamona', for example, rendered 'as often as we forsake and leave honourynge of erthely richesse' (pp. 30–31). The panacea for these ills rests in a rejection of the source of 'erthely' power and wealth in favor of a personal, and highly emotive, relationship with the Divinity, emphasized through Margaret's abundant addition of vocatives; 'Audi pater spiritum' becoming, for instance, 'O father of spyrites' (pp. 14–15). That these ideas may have been recognized by contemporaries as cutting close to the political bone is indicated by the fact that Margaret's translation was investigated for heresy by the Bishop of London's vicar general, Richard Foxford, in 1526.[33] A precursor to the book which Lockey's painting entrusts to More's beloved daughter, this Erasmian text, placed in a woman's hands, constitutes a public declaration of Margaret's role as the humanists' co-collaborator and co-equal on an international stage.

Despite Cresacre More's insistence that Margaret had intended to publish her father's works,[34] this highly political task was left to others to accomplish, among them her daughter Mary Clarke Basset who added her own translation of More's *De Tristitia* to his printed *Workes* in 1557, defining her status as her grandfather's heir 'in kynred, vertue and litterature'.[35] It was, however, Basset's earlier translation of Eusebius's *Ecclesiastical History* which signaled an evolution in the self-conception of the female author. In her dedicatory epistle to the Catholic Mary Tudor, she confidently presented her ability to recuperate the histories 'of sundrye Greke aucthors' which would 'have bene lost [...] to owr knowledge'. Her desire to restore the valuable works which were only available to her contemporaries in 'wonderfully unperfecte and corrupte' form became coterminous with the task of establishing the providentially ratified status of the true church.[36] Margaret More Roper's legacy had given birth to the English woman of letters, aware of her interventionist role in the making of history.

Radical interventions: women as translators of religious texts

In 1570 Queen Elizabeth I attended one of the most memorable lectures of her life. After attacking the 'abominations' of a corrupt church hierarchy the speaker, the Cambridge Puritan Edward Dering, accused his royal auditor of turning a blind eye 'while that all these whordoms are committed'. A failure to 'be zealous as good King David' to 'reforme evill Patrones', he warned, would bring down the vengeance of a 'righteous God' who 'will one day call you to your reckoning'.[37] The Queen's displeasure continued unabated for two years, at which point a group of radical women joined forces in an attempt to regain some royal favor on Dering's behalf by offering as a gift a manuscript of a scientific treatise by Bartholo Sylva of Turin, the *Giardino cosmografico coltivato*. This included prefatory verses composed by Anne Lock, who was Dering's wife, and the Cooke sisters, which mobilized the metaphor of the 'well-ordered [...] garden' as an emblem of the cosmic unity towards which this Protestant community was working.[38] This was reinforced by dazzling illuminations charting the journey of creation from chaos to universal harmony (Figure 13.5).

Four years later the translator James Sandford adopted this imagery in his praise of England's 'learned and eloquente Queene' as the 'best knot in this Garden, that holdeth Englishmen together'. Contrasted to the 'Papistes' who are 'sowers of dissention', Elizabeth is encouraged to 'do greater things' in her role as 'a mightie piller of Gods Church', safe in the knowledge that she will be aided by 'noble Gentlewomen famous for their learning, as the right honourable my Lady Burleigh, my Lady

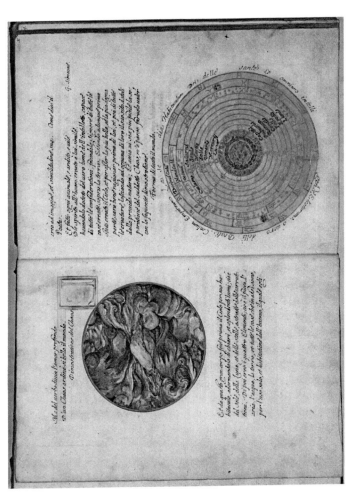

Figure 13.5 Bartholo Sylva of Turin, *Giardino cosmografico coltivato* (c.1572), pages showing diagrammatic renderings of chaos and the cosmos. MS Ii.5.37, fols. 9ᵛ–10ᵛ. Reproduced by kind permission of the Syndics of Cambridge University Library.

Russel, My Lady Bacon, Mistresse Dering, with others'.[39] Both the Sylva manuscript and Sandford's text present the same female community as the wellspring of concord and mutual support. This rhetorical strategy, which pointedly addressed problems at the forefront of foreign and domestic policy for over a decade, was intended to remind the Queen of the instrumental involvement of these well-connected women in the establishment of the Elizabethan constitution.

On 6 May 1561 the Spanish King's ambassador reported his fury at the Queen's closest advisors whom he believed had prevented her participation in negotiations with Catholic representatives at the Council of Trent. Chief among these was the Lord Treasurer, Sir William Cecil, and the Keeper of the Royal Seal, Sir Nicholas Bacon, the former of whom confirmed a week later that he had commissioned an 'apology' in defense of the established church against rumors spread by the Papacy that it had become a factional institution divided within itself.[40] Cecil and Bacon were the husbands of two of the celebrated daughters of Sir Anthony Cooke whose home, Gidea Hall in Essex, had come to be known as a 'little university' (*parua[m]* [...] *academiam*) where 'the studies of women were thriving'.[41] Mildred Cecil's relationship with her husband was, in her own words, driven by 'divine philanthropy' for the 'benefit of the church'.[42] Praised by Roger Ascham in 1550 for her 'surpassing knowledge' of Greek,[43] she translated, perhaps around the same year, *An Homilie or Sermon of Basile the Great*, in which she maintained that because she had 'sup[er]stitiosely observed the nature of the Greke phrase' without 'omittyng the congruity of English speche', she was able to preserve the 'efficacie & value' of a work which would acquire new significance for its English patron's political and pedagogical circle. The text itself opened with a justification of speech made 'profitable' by God who gives 'a voice of some signification' to the 'counsells of oure hartes'.[44] By dedicating it to the Protestant Duchess of Somerset, Mildred was signaling her allegiance to the Edwardian reforming agenda of Cooke's school whose pupils included both Edward VI and the son of the Lord Protector, Duke of Somerset.[45]

Cooke's commitment to the 're-establishing [of] true religion' upon Elizabeth's accession,[46] made Mildred's sister, Anne Bacon, a particularly fitting conduit for John Jewel's *Apologia Ecclesiae Anglicanae* in the English tongue. Published in 1564, her *Apologie* would prove the most compelling propagandist tool of the fledgling Elizabethan establishment. Anne had already helped disseminate Calvinistic teaching between 1548 and 1551 through her Englishing of the sermons of the Italian scholar Bernadino Ochino, defending the international reach of her learning as an endeavor 'co[n]verted to [...] good use in me'.[47] This utilitarian theme was more forcefully re-echoed by Archbishop Matthew Parker, who lauded the translator's achievement as 'publikely beneficiall' because it circumvented 'the perils of ambiguous and doubtful constructions'.[48] A stimulus to universal Protestant consensus, the *Apologie* countered claims that Elizabeth's ministers were 'devided into contrarye partes and opinions' and had 'utterly dyssolved the concorde of the Churche'. Leveling the charge at the Catholics who 'hardly at any time [...] agree betweene themselves', the enumeration of their shameful 'strifes' and 'debates' formed the pretext for a critique of 'corrupt [...] Councielles' deftly designed to justify England's opting out of the Council of Trent.[49]

As the Puritan movement began to gather ground, the very women whom Sandford praised as the Elizabethan regime's supporting pillars strained the coherence of the reformed community through their religious activism. Foremost among these was Anne's sister, the redoubtable Elizabeth Russell, whom Thomas Lodge would dub the 'English Sappho'.[50] In 1605 she published her translation of Bishop Jean Ponet's *Diallacticon viri boni* [...] *Christi in eucharistia*, which had been issued in its Latin original by her father in Strasbourg in 1557.[51] In a private letter to her nephew Robert Cecil she presented her translation as a continuation of the work of Cooke's reforming circle, which had included Ponet, by offering her rendering of 'a Book of his [her father's] own making in Germany' as a 'token' to Cecil for 'so much honouring his Cooke's blood'.[52] While she claimed in the printed version that her purpose in delivering a treatise which harmonized seemingly contradictory Eucharistic doctrines had been to 'study to make enemies friends', the original circumstances in which it circulated in manuscript may have stimulated a more subversive reading.[53] Probably born around 1539–40, not 1528 as has (almost certainly erroneously) been commonly thought, it is possible that Elizabeth Russell translated the work some time between the Strasbourg printing and her father's death in 1576.[54] If this is the case, the text's appeal to 'Princes and Magistrates' to prevent 'the cruell vexation of their Subjects' by removing from 'Ministers of the Church, the [...] desire to strive and rule', would have lit the touchpaper of Presbyterian sentiment circulating among the Puritan faction in the first years of Elizabeth's reign.[55]

At the center of the storm was one of Russell's closest allies, Thomas Cartwright, whose program of radical reform would send shock-waves through the government of the early 1570s, triggering the Admonition Controversy.[56] In his illegally published *Replye* to a tract by Archbishop John Whitgift, the conservative establishment's hammer against the Puritans, Cartwright solidified the terms for the 'spirituall warfare' which was to force him into hiding.[57] Among his many female defenders was Dorcas Martin, who reputedly concealed him from the authorities and, more audaciously, acted as 'the stationer for the first impressions' of his book.[58] Dorcas, who had facilitated the marriage between Anne Lock and Cartwright's follower, Edward Dering, in 1572, was a translator in her own right.[59] Her work had appeared in Thomas Bentley's *Monument of Matrones* (1582), in which she was grouped among the 'heroicall authors' working 'for the common benefit of their countrie'.[60] Over the years Elizabeth Russell would also come to the rescue of many of Cartwright's supporters, among them the Cambridge scholar Edmund Rockray, and James Morrice who, like Russell, was a conscientious objector of Whitgiftian policy.[61] With strictures on the Puritans' activities tightening throughout the 1580s, Anne Bacon decided to petition the Queen to look more favorably on beleaguered nonconformist ministers with the caveat that she 'refuse ye Bishops, for judges, who are parties, partial in their own defence', motivated solely by 'worldly ambition'.[62] Little relief was forthcoming, however, and by 1590 Cartwright was incarcerated in the Fleet Prison from where he sought the aid of Elizabeth Russell whose 'honourable mediation' eventually led to his release some time before 21 May 1592.[63]

It was in 1590 that Anne Lock published her translation of Jean Taffin's Calvinistic text, *Of the markes of the children of God*, refashioning the history of the sufferings of Protestants in the Low Countries in response to the hardships of English Puritans.[64] Perhaps deliberately intended to stir up memories of the Admonition Controversy, her dedicatory epistle to Elizabeth Russell's sister-in-law, the influential Protestant patroness Anne Russell, called upon the faithful to 'admonish' their brothers and sisters so that they may 'awake' from their 'Lethargie' and 'prepare [...] [for] the day of trial'.[65] This advice echoes Dering's admonitions to the many godly women with whom he corresponded – including another of the Cooke sisters, Katherine Killigrew – to imitate biblical figures like Job and David, whose example would encourage them to seek 'remedie in the day of triall'.[66] However, perhaps the most radical appropriation of King David by an author of the Renaissance appears in another of Lock's publications over a decade before her marriage to Dering. In November 1557 Lock was in Geneva, working alongside John Knox, when Calvin delivered his sermons on Isaiah 38. After returning to England, where she helped disseminate Knox's writings, one of Anne Bacon's early publishers, the reformer John Day, issued her translation of the *Sermons of John Calvin* in 1560.[67] Dedicated to the activist Protestant Duchess of Suffolk, it included, arguably, the first sonnet sequence published in English, a verse paraphrase of the text which became synonymous with

Protestant martyrology: Psalm 51. Lock's translation thus participated in a reorientation of English historiographical consciousness for which the Foxean martyrological project served as the catalyst.

Foxe's *Acts and Monuments*, which would also be published by John Day in 1563, was originally issued in a Latin precursor, the *Rera in Ecclesia Gestarum*, in 1559. This text's providential machinery plotted God's unfolding of history not through the actions of a succession of great men, or even, as in the Catholic tradition, individual saints, but through the sufferings of communities of ordinary men and women whose activities united them across social, sexual, and geographical divides. Lock's textual 'medicine' for the 'afflictions' of God's elect merged the monarchical voice and the (potentially female) utterance of the translator with the cries of those who died 'with open mouth' reciting Psalm 51.[68] This may have influenced the Genevan-inspired Psalms of Mary Sidney Herbert, Countess of Pembroke, a generation later in the late 1580s and 1590s.[69] Expanding upon David's exhortation to God to 'Unlock my lipps' (Psalm 51, l. 43),[70] Sidney Herbert appropriates the psalmist's advice to, even admonition of, kings and princes. God's ear is assailed by the suppliant who calls on him to 'Teach' princes how 'to rule thy Realme as justice shall decree' (Psalm 72, ll. 1–3), and more provocatively: 'How long will ye just doome neglect? | how long [...] bad men respect? | ... err not princes you as men must dy' (Psalm 82, ll. 6–28). Such biblical authorization of the right to speak, teach, and admonish could serve as a compelling ratification of female translators' own political activism, drawing the Queen, close to whose court and council they operated, into sympathy with the tormented communities of which they and their (often female) patrons were the representatives.

Sensitive to trends in historiographical inscription, these women exploited the 'catechizing' practices which allowed them to turn communal activity into a galvanizing force for historical and political change. This model gave shape to the radical mission of the Puritan women who gathered around the fiery divine Stephen Egerton, whose 'great congregacion', at the Church of St Anne in the Blackfriars, was an 'auditory, being most of women' which included Elizabeth Russell and her daughter-in-law Margaret Hoby.[71] This ethos also informed the compilation of a *Register* which documented the ordeals of the Puritans in a manner reminiscent of Foxe's *Book of Martyrs*, probably commandeered by Anne Bacon, part of which was illegally published abroad in 1593.[72] These far-reaching networks allowed both Anne and her sister Elizabeth to influence the structure of the intelligence services. Intervening in the titan political struggles between Robert Cecil and the Earl of Essex in the 1590s, they spoke out against 'bad and lewd' suspected double-agents like Anthony Standen and Thomas Wright, and the 'Bloody' and 'prophane, costly fellow' Antonio Pérez.[73] Serving as the unacknowledged national historiographers of their age, the Cooke sisters, and the women who worked alongside them, recorded and disseminated both the trials of their fellow radicals and the spurious intelligencing histories of their powerful political enemies, waging their holy wars on an international battleground.

Secular transactions: women as translators of history

Whenever Henry VIII stood before his grand tapestry which depicted the *Triumph of Fame* he must have been struck by the figure of the King who, sharing the fate of Pope and Cardinal, lies crushed beneath the wheels of Death's chariot (Figure 13.6), a scene adorned with the motto: 'Fame proclaims the great deeds of the dead, so that the actions of those, who by their greatness have deserved glory, shall be remembered after their death'.[74] The tapestry was one of a series based on Petrarch's influential *I Trionfi*, composed between 1352 and 1374, which bodied forth the poet's love of Laura through a series of allegorical 'triumphs'. Flanked on either side by vignettes showing the conquering of Chastity by Death and the succeeding triumph of a winged Fame, a mysterious female figure looks out at the viewer from the center of the tapestry. Dressed in ermine, a traditional symbol of purity, she is crowned and holds aloft a sword, echoing emblematic representations of Justice. The tapestry offers the ruler a choice: be the humiliated victim trampled under Death's triumphal car or seize the immortality conferred by monumental acts of greatness.

When Mary Sidney Herbert, Countess of Pembroke, decided to translate Petrarch's *Triumph of Death*, she was appropriating a text which came to be as closely associated with the Elizabethan as it was with the Henrician court. In her youth Elizabeth I may have translated part of the *Trionfo della Divinità* and, when she became the great Virgin Queen, she would be entertained with pageants embellished with Petrarchan motifs, particularly those deriving from the *Trionfo della Castità* which was raided for her progress to Suffolk in 1578 and, three years later, for her Accession Day tilt in which Mary Sidney Herbert's brother, Philip Sidney, participated.[75] This iconographical program also infiltrated royal portraiture, including the 'Ermine Portrait' (1585), attributed to William Segar (Figure 13.7).[76] Mary Sidney Herbert's *Triumph of Death* succeeds the symbolic repertoire of Chastity's victories which formed such a potent vehicle for the Queen's public image in her youth. As Danielle

313

Figure 13.6 Tapestry depicting Petrarch's *Triumph of Fame*, virtually identical to one owned by Henry VIII. ©V&A Images/ Victoria and Albert Museum, London.

Figure 13.7   The 'Ermine Portrait', atributed to Wiliam Segar. By permission of the Marquess of Salisbury/Hatfield House.

Clarke suggests, this 'pointed to, rather than concealed Elizabeth's own decline into mortality', recalling the kind of panegyric or epideictic poetry which intermingled 'praise with blame, flattery with criticism'.[77] This is indicative of the ambiguous royal praise versified by Edmund Spenser in the 1590s. In the *Faerie Queene*, the 'Mutabilite Cantos' present a triumphal procession, modeled on the *I Trionfi*, headed by Mutabilitie who offers a startling critique of Elizabeth's mythic avatar Cynthia as one 'mortall borne' whose 'face and countenance every day | We changed see [...] | Now hornd [...] now bright, now brown and gray'.[78] This certainly appears to match Sidney Herbert's presentation of Laura who, bearing a triumphal banner of 'Snowie Ermiline' (part I, l. 19), which would have recalled images of Elizabeth I, returns 'from hir warre's a joyefull Conqueresse' (part I, l. 4) to be confronted by Death who ridicules her for 'Standing upon thy youth, and beawties state' while 'of thy life, the limit's doest not knowe' (part I, ll. 35–36). However, Spenser skillfully balances Mutabilitie's unflattering portrait of Cynthia with a Petrarchan triumph of 'Eternity', the closing appeal to 'the God of Sabbaoth' hinting at the immortal repose which succeeds the divine accomplishment of the six days' work of creation.[79] Sidney Herbert's *Triumph*, I suggest, functions analogously to prompt Elizabeth to her own great work of decisive political action for the Protestant cause by manipulating flattering and critical mirror-images of monarchical rule.

When Mary Sidney Herbert translates Laura's defiant response to Death she renders Petrarch's 'che fu nel mondo una' as 'Replide then she, who in the world was one' (part I, l. 51), a version which G. F. Waller calls 'rather flat'.[80] In the *Tryumphes of Fraunces Petrarcke* by Henry Parker, Lord Morley, a full translation of the *I Trionfi* published in 1554, the same line is Englished with a logical paraphrase as 'This excellent Lady having no peare'.[81] Rather than being a bad choice of phrasing on Sidney Herbert's part, it is possible that she was intentionally alluding to Elizabeth I's motto *Semper Eadem* ('Always One'). Drawing attention to this well-recognized emblem of the Virgin Queen's singularity allowed Sidney Herbert to mobilize alternative portraits of royalty in a more provocative fashion. In Morley's poem Laura engages in a dialogue with a clearly male 'fury' of Death (sig. G2ʳ) while Sidney Herbert's Laura is accosted by a female figure who is given the paraphernalia of queenship in the form of a 'scepter' (part I, l. 63), a detail which is missing in the earlier English text (sig. G3ʳ). Shattering the icon of royal unity she has conjured, Sidney Herbert offers an image of 'cruell' Death (part I, l. 58) as demonic monarch followed almost immediately by the tragic visionary bathos of 'Popes, Emperors, and kings [...] | All naked now, all needie beggars all' who, dying, will 'hardlie leave your verie names behinde' (part I, ll. 80–90). The social instability which proceeds from an ill-governed state, alluded to throughout the poem, is given a historical locus in Petrarch's itemization of 'tyrauntes' rendered by Morley as 'Silla, Nero, Cayus, and Maryus' (sig. H2ʳ). Sidney Herbert, however, detaches her interpretation from its classical specificity by reducing this to 'Tyrrants olde' (part II, l. 43), opening up possibilities of association with Protestant sufferings through her Christological allusion to 'the crosse' which 'extreemelie martireth' and 'the panting soule [which] in God take's breath', the latter lifted from Philip Sidney's paraphrase of Psalm 42 (part II, ll. 46–49).[82]

As critics have recognized, Sidney Herbert's expansion of her brother's Psalms, as well as her interest in translating works associated with the memento mori tradition, allowed her to combine her role as a memorializer of the man who came to be known as the 'English Petrarque'[83] with the continuation of their shared religious activism.[84] In her Englishing of Robert Garnier's 1585 edition of *Marc Antonie*, Cleopatra becomes the living embodiment of the 'funerals' and 'oblations' due to Antony's 'Image great', urging her women to become 'Martir[s]' (ll. 1981–2009) to his memory in ways which resonate with Abraham Fraunce's descriptions of the mourning rites practiced by Sidney Herbert and her female coterie in his *Ivychurch*.[85] Recontextualizing images of a collapsing political constitution originally relevant to Garnier's France, Sidney Herbert presents Cleopatra's noble stoicism through the prism of a Calvinistic resilience in the face of prolonged suffering.[86] It is perhaps significant that Sidney Herbert's *Antonius* was published in 1592 with her translation of the *Discours de la Vie et de la Mort* (1576) by Philippe du Plessis-Mornay, a close friend of Philip Sidney and co-sympathizer with the Huguenot cause.[87] Detailing the corruptions of a series of historical and biblical kings (ll. 353–459), Mornay advises those in public service in particular 'to serve God' (l. 948) who will give them the courage to face the 'threatnings of tyrants' and 'the swords of [...] enemies' (ll. 910–11). Mary Sidney Herbert's *Triumph* continues the agenda of her wider textual enterprise, mobilizing her personal history, as the guardian of her brother's memory, for the purpose of authorizing her reinterpretation of literary discourses which had become powerfully emblematic of English national history. The trajectory of this mission is perhaps best summed up in her rendering of Petrarch's heartfelt plea to Laura: 'Ma'l viver senza voi m'è duro e greve'. Literally translated as 'It is hard for me to live without you', a sense followed closely by Morley (sig. 11ʳ), Sidney Herbert reinterprets it in a way which has perplexed critics: 'But what is left of yow to live behind' (part II, l. 186).[88] Recapitulating the kind of politically charged allegorical strategies which were woven into Henry VIII's *Fame* tapestry, Sidney Herbert's liberty with her original allows her to place a direct challenge before her Queen, encouraging her to accomplish a great work in the service of true religion before her death. With such a work the great Gloriana would 'live behind' a legacy that would deserve the praise of Fame.

By translating a secular work in the 'triumph' tradition, with all its warlike associations, Mary Sidney Herbert was engaging, in more pointedly political fashion, with the critique delivered by Margaret Tyler in her bold preface to *The Mirrour of Princely Deedes and Knighthood* (c.1578), her translation of the first part of Diego Ortúñez de Calahorra's *Espejo de principes y cavalleros*. Tyler offers a provocative challenge to men's 'claim to be sole possessioners of knowledge' by advancing the idea that the 'report of armes' should not only be the preserve of 'you men which [...] are fighters' but should concern 'us women, to whom the benefit in equal part apperteineth of your victories'.[89] Sharing the concerns of many of the female translators we have been exploring, Anne Dowriche provided a yet more daring intervention in the historiography of political and religious conflict in her *French Historie* (1589), a verse adaptation of Thomas Tymme's *Three Partes of the Commentaries* [...] *of the Civill Warres of Fraunce* (1574), itself a translation of Jean de Serres's monumental Latin *Commentariorum* begun in 1572.[90] In her survey of female historical writers Natalie Zemon Davies lamented that 'When Queen Elizabeth had Cecil commission a historian for her reign, no female was entrusted with that task.'[91] It was, however, a task which Anne Dowriche had taken upon herself.

In the same year in which her full name confidently appeared on her *Historie*, Timothy Bright published a work which closely matched hers in its relation to an epoch-defining *ur*-text. In his *Abridgement of the Booke of Acts and Monumentes*, Bright sought to stimulate in the reader 'an assay, and appetite, to know further' which would lead them to a better engagement with Foxe's, more perfect, text.[92] In contrast, Dowriche described her own creative process as an active 'collecting & framing' of source material whose 'substance', too 'lightly touched' by the original authors, she had 'amplified' through a series of highly dramatized speeches intended to reveal 'of purpose the nature both of the person that speaks and also of the matter that is spoken [...] lively set downe'.[93] Offering, through the lips of a French exile, an emotive rendering of the sufferings of the Huguenots and the St Bartholomew's Day Massacre of 24 August 1572, Dowriche expands upon the providentialist reframing of biblical and martyrological narrative undertaken in Tymme's first act of translation. Beginning with the pre-Christian 'Fathers' of the Old Testament, Tymme reorients the history of Huguenot persecution into alignment with English national consciousness by tracing the gradual revelation of 'Christes Churche' from 'the common wealth of the Lordes Israell' to 'our time', represented by the father of English Protestant hagiography 'Maister John Foxe oure Countrey man'.[94] Dowriche, I suggest, unsettles Tymme's patriarchal historiography through a politicized staging of royal femininity activated by a new context. After the defeat of the Spanish Armarda, with England's financial resources strained by a new anti-Spanish military offensive, the nation's fate rested on Elizabeth I's willingness to support Henri IV's campaign against the Catholic League which, in receipt of Spanish funds, was threatening to conquer France.[95] With the League poised to seize a doorway to the rest of Europe, Dowriche's presentation of the two powerful female figures who preside, either explicitly or implicitly, over her *Historie* – Katherine de Medici, the Queen Mother, and Queen Elizabeth I – takes on a poignant urgency.

Katherine de Medici is given a central place in Dowriche's narrative as the prime agent of the gravest horrors visited upon the Protestants. When she sets her 'bloodie plot' in motion, she uncannily comes to epitomize the dramatizing tendencies of the *Historie* itself: 'But here the Prologue ends, and here begins the plaie [...] | The Mother Queene appears now first upon the Stage' (sigs. G3ʳ–G3ᵛ). This curious mirroring is intensified through the text's almost Machiavellian self-consciousness. Dowriche follows her contemporaries by drawing on the stereotypes attached to Katherine's Florentine background. Hotman, for example, maintained that 'since the Administration of the Realme was co[m]mitted to the Queene mother' it has become 'a common sinke of *Italie*',[96] while Henry Estienne associated Katherine's 'cruel tyranny' with the 'histories of *Florence*', Italy's wellspring of Machiavellian 'craft and subtiltie'.[97] Dowriche's Katherine is also presented as a dedicated 'scholar' of the Florentine controversialist and her speech is interlaced with marginal annotations glossing the Machiavellian precepts which fill her 'womans minde', including his well-known injunction to 'the Prince to plaie the Foxe, | And Lion-like to rage', the model which most exemplifies the 'wisedome matcht with policie' with which she hopes to effect her political machinations (sigs. G3ᵛ–G4ʳ). In her dedicatory epistle Dowriche uses the same Machiavellian terminology, describing her poem as a document 'worthie [...] for policie the observing' (sig. A2ᵛ). Her belief that her text can provide a valuable training in 'policie' echoes the instruction Katherine de Medici has herself undergone, as a pupil of Machiavelli, and which the reader similarly undergoes in her/his consumption of the poem's marginal apparatus. It is within this strange slippage that the potentially radical import of Dowriche's interest in female power inheres.

Randall Martin interprets Dowriche's Machiavellian allusions collectively as a form of strategic moral coding which serves to pit the

Figure 13.8 The Marian Hanging, embroidered with the motto *Virescit Vulnere Virtus*. ©V&A Images/Victoria and Albert Museum, London.

Huguenots' 'nonaggressive self-possession and communitarian human-ity' against Katherine de Medici's 'gender-specific and rhetorical activ-ism'.[98] Dowriche deliberately evokes only to overturn this binary model in her closing appeal to the English Queen to act both as 'chiefe Pastor of thy sheepe' and wily predator who will 'finde oute, and hunt with perfect hate | The Popish hearts of fained frends before it be too late' (sig. L1[r]). Her textual labors therefore become a transaction in which direct political action will form the reciprocating gesture. Significantly, the emblem of the 'hunt' for the hart/heart, with its connotations of violence and anatomical violation, reverberates on the final page of the *Historie* in a cartouche bearing the Latin motto *Virescit Vulnere Veritas* (Truth flourishes through a wound/Truth flourishes by wounding). Ambiguously exhorting either patient suffering or justified aggression, the motto conceals a subversive political history. Mary Queen of Scots, for example, used a variation of this dictum – replacing *Veritas* (Truth) with *Virtus* (Virtue) – in a piece of needlework which may have carried an insidious coded plea to her co-conspirators to cut away the fruitless branch of her bloodline (Figure 13.8). Whether the *Historie* articulates a 'warning' to Elizabeth[99] or a demand for a more ruthless domestic, and ultimately foreign, policy, Dowriche's dramatization of queenly authority deftly calls for an appropriation and moralized redefinition (rather than a complete rejection) of Machiavellian teaching for the benefit of God's elect. The Queen must play the fox and the lion. Dowriche is a more sophisticated analyst of political historiography than she has often been given credit for. By choosing to write a history she adopted a reactive medium which, as Thomas Blundeville noted in his *Methode of Wryting and Reading Hystories* (1574), 'direct[ed]' the reader's 'private action' with the intention of influencing 'publyke causes'.[100]

The women we have encountered in this chapter all wielded their pens in order to become active shapers of the – sometimes subversive, always turbulent – intellectual, political, and national histories which the interventionist power of their extraordinary learning placed within their hands.

Acknowledgments

Thanks are due to the British Academy for their support; Caroline Bicks, Jennifer Summit and Ema Vyroubalova; the Marquess of Salisbury and Robin Harcourt Williams of Hatfield House; Cressida Williams and Amy Jones of Canterbury Cathedral Archives; Jaime Goodrich; and Benjamin Doyle and Jo North of Palgrave Macmillan.

Notes

1. Jonathan Goldberg counters this notion in his *Desiring Women Writing: English Renaissance Examples* (Stanford: Stanford University Press, 1997), p. 75. For a similarly valuable revisionist reading see Micheline White, 'Renaissance Englishwomen and Religious Translations: The Case of Anne Lock's *Of the Markes of the Children of God* (1590)', *English Literary Renaissance* 29 (September, 1999), 375–400. On the prestige of Renaissance translation see Flora Ross Amos, *Early Theories of Translation* (1920) (Charleston: Bibliobazaar, 2007), pp. 81–121. A concise survey of female translators appears in Paul Salzman's *Reading Early Modern Women's Writing* (Oxford: Oxford University Press, 2006), pp. 12–14.
2. Luise von Flotow, 'Translation in the Politics of Culture', in *The Politics of Translation in the Middle Ages and Renaissance*, ed. Renate Blumenfeld-Kosinski, Luise von Flotow, and Daniel Russell (Ottawa: University of Ottawa Press, 2001), pp. 9–15. The etymological root of translation is explored in ibid. by Renate Blumenfeld-Kosinski and Daniel Russell, pp. 16 and 29.
3. Joan Kelly, 'Did Women Have a Renaissance?', in *Women, History, and Theory: The Essays of Joan Kelly* (Chicago and London: Chicago University Press, 1984), p. 35.
4. Louise Schleiner, *Tudor and Stuart Women Writers* (Bloomington and Indianapolis: Indiana University Press, 1994), p. 51; Elaine Beilin, *Redeeming Eve: Women Writers of the English Renaissance* (Princeton: Princeton University Press, 1987), p. xxii; Tina Krontiris, *Oppositional Voices: Women as Writers and Translators of Literature in the English Renaissance* (London: Routledge, 1992), p. 10.
5. Margaret W. Ferguson, 'Renaissance Concepts of the "Woman Writer"', in *Women and Literature in Britain 1500–1700*, ed. Helen Wilcox (Cambridge: Cambridge University Press, 1996), p. 159.
6. The archaeological report and investigation of the vault's human remains are held in the Canterbury Cathedral Archives, CCA-DC6-E/F/Canterbury, St. Dunstan/37. See also Tim Tatton-Brown, 'The Roper Chantry in St Dunstan's Church, Canterbury', Canterbury Cathedral Archives, 76/18.
7. Thomas Stapleton, *The Life and Illustrious Martyrdom of Sir Thomas More*, trans. Philip E. Hallett, ed. E. E. Reynolds (London: Burns and Oates, 1966), pp. 103–04.
8. On the use of figures like St Augustine and St Jerome by the humanists see Lisa Jardine, *Erasmus, Man of Letters: The Construction of Charisma in Print* (Princeton: Princeton University Press, 1993), pp. 55–82.
9. Stapleton, *Life*, pp. 147–63. See *Calendar of State Papers, Foreign and Domestic, of the Reign of Henry VIII, 1534*, ed. J. Gairdner, 21 vols (London: Longman & Co., 1862–1932), VII (1883), entries 575, 1114, 1117–19, and ibid. VIII (1885), for 1535, entries 659 and 815, for examples of these political debates. See also Peter Iver Kaufman's 'Absolute Margaret: Margaret More Roper and "Well Learned Men"', *Sixteenth Century Journal* 20.3 (Autumn, 1989), 443–56. It was More who referred to his children collectively as his 'school': Stapleton, *Life*, p. 97.
10. Stapleton, *Life*, pp. 191–93.
11. H. O. Albin, 'Opening of the Roper Vault in St Dunstan's, Canterbury and Thoughts on the Burial of William and Margaret Roper', *Moreana* 63 (1979), 29–35, and *Thomas More and Canterbury*, ed. Hugh O. Albin (Bath: Downside Abbey, 1994).

322 *The History of British Women's Writing, 1500–1610*

12. From the translations in E. E. Reynolds, *Margaret Roper, Eldest Daughter of St. Thomas More* (London: Burns & Oates, 1960), pp. 53–55.

13. Plato, *Republic*, trans. Robin Waterfield (Oxford: Oxford University Press, 1993), pp. 208–11. For the identification of Seneca's text see John Guy, *A Daughter's Love: Thomas and Margaret More* (London: Fourth Estate, 2008), pp. 174–75.

14. Thomas More, *Utopia*, trans. Paul Turner (Harmondsworth: Penguin, 1965), pp. 63–64.

15. Jardine, *Erasmus*, pp. 28–29. For the translation of More's poem see David R. Carlson, *English Humanist Books: Writers and Patrons, Manuscript and Print, 1475–1525* (Toronto: University of Toronto Press, 1993), p. 145.

16. For a reading which focuses more specifically on the role of male friendship throughout Erasmus's career see Jardine, *Erasmus*, pp. 27–34.

17. Letters from More to Roper, dated between 1522 and 1523, *St Thomas More: Selected Letters*, ed. Elizabeth Frances Rogers (New Haven: Yale University Press, 1961), pp. 151–54.

18. Cresacre More, *The Life and Death of Sir Thomas Moore* (Antwerp[?], 1631), p. 184, BL, 1130.f.30. See also Stapleton, *Life*, pp. 103–04. For Margaret's training as a translator see John Archer Gee, 'Margaret Roper's English Version of Erasmus' *Precatio Dominica* and the Apprenticeship behind Early Tudor Translation', *Review of English Studies* 12 (1937), 257–71.

19. Letter to Guillaume Budé, P. S. Allen, *Opus Epistolarum Des Erasmi Roterodami*, 12 vols (Oxford: Clarendon Press, 1965), IV, Ep. 1233, pp. 578–79.

20. Elizabeth McCutcheon, 'The Learned Woman in Tudor England: Margaret More Roper', in *Women Writers of the Renaissance and Reformation*, ed. Katharina M. Wilson (Athens: University of Georgia Press, 1987), p. 461.

21. *A Devout Treatise upon the Pater Noster* (London, c.1526), sig. A4ᵛ, BL, C.37e. a.6(1).

22. Rogers (ed.), *Selected Letters*, pp. 103–05 and 155.

23. See Gloria Kaufman, 'Juan Luis Vives on the Education of Women', *Signs* 3 (1978), 891–96, and J. K. Sowards, 'Erasmus and the Education of Women', *Sixteenth Century Journal* 13 (1982), 77–89.

24. Ulinka Rublack, *Reformation Europe* (Cambridge: Cambridge University Press, 2005), pp. 27 and 72–73; Guy, *A Daughter's Love*, pp. 138–39.

25. *The Colloquies of Erasmus*, trans. Craig R. Thompson (Chicago and London: University of Chicago Press, 1965), pp. 269–70 and 283.

26. *The Praise of Folly and Other Writings*, trans. Robert M. Adams (New York: W.W. Norton & Co., 1989), pp. 224–25.

27. For an alternative view which presents the *Colloquies* as strategically exploiting 'the horror of effeminacy', see Barbara Correll, 'Malleable Material, Models of Power: Woman in Erasmus's "Marriage Group" and *Civility in Boys*', *English Literary History* 57 (1990), 241–62 (p. 258).

28. Robert P. Adams, 'Designs by More and Erasmus for a New Social Order', *Studies in Philology* 42 (1945), 131–45.

29. Plutarch, *Moralia*, trans. Frank Cole Babbitt, 15 vols (Cambridge, MA: Harvard University Press, 1936), IV, p. 397.

30. From the parallel translation in 'Erasmus' paraphrase of the *Pater Noster* (1523) with its English translation by Margaret Roper (1524)', *Moreana* 7 (1965), 9–64 (p. 15). Hereafter page numbers will appear in parentheses.

31. John Guy, *Tudor England* (Oxford: Oxford University Press, 1988), pp. 105–08.
32. These terms had political (courtly) import throughout the sixteenth and seventeenth centuries. For examples see Anon., *A Plaine Description of the Auncient Petigree of Dame Slaunder [...] Lying, Flattering, Backebyting* (London, 1573), BL, 245.d.4; Nicholas Breton, *A Murmurer* (London, 1607), BL, C.27. d.7; and Edmund Spenser's description of Sclaunder in *The Faerie Queene*, ed. A. C. Hamilton (London and New York: Longman, 1977), IV.8.24–26.
33. Goldberg, *Desiring Women Writing*, pp. 108–09.
34. McCutcheon, 'The Learned Woman in Tudor England', p. 456.
35. *The Workes of Sir Thomas More Knyght* (London, 1557), in *The Early Modern Englishwoman: A Facsimile Library of Essential Works, Early Tudor Translators: Margaret Beaufort, Margaret More Roper and Mary Basset*, Series I, Printed Writings, 1500–1640: Part 2, ed. Lee Cullen Khanna (Aldershot: Ashgate, 2001), publisher's preface, p. 1350.
36. London, British Library, Harleian MS 1860, fol. 5ʳ.
37. *M. Derings Workes [...]* (London, 1597), pp. 27–28, BL, 3755.aa.7. See also William Haller, *The Rise of Puritanism* (New York: Harper and Brothers, 1957), pp. 13–14.
38. Cambridge, Cambridge University Library MS Ii.5.37. This is my own translation from the Greek poem offered by Elizabeth (Cooke) Russell. A translation by Lynn Roller of the full poem appears in Schleiner, *Tudor and Stuart Women Writers*, p. 41.
39. James Sandford, *Houres of recreation, or Afterdinners, Which may aptly be called The Garden of Pleasure [...]* (London, 1576), sigs. A4ᵛ–A7ᵛ, BL, 12316.aa.27. See also Susan M. Felch, '"Noble Gentlewomen famous for their learning": The London Circle of Anne Vaughan Lock', *ANQ* 16 (2003), 14–16.
40. Kew, National Archives, SP 70/26, fol. 59ᵛ. An account of the context in which the *Apology* was written appears in J. E. Booty's introduction to *An Apology of the Church of England By John Jewel* (Ithaca: Cornell University Press, 1963).
41. Walter Haddon, *Lucubrationes, Epistolae, Poemata [...]* (London, 1567), p. 131 (the translation is my own), BL, 90.h.17. On the education of the Cooke daughters see Mary Ellen Lamb, 'The Cooke Sisters: Attitudes toward Learned Women in the Renaissance', in *Silent But for the Word: Tudor Women as Patrons, Translators, and Writers of Religious Works*, ed. Margaret P. Hannay (Kent, OH: Kent State University Press, 1985), pp. 108–25.
42. London, British Library, Landsdowne MS 104, c.1571, fol. 158ʳ. From a Greek letter written by Mildred Cecil (the translation from the original Greek is my own).
43. *The Whole Works of Roger Ascham*, ed. Rev. Dr Giles, 3 vols (London: John Russell Smith, 1865), I, part 1, p. lxxi.
44. London, British Library, Royal MS 17Bxviii, Dedicatory Epistle, 2ᵛ, and fols. 3ʳ–4ʳ respectively.
45. 'Letters of Lady Elizabeth Russell (1540–1609)', ed. Elizabeth Farber (unpublished doctoral dissertation, Columbia University, 1977), p. 14.
46. Sir Anthony Cooke to Peter Martyr, London, 12 February 1559, *The Zurich Letters (Second Series), 1558–1602*, ed. Hastings Robinson (Cambridge: Cambridge University Press, 1845), p. 13.

47. *Certayne Sermons of* [...] *B Ochine* (London: 1550[?]), Dedicatory Epistle, BL, 3901.a.31. For the printing history of Anne Bacon's Ochino translations see Alan Stewart, 'The Voices of Anne Cooke, Lady Anne and Lady Bacon', in *'This Double Voice': Gendered Writing in Early Modern England*, ed. Danielle Clarke and Elizabeth Clarke (Basingstoke and New York: Macmillan, 2000), pp. 88–102.
48. *An Apologie or Answere in Defence of the Churche of Englande* (London, 1564), Dedicatory Epistle, BL, C.12.c.12. C.S.
49. Ibid., sigs. A4^v, C5^r–C6^v and M8^r.
50. *A Margarite of America* (London, 1596), Dedicatory Epistle, BL, C.14.a.2.
51. On Cooke's connection to Ponet see Marjorie Keniston McIntosh, 'Sir Anthony Cooke: Tudor Humanist, Educator, and Religious Reformer', *Proceedings of the American Philosophical Society* 119 (1975), 233–50.
52. Hatfield House, Cecil Papers 197.53.
53. *A Way of Reconciliation* [...] *Touching* [...] *the Sacrament* (London, 1605), *The Early Modern Englishwoman: A Facsimile Library of Essential Works, Protestant Translators: Anne Lock Prowse and Elizabeth Russell*, Series I, Printed Writings, 1500–1640: Part 2, vol. 12, ed. Elaine Beilin (Aldershot: Ashgate, 2001), sig. A1^v.
54. For Elizabeth Russell's birth date see Farber, *Letters*, and Helen Gladstone, 'Building an Identity: Two Noblewomen in England 1556–1666' (unpublished doctoral thesis, Open University, 1989). The erroneous date of 1528 appears in both the *DNB* and *ODNB*. Russell's claim, in her *Reconciliation's* dedicatory epistle, that her translation had been 'approved' by 'the dead [...] in his life', could refer either to Ponet or her father, indicating that either one had seen or merely consented to the text's Englishing. Cooke had purchased Ponet's entire library after his death in 1556: see letter from Maria Ponet to Peter Martyr, Strasbourg, 15 July 1557, *Original Letters Relative to the English Reformation*, ed. Hastings Robinson, 2 vols (Cambridge: Cambridge University Press, 1846), II, pp. 118–19.
55. Russell, *A Way of Reconciliation*, pp. 103–04.
56. For this episode in Cartwright's career see M. M. Reese, *The Tudors and Stuarts* (London: Edward Arnold, 1940), pp. 148–49; Conyers Read, *Lord Burghley and Queen Elizabeth* (London: Jonathan Cape, 1960), pp. 112–13; and Haller, *Rise of Puritanism*, pp. 11–12.
57. *A Replye to an Answere made of M. Doctor Whitegifte* [...] (London, c.1573), sig. B4^r, BL, T.2108(1). For more on the Admonition Controversy see Patrick Collinson, *The Elizabethan Puritan Movement* (London: Jonathan Cape, 1967), pp. 131–45, and A. F. Scott Pearson, *Thomas Cartwright and Elizabethan Puritanism 1535–1603* (Cambridge: Cambridge University Press, 1925), pp. 83–104.
58. *The Remains of Edmund Grindal*, ed. William Nicholson (Cambridge: Cambridge University Press, 1843), pp. 347–48.
59. Micheline White, 'A Biographical Sketch of Dorcas Martin: Elizabethan Translator, Stationer, and Godly Matron', *The Sixteenth Century Journal* 30 (Autumn, 1999), 775–92. For Dering's support of Cartwright see his letter to William Cecil, London, British Library, Landsdowne MS 12.86, dated 18 November 1570.
60. *The Monument of Matrones* (London, 1582), sig. B1^r, BL, 845.c.21.
61. Letter from Elizabeth Russell to William Cecil, Kew, National Archives, SP, Domestic, 12/77.11, dated 31 January 1571; and letter to Robert Cecil,

Hatfield House, Cecil Papers 170.53, dated May 1593. For Elizabeth Russell's criticism of Whitgift's policies see her letter to Robert Cecil, Hatfield House, Cecil Papers 25.51, dated 24 February 1595, and the account of her political activities in Chris Laoutaris, 'The Radical Pedagogies of Lady Elizabeth Russell', in *Performing Pedagogy in Early Modern England: Gender, Instruction, and Performance*, ed. Kathryn M. Moncrief and Kathryn R. McPherson (forthcoming from Ashgate).

62. Letter to William Cecil, London, British Library, Lansdowne MS 115, fol. 125ʳ, dated 26 February 1584.

63. Letter from Thomas Cartwright to Elizabeth Russell, London, British Library, Landsdowne MS 68.58, dated 13 August 1591. The letter is printed in appendix XXIX of Pearson, *Thomas Cartwright*, pp. 467–70.

64. White, 'Renaissance Englishwomen and Religious Translations', p. 384.

65. *Of the markes of the children of God, and of their comforts in afflictions* (London, 1590), sigs. A2ʳ–A4ʳ, BL, C.119.dd.41.

66. Edward Dering, *Certaine goldy and very comfortable letters* (1590), in *M. Derings Workes* [...] (London, 1597), sig. A7ᵛ, and sigs. B5ᵛ, B7ʳ, B8ʳ, C2ʳ, C4ʳ, C8ʳ, and D2ʳ, for examples of Dering's use of Job and David, BL, 3755.aa.7.

67. Patrick Collinson, 'The Role of Women in the English Reformation Illustrated by the Life and Friendships of Anne Locke', in *Studies in Church History*, ed. G. J. Cuming (London: Thomas Nelson and Sons, 1965), II, pp. 258–72.

68. *Sermons of John Calvin* (London, 1560), Beilin, *Early Modern Englishwoman*, sigs. A2ʳ, A3ᵛ, and H7ʳ. For the use of Psalm 51 by women in Foxe's later English version of the *Book of Martyrs* see Ellen Macek, 'The Emergence of a Feminine Spirituality in the *Book of Martyrs*', *Sixteenth Century Journal* 19 (1988), 63–80. For Lock's possible appeal to Queen Elizabeth and the debate surrounding her composition of the sonnet sequence see Rosalind Smith, '"In a mirrour clere": Protestantism and Politics in Anne Lok's *Miserer mei Deus*', in *'This Double Voice'*, pp. 41–60, and Teresa Lanpher Nugent, 'Anne Lock's Poetics of Spiritual Abjection', *English Literary Renaissance* 39 (2009), 3–23.

69. On Mary Sidney Herbert's knowledge of Lock's sonnet sequence see the introduction to *The Psalmes of David*, in *The Collected Works of Mary Sidney Herbert, Countess of Pembroke*, ed. Margaret P. Hannay, Noel J. Kinnamon, and Michael G. Brennan, 2 vols (Oxford: Clarendon Press, 1998), II, pp. 7–8. All references to Mary Sidney Herbert's *Psalmes* will be from this edition.

70. For a comparison of Lock and Sidney Herbert see Margaret P. Hannay, '"Unlock my lipps": The *Miserer mei Deus* of Anne Vaughan Lock and Mary Sidney Herbert, Countess of Pembroke', in *Privileging Gender in Early Modern England*, ed. Jean R. Brink, *Sixteenth Century Essays and Studies* (Michigan: Edwards Brothers, 1993), pp. 29–36.

71. *Diary of John Mannigngham*, ed. John Bruce (Westminster: J. B. Nichols and Sons, 1868), pp. 74 and 101–2; *The Private Life of an Elizabethan Lady: The Diary of Lady Margaret Hoby 1599–1605*, ed. Joanna Moody (Gloucestershire: Sutton Publishing, 1998), pp. 119–20, 124, 134, 136, 205, and 207.

72. William Muss-Arnolt, 'Puritan Efforts and Struggles, 1550–1603: A Bio-Bibliographical Study', *American Journal of Theology* 23.4 (October, 1919), 471–99 (p. 473).

73. Letter from Elizabeth Russell to Anthony Bacon, dated 8 September 1596, *Memoirs of the Reign of Queen Elizabeth* [...], 2 vols (London: A. Millar,

1754), II, p. 129; Letter from Anne Bacon to Anthony Bacon, dated 27 April 1594, *A Spaniard in Elizabethan England: The Correspondence of Antonio Pérez's Exile*, ed. Gustav Ungerer, 2 vols (London: Tamesis Books, 1974), I, p. 219.

74. The tapestry (Victoria and Albert Museum, London) was produced *c*.1520 and is virtually identical to that which Henry VIII once owned. See Thomas P. Campbell, *Tapestry in the Renaissance: Art and Magnificence* (New Haven: Yale University Press, 2002), pp. 151–55. The translation of the motto appears on ibid., p. 154.

75. In *Elizabeth I: Translations, 1544–1589* (Chicago and London: Chicago University Press, 2009), Janel Mueller and Joshua Scodel argue against Elizabeth I's authorship of the *Trionfo della Divinità* (also known as the *Trionfo dell'Eternità*), pp. 459–68. I would like to thank Jaime Goodrich for bringing this to my attention. For the use of Petrarchan motifs in Elizabeth I's court see June Osborne, *Entertaining Elizabeth I: The Progresses and Great Houses of Her Time* (London: Bishopsgate Press, 1989), pp. 82–83; Robert Coogan, '"Trionfi" and the English Renaissance', *Studies in Philology* 67 (1970), 306–27. See also the introduction to Sidney Herbert's *Triumph of Death* in *Collected Works*, ed. Hannay, Kinnamon, and Brennan, I, pp. 255–67. All subsequent references to Sidney Herbert's translations will be taken from this volume.

76. Roy Strong, *Gloriana: The Portraits of Queen Elizabeth I* (London: Pimlico, 1987), pp. 112–15.

77. Danielle Clarke, '"Lover's Songs Shall Turne to Holy Psalmes": Mary Sidney Herbert and the Transformation of Petrarch', *Modern Language Review* 92 (April, 1997), 282–94.

78. *Faerie Queene*, ed. Hamilton, VII.50. For Spenser's double-edged praise of Elizabeth I see Helen Hackett, *Virgin Mother, Maiden Queen: Elizabeth I and the Cult of the Virgin Mary* (Basingstoke: Macmillan, 1995), pp. 191–97.

79. *Faerie Queene*, ed. Hamilton, VIII, 2.

80. G. F. Waller, *Mary Sidney, Countess of Pembroke: A Critical Study of her Writings and Literary Milieu* (Salzburg: Institut für Anglistik und Amerikanistik, 1979), p. 148.

81. *Tryumphes of Fraunces Petrarcke* (London, 1554 [I am using the BL's edition dated 1565]), sig. G2ᵛ, BL, C.12.a.7(2). All subsequent references to this text will appear in parentheses.

82. *Collected Works*, ed. Hannay, Kinnamon, and Brennan, pp. 271–72.

83. John Harington, *Orlando Furioso* (London, 1591), p. 126, BL, C.70.g.1.

84. For more on this aspect of the Sidneys' literary activities see Margaret P. Hannay, *Philip's Phoenix: Mary Sidney, Countess of Pembroke* (Oxford: Oxford University Press, 1990); Wendy Wall, *The Imprint of Gender: Authorship and Publication in the English Renaissance* (Ithaca: Cornell University Press, 1993), pp. 311–19; Waller, *Mary Sidney*, pp. 75–151; and Mary Ellen Lamb's cautionary 'The Myth of the Countess of Pembroke: The Dramatic Circle', *Yearbook of English Studies* 11 (1981), 194–202.

85. Mary Sidney, *Antonius*, in *Collected Works*, ed. Hannay, Kinnamon, and Brennan. See also *The Third Part of the Countess of Pembrokes Yvychurch* (London, 1592), BL, 80.a.28 (2), and Schleiner, *Tudor and Stuart Women Writers*, pp. 52–60. For women's manipulation of the rituals of commemoration see Chris Laoutaris, 'Speaking Stones: Memory and Maternity in the

Theatre of Death', in *Shakespearean Maternities: Crises of Conception in Early Modern England* (Edinburgh: Edinburgh University Press, 2008), pp. 212–67.

86. Waller, *Mary Sidney*, p. 115, and *Three Tragedies by Renaissance Women*, ed. Diane Purkiss (Harmondsworth: Penguin, 1998), p. xxxiv.

87. See *Collected Works*, ed. Hannay, Kinnamon, and Brennan, pp. 208–09.

88. Ibid., p. 344 n. 186.

89. *The Early Modern Englishwoman: A Facsimile Library of Essential Works, Margaret Tyler, Printed Writings, 1500–1640: Part I, vol. 8*, ed. Kathryn Coad (Aldershot: Ashgate, 1996), sig. A3ᵛ–A4ʳ.

90. Dowriche based the bulk of her narrative on François Hotman's *A true and plaine report of the Furious outrages of Fraunce* (1573) which appeared as Book 10 of the *Commentaries*.

91. Natalie Zemon Davies, 'Gender and Genre: Women as Historical Writers, 1400–1820', in *Beyond Their Sex: Learned Women of the European Past*, ed. Patricia H. Labalme (New York and London: New York University Press, 1984), pp. 153–82.

92. *An Abridgement of the Booke of Acts and Monumentes of the Church Written by* [...] *John Fox* (London, 1589), Epistle to the Reader, BL, C.123.k.13.

93. *The French Historie* (London, 1589), Epistle to the Reader, sigs. A3ᵛ–A4ʳ, BL, C.95.aa.2. All subsequent references to this text will appear in parentheses.

94. Thomas Tymme, *Three Partes of the Commentaries Containing the Whole and Perfect Discourse of the Civill Warres of Fraunce* (London, 1574), Dedicatory Epistle, sig. A2ʳ, BL, 286.c.29.

95. Anne Somerset, *Elizabeth I* (London: Ted Smart, 1991), pp. 606–14.

96. *Commentaries*, Book 10, sig. C2ʳ.

97. *A Mervaylous discourse upon the lyfe, deedes, and behaviours of Katherine de Medicis, Queene mother* (Heidelberg, 1575), pp. 4–6, BL, 285.a.21.

98. Randall Martin, 'Anne Dowriche's *The French History*, Christopher Marlowe, and Machiavellian Agency', *Studies in English Literature* 39 (1999), 69–87 (p. 84).

99. Megan Matchinske suggests that Dowriche justifies 'rebellion and regicide': 'Moral, Method, and History in Anne Dowriche's *The French Historie*', *English Literary Renaissance* 34 (2004), 176–200 (p. 187).

100. *The True Order and Methode of Wryting and Reading Hystories* (London, 1574), sig. A2ʳ, BL, C.32.a.2.

Select Bibliography

Amussen, Susan D. and Adele Seeff (eds), *Attending to Early Modern Women* (Newark: University of Delaware Press/London: Associated University Presses, 1998)

Archer, Jayne Elizabeth, Elizabeth Goldring, and Sarah Knight (eds), *The Progresses, Pageants and Entertainments of Queen Elizabeth* (Oxford: Oxford University Press, 2007)

Beal, Peter and Margaret J. M. Ezell, *Writings by Early Modern Women*, English Manuscript Studies, 9 (London: British Library, 2003)

Beal, Peter and Grace Ioppolo (eds), *Elizabeth I and the Culture of Writing* (London: British Library, 2007)

Beilin, Elaine, *Redeeming Eve: Women Writers of the English Renaissance* (Princeton: Princeton University Press, 1987)

Bennett, Lynn, *Women Writing of Divinest Things: Rhetoric and the Poetry of Pembroke, Wroth and Lanyer* (Pittsburgh: Duquesne University Press, 2004)

Benson, Pamela Joseph and Victoria Kirkham (eds), *Strong Voices, Weak History: Early Women Writers and Canons in England, France, and Italy* (Ann Arbor: University of Michigan Press, 2005)

Bicks, Caroline, *Midwiving Subjects in Shakespeare's England* (Burlington, VT: Ashgate, 2003)

Blumenfeld-Kosinski, Renate, Luise von Flotow, and Daniel Russell (eds), *The Politics of Translation in the Middle Ages and Renaissance* (Ottawa: University of Ottawa Press, 2001)

Boesky, Amy and Mary Thomas Crane (eds), *Form and Reform in Renaissance England: Essays in Honor of Barbara Kiefer Lewalski* (Newark: University of Delaware Press, 2000)

Brayman Hackel, Heidi, *Reading Material in Early Modern England: Print, Gender, and Literacy* (Cambridge: Cambridge University Press, 2005)

Brayman Hackel, Heidi and Catherine E. Kelly (eds), *Reading Women: Literacy, Authorship, and Culture in the Atlantic World, 1500–1800* (Philadelphia: University of Pennsylvania Press, 2008)

Brennan, Michael G., *The Sidneys of Penshurst and the Monarchy, 1500–1700* (Aldershot: Ashgate, 2006)

Brink, Jean (ed.), *Privileging Gender in Early Modern England* (Kirksville, MO: Sixteenth Century Journal Publishers, 1993)

Broomhall, Susan, *Women and the Book Trade in Sixteenth-Century France* (Burlington, VT: Ashgate, 2002)

Brown, Pamela Allen, *Better a Shrew than a Sheep: Women, Drama and the Culture of Jest* (Ithaca, NY: Cornell University Press, 2003)

Brown, Pamela Allen and Peter Parolin, *Women Players in England, 1550–1660: Beyond the All-Male Stage* (Aldershot and Burlington, VT: Ashgate, 2005)

Burke, Mary E., Jane Donawerth, Linda L. Dove, and Karen Nelson (eds), *Women, Writing and the Reproduction of Culture in Tudor and Stuart Britain* (Syracuse: Syracuse University Press, 2000)

Burke, Victoria E. and Jonathan Gibson (eds), *Early Modern Women's Manuscript Writing: Selected Papers from the Trinity/Trent Colloquium* (Aldershot: Ashgate, 2004)

Callaghan, Dympna (ed.), *The Impact of Feminism in English Renaissance Studies* (Basingstoke: Palgrave Macmillan, 2007)

Cerasano, S. P. and Marion Wynne-Davies, *Readings in Renaissance Women's Drama: Criticism, History, and Performance, 1594–1998* (London: Routledge, 1998)

Chedgzoy, Kate, Melanie Hansen, and Suzanne Trill (eds), *Voicing Women: Gender and Sexuality in Early Modern Writing* (Keele: Keele University Press, 1996)

Clarke, Danielle and Elizabeth Clarke (eds), *'This Double Voice': Gendered Writing in Early Modern England* (Basingstoke: Macmillan, 2000)

Coldiron, A. E. B., *English Printing, Verse Translation, and the Battle of the Sexes, 1476–1557* (Burlington, VT: Ashgate, 2009)

Coleman, Linda S. (ed.), *Women's Life Writing* (Bowling Green: Bowling Green State University Popular Press, 1997)

Coles, Kimberly, *Religion, Reform, and Women's Writing in Early Modern England* (Cambridge: Cambridge University Press, 2008)

Cressy, David, *Literacy and the Social Order: Reading and Writing in Tudor and Stuart England* (Cambridge: Cambridge University Press, 1980)

Daybell, James (ed.), *Early Modern Women's Letter Writing, 1450–1700* (Basingstoke: Palgrave Macmillan, 2001)

Daybell, James (ed.), *Women and Politics in Early Modern England, 1450–1700* (Aldershot: Ashgate, 2004)

Daybell, James, *Women Letter-Writers in Tudor England* (Oxford: Oxford University Press, 2006)

Demers, Patricia, *Women's Writing in English: Early Modern England* (Toronto: University of Toronto Press, 2005)

Dolan, Frances E., *Whores of Babylon: Catholicism, Gender, and 17th-Century Print Culture* (Notre Dame, IN: Notre Dame University Press, 1999)

Dowd, Michelle and Julie Eckerle (eds), *Genre and Women's Life Writing in Early Modern England* (Aldershot: Ashgate, 2007)

Erler, Mary C., *Women, Reading, and Piety in Late Medieval England* (Cambridge: Cambridge University Press, 2002)

Ferguson, Margaret W., *Dido's Daughters: Literacy, Gender, and Empire in Early Modern England and France* (Chicago: University of Chicago Press, 2003)

Ferguson, Margaret W., Maureen Quilligan, and Nancy J. Vickers (eds), *Rewriting the Renaissance: The Discourse of Sexual Difference in Early Modern Europe* (Chicago: University of Chicago Press, 1986)

Findlay, Alison, *Playing Spaces in Early Women's Drama* (Cambridge: Cambridge University Press, 2006)

Fleming, Juliet, *Graffiti and the Writing Arts of Early Modern England* (London: Reaktion Books, 2001)

Floyd-Wilson, Mary, *English Ethnicity and Race in Early Modern Drama* (Cambridge: Cambridge University Press, 2003)

Fox, Adam, *Oral and Literate Culture in England, 1500–1700* (Oxford: Oxford University Press, 2000)

Frye, Susan and Karen Robertson (eds), *Maids and Mistresses, Cousins and Queens: Women's Alliances in Early Modern England* (New York: Oxford University Press, 1999)

Fumerton, Patricia, *Unsettled: The Culture of Mobility and the Working Poor in Early Modern England* (Chicago: University of Chicago Press, 2006)

Goldberg, Jonathan, *Desiring Women Writing: English Renaissance Examples* (Stanford: Stanford University Press, 1997)

Gowing, Laura, *Domestic Dangers: Women, Words and Sex in Early Modern London* (Oxford and New York: Oxford University Press, 1996)

Grossman, Marshall (ed.), *Aemilia Lanyer: Gender, Genre, and the Canon* (Kentucky: University of Kentucky Press, 1998)

Guy, John, *A Daughter's Love: Thomas and Margaret More* (London: Fourth Estate, 2008)

Hackett, Helen, *Virgin Mother, Maiden Queen: Elizabeth I and the Cult of the Virgin Mary* (Basingstoke: Macmillan, 1995)

Hackett, Helen, *Women and Romance Fiction in the English Renaissance* (Cambridge: Cambridge University Press, 2000)

Hageman, Elizabeth H. and Katherine Conway (eds), *Resurrecting Elizabeth I in Seventeenth-Century England* (Madison: Fairleigh Dickinson University Press, 2007)

Hall, Kim F., *Things of Darkness: Economies of Race and Gender in Early Modern England* (Ithaca, NY: Cornell University Press, 1996)

Hallett, Nicky, *Lives of Spirit: English Carmelite Self-Writing of the Early Modern Period* (Aldershot: Ashgate, 2007)

Hannay, Margaret P. (ed.), *Silent But for the Word: Tudor Women as Patrons, Translators, and Writers of Religious Works* (Kent, OH: Kent State University Press, 1985)

Hannay, Margaret P., *Philip's Phoenix: Mary Sidney, Countess of Pembroke* (Oxford: Oxford University Press, 1990)

Hannay, Margaret P., Noel Kinnamon, and Michael Brennan (eds), *Domestic Politics and Family Absence: The Correspondence (1588–1621) of Robert Sidney, First Earl of Leicester, and Barbara Gamage Sidney, Countess of Leicester* (Aldershot: Ashgate, 2005)

Haselkorn, Anne and Betty S. Travitsky, *The Renaissance Englishwoman in Print: Counterbalancing the Canon* (Amherst, MA: University of Massachusetts Press, 1999)

Henderson Usher, Katherine and Barbara McManus (eds), *Half Humankind: Contexts and Texts of the Controversy About Women in England, 1540–1640* (Urbana: University of Illinois Press, 1985)

Hendricks, Margo and Patricia Parker (eds), *Women, 'Race' and Writing in the Early Modern Period* (London: Routledge, 1993)

Herman, Peter C. (ed.), *Reading Monarch's Writing: The Poetry of Henry VIII, Mary Stuart, Elizabeth I, and James VI/I* (Tempe: Arizona Center for Medieval and Renaissance Studies, 2002)

Holland, Peter and Stephen Orgel (eds), *From Script to Stage in Early Modern England* (Basingstoke and New York: Palgrave Macmillan, 2004)

Howard, Jean E., *Theater of a City: The Places of London Comedy, 1598–1642* (Philadelphia: University of Pennsylvania Press, 2007)

Howe, Florence, *Tradition and the Talents of Women* (Urbana: University of Illinois Press, 1991)

Hull, Suzanne W., *Chaste, Silent, and Obedient: English Books for Women, 1475–1640* (San Marino, CA: Huntington Library, 1982)

Iyengar, Sujata, *Shades of Difference: Mythologies of Race and Skin-Color in Early Modern England* (Philadelphia: University of Pennsylvania Press, 2005)

James, Susan E., *Kateryn Parr: The Making of a Queen* (Aldershot: Ashgate, 1999)

Jones, Ann Rosalind and Peter Stallybrass, *Renaissance Clothing and the Materials of Memory* (Cambridge: Cambridge University Press, 2000)

Jordan, Constance, *Renaissance Feminism: Literary Texts and Political Models* (Ithaca, NY: Cornell University Press, 1990)

Justice, George L. and Nathan Tinker, *Women's Writing and the Circulation of Ideas: Manuscript Publication in England, 1550–1800* (Cambridge: Cambridge University Press, 2002)

Kastan, David Scott and Peter Stallybrass, *Staging the Renaissance: Reinterpretation of Elizabethan and Jacobean Drama* (London: Routledge, 1991)

Kermode, Jennifer and Garthine Walker, *Women, Crime and the Courts in Early Modern England* (London: University College of London Press, 1994; 2nd edn, 2005)

Korda, Natasha, *Shakespeare's Domestic Economies* (Philadelphia: University of Pennsylvania Press, 2002)

Krontiris, Tina, *Oppositional Voices: Women as Writers and Translators of Literature in the English Renaissance* (New York: Routledge, 1992)

Krug, Rebecca, *Reading Families: Women's Literate Practice in Late Medieval England* (Ithaca, NY: Cornell University Press, 2002)

Lamb, Mary Ellen, *Gender and Authorship in the Sidney Circle* (Madison: University of Wisconsin Press, 1991)

Lamb, Mary Ellen and Karen Bamford, *Oral Traditions and Gender in Early Modern Literary Texts* (Aldershot: Ashgate, 2008)

Laoutaris, Chris, *Shakespearean Maternities: Crises of Conception in Early Modern England* (Edinburgh: Edinburgh University Press, 2008)

Levin, Carole and Patricia A. Sullivan (eds), *Political Rhetoric, Power, and Renaissance Women* (Albany: State University of New York Press, 1995)

MacDonald Green, Joyce, *Women and Race in Early Modern Texts* (Cambridge: Cambridge University Press, 2002)

Magnusson, Lynne, *Shakespeare and Social Dialogue: Dramatic Language and Elizabethan Letters* (Cambridge: Cambridge University Press, 1999)

Malcolmson, Cristina and Mihoko Suzuki (eds), *Debating Gender in Early Modern England, 1500–1700* (New York: Palgrave Macmillan, 2002)

Mason Vaughan, Virginia, *Performing Blackness on English Stages, 1500–1800* (Cambridge: Cambridge University Press, 2005)

McGrath, Lynette, *Subjectivity and Women's Poetry in Early Modern England: 'Why on the ridge should she desire to go?'* (Aldershot: Ashgate, 2002)

Meale, Carol (ed.), *Women and Literature in Britain, 1150–1500* (Cambridge: Cambridge University Press, 1993)

Mendelson, Sara and Patricia Crawford, *Women in Early Modern England* (Oxford: Clarendon Press, 1998)

Montrose, Louis, *The Subject of Elizabeth: Authority, Gender, Representation* (Chicago: University of Chicago Press, 2006)

O'Day, Rosemary, *Women's Agency in Early Modern Britain and the American Colonies: Patriarchy, Partnership, and Patronage* (Harlow: Pearson Longman, 2007)

O'Malley, Susan, *Custom Is an Idiot: Jacobean Pamphlet Literature on Women* (Urbana: University of Illinois Press, 2004)

Ostovich, Helen and Elizabeth Sauer (eds), *Reading Early Modern Women: An Anthology of Texts in Manuscript and Print, 1550–1700* (New York: Routledge, 2004)

Pacheco, Anna (ed.), *A Companion to Early Modern Women's Writing* (Malden, MA: Blackwell Publishing, 2002)

Peters, Christine, *Patterns of Piety: Women, Gender, and Religion in Late Medieval and Reformation England* (Cambridge: Cambridge University Press, 2003)

Pollock, Linda, *Forgotten Children: Parent–Child Relations from 1500 to 1900* (Cambridge: Cambridge University Press, 1983)

Pollock, Linda, *With Faith and Physic: The Life of a Tudor Gentlewoman Lady Grace Mildmay, 1552–1620* (London: Collins and Brown, 1993)

Richardson, Catherine, *Domestic Life and Domestic Tragedy* (Manchester: Manchester University Press, 2006)

Salzman, Paul, *Reading Early Modern Women's Writing* (Oxford: Oxford University Press, 2006)

Sanders, Eve Rachele, *Gender and Literacy on Stage in Early Modern England* (Cambridge: Cambridge University Press, 1998)

Schleiner, Louise, *Tudor and Stuart Women Writers* (Bloomington: Indiana University Press, 1994)

Shell, Marc, *Elizabeth's Glass: With 'The Glass of the Sinful Soul' (1544) by Elizabeth I and 'Epistle Dedicatory' and 'Conclusion' (1548) by John Bale* (Lincoln: University of Nebraska Press, 1993)

Smith, Bruce R., *The Acoustic World of Early Modern England: Attending to the O-factor* (Chicago: University of Chicago Press, 1999)

Stevenson, Jane and Peter Davidson (eds), *Early Modern Women Poets (1520–1700): An Anthology* (Oxford: Oxford University Press, 2001)

Stewart, Alan and Heather Wolfe, *Letterwriting in Renaissance England* (Washington: Folger Shakespeare Library, 2004)

Stone, Lawrence, *Family, Sex and Marriage in England, 1500–1800* (London: Weidenfeld and Nicolson, 1977)

Straznicky, Marta, *Privacy, Playreading, and Women's Closet Drama, 1550–1700* (Cambridge: Cambridge University Press, 2004)

Stretton, Timothy, *Women Waging Law in Elizabethan England* (Cambridge: Cambridge University Press, 1998)

Strong, Roy, *Gloriana: The Portraits of Queen Elizabeth I* (London: Pimlico, 1987)

Summers, Claude J. and Ted-Larry Pebworth (eds), *Literary Circles and Cultural Communities in Renaissance England* (Columbia: University of Missouri Press, 2000)

Summit, Jennifer, *Lost Property: The Woman Writer and English Literary History, 1380–1589* (Chicago: University of Chicago Press, 2000)

Summit, Jennifer, *Memory's Library: Medieval Books in Early Modern England* (Chicago: University of Chicago Press, 2008)

Traub, Valerie, M. Lindsey Kaplan, and Dympna Callaghan (eds), *Feminist Readings of Early Modern Culture: Emerging Subjects* (Cambridge: Cambridge University Press, 1996)

Travitsky, Betty S. and Anne Lake Prescott, *Female and Male Voices in Early Modern England: An Anthology of Renaissance Writing* (New York: Columbia University Press, 2000)

Trill, Suzanne, Kate Chedgzoy, and Melanie Osborne (eds), *Lay By Your Needles Ladies, Take the Pen: Writing Women in England, 1500–1700* (London and New York: Arnold, 1997)

Walker, Claire, *Gender and Politics in Early Modern Europe: English Convents in France and the Low Countries* (New York: Palgrave Macmillan, 2003)

Wall, Wendy, *The Imprint of Gender: Authorship and Publication in the English Renaissance* (Ithaca, NY: Cornell University Press, 1993)

Waller, Gary, *The Sidney Family Romance: Mary Wroth, William Herbert, and the Early Modern Construction of Gender* (Detroit: Wayne State University Press, 1993)

Walsham, Alexandra, *Church Papists: Catholic Conformity and Confessional Polemic in Early Modern England* (Woodbridge: Boydell, 1993)

Warren, Nancy Bradley, *Women of God and Arms: Female Spirituality and Political Conflict, 1380–1600* (Philadelphia: University of Pennsylvania Press, 2005)

Wilcox, Helen (ed.), *Women and Literature in Britain, 1500–1700* (Cambridge: Cambridge University Press, 1996)

Williams, Deanne, *The French Fetish from Chaucer to Shakespeare* (Cambridge: Cambridge University Press, 2007)

Wilson, Katharina M. (ed.), *Women Writers of the Renaissance and Reformation* (Athens: University of Georgia Press, 1987)

Wiltenburg, Joy, *Disorderly Women and Female Power in the Street Literature of Early Modern Germany and England* (Charlottesville: University of Virginia Press, 1992)

Wolfe, Heather (ed.), *The Literary Career and Legacy of Elizabeth Cary, 1613–1680* (London: Palgrave Macmillan, 2007)

Woods, Susanne and Margaret P. Hannay, *Teaching Tudor and Stuart Women Writers* (New York: MLA, 2000)

Würzbach, Natascha, *The Rise of the English Street Ballad, 1550–1650* (Cambridge: Cambridge University Press, 1990)

Wynne-Davies, Marion, *Women Writers and Familial Discourse in the English Renaissance* (Basingstoke: Palgrave Macmillan, 2007)

Index

Erasmus, Desiderius – *continued*
  The New Mother, 304
  portrait, 300, 302
  Precatio Dominica, 301, 303
Erdmann, Axel, 72, 74
Erler, Mary 25, 26, 72
Euripides, 9, 184
  Iphigeneia at Aulis, 9–10, 181
executions, 159–60, 177, 180;
  see also speeches
Ezell, Margaret, J. M., 14 n.6, 35, 72,
  73, 98

Fane, Francis, first Earl of
  Westmorland, 115
Fane, Mary (Lady Mary Mildmay
  Fane), Countess of Westmorland,
  8, 113, 115,
  116
  Book of Advice to the Children, 115
Fane, Mary (Lady Mary Neville Fane),
  Baroness le Despencer, 111
Fane, Mildmay, second Earl of
  Westmorland, 115, 116, 117
Fane, Rachel, fourth Countess of
  Westmorland, 116
Fane, Vere, 116
Felch, Susan, 44, 45
Fenton, Geoffrey, 41, 44
Ferguson, Margaret W., 20, 182,
  191, 217
Field, John, 43, 44, 45, 50
Findlay, Alison, 176, 182, 188
Fitzalan, Henry, twelfth Earl of
  Arundel, 10, 181–82, 183
Fleming, Juliet, 21
Floyd-Wilson, Mary, 291
Fonte, Moderata, 96
Foster, Seth, 262
Fouquart, Antoine, *The Gospelles of
  Dystaues*, 67
Fox, Adam, 20, 102, 166–67
Foxe, John, 9, 172 n.15, 180, 191,
  201, 260
  Acts and Monuments, 114, 165, 166,
  177, 205, 311
  Book of Martyrs, 27, 28, 114, 156,
  256, 311
Foxford, Richard, 305
Fraunce, Abraham, *Ivychurch*, 316

Frith, John, 202
Fumerton, Patricia, 158, 228

Gardiner, Stephen, Bishop of
  Winchester, 203–04, 205,
  206, 260
Garnier, Robert, *Marc Antoine*
  (*The Tragedie of Antonie*), 10, 184,
  186
gender
  authorship, 7, 73, 176
  difference, 5, 10, 122
  identity, 101, 185, 186, 227, 249
  ideology, 157, 225, 240
  inequality, 68, 227
  language, viii, 131, 137, 254–55
  print culture, viii, 61, 63, 65
  relations, 270, 290
  roles, 6, 10, 24, 68, 90, 91, 110,
    157, 176, 186, 187, 190, 225,
    240, 305
  'woman question', 6, 60, 77
Geneva Bible (1560), 280, 282
genre(s)
  acceptable, 23
  choice, 19, 200, 212
  hybridity, 2, 288
  literary, 47, 65, 68, 90, 92, 93, 98, 108,
    132, 143, 145, 146, 147, 164, 168,
    174 n.49, 175, 188, 200, 202, 206,
    210, 215, 218, 228, 231, 236, 248,
    252, 259, 288, 289, 291
Gifford, George, 50
Gilles, Peter, 300, 301
Godet, Gyles, 104
Goodrich, Jaime, 39, 42
Gouge, William, 91
  Of domesticall duties, 105 n.6
Gowing, Laura, 206–07
graffiti, 9, 156
Grafton, Anthony, 40
Greenblatt, Stephen, 14 n.2
Greene, Roland, 43
Greenham, Richard, 50
Greville, Fulke, 49
Grey, Lady Jane, 10, 161, 177–78, 181,
  182, 183
Grindal, William, 225
Gringore, Pierre, *The Castle of Labour*,
  68–69, 77

CPSIA information can be obtained at www.ICGtesting.com
Printed in the USA
LVOW102149070313

323266LV00015B/141/P